The Popular Music Teaching Handbook

An Educator's Guide to Music-Related Print Resources

B. Lee Cooper and
Rebecca A. Condon

UNLIMITED

A Member of the Greenwood Publishing Group

Westport, Connecticut • London

Library of Congress Cataloging-in-Publication Data

Cooper, B. Lee.
  The popular music teaching handbook : an educator's guide to music-related print
  resources / B. Lee Cooper and Rebecca A. Condon.
    p. cm.
  Includes bibliographical references and indexes.
  ISBN 1–59158–039–0
    1. Popular music—Instruction and study. 2. School music—Instruction and study. I.
  Condon, Rebecca A., 1954– II. Title.
  ML3470.C66 2004
  16.78164'071—dc20   2003065947

British Library Cataloguing in Publication Data is available.

Library of Congress Catalog Card Number: 2003065947
ISBN: 1–59158–039–0

First published in 2004

Libraries Unlimited, 88 Post Road West, Westport, CT 06881
A Member of the Greenwood Publishing Group, Inc.
www.lu.com

Printed in the United States of America

⊗™

The paper used in this book complies with the
Permanent Paper Standard issued by the National
Information Standards Organization (Z39.48–1984).

10   9   8   7   6   5   4   3   2   1

Contents

Acknowledgments

Students and teachers dwell together in a culture bristling with popular music. Integration of sound recording lyrics and pop performers and composers during classroom discussions, in writing assignments, or as co-curricular pursuits are increasingly common practices in schools and colleges. Debates about contemporary music quality and lyrical censorship also abound. Former notions of banning the examination of popular music topics from classes have yielded to the reality of cross-disciplinary involvement concerning audio products of the commercial recording industry. Art students investigate rock poster designs; business classes ponder performer contract packages and music marketing techniques; geographers investigate the impact of radio-signal power on the sales and distribution of various recorded cultural contexts; historians trace the backgrounds of financial scandals ("payola") and commercial successes (rags-to-riches tales about record labels and their artists); and social studies students look for trends in songs concerning military involvement, urban life, and even baseball heroes. The ubiquitous song lyric is the new teacher's pet. This compilation of bibliographic resources features hundreds of books, articles, anthologies, and other sources that speak to the integration of popular music and classroom teaching. This volume also enumerates specific resources and recommended instructional approaches designed to increase the utilization of sound recordings. We are grateful to Libraries Unlimited for their support in publishing this study. The opportunity to extol and illustrate the extensive cultural influence of popular music in American life is genuinely appreciated.

Teachers and writers are highlighted throughout this study. Pedagogical scholarship informs every page, every instructional interpretation featured here, and we wish to acknowledge intellectual debts. In the realm of lyric theme identification, trailblazers of merit include Bill Ayres, Peter Fornatale, Jeff Green, Bob Macken, Anthony and Ann Stecheson, and Larry Stidom. In the field of teaching about popular culture, key thinkers are Carl Bode, Ray B. Browne, John Cawelti, Marshall W. Fishwick, H. L. Goodall, Jr., Charles F. Gritzner, Lawrence Grossberg, M. Thomas Inge, Lawrence W. Levine, George Lipsitz, Russel B. Nye, Charles Panati, William D. Romanowski, and Fred E. H. Schroeder. In the area of using popular music as cultural commentary, insightful intellectuals include Michael Bane, Stephen Barnard, Stanley Booth, Lee Cotton, Howard DeWitt, Philip H. Ennis, Colin Escott, Simon Frith, Reebee Garafalo, Charlie Gillett, Theodore Gracyk, Peter Guralnick, Jeff Hannusch (aka Almost Slim), David Hatch, George H. Lewis, Stephen Millward, Richard A. Peterson, George Plasketes, Robert Pruter, Jerome L. Rodnitzky, Timothy

Scheurer, Nick Tosches, and Brian Ward. In the arenas of record chart compilations and discographic research, remarkable works have been compiled by George Albert, Fred Bronson, Mike Callahan, Michael Erlewine, Robert Ferlingere, Paul Gambaccini, Jeff Kreiter, Paul C. Mawhinney, David A. Milberg, Tim Neely, Jerry Osborne, Craig W. Pattillo, Al Pavlow, Bruce Pollock, Michael Ruppli, Frank Scott, Nat Shapiro, Dean Tudor, Neal Umphred, and Joel Whitburn. Finally, in the area of music encyclopedias and bibliographies, highly useful contributions have been made by Mark W. Booth, Tim Brooks, Galen Gart, Jeffrey N. Gatten, Phil Hardy, Frank Hoffmann, David Horn, Gary M. Krebs, D.W. Krummel, Michael L. LaBlanc, David Laing, Colin Larkin, Brady J. Leyser, Guy A. Marco, Irwin Stambler, and Paul Taylor.

Writers draw inspiration, ideas, criticism, and assistance from fellow authors, teaching colleagues, and other professional colleagues. Scholarly work is invariably a symphony of voices rather than a solo performance. This volume is informed by personal commentaries, books, articles, and conference papers produced by Gary Burns, Ronald Butchart, George O. Carney, George Chilcoat, Howard A. DeWitt, Peter Guralnick, Frank W. Hoffmann, Steve Kneeshaw, George H. Lewis, David A. Milberg, David Pichaske, Roger B. Rollin, Tim Scheurer, Larry Stidom, and Chas "Dr. Rock" White. For discographic support, the backbone of any lyric analyst's research, we have benefited from more than thirty years of professional discussions and personal attention by sound recordings archivist William L. Schurk. As a college professor and a school library media specialist, we have also drawn encouragement from many students, staff, faculty members, and fellow administrators. These folks include Donna Brummett, Roger Buese, Dolores Chapman, Neil and Karen Clark, Colby Currier, Shirley Erickson, Joy Farmer, Pam Glasgow, Cindy Goldsmith, Susan Gray, Wayne Haney, Peggy Haun, Don Hardy, Elna Hensley, Tracy McGarey, Liz Moore, Don and Zella Morris, Jack and Anne Patterson, Angela Ratcliff, Todd and Connie Reynolds, Audrey Thompson, Stewart Tubbs, Don Walker, and Wayne Wiegand. Finally, the authors benefit from the loving, uncritical support of a wife, a husband, children, grandchildren, parents, and siblings. This indispensable sustenance has been provided by Dozier Allen, Peggy Allen, Thad Allen, Willodene Allen, Curt Condon, Gen Condon, Jack Condon, Lexi Condon, Steve Condon, Jill Cooper, Michael Cooper, Julie Cooper, Dustin Cooper, Nicholas Cooper, Kathleen M. Cooper, Charles A. Cooper, Patty Jo Cooper, Larry W. Cooper, Erin Condon Gonyea, Brian Mioduszewski, Laura Mioduszewski, Lauren Mioduszewski, Sam Mioduszewski, and Wendy Allen Williams.

Introduction

Nearly two decades have passed since *The Popular Music Handbook: A Resource Guide for Teachers, Librarians, and Media Specialists* (Libraries Unlimited, 1984) first appeared in print. Since then, a host of thorough bibliographic guides focusing on contemporary music resources have been published. These reference compendiums detail lengthy lists of artist profiles, general and critical discographies, dictionaries and encyclopedias, almanacs and chronologies, and alphabetical lists of scholarly periodicals and popular music magazines. *A Guide to Popular Music Reference Books* (Greenwood, 1995) by Gary Haggerty and *The Rock and Roll Reader's Guide* (Billboard, 1997) by Gary M. Krebs are fine examples of the general bibliographic resources currently on the market. The best biographical compilations are *Rock Stars/Pop Stars: A Comprehensive Bibliography, 1955-1994* (Greenwood, 1994) by Brady J. Leyser and *Popular Singers of the Twentieth Century* (Greenwood, 1999) by Robert H. Cowden. Finally, the most outstanding study on music-related research and writing within the academic disciplines of communication, education, ethnomusicology, history, literature and the arts, music, politics, psychology, religion, and sociology is *Rock Music Scholarship: An Interdisciplinary Bibliography* (Greenwood, 1995) by Jeffrey N. Gatten.

This concise volume from Libraries Unlimited fills a bibliographic void. It addresses the function of print resources as instructional guides and descriptors of popular music pedagogy. The motivation for assembling this compilation of books and articles is the realization that more and more public school teachers and college-level faculty members are introducing and utilizing music-related educational approaches in their classrooms. I documented this trend in two recent publications: "Teaching with Popular Music Resources: A Bibliography of Interdisciplinary Instructional Approaches, *Popular Music and Society* XXII (summer 1998), 85–115 and *American Culture Interpreted Through Popular Music: Interdisciplinary Teaching Approaches* (Bowling Green State University Popular Press, 2000). This Libraries Unlimited volume enhances these two studies by focusing directly on the growing spectrum of published scholarship that is available to instructors in specific teaching fields (art, geography, social studies, urban studies, and so on) as well as on the multitude of general resources (including biographical directories and encyclopedias of artist profiles) that are especially appropriate for fueling classroom investigations.

The Popular Music Teaching Handbook is limited in scope. There are no audiovisual or computer database resources identified. It focuses on print resources only. It also champions a pedagogical perspective within rock and educational literature with an eye toward assisting teachers, professors, researchers, reference librarians, media specialists, and their students. Sound recordings from 1920 through the present day are deemed to be reasonable tools for study. Rock era students and their post–World War II era instructors are already integrating music and many other popular media resources into multidisciplinary teaching styles and reflective learning pursuits. Items omitted from this volume are the following:

♫ Works of rock-related literary fiction, both short stories and novels

♫ Comics and cartoon format studies about rock artists

♫ Studies on classical performers or art music personalities

♫ References to Internet teaching functions and Web site locations of music sources

♫ Specialized discography lists of artists or record labels

♫ "Opening Day Collection" recommendations of books and compact discs for music archives

♫ Articles describing record collecting techniques, sound recording price guides, or popular music memorabilia materials

♫ Pop magazine and fanzine identifications or fan club lists

♫ Tourbooks

♫ Quiz books, trivia question volumes, or rock star birthday lists

Despite these omissions, the topical bibliographies in this volume are well populated with references to art (photographs, album covers, and poster drawings), biographical references (autobiographies, interviews, and critical character studies), history (chronologies, timelines, and almanacs), journalism (rock writers, music periodicals, and cultural critics), and speech communications (protest, humor, novelty tunes, and song parodies).

This volume is divided into four sections. The first chapter lists resources that illustrate various applications of music-related topics within traditional academic areas. More than thirty educational fields—from architecture to women's studies—are included. The second chapter provides an array of encyclopedia and biographical directory references, along with a selected listing of influential popular music performers and composers. At least ten references on the careers and musical contributions of each person or group are listed. The third chapter offers selected references related to the vast array of popular musical styles and dance crazes that have surfaced during the past sixty years. Finally, the fourth chapter is an extended bibliographic section that denotes key music teaching resources found in books, articles, songbooks, lyric anthologies, and archival collections.

The relative brevity of this reference work is by design. No annotations are provided. All citations are consistent, but minimal. For books, references include author, title, place of publication, publishing company, and year of release. Citations for periodicals are similarly concise, listing author, title of the article, journal name, volume number, month and year of release, and page numbers. The goal of this resource guide is not to duplicate the more expansive works of other fine general music bibliographers. Instead, *The Popular Music Teaching Handbook* is a clearly delineated instructional reference to other guidebooks, essays, and book-length commentaries on educational approaches that integrate sound recordings, popular music performers, or other music-related materials with traditional disciplinary teaching methodologies.

B. Lee Cooper

Interdisciplinary Applications of Popular Music for Classroom Teaching Activities and Student Research Projects

Popular recordings are pieces of oral history. Of course, contemporary lyrics offer only partial, fragmented visions of American society. The limited perspective provided in recorded songs is magnified by several factors. First, the physical nature of a single sound recording restricts the duration of a singer's commentary to an extremely brief time. An average tune is less than three minutes long. Second, the achievement of "popularity" for a specific recording indicates broad public acceptance for a particular song. This market-oriented reality tends to limit extremes of lyrical deviance. Third, the radio-play life span for most songs is quite brief. A particular tune may be a frequently played, much discussed commodity for six to ten weeks, then it can disappear from the music charts forever. Finally, songs may either consciously or unconsciously address significant historical conditions or personal concerns. Various listening audiences may accept, reject, ignore, or be totally unaware of the lyrical commentary being presented. This means that intent, content, and influence via recorded music are rarely synonymous.

Recognizing these limitations in assessing the impact of sound recording communications, why should songs be considered valuable instructional resources? As a communication medium, lyrics do not systematically propagandize listeners. Likewise, they do not function as flawless historical mirrors. Such polarized perspectives on songs ignore the inherent pluralism of contemporary lyrics, a pluralism that is a logical by-product of the intellectual (and sometimes anti-intellectual) variety found in modern society. Popular songs replicate in unsystematic, segmented fashions a multiplicity of facts, ideas, and values. In contemporary culture, they form an unpredictable, ever-changing audio collage. Lyrics resemble the historical remnants available in an Indian burial mound. Just as an archeologist must reconstruct cultural reality from innumerable fragments left by a former Native American civilization—pieces of pottery, projectile points, tools for building, stone drawings, ancient toys and games, eating utensils, religious tokens, and death masks—contemporary soundscape researchers must examine many, many recordings produced over an extended time span to identify persistent ideas, attitudes, themes, and patterns.

Some subjects of rock lyrics are overwhelmingly available for scrutiny. For example, the standard courtship theme—boy meets girl, boy dates girl, love blooms, marriage beckons, and a wedding occurs—is ubiquitous in popular music. Numerous variations on this typical love-and-marriage scenario have also appeared, however. Women's liberation, birth control, generation gaps, social mobility, economic independence, the sexual revolution, and dozens of other social trends and personal situations in post-1950 U.S. history have dramatically altered and complicated the previously simple courtship theme. These same social and political realities have generated an enlarged spectrum of lyrical commentary within many popular music themes.

Since 1950, U.S. society has been verbally photographed by innumerable itinerant tunesmiths and displayed in audio galleries across this continent and throughout the world. Radios, jukeboxes, cable television (MTV), cassette recordings, motion picture soundtracks, compact discs, and millions and millions of records sound a clarion call to students and teachers. The irony is that so few educators utilize recorded resources. Just as armies of archeologists have successfully reconstructed the fabric of ancient cultures by carefully examining buried relics, it is vital that modern teachers apply their logical analyses and reasoned perspectives to the audio remnants of the American music industry.

Is popular music a legitimate resource for investigating contemporary society? For Dick Clark, Wolfman Jack, and Casey Kasem, maybe so; but what about for the thousands of teachers and millions of students in secondary schools and college classrooms across this country? The answer should be a resounding "Yes!" This does not imply that rock music is either the *only* or the *best* resource for examining contemporary social and political events. Televised speeches, printed articles from newspapers and magazines, lectures by teachers, scholars, politicians, and businessmen, and innumerable other oral and written communication vehicles can stimulate student thought, reflection, decision making, and action. In contrast, rock lyrics are "ear candy" to most youngsters, offering relief from the bland pabulum they perceive traditional textbooks to be.

Because few teachers consider rock to be "serious music"—let alone "serious history"—few classes have explored the sociopolitical imagery contained in songs by Elvis Presley, Chuck Berry, or the Coasters. Beyond these early rockers, though, the idea of Mick Jagger, John Lennon, Burton Cummings, Pete Townsend, Carole King, Bob Dylan, Elvis Costello, Tracy Chapman, or John Cougar Mellencamp making political and social declarations is not nearly as unexpected. Popular music is, after all, the rhythmic voice of the young. Obviously, love themes, dancing, partying, and other less-than-polemic ideas dominate rock's frantic media message. Yet individuals such as Bruce Springsteen, Paul Simon, David Bowie, and Billy Joel and groups like the Beatles, the Rolling Stones, the Who, the Cure, and U2 defy traditional society and explain modern history with statements of meaning and substance in their hit recordings.

The most productive approach to examining U.S. history through popular music is to focus on specific ideas and themes that have been identified and explored by innovative, creative classroom teachers. The following pedagogical bibliography is designed to be illustrative rather than comprehensive. The focus is on specific academic areas—art, business, geography, history, language arts, philosophy, speech, and women's studies. Thirty-two fields of study are represented. The goal of presenting a listing of reports dealing with popular music resources as classroom teaching materials is to stimulate further thought among students and teachers. This extensive bibliography will not have fulfilled its mission unless readers conclude that the soundscape of American life is a worthy field for further educational investigation.

General Teaching Commentaries

Jane A. Ahekvist, "Music and Cultural Analysis in the Classroom," *Teaching Sociology* XXVII (1999), 126–44.

James E. Akenson, "Teaching Country Music," in *Country Music Annual 2000*, edited by Charles K. Wolfe and James E. Akenson. Lexington: University Press of Kentucky, 2000, 151–72.

Richard Aquila, "A Scholar Takes His Views on Rock 'n' Roll to the Air," *Chronicle of Higher Education* XLVIII (January 31, 1997), B7.

Patricia Averill, "How to Teach the Rock and Roll Generation What They Don't Know They Want to Hear," *Popular Culture Methods* III, no. 1 (spring 1976), 31–36.

Robert D. Barr, "Youth and Music," in *Values and Youth: Teaching Social Studies in an Age of Crisis—No. 2* (Washington, D.C.: National Council for the Social Studies, 1971), 99–103.

David Ross Baskerville, "Black Music, Pop, and Rock vs. Our Obsolete Curricula," *National Association of Jazz Education Educator* III (April-May 1971), 5–7, 27–28.

Alf Bjornberg, "Teach You to Rock? Popular Music in the University Music Department," *Popular Music* XII (January 1993), 69–77.

Elsa M. Bowman, "The Relationship of Music and Popular Culture in Schooling," *Perspectives of New Music* XXVII (winter 1989), 118–23.

Gary Burns, "*Popular Music and Society* and the Evolving Discipline of Popular Music Studies," *Popular Music and Society* XXI (spring 1997), 123–31.

Gary Burns, "Where Have All the Records Gone, or When Will We Ever Learn?" *Popular Culture in Libraries* II, no. 4 (1994), 1–9.

Ronald E. Butchart and B. Lee Cooper, "Perceptions of Education in the Lyrics of American Popular Music, 1950-1980," *American Music* V (fall 1987), 31–41.

Iain Chambers, "Pop Music: A Teaching Perspective," *Screen Perspectives* XXXIX (1987), 35–46.

Floyd T. Christian, "Rock 'n' Roll Gets through to Them—Why Can't We?" *Grade Teacher* LXXXIV (October 1966), 32–38.

John Comer, "How Can I Use the Top Ten?" in *Pop, Rock and Ethnic Music in School*, edited by Graham Vulliamy and Edward Lee. Cambridge: Cambridge University Press, 1982, 7–23.

B. Lee Cooper (ed.), "American Culture Interpreted through Popular Music: Interdisciplinary Teaching Approaches," *Popular Music and Society* XXIII (winter 1999), 1–129.

B. Lee Cooper, "Can Music Students Learn Anything of Value by Investigating Popular Recordings?" *International Journal of Instructional Media* XX, no. 3 (1993), 273–84.

B. Lee Cooper, "It's Still Rock 'n' Roll to Me: Reflections on the Evolution of Popular Music and Rock Scholarship," *Popular Music and Society* XXI (spring 1997), 101–8.

B. Lee Cooper, "Teaching with Popular Music Resources: A Bibliography of Interdisciplinary Instructional Approaches," *Popular Music and Society* XXII (summer 1998), 85–115.

Richard Corliss, "A Beatle Metaphysic," *Commonwealth* (May 12, 1967), 234–6.

Robert A. Cutietta, "Popular Music: An Ongoing Challenge," *Music Educators Journal* LXXVII (April 1991), 26–29.

Frederick E. Danker, "Folksongs in the High School Classroom," *Sing Out!* XIII (February-March 1963), 16–17.

Harris Danzinger, "The Role of Popular Music in the Schools," *National Music Council Bulletin* XXX (spring/summer 1970), 16–17.

Kevin J. H. Dettmar, "An Introduction to Postmodernism: Just Let Them Hear Some of That Rock 'n' Roll Music," *Chronicle of Higher Education* XLV (September 25, 1998), B4, B5.

"Does Popular Music Have Educational Value?" *Music Educators Journal* LXVI (December 1979), 60–65.

David Dufty and John Anthony Scott, "How to Use Folk Songs." Washington, D.C.: National Council for the Social Studies, 1969.

Mary Ellison, "Teaching Popular Music," *Popular Music* IX (October 1990), 370–1.

Glenn Famous and Barbara Sargent, "Rockin' 'Round the USA," *Learning* XXI (November 1992), 34–37.

David Feldman, "How to Teach Students about Something They Already Know More about Than You Do: Some Approaches to Teaching Rock Music," *Popular Culture Methods* III (spring 1976), 22–31.

Henrietta Fleek, "Learning from Rock," *Forecast for Home Economics* XVI (October 1970), 50–57.

Glenn Gass, "Why Don't We Do It in the Classroom?" in *Present Tense: Rock and Roll Culture*, edited by Anthony DeCurtis. Durham, NC: Duke University Press, 1992, 93–100.

Andrew Goodwin, "On Being a Professor of Pop," *Popular Music and Society* XXI (spring 1997), 43–52.

Andrew Goodwin, "Pop Goes the Academy: On Teaching, DJing, and What's in Between," *Pulse* CLIV (November 1996), 20, 64.

Mark Gordon and Jack Nachbar (comps.), *Currents of Warm Life: Popular Culture in American Higher Education*. Bowling Green, OH: Bowling Green State University Popular Press, 1980.

William Graebner, "Teaching 'The History of Rock 'n' Roll'," *Teaching History: A Journal of Methods* IX (spring 1984), 2–20.

Gene Grier, *The Conceptual Approach to Rock Music: A Teacher's Manual*. Valley Forge, PA: Charter, 1974.

Scott Heyman, "And Music," in *Humanities and the Social Studies*, edited by Thomas F. Powell. Washington, D.C.: National Council for the Social Studies, 1969, 80–87.

David Horn, "Institute of Popular Music," *Popular Music* VII (October 1988), 333–5.

Glenn M. Hudak, et al. (edited by Joe Kincheloe and Shirley Steinberg), *Student Identity and Popular Music in the Context of School.* New York: Garland Books, 1997.

Phil Jochem, "Some Popular Songs Rip into Teachers," *Instructor* LXXXV (October 1975), 40–42.

Eric P. Johnson, "The Use of Folk Songs in Education: Some Examples of the Use of Folk Songs in the Teaching of History, Geography, Economics, and English Literature," *The Vocational Aspect of Education* XXI (summer 1969), 89–94.

Norman A. Josephs, "Reflections on Teaching American Popular Music in Britain . . .," *Popular Music and Society* VI (fall 1979), 229–33.

"Keeping Up with Rock 'n' Roll," *Ohio Schools* L (February 25, 1972), 21.

Greta B. Lipson and Doris Richards, "Today's Music: Society Reflected," *The Clearing House* LII (December 1978), 163–6.

Thomas J. Meyer, "In This Course, 'Dare to Be Stupid' Can Be the Route to Intellectual Growth," *Chronicle of Higher Education* XXX (November 6, 1985), 1, 35.

Richard Middleton, *Studying Popular Music.* Milton Keynes, England: Open University Press, 1989.

Allan F. Moore, *Rock, The Primary Text: Developing a Musicology of Rock.* Philadelphia: Open University Press, 1993.

Robert Myers, "There Are Right Reasons and Wrong Reasons for Studying Rock," *Chronicle of Higher Education* XXXVI (February 14, 1990), B2, B3.

Jack Nachbar and Marc Hugunin (eds.), "Teaching Popular Music: Courses, Sources, Approaches," *Popular Culture Association Newsletter* X (July 1981), 14–25.

Daniel Newsom, "Rock's Quarrel with Tradition: Popular Music's Carnival Comes to the Classroom," *Popular Music and Society* XXII, no. 3 (fall 1998), 1–20.

Susan L. Porter, "American Music: A Teaching Questionnaire," *The Sonneck Society Bulletin* XV (summer 1989), 51–56.

Alan Raph, "An Educator's Guide to Rock Music," *Education Digest* XXXVIII (February 1973), 36–39.

Motti Regev, "Popular Music Studies: The Issue of Musical Value," *Tracking: Popular Music Studies* IV (spring 1992), 22–27.

Robert Reid, *Understanding Music*. Portland, ME: J. Weston Walch, 1972.

Jerome J. Rodnitzky, "Popular Music in American Studies," *History Teacher* VII (August 1974), 503–10.

Keith Roe, "The School and Music in Adolescent Socialization," in *Popular Music and Communication*, edited by James Lull. Newbury Park, CA: Sage, 1987, 212–30.

Jimmie N. Rogers, *The Country Music Message: All about Lovin' and Livin'*. Englewood Cliffs, NJ: Prentice Hall, 1983.

Jimmie N. Rogers, *The Country Music Message: Revisited*. Fayetteville: University of Arkansas Press, 1989.

Emmett R. Sarig, "Ignoring Rock Won't Make It Go Away," *Music Educators Journal* LVI (November 1969), 46–47.

James Von Schilling, "Popular Music in the College Classroom," *Popular Culture Association Newsletter* X (July 1981), 14–19.

Tom Schoenberg, "Professor's Research Inspires a Rock Star," *Chronicle of Higher Education* XLII (January 19, 1996), A7.

Quentin J. Schultze, Roy M. Anker, James D. Bratt, William D. Romanowski, John W. Worst, and Lambert Zuidervaart, *Dancing in the Dark: Youth, Popular Culture, and the Electronic Media*. Grand Rapids, MI: William B. Eerdmans, 1991.

Jane Scott, "Rock Goes to College," *The* [Cleveland] *Plain Dealer* (March 29, 1987), 2H.

John Anthony Scott, *Teaching for a Change*. New York: Bantam Books, 1972.

John Shepherd, Phil Virden, Graham Vulliamy, and Trevor Wishart, *Whose Music? A Sociology of Musical Languages*. New Brunswick, NJ: Transaction, 1980 (first published 1977).

Roy Shuker, *Understanding Popular Music*. London: Routledge, 1994.

William A. Sievert, "Progressive Rock: Poetry, Politics, and Powerful Music," *Chronicle Review* XVII (February 20, 1979), 22–23.

Christopher Small, *Music-Society-Education: An Examination of the Function of Music in Western, Eastern, and African Cultures with Its Impact on Society and Its Use in Education*. New York: Schirmer Books, 1977.

Doug Stewart, "Now Playing in Academe: The King of Rock 'n' Roll," *Smithsonian* XXVI (November 1995), 56–67.

Keith Swanwick, *Popular Music and the Teacher*. London: Pergamon Press, 1968.

Dick Thompson, "Plugged into Pop at the Junior High Level," *Music Educators Journal* LXVI (December 1979), 54–59.

Art Tipaldi, "Blues in the Schools," *Blues Revue*, no. 42 (November 1998), 27–32.

Graham Vulliamy and Edward Lee (eds.), *Pop Music in School* (rev. ed.). Cambridge: Cambridge University Press, 1980.

Graham Vulliamy and Edward Lee (eds.), *Pop, Rock, and Ethnic Music in School*. Cambridge: Cambridge University Press, 1982.

Graham Vulliamy and Edward Lee, *Popular Music: A Teacher's Guide*. London: Routledge and Kegan Paul, 1982.

Neal Weiss, "Listen to Their Music? A Problem in Teaching Popular Music," *Popular Culture Association Newsletter* X (July 1981), 22–25.

Mathias Wexler, "Teaching Music Students to Make Music for Love, Not for a Living," *Chronicle of Higher Education* XLVI (July 28, 2000), 136–37.

Karen J. Winkler, "Slowly, Country Music Wins Scholarly Respectability," *Chronicle of Higher Education* XLIV (May 1, 1998), A18–A19.

"Youth Music—a Special Report," *Music Educators Journal* LVI (November 1969), 43–73.

Architecture

B. Lee Cooper, "Building, Burning, Crossing . . . and Feeling Groovy: Examining the Human Condition through Bridge Songs," *International Journal of Instructional Media* XXVII, no. 3 (2000), 315–26.

B. Lee Cooper, "Cross over the Bridge: Images of Bridges in Popular Recordings" (photocopied lyrics and discography of an audio presentation from the 23rd annual convention of the American Culture Association, April 11, 2001, Philadelphia), 1–10.

Alan Hess, *Googie: Fifties Coffee Shop Architecture*. San Francisco: Chronicle Books, 1986.

John Sweetman, *The Artist and the Bridge, 1700–1920*. Brookfield, VT: Ashgate, 1999.

Emily Thompson, *The Soundscape of Modernity: Architectural Acoustics and the Culture of Listening in America, 1900–1933*. Cambridge: MIT Press, 2002.

Art and Photography

K. Abé (comp.), *Jazz Giants: A Visual Retrospective*. New York: Billboard Books, 1988.

Peter Bastine (comp.), *The Book of Shapes—Art in Records: The History of Shaped Records, 1930–Today*. Hamburg, Germany: P. Bastine, 1986.

Peter Belsito, Bob Davis, and Marian Kester, *Streetart: The Punk Poster in San Francisco, 1977–1981*. San Francisco: Last Gasp Press, 1981.

Brad Benedict and Linda Barton (comps.), *Phonographics: Contemporary Album Cover Art and Design*. New York: Collier Books, 1977.

Alan Betrock (comp.), *Rock 'n' Roll Movie Posters*. New York: Shake Books, 1979.

Mal Burns (comp.), *Visions of Rock: Artists Interpretations of the World's Foremost Rock Stars*. London: Proteus Press, 1981.

Stephanie Chernikowski, *Dream Baby Dream: Images from the Blank Generation*. Los Angeles: 2.13.61, 1996.

Anthony Connor and Robert Neff, *The Blues in Images and Interviews*. New York: Cooper Square Press/Rowman and Littlefield, 1999 (first published 1975).

Lisa Day (ed.), *Chicago Blues—As Seen from the Inside: The Photographs of Raeburn Flerlage*. Etobicoke, Ontario: ECW Press, 2000.

Roger Dean and David Howells (comps.), *The Ultimate Album Cover Album*. New York: Prentice Hall, 1987.

George W. Denham and Burt Barack (comps.), *Thirty Years of 45 r.p.m. Picture Sleeves*. Avon, MA: Lorell Press, 1983.

Paul Dowling, *Elvis: The Ultimate Album Cover Book*. New York: Harry N. Adams, 1996.

Spencer Drate, *Rock Art: A Collection of CDs, Albums, and Posters*. Glen Cove, New York: PBC International, 1993.

Frank Driggs and Harris Lewine, *Black Beauty, White Heat: A Pictorial History of Classic Jazz, 1920–1950*. New York: William Morrow, 1982.

Rush Evans, "Concert Poster Art: Austin, Texas Style," *DISCoveries*, no. 94 (March 1996), 29–35.

Holly George-Warren (ed.), *Rolling Stone: The Complete Covers, 1967–1997*. New York: Harry N. Abrams, 1998.

Frank Goldmann and Klaus Hiltscher (eds.), *Grimmix Book of Records: An Almanac of Unusual Records, Sleeves, and Picture Discs*. London: Virgin Books, 1981.

Paul D. Grushkin (artworks photographed by Jon Sievert), *The Art of Rock: Posters from Presley to Punk*. New York: Abbeville Press, 1987.

Walter Herdeg (ed.), *Graphis: Record Covers—The Evolution of Graphics Reflected in Record Packaging*. Zurich: Graphis Press, 1974.

Piet Klaase (text by Mark Gardner and J. Bernlef), *Jam Session: Portraits of Jazz and Blues Musicians Drawn on the Scene*. Newton Abbot: David and Charles, 1985.

Joe Lindsay, "The Beatles International Picture Discography," *DISCoveries* II (February 1989), 24–27.

Graham Marsh and Barrie Lewis (eds.), *The Blues: Album Cover Art*. San Francisco: Chronicle Books, 1996.

Michael Ochs, *Rock Archives: A Photographic Journey through the First Two Decades of Rock and Roll*. New York: Doubleday, 1984.

David Oxtoby (edited by David Sandison), *Rockvisions: The Art of David Oxtoby*. New York: E. P. Dutton, 1978.

Guy Peellaert and Nik Cohn, *Rock Dreams*. New York: Popular Library, 1973.

Charles Reinhart, "Colored Vinyl and The Beatles," *Goldmine*, no. 267 (October 19, 1990), 26–28, 32.

Charles Reinhart, "The Solo Beatles Picture Disc Discography," *Goldmine*, no. 267 (October 19, 1990), p. 23, 102.

Michael P. Smith, *A Joyful Noise: A Celebration of New Orleans Music*. Dallas, TX: Taylor, 1990.

Lynn Wenzel and Carol J. Binkowski, *I Hear America Singing: A Nostalgic Tour of Popular Sheet Music*. New York: Crown, 1989.

Christine Wilson, *All Shook Up: Mississippi Roots of American Popular Music*. Jackson: Mississippi Department of Archives and History, 1995.

Audio Technology

Michael G. Corenthal, *The Iconography of Recorded Sound, 1886–1986: One Hundred Years of Commercial Entertainment and Collecting Opportunity*. Milwaukee, WI: Yesterday's Memories, 1986.

Evan Eisenberg, *The Recording Angel: Music, Records, and Culture from Aristotle to Zappa*. New York: McGraw-Hill, 1988 (first published 1987).

John Harvith and Susan Harvith (eds.), *Edison, Musicians, and the Phonograph: A Historical Guide*. Westport, CT: Greenwood, 1987.

Allen Koenigsberg, *The Patent History of the Phonograph* (rev. and enlarged ed.). New York: Antique Phonographs, 1992.

Andre Millard, *America on Record: A History of Recorded Sound*. Cambridge: Cambridge University Press, 1995.

Russell Miller and Roger Boar (edited by Jacques Lowe), *The Incredible Music Machine: 100 Glorious Years*. London: Quartet/Visual Arts, 1982.

Oliver Read and Walter Welch, *From Tin Foil to Stereo: Evolution of the Phonograph*. Indianapolis, IN: Bobbs-Merrill, 1959.

Eric L. Reiss, *The Compleat Talking Machine*. New York: Vestal Press, 1986.

James R. Smart and Jon W. Newsom, *"A Wonderful Invention": A Brief History of the Phonograph from Tinfoil to the LP*. Washington, D.C.: Library of Congress, 1977.

Black Studies

Joseph K. Adjaye and Adrianne R. Andrews (eds.), *Language, Rhythm, and Sound: Black Popular Cultures into the Twenty-First Century*. Pittsburgh: University of Pittsburgh Press, 1997.

Paul Allen Anderson, *Deep River: Music and Memory in Harlem Renaissance Thought*. Durham, NC: Duke University Press, 2001.

Houston A. Baker, Jr., *Black Studies, Rap, and the Academy*. Chicago: University of Chicago Press, 1993.

William Barlow and Cheryl Finley, *From Swing to Soul: An Illustrated History of African American Popular Music from 1930 to 1960*. Washington, D.C.: Elliott and Clark, 1994.

David Ross Baskerville, "Black Music, Pop, and Rock vs. Our Obsolete Curricula," *NAJE Educator* III (April-May 1971), 5–7, 27–28.

B. Lee Cooper, "Popular Music: An Untapped Resource for Teaching Contemporary Black History," *Journal of Negro Education* XLVIII (winter 1979), 20–36.

B. Lee Cooper, "Promoting Social Change through Audio Repetition: Black Musicians as Creators and Revivalists, 1953–1978," *Tracking: Popular Music Studies* II (winter 1989), 26–46.

B. Lee Cooper, "Repeating Hit Tunes, A Cappella Style: The Persuasions as Song Revivalists, 1967–1982," *Popular Music and Society* XIII (fall 1989), 17–27.

Ralph Cooper, with Steve Dougherty, *Amateur Night at the Apollo: Ralph Cooper Presents Five Decades of Great Entertainment*. New York: Harper Collins, 1990.

Sam Dennison, *Scandalize My Name: Black Imagery in American Popular Music*. New York: Garland, 1982.

Mary Ellison, *Lyrical Protest: Black Music's Struggle against Discrimination*. New York: Praeger Books, 1989.

Samuel A. Floyd, Jr. (ed.), *Black Music in the Harlem Renaissance: A Collection of Essays*. Westport, CT: Greenwood, 1990.

Samuel A. Floyd, Jr., *The Power of Black Music: Interpreting Its History from Africa to the United States*. New York: Oxford University Press, 1995.

Ted Fox, *Showtime at the Apollo: 50 Years of Great Entertainment from Harlem's World Famous Theatre*. New York: Holt, Rinehart, and Winston, 1983.

Paul Fryer, " 'Can You Blame the Colored Man?': The Topical Song in Black American Popular Music," *Popular Music and Society* VIII (1981), 19–31.

Phyl Garland, *The Sound of Soul: The History of Black Music*. Chicago: Henry Regnery, 1969.

Michael Haralambos, *Right On: From Blues to Soul in Black America*. New York: Drake, 1975.

Jim Haskins, *The Cotton Club*. New York: Hippocrene Books, 1994.

Frank W. Hoffmann, "Popular Music and Its Relationship to Black Social Consciousness," *Popular Music and Society* VIII, nos. 3 and 4 (1982), 55–61.

Jerah Johnson, "Jim Crow Laws of the 1890s and the Origins of New Orleans Jazz," *Popular Music* XIX (April 2000), 243–51.

Lawrence W. Levine, *Black Culture and Black Consciousness: Afro-American Folk Thought from Slavery to Freedom*. New York: Oxford University Press, 1977.

George H. Lewis, "Protest and Social Change in Black American Popular Music," *Billboard* LXXXVIII (July 4, 1976), 147, 150.

W. T. Lhamon, Jr., *Raising Cain: Blackface Performance from Jim Crow to Hip Hop*. Cambridge: Harvard University Press, 1998.

David Margolick, *Strange Fruit: Billie Holiday, Café Society, and an Early Cry for Civil Rights*. Philadelphia: Running Press, 2000.

Jeffrey Melnick, *A Right to Sing the Blues: African Americans, Jews, and American Popular Song*. Cambridge: Harvard University Press, 1999.

Bob Merlis and David Seay, *Heart and Soul: A Celebration of Black Music Style in America, 1930–1975*. New York: Stewart Tabor and Chang, 1997.

Lorenzo Middleton, "The Sorrowful Songs That Saved a College," *Chronicle of Higher Education* XX (April 7, 1980), 3.

Bob Millard, "School House Blues: An African American Art Form Offers New Lessons in Harmony," *Teaching Tolerance* (spring 1999), 17–23.

Peter Monaghan, "The Riffs of Jazz Inspire Social and Political Studies of Black Music," *Chronicle of Higher Education* XLIV (May 1, 1998), A16–A17.

Mark Anthony Neal, *What the Music Said: Black Popular Music and Black Public Culture*. New York: Rutledge, 1999.

Paul Oliver, *Songsters and Saints: Vocal Traditions on Race Records*. New York: Cambridge University Press, 1984.

Alan Pomerance, *Repeal of the Blues: How Black Entertainers Influenced Civil Rights*. Secaucus, NJ: Citadel Press, 1988.

Horace A. Porter, *Jazz Country: Ralph Ellison in America*. Iowa City: University of Iowa Press, 2001.

Ronald M. Radano and Philip Bohlman (eds.), *Music and the Racial Imagination*. Chicago: University of Chicago Press, 1998.

Charlene Regester, "The Construction of an Image and the Destruction of a Star: Josephine Baker Racialized, Sexualized, and Politicized in the African-American Press, The Mainstream Press, and FBI Files," *Popular Music and Society* XXIV (spring 2000), 31–84.

Kerran L. Sanger, *'When the Spirit Says Sing!': The Role of Freedom Songs in the Civil Rights Movement*. New York: Garland Books, 1995.

Jack Schiffman, *Harlem Heyday: A Pictorial History of Modern Black Show Business and the Apollo Theatre*. New York: Promotheus Books, 1984.

Jack Schiffman, *Uptown: The Story of Harlem's Apollo Theatre*. New York: Cowles Book, 1971.

Allen Schoener (ed.), *Harlem on My Mind: Cultural Capitol of Black America, 1900–1968*. New York: Random House, 1968.

Arnold Shaw, *Black Popular Music in America: From the Spirituals, Minstrels, and Ragtime to Soul, Disco, and Hip-Hop*. New York: Schirmer Books, 1986.

Ben Sidran, *Black Talk: How the Music of Black America Created a Radical Alternative to the Values of Western Literary Tradition*. New York: Holt, Rinehart, and Winston, 1971.

Christopher Small, *Music of the Common Tongue: Survival and Celebration in Afro-American Music*. New York: River-Run Press, 1987.

Eileen Southern and Josephine Wright (comps.), *African-American Traditions in Song, Sermon, Tale, and Dance, 1600–1920*. Westport, CT: Greenwood, 1991.

Eileen Southern, *The Music of Black Americans: A History* (3d ed.). New York: W. W. Norton, 1997.

Jon Michael Spencer, *The New Negroes and Their Music: The Success of the Harlem Renaissance*. Knoxville: University of Tennessee Press, 1997.

Jon Michael Spencer, *Re-Searching Black Music*. Knoxville: University of Tennessee Press, 1996.

Philip Tagg, "Open Letter—'Black Music', 'Afro-American Music' and 'European Music'," *Popular Music* VIII (October 1989), 285–98.

Steve Tomashefsky, "The Apollo Theater," *Living Blues*, no. 27 (May/June 1976), 12–17.

Steven C. Tracy, *Langston Hughes and the Blues*. Champaign: University of Illinois Press, 2001.

Jessie Walker, *The Apollo Theater Story*. New York: Apollo Operations, 1966.

Business and Economics

Jacques Attali, *Noise: The Political Economy of Music*. Minneapolis: University of Minnesota Press, 1985.

David Baskerville, *Music Business Handbook and Career Guide* (6th ed.). Thousand Oaks, CA: Sage, 1995.

Peter Benjaminson, *The Story of Motown*. New York: Grove Press, 1979.

H. Stith Bennett, *On Becoming a Rock Musician*. Amherst: University of Massachusetts Press, 1980.

Peter W. Bernstein, "Record Business: Rocking to the Big Money Beat," *Fortune* XLIX (April 23, 1979), 58–68.

David Bianco, *Heat Wave: The Motown Fact Book*. Ann Arbor, MI: Pierian Press, 1988.

Rob Bowman, "The Academic at the Crossroads of Commerce," *Popular Music and Society* XXI (spring 1997), 5–10.

Ashley Brown, "The Industry at Work," *The History of Rock*, no. 14 (1982), 261.

Ashley Brown and Michael Heatley (eds.), *The Motown Story*. London: Bedford Press, 1985.

Robert Burnett, *The Global Jukebox: The International Music Industry*. London: Routledge Books, 1995.

Robert Burnett, "The Popular Music Industry in Transition," *Popular Music and Society* XVII (spring 1993), 87–114.

Joseph R. Carlton (comp.), *Carlton's Complete Reference Book of Music*. Studio City, CA: Carlton, 1980.

Steve Chapple and Reebee Garofalo, *Rock 'n' Roll Is Here to Pay: The History and Politics of the Music Industry*. Chicago: Nelson-Hall, 1977.

Michael Christiansen, "Cycles of Symbol Production? A New Model to Explain Concentration, Diversity, and Innovation in the Music Industry," *Popular Music* XIV (January 1995), 55–93.

Nadine Cohodas, *Spinning Blues into Gold: The Chess Brothers and the Legendary Chess Records*. New York: St. Martin's Press, 2000.

John Collis, *The Story of Chess Records*. New York: Bloomsbury, 1998.

B. Lee Cooper, "Family Businesses," in *Rock Music in American Popular Culture: Rock 'n' Roll Resources*, by B. Lee Cooper and Wayne S. Haney (New York: Haworth Press, 1995), 97–102.

B. Lee Cooper, "Review of *Capricorn Records Presents the Fire/Fury Story*," *Popular Music and Society* XVII (fall 1993), 113–14.

B. Lee Cooper, "Review of *Club Date Musicians: Playing the New York Party Circuit*, by Bruce A. MacLeod," *Popular Culture in Libraries* II, no. 4 (1994), 111–13.

B. Lee Cooper, "Review of *Duke/Peacock Records: An Illustrated History with Discography*, by Galen Gart and Roy C. Ames, with Ray Funk, Rob Bowman, and David Booth," *Popular Culture in Libraries* I, no. 1 (1993), 154–5.

B. Lee Cooper, "Review of *Heat Wave: The Motown Fact Book*, by David Bianco," *Tracking: Popular Music Studies* II (winter 1989), 47–49.

B. Lee Cooper, "Review of *Jailhouse Rock: The Bootleg Records of Elvis Presley, 1979–1983*, by Lee Cotton and Howard DeWitt," *JEMF Quarterly* XIX (summer 1983), 141–3.

B. Lee Cooper, "Review of *The King Labels: A Discography* (2 vols.), by Michel Ruppli, with the assistance of Bill Daniels," *Popular Music and Society* XI (summer 1987), 114–15.

B. Lee Cooper, "Review of *The Minit/Instant Story*," *Popular Music and Society* XXI (winter 1997), 132–4.

B. Lee Cooper, "Review of *Music Man: Ahmet Ertegun, Atlantic Records, and the Triumph of Rock 'n' Roll*, by Dorothy Wade and Justine Picardie," *Popular Music and Society* XVI (winter 1992), 89–91.

B. Lee Cooper, "Review of *Rock Culture in Liverpool: Popular Music in the Making* by Sara Cohen and *The Rock File: Making It in the Music Business* by Norton York," *Popular Music and Society* XVI (spring 1992), 102–3.

B. Lee Cooper, "Review of *The Stax Story*," *Rock and Blues News*, no. 15 (April-May 2001), 46.

B. Lee Cooper, "Review of *Trumpet Records: An Illustrated History with Discography* by Marc Ryan," *Popular Music and Society* XVI (winter 1992), 93–94.

Don Cusic, *Music in the Market*. Bowling Green, OH: Bowling Green State University Popular Press, 1995.

Bill Dahl, *Motown: The Golden Years*. Iola, WI: Goldmine/Krause, 2002.

Fredric Dannen, *Hit Men: Power Brokers and Fast Money Inside the Music Business*. New York: Times Books, 1990.

Andy Davis, "The Beatles on Apple," *Record Collector*, no. 151 (March 1992), 3–8.

Clive Davis, with James Willwerth, *Clive: Inside the Record Business*. New York: William Morrow, 1975.

Sharon Davis, *Motown: The History*. New York: Sterling Books, 1989.

R. Serge Denisoff, "The Vinyl Crap Game: The Pop Record Industry," *Journal of Jazz Studies* I (June 1974), 3–26.

Richard DiLello, *The Longest Cocktail Party: An Insider's Diary of the Beatles, Their Million-Dollar Apple Empire and Its Wild Rise and Fall*. Chicago, Illinois: Playboy Press, 1972.

Peter Doggett, "The Apple Label," *Record Collector*, no. 46 (June 1983), 4–12.

Peter Doggett, "Apple Records: The Beatles' Great Experiment!" *Record Collector*, no. 108 (August 1988), 3–7.

Mark Duffett, "Transcending Audience Generalizations: Consumerism Reconsidered in the Case of Elvis Presley Fans," *Popular Music and Society* XXIV (summer 2000), 75–91.

Gerald Early, *One Nation under a Groove: Motown and American Culture.* Hopewell, NJ: ECCO Press, 1995.

Marc Eliot, *Rockonomics: The Time behind the Music.* New York: Watts Press, 1989.

Colin Escott and Martin Hawkins, *Sun Records: The Brief History of the Legendary Record Label.* New York: Quick Fox, 1980.

Jory Farr, *Moguls and Madmen. The Pursuit of Power in Popular Music.* New York: Simon & Schuster, 1994.

Bill Flanagan and Jock Baird, "The Failure of Corporate Rock," *Musician*, no. 50 (December 1982), 72–80.

Henrietta Fleek, "Learning from Rock," *Forecast for Home Economics* XVI (October 1970), F-57.

Peter Gammond and Raymond Horricks (eds.), *The Music Goes Round and Round: A Cool Look at the Record Industry.* London: Quartet Books, 1980.

Simon Garfield, *Money for Nothing: Greed and Exploitation in the Music Industry.* New York: Faber and Faber, 1986.

Galen Gart and Roy C. Ames, with contributions from Ray Funk, Rob Bowman and David Booth, *Duke/Peacock Records: An Illustrated History with Discography.* Milford, NH: Big Nickel, 1990.

Nelson George, *Where Did Our Love Go? The Rise and Fall of the Motown Sound.* New York: St. Martin's Press, 1985.

Charlie Gillett, *Making Tracks: Atlantic Records and the Growth of a Multi-Billion-Dollar Industry.* New York: E. P. Dutton, 1974.

Goldmine Publishers (comps.), *2002 Independent Label Directory.* Iola, WI: Krause, 2002.

Peter D. Goldsmith, *Making People's Music: Moe Asch and Folkways Records.* Washington, D.C.: Smithsonian Institution Press, 1998.

Fred Goodman, *The Mansion on the Hill: Dylan, Young, Geffen, Springsteen and the Head-on Collision of Rock and Commerce.* New York: Times Books/Random House, 1997.

Berry Gordy, *To Be Loved: The Music, the Magic, the Memories of Motown—an Autobiography*. New York: Warner Books, 1994.

Clark Halker, " A History of Local 208 and the Struggle for Racial Equality in the American Federation of Musicians," *Black Music Research Journal* VIII (fall 1988), 207–22.

John Hammond, with Irving Townsend, *John Hammond on Record: An Autobiography*. New York: Ridge Press, 1977.

Bruce Haring, *Off the Charts: Ruthless Days and Reckless Nights Inside the Music Industry*. Secaucus, NJ: Birch Lane Press, 1996.

Dave Harker, *One for the Money: Politics and the Popular Song*. London: Hutchinson, 1980.

Hans W. Heinsheimer, "Music From the Conglomerates," *Saturday Review* LII (February 22, 1969), 61–64, 77.

Frank Hoffmann, "Popular Culture, Ink: A Vital New Publishing House for Students, Scholars, and Enthusiasts," *Popular Culture in Libraries* I, no. 2 (1993), 1–10.

Jac Holzman and Gavan Daws, *Follow the Music: The Life and High Times of Elektra Records in the Great Years of American Pop Culture*. Santa Monica, CA: First Media Books, 1998.

Marc Hugunin, "ASCAP, BMI, and the Democratization of American Popular Music," *Popular Music and Society* VII (1979), 8–17.

John A. Jackson, *American Bandstand: Dick Clark and the Making of a Rock 'n' Roll Empire*. New York: Oxford University Press, 1997.

Larry Jaffee, "K-Tel's Place in the Music Industry: Where Have All the One-Hit Wonders Gone?" *Popular Music and Society* X (winter 1986), 43–50.

William Knoedelseder, *Stiffed: A True Story of MCA, the Music Business, and the Mafia*. New York: HarperCollins, 1993.

Mike A. Leadbitter, *From the Bayou: The Story of Goldband Records*. Bexhill-on-Sea, England: Blues Unlimited, 1969.

McKinley "Malik" Lee, Jr., with Frank B. Williams, *Chosen by Fate: My Life Inside Death Row Records*. West Hollywood, CA: Dove Books, 1997.

Paul D. Lopes, "Innovation and Diversity in the Popular Music Industry, 1969–1990," *American Sociological Review* LVII (February 1992), 56–71.

Bruce A. MacLeod, *Club Date Musicians: Playing the New York Party Circuit*. Urbana: University of Illinois Press, 1993.

Jules Malamud, "The Merchandising of Music," *Popular Music and Society* II (summer 1973), 291–6.

Peter McCabe and Robert D. Schonfeld, *Apple to the Core: The Unmaking of the Beatles*. New York: Pocket Books, 1972.

Bill Millar, "Motown/Magician," *The History of Rock*, no. 24 (1982), 470–3.

Elvis Mitchell, *The Motown Album: An American Story*. London: Virgin Books, 1990.

David Morse, *Motown and the Arrival of Black Music*. New York: Collier Books, 1971.

Bert Muirhead, *Stiff: The Story of a Record Label, 1976–1982*. Poole, Dorset, England: Blandford Press, 1983.

R. Michael Murray, *The Golden Age of Walt Disney Records, 1933–1988*. Dubuque, IA: Antique Trader Books, 1997.

Mark Anthony Neal, "Sold Out on Soul: The Corporate Annexation of Black Popular Music, "*Popular Music and Society* XXI (fall 1997), 117–35.

Keith Negus, *Producing Pop: Culture and Conflict in the Popular Music Industry*. New York: Edward Arnold, 1992.

Sean O'Neal, *Elvis, Inc.: The Fall and Rise of the Presley Empire*. Rocklin, CA: Prima, 1996.

Joe Owens, *Welcome to the Jungle: A Practical Guide to Today's Music Business*. New York: HarperCollins, 1992.

Marianne Partridge (ed.), *The Motown Album: The Sound of Young America*. New York: St. Martin's Press, 1990.

Donald S. Passman, *All You Need to Know about the Music Business* (rev. ed.). New York: Simon & Schuster, 1997.

Robert R. Prechter, "Elvis, Frankenstein, and Andy Warhol: Using Pop Culture to Forecast the Stock Market," *Barron's* LXV (September 9, 1985), 6–7, 28.

Harvey Rachlin, *Encyclopedia of the Music Business*. New York: Harper& Row, 1981.

Ronin Ro, *Gangsta: Merchandising the Rhymes of Violence*. New York: St. Martin's Press, 1996.

Ronin Ro, *Have Gun Will Travel: The Spectacular Rise and Violent Fall of Death Row Records*. New York: Doubleday, 1998.

Robert L. Root, Jr., *The Rhetorics of Popular Culture: Advertising, Advocacy, and Entertainment*. Westport, CT: Greenwood, 1987.

Eric W. Rothenbuhler and John W. Dimmick, "Popular Music: Concentration and Diversity in the Industry, 1974–1980," *Journal of Communication* XXXII (winter 1982), 143–9.

John W. Rumble, "Roots of Rock and Roll: Henry Glover at King Records," *Journal of Country Music* XIV, no. 2 (1992), 30–42.

Jack Ryan, *Recollections—The Detroit Years: The Motown Sound by the People Who Made It*. Detroit, MI: J. Ryan (Data Graphics/Whitlaker Marketing), 1982.

John Ryan, *The Production of Culture in the Music Industry: The ASCAP-BMI Controversy*. Lanham, MD: University of America, 1985.

Marc Ryan, *Trumpet Records: An Illustrated History with Discography*. Milford, NH: Big Nickel, 1992.

Russell Sanjek, *American Popular Music and Its Business—The First Four Hundred Years: Volume One, The Beginning to 1790*. New York: Oxford University Press, 1988.

Russell Sanjek, *American Popular Music and Its Business—The First Four Hundred Years: Volume Two, 1790–1909*. New York: Oxford University Press, 1988.

Russell Sanjek, *American Popular Music and Its Business—The First Four Hundred Years: Volume Three, 1900–1984*. New York: Oxford University, Press, 1988.

Russell Sanjek, *From Print to Plastic: Publishing and Promoting America's Popular Music, 1900–1980*. Brooklyn, NY: Institute for Studies in American Music in the Conservatory of Music at Brooklyn College, City University of New York, 1983.

Russell Sanjek and David Sanjek, *The American Popular Music Business in the 20th Century*. New York: Oxford University Press, 1991.

Russell Sanjek (updated by David Sanjek), *Pennies from Heaven: The American Popular Music Business in the Twentieth Century*. New York: Da Capo Press, 1996 (first published 1988).

Kerry Segrave, *Payola in the Music Industry: A History, 1880–1991*. Jefferson, NC: McFarland, 1994.

George Seltzer, *Music Matters: The Performer and the American Federation of Musicians*. Metuchen, NJ: Scarecrow Press, 1989.

Sidney Shemel and William Krasilovsky, *This Business of Music: A Practical Guide to the Music Industry for Publishers, Writers, Record Companies,*

Producers, Artists, and Agents (5th ed., rev. and enlarged). New York: Billboard Books, 1988.

Raynoma Gordy Singleton, with Bryan Brown and Mim Eichler, *Berry, Me, and Motown*. Chicago: Contemporary Books, 1990.

Joe Smith (edited by Mitchell Fink), *Off the Record: An Oral History of Popular Music*. New York: Warner Books, 1988.

Suzanne E. Smith, *Dancing in the Street: Motown and the Cultural Politics of Detroit*. Cambridge: Harvard University Press, 1999.

Susan Smulyan, *Selling Radio: The Commercialization of American Broadcasting, 1920–1934*. Washington, D.C.: Smithsonian Institution Press, 1994.

Robert Stephen Spitz, *The Making of Superstars: Artists and Executives of the Rock Music Business*. Garden City, NY: Anchor Books/Doubleday, 1978.

Geoffrey Stokes, *Starmaking Machinery: Inside the Business of Rock and Roll*. New York: Vintage Books, 1976.

Peter Stromberg, "Elvis Alive? The Ideology of American Consumerism," *Journal of Popular Culture* XXIV (winter 1990), 11–19.

J. Randy Taraborrelli, *Motown: Hot Wax, City Cool, and Solid Gold*. Garden City, NY: Doubleday, 1986.

Bob Thiele, with Bob Golden, *What a Wonderful World: A Lifetime of Recordings*. New York: Oxford University Press, 1995.

Neal Umphred, "Milli Vanilli and the Integrity of the Popular Music Industry," *Goldmine*, no. 274 (January 25, 1991), 5.

Dorothy Wade and Justine Picardie, *Music Man: Ahmet Ertegun, Atlantic Records, and the Triumph of Rock 'n' Roll*. New York: W. W. Norton, 1990.

Don Waller, *The Motown Story: The Inside Story of America's Most Popular Music*. New York: Scribner's, 1985.

Norton York (ed.), *The Rock File: Making It in the Music Business*. New York: Oxford University Press, 1991.

Criminal Justice and Law Enforcement

Werner G. Albert, "Dimensionality of Perceived Violence in Rock Music: Musical Intensity and Lyrical Violence Content," *Popular Music and Society* VI (1978), 27–38.

Burnett Anderson, "Counterfeits, Bootlegs, the Law and You," *Goldmine*, no. 258 (June 1, 1990), 6–7.

Jim Berkenstadt and Belmo, *Black Market Beatles: The Story Behind the Lost Recordings*. Burlington, Ontario: Collector's Guide, 1995.

Roy Blount, Jr., "Whiskey and Blood," *Journal of Country Music* VIII (August 1980), 2, 15–28.

"Bootlegs, Pirates, and Counterfeits: Why Is It Illegal to Manufacture and Sell Some Records by Top Artists?" *Record Collector*, no. 149 (January 1992), 30–32.

Gary Burns, "Marilyn Manson and the Apt Pupils of Littleton," *Popular Music and Society* XXIII (fall 1999), 3–7.

B. Lee Cooper, "Review of *Stop Handgun Violence: Volume One* by Various Artists," *Rock and Blues News*, no. 14 (February-March 2001), 29.

Lee Cotten and Howard A. DeWitt, *Jailhouse Rock: The Bootleg Records of Elvis Presley, 1970–1983*. Ann Arbor, MI: Pierian Press, 1983.

Bruce Eder, "Beatles Bootlegs," *Goldmine*, no. 224 (February 24, 1989), 24–26.

Simon Frith, "Copyright and the Music Business," *Popular Music* VII (January 1988), 57–75.

Galen Gart, "Booting the Blues: Record Piracy in the Late 1940s," *Goldmine*, no. 165 (November 21, 1986), 28–29.

Clinton Heylin, *Bootleg: The Secret History of the Other Recording Industry*. New York: St. Martin's Press, 1994.

James A. Inciardi and Juliet L. Dee, "From the Keystone Cops to *Miami Vice*: Images of Policing in American Popular Culture," *Journal of Popular Culture* XXI (fall 1987), 84–102.

L. R. E. King, *Do You Want to Know a Secret? Making Sense of the Beatles' Unreleased Recordings*. Tucson, AZ: Storyteller Productions, 1988.

L. R. E. King, *Fixing A Hole: A Second Look at the Beatles' Unauthorized Recordings*. Tucson, AZ: Storyteller Productions, 1989.

Jim Leary, " 'Pretty Boy Floyd': An Aberrant Outlaw Ballad," *Popular Music and Society* III (fall 1974), 215–26.

Jamie Melanowski, "Jailhouse Rock," *Spin* II (October 1986), 62–67, 89.

Gary Warren Melton, "An Examination of the Bootleg Record Industry and Its Impact upon Popular Music Consumption," *Tracking: Popular Music Studies* IV (winter 1991), 16–25.

George Plasketes, "Things to Do in Littleton When You're Dead: A Post Columbine Collage," *Popular Music and Society* XXIII (fall 1999), 9–24.

Charles Reinhart, "Beatles Bootleg Update: Reviews of the Latest Vinyl and CD Releases," *Goldmine*, no. 267 (October 19, 1990), 19–22, 112.

Charles Reinhart, *You Can't Do That! Beatles Bootlegs and Novelty Records, 1963–1980*. Ann Arbor, MI: Pierian Press, 1981.

Ronin Ro, *Gangsta: Merchandising the Rhymes of Violence*. New York: St. Martin's Press, 1996.

Ray Schultz, "I'll Stick My Knife Right Down Your Throat . . . : Rock and Violence—The Wave of the 70's and the Legacy of the 50's," *Rock* XI (December 14, 1970), 16–17, 28–29.

Kenneth D. Tunnell, "99 Years Is Almost for Life: Punishment for Violent Crime in Bluegrass Music," *Journal of Popular Culture* XXVI (winter 1992), 165–81.

Dick Weissman, "Some Thoughts on the Columbine Shootings," *Popular Music and Society* no. 3 (fall 1999), 29–30.

Raymond R. Wile, "Record Piracy: The Attempts of the Sound Recording Industry to Protect Itself Against Unauthorized Copying, 1890–1978," *ARSC Journal* XVII (1985), 18–40.

Robert Wright, " 'I'd Sell You Suicide': Pop Music and Moral Panic in the Age of Marilyn Manson," *Popular Music* XIX (October 2000), 365–85.

Clive Young, "Despite Industry Crackdowns, Bootlegs Thrive in the Age of the CD," *Goldmine*, no. 401 (December 8, 1995), 164, 166, 168.

Culinary Arts

Warren James Belasco, "Toward a Culinary Common Denominator: The Rise of Howard Johnson's, 1925–1940," *Journal of American Culture* II (fall 1979), 503–18.

B. Lee Cooper and William L. Schurk, "Food for Thought: Investigating Culinary Images in Contemporary American Recordings," *International Journal of Instructional Media* XIV, no. 3 (1987), 251–62.

B. Lee Cooper and William L. Schurk, "There's a Surfeit of Java in Rio: Coffee Songs as Teaching Resources," *International Journal of Instructional Media* XXVI, no. 2 (1999), 231–6.

Robin LeMesurier and Peggy Sue Honeyman-Scott, *Rock 'n' Roll Cuisine*. New York: Billboard Books, 1988.

Mark Pendergrast, *For God, Country, and Coca-Cola: The Unauthorized History of the Great American Soft Drink and the Company That Makes It*. New York: Touchstone Books/Simon & Schuster, 1997.

Mark Pendergrast, *Uncommon Grounds: The History of Coffee and How It Transformed Our World*. New York: Basic Books, 1999.

Mark Schapiro, "Muddy Waters: The Lore, the Lure, the Lowdown on America's Favorite Addiction," *UTNE Reader*, no. 66 (November-December 1994), 58–66.

William L. Schurk, "Did Skinny Minnie Dance the Too Fat Polka? To Eat or Not to Eat in American Popular Song," (unpublished paper from the 9th annual meeting of the American Culture Association, 25–29 March 1987, Montreal, Canada).

William L. Schurk, "Get Your Biscuits in the Oven and Your Buns in the Bed: The Bakery Trade in Popular Song," (unpublished paper from the 13th annual meeting of the American Culture Association, 27–30 March 1991, San Antonio, Texas).

Drama, Film, and Theatre Studies

Barry Brady, *Reelin' and Rockin': The Golden Age of Rock 'n' Roll Movies*. Australia: Printing Place, 1982.

Alan Clark (comp.), *Rock and Roll in the Movies—Number One*. West Covina, CA: Alan Lungstrum, 1986.

Alan Clark (comp.), *Rock and Roll in the Movies—Number Two*. West Covina, CA: Alan Lungstrum, 1987.

Alan Clark (comp.), *Rock and Roll in the Movies: Number Three*. West Covina, CA: Alan Lungstrum, 1988.

Alan Clark (comp.), *Rock and Roll in the Movies—Number Four*. West Covina, CA: Alan Lungstrum/National Rock 'n' Roll Archives, 1989.

Alan Clark (comp.), *Rock and Roll in the Movies—Number Five*. West Covina, CA: National Rock and Roll Archives, 1993.

B. Lee Cooper, "Dracula and Frankenstein in the Classroom: Examining Theme and Character Exchanges in Film and Music," *International Journal of Instructional Media* XIX, no. 4 (1992), 339–47.

B. Lee Cooper, "A Review Essay and Bibliography of Studies on Rock 'n' Roll Movies, 1955–1963," *Popular Music and Society* XVI (spring 1992), 85–92.

B. Lee Cooper, "Review of *Laughter on Record: A Comedy Discography* by Warren Debenham and *Film, Television, and Stage Music on Phonograph Records: A Discography* by Steve Harris," *Popular Music and Society* XVII (fall 1993), 106–7.

B. Lee Cooper, "Review of *Risky Business: Rock in Film* by R. Serge Denisoff and William D. Romanowski," *Journal of Popular Culture* XXVI (spring 1993), 207–8.

Marshall Crenshaw (edited by Ted Mico), *Hollywood Rock: A Guide to Rock 'n' Roll in the Movies*. New York: HarperCollins, 1994.

R. Serge Denisoff and William D. Romanowski, *Risky Business: Rock in Film*. New Brunswick, NJ: Transaction, 1991.

Didier C. Deutsch (ed.), *VideoHound's Soundtracks: Music from the Movies, Broadway, and Television*. Detroit, MI: Visible Ink Press, 1998.

Thomas Doherty, *Teenagers and Teenpics: The Juvenilization of American Movies in the 1950s*. Boston: Unwin Hyman Books, 1988.

David Ehrenstein and Bill Reed, *Rock on Film*. New York: Delilah Books, 1982.

Krim Gabbard, *Jammin' at the Margins: Jazz in the American Cinema*. Chicago: University of Chicago Press, 1996.

Barry K. Grant, "The Classic Hollywood Musical and the 'Problem' of Rock 'n' Roll," *Journal of Popular Film and Television* XIII (winter 1986), 195–205.

Philip Jenkinson and Alan Warner, *Celluloid Rock: Twenty Years of Movie Rock*. London: Lorrimer, 1974.

William P. Kelly, "Running on Empty: Reimagining Rock and Roll," *Journal of American Culture* IV (winter 1981), 152–9.

Mark Thomas McGee, *The Rock and Roll Movie Encyclopedia of the 1950s*. Jefferson, NC: McFarland, 1990.

Jon Radwan, "A Generic Approach to Rock Film," *Popular Music and Society* XX (summer 1996), 155–71.

William D. Romanowski and R. Serge Denisoff, "Money for Nothin' and the Charts for Free: Rock and the Movies," *Journal of Popular Culture* XXI (winter 1987), 63–78.

Jonathan Romney and Adrian Wootton (eds.), *Celluloid Jukebox: Popular Music and the Movies since the 1950s*. London: British Film Institute, 1995.

Linda J. Sandahl, *Encyclopedia of Rock Music on Film: A Viewer's Guide to Three Decades of Musicals, Concerts, Documentaries, and Soundtracks, 1955–1986*. Poole, England: Blandford Press, 1987.

Jeff Smith, *The Sounds of Commerce: Marketing Popular Film Music*. New York: Columbia University Press, 1998.

Jan Stacy and Ryder Syvertsen, *Rockin' Reels: An Illustrated History of Rock and Roll Movies*. Chicago: Contemporary Books, 1984.

Dave Thompson, "Rock 'n' Roll Movies: The First 25 Years," *Goldmine*, no. 456 (January 16, 1998), 22–6, 102–8.

Education

Ronald E. Butchart and B. Lee Cooper, "Perceptions of Education in the Lyrics of American Popular Music, 1950–1980," *American Music* V (fall 1987), 271–81.

B. Lee Cooper, " 'It's a Wonder I Can Think at All': Vinyl Images of American Public Education, 1950–1980," *Popular Music and Society* IX (winter 1984), 47–65.

Geography and Environmental Studies

Richard Aquila, "Images of the West in Rock Music," *Western Historical Quarterly* XI (October 1980), 415–32.

Richard Aquila (ed.), *Wanted Dead or Alive: The American West in Popular Culture*. Urbana: University of Illinois Press, 1996.

David Bacon and Norman Maslov, *The Beatles' England: There Are Places I'll Remember*. San Francisco: 910 Press, 1982.

Earl F. Bargainneer, "Tin Pan Alley and Dixie: The South in Popular Song," *Mississippi Quarterly* XXX (fall 1977), 527–65.

Jack Barth, *Roadside Elvis: The Complete State-by-State Travel Guide for Elvis Presley Fans*. Chicago: Contemporary Books, 1991.

Richard W. Butler, "The Geography of Rock, 1954–1970," *Ontario Geography* XXIV (1984), 1–33.

George O. Carney, "Bluegrass Grows All Around: The Spatial Dimensions of a Country Music Style," *Journal of Geography* LXXIII (April 1974), 34–55.

George O. Carney, "Country Music and the Radio: A Historical Geographic Assessment," *Rocky Mountain Social Science Journal* XI (April 1974), 19–32.

George O. Carney, "Country Music and the South: A Cultural Geography Perspective," *Journal of Cultural Geography* I (fall/winter 1980), 16–33.

George O. Carney, "Cowabunga! Surfer Rock and the Five Themes of Geography," *Popular Music and Society* XXIII (winter 1999), 3–29.

George O. Carney, "The Diffusion of the All-Country Music Radio Station in the United States, 1971–1974," *JEMF Quarterly* XIII (summer 1977), 58–66).

George O. Carney (ed.), *Fast Food, Stock Cars, and Rock 'n' Roll: Place and Space in American Pop Culture*. Lanham, MD: Rowman and Littlefield, 1995.

George O. Carney, "From Down Home to Uptown: The Diffusion of Country-Music Radio Stations in the United States," *Journal of Geography* LXXVI (March 1977), 104–10.

George O. Carney (comp.), "Geography of Music: A Bibliography," *Journal of Cultural Geography* I (fall/winter 1980), 185–6.

George O. Carney, "Geography of Music: Inventory and Prospect," *Journal of Cultural Geography* X (spring-summer 1990), 35–48.

George O. Carney, "Music and Dance," in *This Remarkable Continent: An Atlas of United States and Canadian Society and Cultures*, edited by John F. Rooney, Jr., Wilbur Zelinsky, and Dean R. Louder. College Station: Texas A&M University Press, 1982, 234–53.

George O. Carney, *Oklahoma's Folk Music Traditions: A Resource Guide*. Stillwater: Oklahoma State University Press, 1979.

George O. Carney, "T for Texas, T for Tennessee: The Origins of American Country Music Notables," *Journal of Geography* LXXVIII (November 1979), 218–25.

George O. Carney, *The Sounds of People and Places: A Geography of American Folk and Popular Music* (3d ed.). Lanham, MD: Rowman and Littlefield, 1994.

Anne Cheney, "Deadheads, Dylan Fans, and Pearl Jammers: Rock Studies in the South," *Popular Culture in Libraries* III, no. 1 (1995), 77–86.

James M. Cobb, "From Muskogee to Luckenbach: Country Music and the Southernization of America," *Journal of Popular Culture* XVI (winter 1982), 81–91.

B. Lee Cooper, "Music and the Metropolis: Lyrical Images of Life in American Cities, 1950–1980," *Teaching History: A Journal of Methods* VI (fall 1981), 72–84.

B. Lee Cooper, "Regional Music," in *Rock Music in American Popular Culture II: More Rock 'n' Roll Resources*, by B. Lee Cooper and Wayne S. Haney (New York: Haworth Press, 1997), 249–66.

B. Lee Cooper, "Review of *Songs of the West*," *Popular Music and Society* XVIII (fall 1994), 97–99.

James R. Curtis, "Woody Guthrie and the Dust Bowl," *Places* III (July 1976), 12–18.

James R. Curtis and Richard F. Rose, "The Miami Sound: A Contemporary Latin Form of Place-Specific Music," *Journal of Cultural Geography* IV (fall-winter 1983), 110–18.

Steven L. Drum, "Country and Western Music as Educational Media," *Journal of Geography* LXX (May 1971), 314.

Larry Ford, "Geography Factors in the Origin, Evolution, and Diffusion of Rock and Roll Music," *Journal of Geography* LXX (November 1971), 455–64.

Larry R. Ford and Floyd M. Henderson, "The Image of Place in American Popular Music, 1891–1970," *Places* I (March 1974), 31–37.

Jon A. Glassgow, "An Example of Spatial Diffusion: Jazz Music," *Geographical Survey* VIII (January 1979), 10–21.

Jeffrey J. Gordon, "How to Teach Comprehensive Geography Skills: 'The Wreck of the Edmond Fitzgerald'," *Social Studies* LXXV (September-October 1984), 186–92.

Jeffrey J. Gordon, "Rock-and-Roll Music: A Diffusion Study." Unpublished master's thesis, Pennsylvania State University, 1970.

Maria Elizabeth Grabe, "Massification Revisited: Country Music and Demography," *Popular Music and Society* XXI (winter 1997), 63–84.

Marcus Gray, *London's Rock Landmarks: The A–Z Guide to London's Rock Geography*. London: Omnibus Books, 1985.

Michael Gray and Roger Osborne, *The Elvis Atlas: A Journey through Elvis Presley's America*. New York: Henry Holt, 1996.

Charles F. Gritzner, Jr., "The Scope of Cultural Geography," *Journal of Geography* LXIV (January 1966), 4–11.

Sheldon Hackney, "The South as a Counter Culture," *American Scholar* XLII (spring 1973), 283–293.

Joe Haertel, "Retracing Elvis' Memphis and Tupelo Footsteps, or How I Spent My Summer Vacation," *Goldmine*, no. 262 (August 10, 1990), 29–38, 131.

Susan Wiley Hardwick and Donald G. Holtgrieve, *Geography for Educators: Standards, Themes, and Concepts*. Upper Saddle River, NJ: Prentice Hall, 1996.

Floyd M. Henderson, "The Image of New York City in American Popular Music, 1890–1970," *New York Folklore Quarterly* XXX (1974), 267–79.

A. Doyne Horsley, "The Spatial Impact of White Gospel Quartets in the United States," *JEMF Quarterly* XV (fall 1979), 91–98.

Cecil Kirk Hutson, "Cotton Pickin', Hillbillies, and Rednecks: An Analysis of Black Oak Arkansas and the Perpetual Stereotyping of the Rural South," *Popular Music and Society* XVII (winter 1993), 47–62.

Ann E. Kellogg, "Spatial Diffusion of Popular Music Via Radio in the United States." Unpublished doctoral dissertation, Michigan State University, 1986.

Douglas Langille, "The Spatial Dynamics and Diffusion of a Culture-Specific Artform: The Geography of Blues." Unpublished bachelor's thesis: University of Guelph, 1975.

John C. Lehr, "Music as an Aid in the Teaching of Geography," *The History and Social Science Teacher* XIX (1984), 223–7.

John C. Lehr, "Texas (When I Die): National Identity and Images of Place in Canadian Country Music Broadcasts," *Canadian Geographer* XXVII (winter 1983), 361–70.

Andrew Leyshon et al., *The Place of Music*. New York: Guilford Press, 1998.

George Lipsitz, *Dangerous Crossroads: Popular Music, Postmodernism, and the Poetics of Place*. New York: Verso Books, 1994.

Kip Lornell, "The Geography of Folk and Popular Music in the United States: An Annotated Bibliography," *Current Musicology* XXXVII/XXXVIII (1984), 127–35.

Hugh MacLean and Vernon Johnson, *An American Rock History—Part Two: The Southwest*. Telford, England: Borderline Productions, 1990.

Bill C. Malone, "The Nationalization of Southern Music," *Journal of Country Music* VIII (August 1980), 29–42.

Ben Marsh, "A Rose-Colored Map," *Harper's Magazine* CCXXV (July 1977), 80–82.

Ben Marsh, "Sing Me Back Home: A Grammar of Places in Country Music Song." Unpublished master's thesis, Pennsylvania State University, 1971.

Douglas K. Meyer, "Country Music and Geographical Themes," *Mississippi Geographer* IV (spring 1976), 65–74.

Patrick Morrow, "The West as Idea in Recent Rock Music," *Indiana Social Studies Quarterly* XXVI (1973/74), 52–64.

Peter Hugh Nash, "Music and Cultural Geography," *The Geographer* XXII (January 1975), 1–14.

Peter Hugh Nash, "Music and Environment: An Investigation of Some of the Spatial Aspects of Production, Diffusion, and Consumption of Music," *Canadian Association of University Schools of Music Journal* V (spring 1975), 42–71.

Peter H. Nash, "Music Regions and Regional Music," *The Deccan Geographer* VI (July-December 1968), 1–24.

Peter Hugh Nash and George O. Carney, "The Seven Themes of Music Geography," *The Canadian Geographer* XL (1996), 69–74.

Alan Nolan, *Rock 'n' Roll Road Trip: The Ultimate Guide to the Sites, the Shrines, and the Legends across America*. New York: Pharos Books, 1992.

Daniel W. Patterson (ed.), *Sounds of the South*. Durham, NC: Duke University Press, 1991.

Tim Perry and Ed Glinert, *Fudor's Rock and Roll Traveler U.S.A.* New York: Fodor's, 1996.

John Platt, *London's Rock Routes*. London: Fourth Estate, 1985.

"The Rockin' Fifties," *The History of Rock* XXI (1982), 410–11.

Neil V. Rosenberg, "From Sound to Style: The Emergence of Bluegrass," *Journal of American Folklore* LXVIII (1965), 245–56.

Piet Schreuders, Mark Lewisohn, and Adam Smith, *The Beatles London: The Ultimate Guide to over 400 Beatles Sites in and around London*. New York: St. Martin's Press, 1994.

Quinta Scott (photographer) and Susan Croce Kelly (author), *Route 66: The Highway and Its People*. Norman: University of Oklahoma Press, 1988.

Tom Snyder, *The Route 66 Traveler's Guide and Roadside Companion*. New York: St. Martin's Press, 1990.

Jean Tavernor, "Musical Themes in Latin American Culture: A Geographic Appraisal," *Bloomsbury Geographer* III (1970), 60–66.

Bruce Thomas, *The Big Wheel: Rock and Roll and Roadside Attractions*. London: Faber and Faber, 1991.

Robert J. Thompson, "Review of Three Books on Route 66," *Journal of American Culture* XVI (spring 1993), 90–91.

Peter Thorpe, "I'm Movin' On: The Escape Theme in Country and Western Music," *Western Humanities Review* XXIV (autumn 1970), 307–18.

Dave Walker, *American Rock 'n' Roll Tour*. New York: Thunder's Mouth Press, 1992.

Michael Wallis, *Route 66: The Mother Road*. New York: St. Martin's Press, 1990.

Eric Weiland, "Woody Guthrie: An Informant of Geographic Themes," *Mississippi Geographer* VI (spring 1978), 32–37.

Christine Wilson, *All Shook Up: Mississippi Roots of American Popular Music*. Jackson: Mississippi Department of Archives and History, 1995.

Richard Wootton, *Honky Tonkin': A Travel Guide to American Music*. Charlotte, NC: East Woods Press, 1980.

William S. Worley, *Beale Street: Crossroads of America's Music*. Kansas City, MO: AODAX, 1998.

Leo Zonn (ed.), *Place Images in Media: Portrayal, Experience, and Meaning*. Savage, MD: Rowman and Littlefield, 1990.

Health Care and Wellness

Joseph K. Albertson and Solomon Goodman, "Music, the Jake Walk, and Jamaica Ginger: Songs about Jake—Leg Paralysis Epidemics in the United States," *Sonneck Society Bulletin* XVI (fall 1990), 103–4.

Ray Astbury, "Drink That Hadacol," *Blues and Rhythm*, no. 53 (July 1990), 4–6.

Jerry C. Brigham and Karlie K. Kenyon, "Hadacol: The Last Great Medicine Show," *Journal of Popular Culture* X (winter 1976), 52–63.

Elizabeth F. Brown and William R. Hendee, "Adolescents and Their Music: Insights into the Health of Adolescents," *Journal of the American Medical Association* CCLXII (September 22–29, 1989), 1659–63.

H. Paul Chalfant and Robert E. Beckley, "Beguiling and Betraying: The Image of Alcohol Use in Country Music," *Journal of Studies on Alcohol* XXXVIII, no. 7 (1977), 1422–33.

David L. Coker and Robert W. Busch, "Some Rock Concerts May Cause Hearing Impairment," *NACUBO Business Officer* XII (March 1979), 29.

B. Lee Cooper, "Examining the Medical Profession through Musical Metaphors," *International Journal of Instructional Media* XXI, no. 2 (1994), 155–63.

B. Lee Cooper, "Processing Health Care Images from Popular Culture Resources: Physicians, Cigarettes, and Medical Metaphors in Contemporary Recordings," *Popular Music and Society* XVII (winter 1993), 105–24.

B. Lee Cooper, "Smokin' Songs: Examining Tobacco Use as an American Cultural Phenomenon through Contemporary Lyrics," *International Journal of Instructional Media* XXI, no. 3 (1994), 261–8.

B. Lee Cooper and Bill Schurk, "Singing, Smoking, and Sentimentality: Cigarette Imagery in Contemporary Recordings," *Popular Music and Society* XXIII (fall 1999), 79–88.

B. Lee Cooper and William L. Schurk, "Symptoms, Illnesses, and Medical Imagery," in *Rock Music in American Popular Culture: Rock 'n' Roll Resources*, by B. Lee Cooper and Wayne S. Haney (New York: Haworth Press, 1995), 287–314.

Andrew E. Curry, "Drugs in Jazz and Rock Music," *Clinical Toxicology* I (June 1968), 236–44.

Mike Douse, "Contemporary Music, Drug Attitudes, and Drug Behavior," *Australian Journal of Social Issues* VIII (February 1973), 74–80.

Andrew L. Gelt (comp.), *Index to Alcohol, Drugs, and Intoxicants in Music.* Albuquerque, NM: A. L. Gelt, 1982.

Don Hagness, "Does Rock Create Deafness?" *Music Journal* XXXI (May 1973), 18.

Charles Jaret and Lyn Thaxton, "Bubbles in My Beer Revisited: The Image of Liquor in Country Music," *Popular Music and Society* VII (1980), 214–22.

Gene Lees, "Music U.S.A.: The Drug Connection," *High Fidelity* XXVIII (October 1978), 22, 24.

George H. Lewis, "Popular Music, Musical Preference, and Drug Use Among Youth," *Popular Music and Society* VII (1980), 176–81.

John P. Morgan and Thomas C. Tulloss, "The Jake Walk Blues: A Toxicologic Tragedy Mirrored in American Popular Music," *Annals of Internal Medicine* LXXXV (December 1976), 804–8.

Robin Lea Pyle, "Elvis Presley and the Western Performing Artist's Unrecognized Role as Social and Self-Healer: Issues of Transformation and Addiction," *Popular Music and Society* XIII (winter 1989), 7–15.

Greg Reibman, "Turn It Down! Hearing Loss: Rock's Ugly Little Secret," *Musician*, no. 102 (April 1987), 114, 110.

John P. Robinson, Robert Pilskaln, and Paul Hirsch, "Protest Rock and Drugs: The Rhetoric of Revolt," *Journal of Communication* XXVI (Autumn 1976), 125–36.

William L. Schurk, "The Rocking Pneumonia and the Boogie Woogie Flu: The Image of the Medical Profession in Popular Song Lyrics." Mimeographed recording list and audio tape presentation given at the annual conference of the Association of Recorded Sound Collections, 3 June 1989, Kansas City, Missouri.

Harry Shapiro, *Waiting for the Man: The Story of Drugs and Popular Music.* New York: William Morrow, 1989.

Stan Soocher, "Rockers Sued for Ear Damage," *Musician*, no. 141 (July 1990), 28–30.

Joseph Turow, *Playing Doctor: Television, Storytelling, and Medical Power.* New York: Oxford University Press, 1989.

Joel Vance, "Review of *Jake Walk Blues* (Stash ST 110)," *Stereo Review* XL (June 1978), 116.

James Harvey Young, *The Medical Messiahs: A Social History of Health Quackery in Twentieth-Century America*. Princeton, NJ: Princeton University Press, 1967.

History

Richard Aquila, "A Scholar Takes His Views on Rock 'n' Roll to the Air," *Chronicle of Higher Education* XLIII (January 31, 1997), B7.

Kenneth J. Bindas, *All of This Music Belongs to the Nation: The W.P.A.'s Federal Music Project and American Society, 1935–1939*. Knoxville: University of Tennessee Press, 1995.

Hugh E. Boyer, "A Report on the Use of Music in the History Classroom," *Network News Exchange* IV (spring 1979), 19–20.

George Chilcoat (comp.), "Teaching about Slavery through Folk Song," *Folksongs in the Classroom* IV (May 17, 1984), 57–81.

George W. Chilcoat, Laurence I. Seidman, Sheldon Brown, and B. Lee Cooper, "Studying U.S. History through Songs," *Social Education* XLIX (October 1985), 579–603.

Nora D. Christianson, "Teaching American History through Its Period Music," *Social Studies* XL (April 1949), 156–65.

Norm Cohen, *Long Steel Rail: The Railroad in American Folksong*. Urbana: University of Illinois Press, 1981.

John P. Coleman, "The Soundtrack of the Past——Popular Music in American History," *School and Community* LXII (March 1976), 13.

B. Lee Cooper, "Audio Musicology: A Discography of Tributes to Musical Styles and Recording Artists," *International Journal of Instructional Media* XXVI, no. 4 (1999), 459–67.

B. Lee Cooper, "Creating an Audio Chronology: Utilizing Popular Recordings to Illustrate Ideas and Events in American History, 1965–1987," *International Journal of Instructional Media* XVI, no. 2 (1989), 167–79.

B. Lee Cooper, "Examining Social Change through Contemporary History: An Audio Media Proposal," *The History Teacher* VI (August 1973), 523–34.

B. Lee Cooper, "Examining the Audio Images of War: Lyrical Perspectives on America's Major Military Crusades, 1914–1991," *International Journal of Instructional Media* XIX, no. 3 (1992), 277–87.

B. Lee Cooper, "Folk History, Alternative History, and Future History," *Teaching History: A Journal of Methods* II (spring 1977), 58–62.

B. Lee Cooper, "Mick Jagger as Herodotus and Billy Joel as Thucydides: A Rock Music Perspective, 1950–1985," *Social Education* XLIX (October 1985), 596–600.

B. Lee Cooper, "Oral History, Popular Music, and American Railroads, 1920–1980," *Social Studies* LXXIV (November/December 1983), 223–31.

B. Lee Cooper, "Oral History, Popular Music, and Les McCann," *Social Studies*, LXVII (May/June 1976), 115–18.

B. Lee Cooper, "Popular Music: An Untapped Resource for Teaching Contemporary Black History," *Journal of Negro Education* XLVIII (winter 1979), 20–36.

B. Lee Cooper, "Popular Music during World War II: Patriotism and Personal Communications," *International Journal of Instructional Media* XXIII, no. 2 (1996), 181–92.

B. Lee Cooper, "Popular Records as Oral Evidence: Creating an Audio Time Line to Examine American History, 1955–1987," *Social Education* LIII (January 1989), 34–40.

B. Lee Cooper, "Record Revivals as Barometers of Social Change: The Historical Use of Contemporary Audio Resources," *JEMF Quarterly* XIV (spring 1978), 38–44.

B. Lee Cooper, "Review of *Born in the U.S.A.: The Myth of America in Popular Music from Colonial Times to the Present* by Timothy E. Scheurer," *Journal of American Culture* XV (summer 1992), 91–92.

B. Lee Cooper, "Review of *The Rolling Stone Illustrated History of Rock and Roll* (3d ed.) by Anthony DeCurtis and James Henke, with Holly George-Warren," *Popular Music and Society* XVI (winter 1993), 134–5.

B. Lee Cooper, "Teaching American History through Popular Music," *AHA Newsletter* XIV (October 1976), 3–5.

B. Lee Cooper and Donald E. Walker, "Review of *The Unofficial Encyclopedia of the Rock and Roll Hall of Fame* by Nick Talevski," *Journal of Popular Culture* XXXIV (summer 2000), 172–5.

B. Lee Cooper and Donald E. Walker, "Teaching American History through Major League Baseball and Popular Music: A Resource Guide," *International Journal of Instructional Media* XVII, no. 1 (1990), 83–87.

Peter Cronin, Scott Isler, and Mark Rowland, "Elvis Presley: An Oral Biography," *Musician*, no. 168 (October 1992), 50–67.

Jim Curtis, *Rock Eras: Interpretations of Music and Society, 1954–1984*. Bowling Green, OH: Bowling Green State University Popular Press, 1987.

Frederick E. Danker, "Folksongs in the High School Classroom," *Sing Out!* XIII (February-March 1963), 16–17.

Paul Desruisseaux, "A Scholar Teaches the History of Rock 'n' Roll—and, in the Process, the Country's," *Chronicle of Higher Education* XXVI (April 20, 1983), 5–6.

Harry Dhand, "Musical Reflections of Canada's History," *Social Education* XXXV (October 1971), 624–7.

John E. DiMeglio, "Music in World History Classes," *The History Teacher* IV (January 1971), 54–56.

David K. Dunaway and Willa K. Baum (eds.), *Oral History: An Interdisciplinary Anthology* (2d ed.). Walnut Creek, CA: AltaMira Press, 1996.

Foster M. Farley, "Music and Liberty," *Musical Heritage Review* I (November 21, 1977), 16–18ff.

Paul Friedlander, *Rock and Roll: A Social History*. Boulder, CO: Westview Press, 1996.

William Graebner, "Teaching 'The History of Rock 'n' Roll'," *Teaching History: A Journal of Methods* IX (spring 1984), 2–20.

John Greenway, "Folk Songs as Socio-Historical Documents," *Western Folklore* XIX (January 1960), 1–9.

Bernard Grun, *The Timetables of History: A Horizontal Linkage of People and Events* (rev. ed.). New York: Touchstone Books/Simon & Schuster, 1982.

Herb Hendler, *Year by Year in the Rock Era: Events and Conditions Shaping the Rock Generations That Reshaped America*. Westport, CT: Greenwood, 1983.

"The History Teacher: 'Piano Man' [Billy] Joel Lights a Fire in the Nation's Classrooms," *Lansing* [Michigan] *State Journal* (January 21, 1990), 1F.

Paul Dennis Hoffmann, "Using Rock Music to Teach History," *OAH Magazine of History* I (April 1985), 10–11.

Eric P. Johnson, "The Use of Folk Songs in Education: Some Examples of the Use of Folk Songs in the Teaching of History, Geography, Economics, and English Literature," *The Vocational Aspect of Education* XXI (summer 1969), 89–94.

Hugo A. Keesing, "Popular Music in American Society—American Studies 298 (3 credits—sixteen-week semester)," in *Currents of Warm Life: Popular Culture in American Higher Education*, edited by Mark Gordon and Jack Nachbar. Bowling Green, OH: Bowling Green State University Popular Press, 1980, 93–97.

John Kimball, "Music and the Teaching of American History," *Social Education* XXVII (January 1963), 23–25.

Stephen Kneeshaw, " 'What If . . .': Alternative History, or Teaching What Might Have Been," *The History and Social Science Teacher* XVIII (fall 1982), 3–7.

Laura Kuhn, *Music Since 1900* (6th ed.). New York: Schirmer Reference, 2001.

Robbie Lieberman, *My Song Is My Weapon: People's Songs, American Communism, and the Politics of Culture, 1930–1950*. Urbana: University of Illinois Press, 1989.

Timothy P. Lynch, *Strike Songs of the Depression*. Jackson: University Press of Mississippi, 2001.

L.R. Meeth and Dean S. Gregory (comps.), *Directory of Teaching Innovations in History*. Arlington, VA: Studies in Higher Education, 1981.

George Mehaffy and Thad Sitton, "Oral History: A Strategy That Works," *Social Education* XLI (May 1977), 378–81.

George L. Mehaffy and Thad Sitton, "Oral History Tells Its Own Story: The 'Loblolly' Project," *Social Studies* LXVIII (November/December, 1977), 231–5.

Richard L. Menzel, "Cognitive Connection: The Rolling Stone Guide to the Teaching of World History," *Social Studies* LXXXI (March 1990), 70–72.

MacDonald Smith Moore, *Yankee Blues: Musical Culture and American Identity*. Bloomington: Indiana University Press, 1985.

"More Scholars Focus on Popular Music as a Key to Examining Culture and History," *Chronicle of Higher Education* XLIV (May 1, 1998), A16.

John Morthland, "The King Remembered: An Oral History," *Country Music* VIII (January-February 1980), 45–55.

Jean W. Mueller, "Rock 'n' Roll Heroes: Letter to President Eisenhower," *Social Education* XLIX (May 1985), 406–8.

Allan Nevins, "Oral History: How and Why It Was Born," *Wilson Library Bulletin* XL (March 1966), 600–1.

Robert Palmer, *Rock and Roll: An Unruly History*. New York: Harmony Books, 1995.

Roy Palmer, *The Sound of History: Songs and Social Comment*. New York: Oxford University Press, 1988.

David R. Pichaske, *A Generation in Motion: Popular Music and Culture in the Sixties*. Granite Falls, MN: Ellis Press, 1989.

Jerome L. Rodnitzky, "Popular Music in American Studies," *History Teacher* VII (August 1974), 503–10.

Timothy E. Scheurer, *Born in the U.S.A.: The Myth of America in Popular Music from Colonial Times to the Present*. Jackson: University Press of Mississippi, 1991.

Jane Scott, "Professor Charles Brown's Rock 'n' Roll 101," *The* [Cleveland] *Plain Dealer* (September 1984), 1C.

John Anthony Scott, *The Ballad of America: The History of the United States in Song and Story*. Carbondale: Southern Illinois University Press, 1983.

Laurence I. Seidman, "Folksongs: Magic in Your Classroom," *Social Education* XLIX (October 1985), 580–7.

Laurence I. Seidman, "Teaching about the American Revolution through Its Folk Songs," *Social Education* XXXVII (November 1973), 653–64.

Thad Sitton, George L. Mehaffy, and O. L. Davis, Jr., *Oral History: A Guide for Teachers (and Others)*. Austin: University of Texas Press, 1983.

Joe Smith (edited by Mitchell Fink), *Off the Record: An Oral History of Popular Music*. New York: Warner Books, 1988.

David P. Szatmary, *Rockin' in Time: A Social History of Rock-and-Roll* (2d ed.). Englewood Cliffs, NJ: Prentice Hall, 1991.

Louis "Studs" Terkel, *Hard Times: An Oral History of the Great Depression*. New York: Pantheon, 1970.

Studs Terkel, *Envelopes of Sound: Six Practitioners Discuss the Method, Theory and Practice of Oral History and Oral Testimony*. New York: Precedent, 1975.

Guido Van Rijn, *Roosevelt's Blues: African-American Blues and Gospel Songs on FDR*. Jackson: University Press of Mississippi, 1997.

Ed Ward, Geoffrey Stokes, and Ken Tucker, *Rock of Ages: The Rolling Stone History of Rock and Roll*. New York: Rolling Stone Press/Summit Books, 1986.

Mitch Yamasaki, "Using Rock 'n' Roll to Teach the History of Post–World War II America," *History Teacher* XXIX (February 1996), 179–93.

International Relations and Military History

Terry H. Anderson, "American Popular Music and the War in Vietnam," *Peace and Change* XI (July 1986), 51–65.

Maxene Andrews, *Over Here, Over There: The Andrews Sisters and the USO Stars in World War II*. New York: Kensington Press, 1993.

Ben H. Auslander, " 'If Ya Wanna End War and Stuff, You Gotta Sing Loud': A Survey of Vietnam-Related Protest Music," *Journal of American Culture* IV (summer 1981), 108–13.

Tony Bacon, *London Live: From the Yardbirds to Pink Floyd to the Sex Pistols—The Inside Story of Live Bands in the Capital's Trail-Blazing Music Clubs*. San Francisco: Balafon Books/Miller Freeman Books, 1999.

Kenneth J. Bindas and Craig Houston, " 'Takin' Care of Business': Rock Music, Vietnam, and the Protest Myth," *The Historian* LII (November 1989), 1–23.

Kent Bowman, "Echoes of Shot and Shell: Songs of the Great War," *Studies in Popular Culture* X, no. 1 (1987), 27–41.

Sheldon Brown, "The Depression and World War II as Seen through Country Music," *Social Education* XLIX (October 1985), 588–94.

George W. Chilcoat, "The Images of Vietnam: A Popular Music Approach," *Social Education* 49 (October 1985), 601–3.

Jennie A. Chinn, " 'There's a Star-Spangled Banner Waving Somewhere': Country-Western Songs of World War II," *JEMF Quarterly* XVI (summer 1980), 74–80.

Charlie Clark, "The Tracks of Our Tears—When Rock Went to War: Looking Back on Vietnam and Its Music," *Veteran* (February 1986), 10–23.

Les Cleveland, *Dark Laughter: War in Song and Popular Culture*. Westport, CT: Praeger Books, 1994.

Les Cleveland, "Singing Warriors: Popular Songs in Wartime," *Journal of Popular Culture* XXVIII (winter 1994), 159–75.

Christopher Connelly, "Voice of America: Rock and Roll with Uncle Sam," *Rolling Stone*, no. 402 (August 18, 1983), 37, 46–47.

B. Lee Cooper, "From 'Love Letters' to 'Miss You': Popular Recordings, Epistolary Imagery, and Romance during War-Time, 1941–1945," *Journal of American Culture* XIX (winter 1996), 15–27.

B. Lee Cooper, "I'll Fight for God, Country, and My Baby: Persistent Themes in American Wartime Songs," *Popular Music and Society* XVI (summer 1992), 95–111.

B. Lee Cooper, "Popular Songs, Military Conflicts, and Public Perceptions of the United States at War," *Social Education* LVI (March 1992), 160–8.

B. Lee Cooper, "Reveille, Riveting, and Romance Remembered: Popular Recordings of the World War II Era," in *Proceedings of the University of Great Falls World War II Symposium (October 2–6, 1995)*, edited by William Furdell. Great Falls, MT: University of Great Falls, 1996, 43–73.

B. Lee Cooper, "Review of *The Omnibus Book of British and American Hit Singles, 1960–1990* by Dave McAleer," *Popular Culture in Libraries* I, no. 2 (1993), 121–2.

B. Lee Cooper, "Review of *The Vietnam Experience: A Concise Encyclopedia of American Literature, Songs, and Film* by Kevin Hillstrom and Laurie Collier Hillstrom," *Popular Music and Society* XXIV (summer 2000), 170–2.

B. Lee Cooper, "Tapping a Sound Recording Archive for War Song Resources to Investigate America's Major Military Involvements, 1914–1991," *Popular Culture in Libraries* I (fall 1986), 29–42.

B. Lee Cooper and Laura E. Cooper, "Commercial Recordings and Cultural Interchanges: Studying Great Britain and The United States, 1943–1967," *International Journal of Instructional Media* XIX, no. 2 (1992), 183–9.

Laura E. Cooper and B. Lee Cooper, "Exploring Cultural Imperialism: Bibliographical Resources for Teaching about American Domination, British Adaptation, and the Rock Music Interchange, 1950–1967," *International Journal of Instructional Media* XVII, no. 2 (1990), 167–77.

Laura E. Cooper and B. Lee Cooper, "From American Forces Network to Chuck Berry, From Larry Parnes to George Martin: The Rise of Rock Music Culture in Great Britain 1943 to 1967 and Beyond—a Biblio-Historical Study," *Popular Culture in Libraries* I, no. 2 (1993), 33–64.

R. Serge Denisoff, "Fighting Prophecy with Naplam: 'The Ballad of the Green Berets'," *Journal of American Culture* XIII (spring 1990), 81–93.

R. Serge Denisoff (comp.), *Songs of Protest, War, and Peace: A Bibliography and Discography*. Santa Barbara, CA: ABC/CLIO Press, 1973.

R. Serge Denisoff and William D. Romanowski, "The Pentagon's Top Guns: Movies and Music," *Journal of American Culture* XII (fall 1989), 67–78.

Robin Denselow, *When the Music's Over: The Story of Political Pop*. London: Faber and Faber, 1990.

Mary Ellison, "War—It's Nothing but a Heartbreak: Attitudes to War in Black Lyrics," *Popular Music and Society* X (fall 1986), 29–42.

Paul Fryer, " 'Everybody's on Top of the Pops': Popular Music on British Television, 1960–1985," *Popular Music and Society* XXI (fall 1997), 153–71.

Gary Graff, "War Likely to Make Music, but Not Like That of '60s," *Detroit Free Press* (February 3, 1991), 1G, 4G.

Bob Groom, "Tiger in the Night," *Blues and Rhythm*, no. 66 (January 1992), 12–15.

Dick Heckstall-Smith, *The Safest Place in the World: A Personal History of Rhythm and Blues*. London: Quartet Books, 1991.

Peter Hesbacher and Les Waffen, "War Recordings: Incidence and Change, 1940–1980," *Popular Music and Society* VIII (summer/fall 1982), 77–101.

Don J. Hibbard and Carol Kaleialoha, "Anti-War Songs," in *The Role of Rock*. Englewood Cliffs, NJ: Prentice Hall, 1983, 55–60.

Anthony Hopkins, *Songs of the Front and Rear: Canadian Servicemen's Songs of the Second World War*. Edmonton, Alberta: Hurtig, 1979.

David E. James, "The Vietnam War and American Music," *Social Text* XXIII (fall-winter 1989), 122–43.

Hugo A. Keesing, "Pop Goes to War: The Music of World War II and Vietnam." Mimeographed paper presented at the 9th national convention of the Popular Culture Association, April 1979, Pittsburgh, Pennsylvania).

Hugo A. Keesing, "Recorded Music and the Vietnam War: The First Twenty-Five Years." Mimeographed paper presented at the 17th national convention of the Popular Culture Association, March 1987, Montreal, Canada).

Hugo A. Keesing (comp.), *World War II's Distaff Army: An Annotated Index of Original Songs about WACs and Nurses*. Columbia, MD: Keesing Musical Archives, 1996.

Hugo A. Kessing (comp.), *Yankee Doodle Girl: Sheet Music's Description of Women in the Military During World War II*. Columbia, MD: Keesing Musical Archives, 1996.

John Lello, "Using Popular Songs of the Two World Wars in High School History," *History Teacher* XIV (November 1980), 37–41.

Jeffrey C. Livingston, "Still Boy-Meets-Girl Stuff: Popular Music and War," in *America's Musical Pulse: Popular Music in Twentieth-Century Society*, edited by Kenneth J. Bindas. Westport, CT: Praeger Books, 1992, 33–42.

Jens Lund, "Country Music Goes to War: Songs for the Red-Blooded American," *Popular Music and Society* I (summer 1972), 210–30.

William K. McNeil, " 'We'll Make the Spanish Grunt': Popular Songs about the Sinking of the *Maine*," *Journal of Popular Culture* II (spring 1969), 537–551.

G. P. Mohrmann and F. Eugene Scott, "Popular Music and World War II: The Rhetoric of Continuation," *Quarterly Journal of Speech* LXII (February 1976), 145–56.

Brian Murdoch, *Fighting Songs and Warring Words: Popular Lyrics of Two World Wars*. London: Routledge, 1990.

Paul Oliver (ed.), *Black Music in Britain: Essays on the Afro-Asian Contributions to Popular Music*. Milton Keynes, England: Open University Press, 1990.

Martin Page (ed.), *Kiss Me Goodnight, Sergeant Major: The Songs and Ballads of World War II*. London: Hart-Davis MacGibbon, 1973.

James Perone, *Songs of the Vietnam Conflict*. Westport, CT: Greenwood, 2001.

Douglas W. Reitinger, "Paint It Black: Rock Music and Vietnam War Film," *Journal of American Culture* XV (fall 1992), 53–59.

Christine Scodari, "Johnny Got His Gun: Wartime Songs of Pacifism, Patriotism, and Life Style in 20th-Century American Culture," *Popular Music and Society* XVIII (spring 1994), 1–17.

Steven Seidenberg, Maurice Sellar, and Lou Jones, *You Must Remember This. . .: Songs at the Heart of the War*. London: Boxtree, 1995.

Les Waffen and Peter Hesbacher, "War Songs: Hit Recordings during the Vietnam Period," *ARSC Journal* XIII, no. 2 (1981), 4–18.

Allen L. Woll, *The Hollywood Musical Goes to War*. Chicago: Nelson-Hall, 1983.

Chris Woodford, "British Beat before the Beatles," *Now Dig This*, no. 126 (September 1993), 9–10.

Chris Woodford, "British Beat before the Beatles," *Now Dig This*, no. 127 (October 1993), 24–26.

Chris Woodford, "British Beat before the Beatles," *Now Dig This*, no. 129 (December 1993), 24–25.

Journalism

Lester Bangs (edited by Greil Marcus), *Psychotic Reactions and Carburetor Dung—The Work of a Legendary Critic: Rock 'n' Roll as Literature and Literature as Rock 'n' Roll*. New York: Knopf, 1988.

Ann P. Basart, *Writing about Music: A Guide to Publishing Opportunities for Authors and Reviewers*. Berkeley, CA: Fallen Leaf Press, 1989.

Steven Blush, "A Talk with Albert Goldman: Rock's Most Vilified Scribe," *Goldmine*, no. 339 (July 23, 1993), 42–44, 149.

Herb Boyd, "A Talk with Gerri Hirshey," *R.P.M.*, no. 7 (September/October 1984), 64–65.

Robert Christgau, "Rock Critics," *Harper's* CCXXXIX (September 1969), 24–28.

Nik Cohn, *Ball the Wall: Nik Cohn in the Age of Rock*. London: Picador Books, 1989.

Maria Columbus, "A Decade of Elvis in Print," *DISCoveries* I (July/August 1988), 34–36.

B. Lee Cooper, "Review of *The Heart of Rock and Soul: The 1001 Greatest Singles Ever Made* by Dave Marsh," *Michigan Academician* XXIII (spring 1991), 203–5.

Anthony DeCurtis, *Rocking My Life Away: Writing about Music and Other Matters*. Durham, NC: Duke University Press, 1998.

Jim DeRogatis, *Let It Blurt: The Life and Times of Lester Bangs, America's Greatest Rock Critic*. New York: Broadway Books/Random House, 2000.

Howard A. DeWitt, "*The New Musical Express* and the Beatles," in *The Beatles: Untold Tales*. Fremont, CA: Horizon Books, 1985, 211–25.

Howard A. DeWitt, "Will the Beatles Please Go Away? *Melody Maker* Reacts to the New Music," in *The Beatles: Untold Tales*. Fremont, CA: Horizon Books, 1985, 183–209.

Robert Draper, *Rolling Stone Magazine: The Uncensored History*. Garden City, NY: Doubleday, 1990.

Linda M. Fidler and Richard S. James (eds.), *International Music Journals*. Westport, CT: Greenwood, 1990.

Chet Flippo, "The History of *Rolling Stone*: Part 1," *Popular Music and Society* III (spring 1974), 159–88.

Chet Flippo, "The History of *Rolling Stone*: Part II," *Popular Music and Society* III (summer 1974), 258–80.

Chet Flippo, "The History of *Rolling Stone*: Part III," *Popular Music and Society* III (summer 1974), 281–98.

Ben Fong-Torres, *Not Fade Away: A Backstage Pass to 20 Years of Rock and Roll*. San Francisco: Miller Freeman Books, 1999.

Murray Forman, "Media Form and Cultural Space: Negotiating Rap 'Fanzines'," *Journal of Popular Culture* XXIX (fall 1999), 171–88.

Gary Giddins, *Faces in the Crowd: Musicians, Writers, Actors, and Filmmakers*. New York: Da Capo Press, 1996.

Gary Giddins, *Rhythm-a-ning: Jazz Tradition and Innovation in the '80s*. New York: Oxford University Press, 1985.

Gary Giddins, *Riding on a Blue Note: Jazz and American Pop*. New York: Oxford University Press, 1981.

David D. Ginsburg, "Fandomania: A Brief History of Fanzines . . .," *Goldmine*, no. 79 (December 1982), 191–3.

David D. Ginsburg, "Jazz and Black Music Bibliographies: Retrospective, Current, and Selective," *Goldmine*, no. 80 (January 1983), 176–7.

Michael Goldberg, "Rock and Roll Fanzines: A New Underground Press Flourishes," *Rolling Stone*, no. 418 (March 29, 1984), 55–59.

Robert Gottlieb (ed.), *Reading Jazz: A Gathering of Autobiography, Reportage, and Criticism From 1919 to Now*. New York: Pantheon Books, 1996.

Joe Gow, "Writing Rock Journalism: An Interview with Charles M. Young," *Popular Music and Society* XVI (summer 1992), 67–74.

Peter Guralnick, "My Back Pages: What Motivates a Music Critic?" *Musician*, no. 126 (April 1989), 27–34, 89.

David Hayles, "Beatles' U.K. Books and Magazines," *Record Collector*, no. 17 (January 1981), 28–33.

Nat Hentoff, *Listen to the Stories: Nat Hentoff on Jazz and Country Music*. New York: Harper Collins, 1995.

Clinton Heylin (ed.), *The Penguin Book of Rock and Roll Writing*. New York: Penguin Books, 1992.

Sally James, *Sally James' Almost Legendary Pop Interviews*. London: Eel Pie, 1981.

Steve Jones, "Popular Music, Criticism, Advertising, and the Music Industry," *Journal of Popular Music Studies* V (1993), 79–91.

Nick Kent, *The Dark Stuff: Selected Writings on Rock Music, 1972–1995*. New York: Da Capo Press, 1995.

Peter Knobler, "On the Nature of Rock Journalism," *Crawdaddy* (February 1973), 28–31.

Jon Landau, *It's Too Late to Stop Now: A Rock and Roll Journal*. San Francisco: Straight Arrow Books, 1972.

Philip Larkin, *Required Writing: Miscellaneous Pieces, 1955–1982*. London: Faber and Faber, 1983.

George H. Lewis, "Won't Get Fooled Again: 25 Years of Pop Recordings and Reviews," *Popular Music and Society* XXI (spring 1997), 109–16.

Kurt Loder, *Bat Chain Puller: Rock and Roll in the Age of Celebrity*. New York: St. Martin's Press, 1990.

Greg Loescher, "What a Long, Strange Trip It's Been: A Brief History of *Goldmine* Magazine," *Goldmine*, no. 501 (October 8, 1999), 38–42.

Robert Love (ed.), *The Best of Rolling Stone: Twenty-Five Years of Journalism on the Edge*. New York: Doubleday, 1993.

Michael Lydon, *Boogie Lightning*. New York: Dial Press, 1974.

Greil Marcus (ed.), *Stranded: Rock and Roll for a Desert Island*. New York: Knopf, 1979.

Bob Margolin, "Musicians vs. Writers," *Blues Revue*, no. 50 (September 1999), 66–67.

Evelyn McDonnell and Ann Powers (eds.), *Rock She Wrote: Women Write about Rock, Pop, and Rap*. New York: Delta Books, 1995.

Kembrew McLeod, " '☆ 1/2 ': A Critique of Rock Criticism in North America," *Popular Music* XX (January 2001), 47–60.

Richard Meltzer, *A Whore Just Like the Rest: The Music Writings of Richard Meltzer*. New York: Da Capo Press, 2000.

Donald C. Meyer, "The Real Cooking Is Done in the Studio: Toward a Context for Rock Criticism," *Popular Music and Society* XIX (spring 1995), 1–15.

Justin Mitchell, "Booking It with Peter Guralnick," *Blues Access*, no. 37 (spring 1999), 50–51.

Charles Shaar Murray (edited by Neil Spencer), *Shots from the Hip*. London: Penguin Books, 1991.

Paul Nelson, "Lester Bangs: 1948–1982," *Rolling Stone*, no. 371 (June 10, 1982), 48.

George M. Plasketes, "My Back Pages: Reflections on Rick (y), Rock Reunions, and Writing Record Reviews," *Popular Music and Society* XXI (spring 1997), 133–40.

Bruce Pollock, *Hipper Than Our Kids: A Rock and Roll Journal of the Baby Boom Generation*. New York: Schirmer Books, 1993.

Robert Pruter, "A History of DooWop Fanzines," *Popular Music and Society* XXI (spring 1997), 11–41.

Jerry Rodnitzky, "A Rocky Road to Respect: Trends in Academic Writing on Popular Music and *Popular Music and Society*," *Popular Music and Society* XXI (spring 1997), 93–96.

Ellen Sander, "The Journalists of Rock," *Saturday Review* LIV (July 31, 1971), 47–49.

Ellen Sander, *Trips: Rock Life in the Sixties*. New York: Scribner's, 1973.

Lydia Sherwood, "Dr. Demento: He's Nuts about His Music," *Goldmine*, no. 145 (February 14, 1986), 80.

John M. Sloop, "The Emperor's New Makeup: Cool Cynicism and Popular Music Criticism," *Popular Music and Society* XXIII (spring 1999), 51–73.

Rob Tannenbaum, "God Helps Those Who Hype Themselves: Never Mind the Music, Build That Press Kit," *Musician*, no. 149 (March 1991), 78–80, 91.

John Tebbel and Mary Ellen Zuckerman, *The Magazine in America, 1741–1990*. New York: Oxford University Press, 1991.

Nick Tosches, "Elvis: Getting the Ink, 1954–1955," *Goldmine*, no. 68 (January 1982), 14.

Jann S. Wenner, *20 Years of Rolling Stone: What a Long, Strange Trip It's Been*. New York: Friendly Press, 1987.

Frederic Wertham, *The World of Fanzines: A Special Form of Communication*. Carbondale: Southern Illinois University Press, 1973.

Charles M. Young, "15 Years of *Musician*: Why We Write about What We Write About," *Musician*, no. 154 (August 1991), 31–33.

Language and Linguistics

Sammy Cahn, *The Songwriter's Rhyming Dictionary*. New York: Facts on File, 1983.

Glenn Collins, "Rap Won't Cross Over, So We're All Getting Hip-Hoppy," *Detroit Free Press* (September 11, 1988), 1, 6.

Maury Dean, "Wo-Uh-Ho Peggy Sue: Exploring a Teenage Queen Linguistically," *Popular Music and Society* II (spring 1973), 244–54.

Edith A. Folb, *Runnin' Down Some Lines: The Language and Culture of Black Teenagers*. Cambridge: Harvard University Press, 1980.

Tom Hibbert (comp.), *Rockspeak: The Dictionary of Rock Terms*. London: Omnibus Books, 1982.

Bruce Horner and Thomas Swiss (eds.), *Key Terms in Popular Music and Culture*. Malden, MA: Blackwell, 1999.

Marshall McLuhan, Kathryn Hutchon, and Eric McLuhan, *Media, Messages, and Language: The World as Your Classroom*. Skokie, IL: National Textbook Company, 1980.

Tim Murphey, *Song and Music in Language Learning: An Analysis of Pop Song Lyrics and the Use of Song and Music in Teaching English to Speakers of Other Languages*. New York: P. Lang, 1990.

Thomas H. Ohlgren and Lynn M. Berk (eds.), *The New Languages: A Rhetorical Approach to the Mass Media and Popular Culture*. Englewood Cliffs, NJ: Prentice Hall, 1977.

Arnold Shaw (comp.), *Dictionary of American Pop/Rock*. New York: Schirmer Books, 1982.

Geneva Smitherman, *Black Language and Culture: Sounds of Soul*. New York: Harper & Row, 1975.

Geneva Smitherman, *Talkin' and Testifyin': The Language of Black America*. Detroit, MI: Wayne State University Press, 1977.

John Stevens and Hazen Schumacher, "Jazzing the Language," *Popular Music and Society* XI (spring 1987), 1–5.

Simon Warner, *Rockspeak! The Language of Rock and Pop*. London: Blandford Press, 1996.

Don B. Wilmeth (comp.), *The Language of American Popular Entertainment: A Glossary of Argot, Slag, and Terminology*. Westport, CT: Greenwood, 1981.

Bob Young and Micky Moody, *The Language of Rock 'n' Roll*. London: Sodgwick and Jackson, 1985.

Language Arts (Composition, Grammar, Literature, Poetry, and Spelling)

Bill Brown, "Rock-and-Roll, Grammatology, and the Teaching of Composition," *OneTwoThreeFour: A Rock 'n' Roll Quarterly* VI (summer 1988), 65–73.

Roger L. Brown and Michael O'Leary, "Pop Music in an English Secondary School System," *American Behavioral Scientist* XIV (January/February 1971), 401–13.

B. Lee Cooper, "The Bridge as Metaphor in Modern Popular Music," *Rock and Blues News*, no. 9 (April-May 2000), 25–27.

B. Lee Cooper, "Controversial Issues in Popular Lyrics, 1960–1985: Teaching Resources for the English Classroom," *Arizona English Bulletin* XXIX (fall 1986), 174–87.

B. Lee Cooper, "Images from Fairy Tales and Nursery Rhymes in the Lyrics of Contemporary Recordings," *International Journal of Instructional Media* XV, no. 2 (1988), 183–93.

B. Lee Cooper, "Please Mr. Postman: Images of Written Communication in Contemporary Lyrics," *International Journal of Instructional Media* XXIII, no.1 (1996), 79–89.

B. Lee Cooper, "Rhythm 'n' Rhymes: Character and Theme Images from Children's Literature in Contemporary Recordings, 1950–1985," *Popular Music and Society* XIII (spring 1989), 53–71.

B. Lee Cooper, "Why Don't You Write Me? A Letter Song Discography, 1945–1995," *Rock and Blues News,* no. 12 (October/November 2000), 37–39.

S. Renee Dechert, " 'Some Things Never Go Out of Style': Recorded Music and the Rhetorical Analysis," *Popular Music and Society* XXIII (winter 1999), 45–59.

Janell R. Duxbury, "Shakespeare Meets the Backbeat: Literary Allusion in Rock Music," *Popular Music and Society* XII (fall 1988), 19–23.

Jim Elledge (ed.), *Sweet Nothings: An Anthology of Rock 'n' Roll in American Poetry*. Bloomington: Indiana University Press, 1994.

Stephen Henderson, *Understanding the New Black Poetry: Black Speech and Black Music as Poetic References*. New York: William Morrow, 1973.

Jill Tedford Jones, "The Delight of Words: The Elizabethan Sonneteers and American Country Lyricists," *Popular Music and Society* XXIV (winter 2000), 63–77.

Anne W. Lyons, "Creative Teaching in Interdisciplinary Humanities: The Human Values in Pop Music," *Minnesota English Journal* X (winter 1974), 23–31.

Anthony Ray Margiane, "The Times They Are a-Changin'," *Elementary English* XLVIII (October 1971), 703–4.

James R. McDonald, "Rockin' in the Classroom: A Literary Alternative," *International Journal of Instructional Media* XIII no. 2 (1986), 145–58.

David E. Morse, "Avant-Rock in the Classroom," *English Journal* LVIII (February 1969), 196–200ff.

Harold F. Mosher, Jr., "The Lyrics of American Pop Music: A New Poetry," *Popular Music and Society* I (spring 1972), 167–76.

Sara Duncan Newsom, "Rock 'n' Roll 'n' Reading," *Journal of Reading* XXII (May 1979), 726–30.

David R. Pichaske, *Beowulf to Beatles and Beyond: The Varieties of Poetry*. New York: Macmillan, 1981.

David R. Pichaske, *The Poetry of Rock: The Golden Years*. Peoria, IL: Ellis Press, 1981.

David R. Pichaske, "Poetry, Pedagogy, and Popular Music: Renegade Reflections," *Popular Music and Society* XXIII (winter 1999), 83–103.

"Popular Culture in the English Classroom" (entire issue), *English Journal* LXVI (March 1976), 28–88.

Michael E. Roos, "The Walrus and the Deacon: John Lennon's Debt to Lewis Carroll," *Journal of Popular Culture* XVIII (summer 1984), 19–29.

Timothy E. Scheurer, "American Popular Music—Humanities 46 (4 credits—15 week trimester)," in *Currents of Warm Life: Popular Culture in American Higher Education*, edited by Mark Gordon and Jack Nachbar.

Bowling Green, OH: Bowling Green State University Popular Press, 1980, 97–101.

Michael Taft, *Blues Lyric Poetry: An Anthology*. New York: Garland, 1983.

Michael Taft, *Blues Lyric Poetry: A Concordance* (3 vols.). New York: Garland, 1984.

Jeff Todd Titon (ed.), *Downhome Blues Lyrics: An Anthology from the Post–World War II Era* (2d ed.). Urbana: University of Illinois Press, 1990.

Terry Volbrecht, *Songsources: Using Popular Music in the Teaching of English*. Cape Town, South Africa: Buchu Books, 1991.

Don L. Wulffson, "Music to Teach Reading," *Journal of Reading* XIV (December 1970), 179–82.

Library Science and Information Services

Tim Brooks, "ARSC: Association for Recorded Sound Collections—An Unusual Organization," *Goldmine* LXXXI (February 1983), 22–23.

B. Lee Cooper, "From the Outside Looking In: A Popular Culture Researcher Speaks to Librarians," *Popular Culture in Libraries* I, no. 1 (1993), 37–46.

B. Lee Cooper, "Information Services, Popular Culture, and the Librarian: Promoting a Contemporary Learning Perspective," *Drexel Library Quarterly* XVI (July 1980), 24–42.

B. Lee Cooper, "Popular Music in Print," *Popular Music and Society* XIX (winter 1995), 105–12.

B. Lee Cooper, "Sex, Songs, and Censorship: A Thematic Taxonomy of Popular Recordings for Music Librarians and Sound Recording Archivists," *Popular Culture in Libraries* II, no. 4 (1994), 11–47.

B. Lee Cooper and William L. Schurk, "A Haunting Question: Should Sound Recordings Archives Promote the Circulation of Horror Material?" *Popular Culture in Libraries* I (1993), 45–58.

B. Lee Cooper, Frank W. Hoffmann, and William L. Schurk, "A Guide to Popular Music Periodicals of the Rock Era, 1953–1983," *International Journal of Instructional Media* II, no. 4 (1983–1984), 369–81.

B. Lee Cooper, Michael Marsden, Barbara Moran, and Allen Ellis, "Popular Culture Materials in Libraries and Archives," *Popular Culture in Libraries* I (1993), 5–35.

Allen Ellis (ed.), *Popular Culture and Acquisitions*. Binghamton, NY: Haworth Press, 1992.

David Evans, "Few Scholars Are Involved in Studying and Preserving the Music We Call the Blues," *Chronicle of Higher Education* XXXV (November 9, 1988), 84.

Christopher D. Geist, with Ray B. Browne, Michael T. Marsden, and Carole Palmer (comps.), *Directory of Popular Culture Collections*. Phoenix, AZ: Oryx Press, 1989.

Leta Hendricks, "A Review of Rap Sound Recordings in Academic and Public Libraries," *Popular Music and Society* XXI (summer 1997), 91–114.

Brad Hill, *The Virtual Musician: A Complete Guide to Online Resources and Services*. New York: Schirmer Books/Simon & Schuster/Macmillan, 1996.

Frank W. Hoffmann (comp.), *Popular Culture and Libraries*. Hamden, CT: Library Professional Publications/Shoe String Press, 1984.

Rebecca Sturm Kelm, "The Lack of Access to Back Issues of the Weekly Tabloids: Does It Matter?" *Journal of Popular Culture* XXIII (spring 1990), 45–50.

Larry N. Lundrum, *American Popular Culture: A Guide to Information Sources*. Detroit, MI: Gale Research, 1982.

James Briggs Murray, "Understanding and Developing Black Popular Music Collections," *Drexel Library Quarterly* XIX (winter 1983), 4–54.

Angus Paul, "New Research Center in Chicago Strives to Preserve and Promote the Legacy of Black Music," *Chronicle of Higher Education* XXXIII (January 28, 1987), 6–7, 10.

John Politis, "Rock Music's Place in the Library," *Drexel Library Quarterly* XIX (winter 1983), 78–92.

Jean Rosenblatt, "From Rock 'n' Roll to Zydeco: Eclectic Archives of Popular Music at Bowling Green State University," *Chronicle of Higher Education* XXXVII (February 6, 1991), 6B, 7B.

Fred E. H. Schroeder (ed.), *Twentieth-Century Popular Culture in Museums and Libraries*. Bowling Green, OH: Bowling Green State University Popular Press, 1981.

Jerry Stevens, "Try 45 rpm's: They're Cheap and Popular," *School Library Journal* XXIII (January 1977), 48.

Gordon Stevenson, "Race Records: Victims of Benign Neglect in Libraries," *Wilson Library Bulletin* L (November 1975), 224–32.

Gordon Stevenson, "The Wayward Scholar: Resources and Research in Popular Culture," *Library Trends* XXV (April 1977), 779–818.

William E. Studwell, "American Popular Culture, Music, and Collection Development in Libraries: Some Comments and Five Examples," *Popular Culture in Libraries* I (1993), 19–27.

Alan Ward, *A Manual of Sound Archive Administration*. Aldershot, England: Gower, 1990.

Wayne A. Wiegand, "Popular Culture: A New Frontier for Academic Libraries," *Journal of Academic Librarianship* V (September 1979), 200–4.

Wayne A. Wiegand (ed.), *Popular Culture and the Library: Current Issues Symposium II*. Lexington: University of Kentucky, 1978.

Wayne A. Wiegand, "Taste Cultures and Librarians: A Position Paper," *Drexel Library Quarterly* XVI (July 1980), 1–11.

Mass Media Communications

Jack Banks, *Monopoly Television: MTV's Quest to Control the Music*. Boulder, CO: Westview Press, 1996.

Jack Banks, "Music Video Cartel: A Survey of Anti-Competitive Practices by MTV and Major Record Companies," *Popular Music and Society* XX (summer 1996), 173–96.

Jack Banks, "Video in the Machine: The Incorporation of Music Video into the Recording Industry," *Popular Music* XVI (October 1997), 293–309.

William Barlow, *Voice Over: The Making of Black Radio*. Philadelphia: Temple University Press, 1999.

Stephen Barnard, *On the Radio: Music Radio in Britain*. Milton Keynes, England: Open University Press, 1989.

James L. Baughman, *The Republic of Mass Culture: Journalism, Filmmaking, and Broadcasting in America Since 1941*. Baltimore: Johns Hopkins University Press, 1992.

Charles M. Berg, "Visualizing Music: The Archaeology of Music Video," *OneTwoThreeFour: A Rock and Roll Quarterly*, no. 5 (spring 1987), 94–103.

Jody Berland, "Radio Space and Industrial Time: Music Formats, Local Narratives, and Technological Mediation," *Popular Music* IX (April 1990), 179–92.

Alan Betrock, *Hitsville: The 100 Greatest Rock 'n' Roll Magazines, 1954–1968*. Brooklyn, NY: Shake Books, 1991.

Frank Biocca, "Media and Perceptual Shifts: Early Radio and the Clash of Musical Cultures," *Journal of Popular Culture* XXIV (fall 1990), 1–15.

Stanley J. Blitz, *Bandstand—The Untold Story: The Years before Dick Clark.* Phoenix, AZ: Cornucopia, 1997.

Robert Burnett and Bert Deivert, "Black or White: Michael Jackson's Video as a Mirror of Popular Culture," *Popular Music and Society* XIX (fall 1995), 19–40.

Gary Burns, "How Music Video Has Changed, and How It Has Not Changed: 1991 vs. 1985," *Popular Music and Society* XVIII (fall 1994), 67–79.

Gary Burns, "Popular Music, Television, and Generational Identity," *Journal of Popular Culture* XXX (winter 1996), 129–41.

Gary Burns and Robert Thompson, "Music, Television, and Video: Historical and Aesthetic Considerations," *Popular Music and Society* XI (fall 1987), 11–25.

Louis Cantor, *Wheelin' on Beale: How WDIA–Memphis Became the Nation's First All-Black Radio Station and Created the Sound That Changed America.* New York: Pharos Books, 1992.

David Carson, *Rockin' Down the Dial: The Detroit Sound of Radio—From Jack the Bellboy to the Big 8.* Troy, MI: Momentum Books, 2000.

Dick Clark, with Fred Bronson, *Dick Clark's American Bandstand.* New York: HarperCollins, 1997.

B. Lee Cooper, "From Anonymous Announcer to Radio Personality, From Pied Piper to Payola: The American Disc Jockey, 1950–1970," *Popular Music and Society* XIV (winter 1990), 89–95.

B. Lee Cooper, "Review of *The Illustrated Price Guide to Scandal Magazines, 1952–1966; The Tabloid Poster Book, 1959–1969; Cult Exploitation Movie Posters, 1940–1973;* and *Unseen America: The Greatest Cult Exploitation Magazines, 1950–1966* by Alan Betrock," *Journal of American Culture* XXIII, no. 2 (summer 1999), 101–2.

B. Lee Cooper, "Review of *Wheelin' on Beale: How WDIA–Memphis Became the Nation's First All-Black Radio Station and Created the Sound That Changed America* by Louis Cantor," *Popular Culture in Libraries* II, no. 2 (1992), 85–86.

B. Lee Cooper, "Revising 'Oldies But Goodies' Playlists: Radio Programming, Market Expansion, and America's Musical Heritage," *Rock and Blues News*, no. 2 (February-March 1999), 19–20.

B. Lee Cooper, Frank W. Hoffmann, and William L. Schurk, "A Guide to Popular Music Periodicals of the Rock Era, 1953–1983," *International Journal of Instructional Media* II (1983–84), 369–81.

B. Lee Cooper, "Having a Screaming Ball in Dracula's Hall," *Popular Music and Society* XV (spring 1991), 103–5.

B. Lee Cooper, "Mass Media," in *Rock Music in American Popular Culture: Rock 'n' Roll Resources*, by B. Lee Cooper and Wayne S. Haney. New York: Haworth Press, 1995 169–86.

B. Lee Cooper, "Terror Translated into Comedy: The Popular Music Metamorphosis of Film and Television Horror, 1956–1991," *Journal of American Culture* XX (fall 1997), 31–42.

Laura E. Cooper and B. Lee Cooper, "The Pendulum of Cultural Imperialism: Popular Music Interchanges between the United States and Britain, 1943–1967," *Journal of Popular Culture* XXVII (winter 1993), 61–78.

R. Serge Denisoff, "The Evolution of Pop Music Broadcasting, 1920–1972," *Popular Music and Society* II (spring 1973), 202–26.

R. Serge Denisoff, "Music Videos and the Rock Press," *Popular Music and Society* X, no. 1 (1985), 59–61.

R. Serge Denisoff, *Inside MTV*. New Brunswick, NJ: Transaction, 1988.

R. Serge Denisoff, "Psychographics and MTV: An Interview with Marshall Cohen," *Popular Music and Society* XI (fall 1987), 27–34.

R. Serge Denisoff, "Ted Turner's Crusade: Economics vs. Morals," *Journal of Popular Culture* XXI (summer 1987), 27–42.

R. Serge Denisoff, "Wodlinger vs. MTV: Sherman-Clayton Antitrust or Publicity Seeking," *Popular Music and Society* XI (fall 1987), 47–56.

R. Serge Denisoff and William D. Romanowski, "MTV Becomes Pastiche: 'Some People Just Don't Get It!' " *Popular Music and Society* XIV (spring 1990), 47–61.

Ben Fong-Torres, *The Hits Just Keep on Coming: The History of Top 40 Radio*. San Francisco: Miller Freeman Books, 1998.

Simon Frith, Andrew Goodwin, and Lawrence Grossberg (eds.), *Sound and Vision: The Music Video Reader*. London: Routledge, 1993.

Paul Fryer, " 'Everybody's on Top of the Pops': Popular Music on British Television, 1960–1985," *Popular Music and Society* XXI (summer 1997), 71–89.

Reebee Garofalo and Steve Chapple, "From ASCAP to Alan Freed: The Pre-History of Rock 'n' Roll," *Popular Music and Society* VI (1978), 72–80.

Steve Gelfand, *Television Theme Recordings: An Illustrated Discography, 1951–1994*. Ann Arbor, MI: Popular Culture, Ink, 1994.

Andrew Goodwin, *Dancing in the Distraction Factory: Music Television and Popular Culture*. Minneapolis: University of Minnesota Press, 1992.

Mark Gottdiener, *The Theming of America: Dreams, Visions, and Commercial Spaces*. Boulder, CO: Westview Press, 1997.

Joe Gow, "Making Sense of Music Video: Research During the Inaugural Decade," *Journal of American Culture* XV (fall 1992), 35–43.

Joe Gow, "Music Video as Communication: Popular Formulas and Emerging Genres," *Journal of Popular Culture* XXVI (fall 1992), 41–70.

Joe Gow, "Political Themes in Popular Music Videos: MTV's 'Top 200, Ever'," *Popular Music and Society* XVIII (winter 1994), 77–89.

Neal and Janice Gregory, "How TV Reacted . . . The Day Elvis Died," *TV Guide* XXIX (August 15, 1981), 4–10.

Pete Grendysa, "No Pay—No Play: The Story of the Music Licensing Societies (Part One)," *Goldmine*, no. 32 (January 1979), 25–26.

Pete Grendysa, "The Forty Year War: The Story of the Music Licensing Societies (Part Two)," *Goldmine*, no. 33 (February 1979), 22–23.

Pete Grendysa, "Paying for Playing: The Story of the Music Licensing Societies (Part Three)," *Goldmine*, no. 34 (March 1979), 30–31.

Lisa St. Clair Harvey, "Temporary Insanity: Fun, Games, and Transformational Ritual in American Music Video," *Journal of Popular Culture* XXIV (summer 1990), 39–50.

Jeffrey Alan Hicks, "Television Theme Songs: A Content Analysis," *Popular Music and Society* XVI (spring 1992), 13–20.

John A. Jackson, *Big Beat Heat: Alan Freed and the Early Years of Rock and Roll*. New York: Schirmer Books, 1991.

Thomas Johansson, "Music Video, Youth Culture, and Postmodernism," *Popular Music and Society* XVI (fall 1992), 9–22.

Steve Jones, "Cohesive but Not Coherent: Music Videos, Narrative, and Culture," *Popular Music and Society* XII (winter 1988), 15–29.

E. Ann Kaplan, *Rocking around the Clock: Music Television, Postmodernism, and Consumer Culture*. New York: McThuen, 1987.

Michael C. Keith, *Voices in the Purple Haze: Underground Radio and the Sixties*. Westport, CT: Praeger Books, 1997.

Ron Lackmann, *The Encyclopedia of American Radio: An A–Z Guide to Radio From Jack Benny to Howard Stern*. New York: Checkmark Books, 2000.

Paul Lepri, *Rocking Radio: Recollections of Sounds That Made the Top 40 Airwaves*. New Haven, CT: P. Lepri, 2001.

Steven Levy, "Ad Nauseam: How MTV Sells Out Rock and Roll," *Rolling Stone*, no. 410 (December 8, 1983), 30–37, 74, 76, 78–79.

George Lipsitz, "A World of Confusion: Music Video as Modern Myth," *OneTwoThreeFour: A Rock and Roll Quarterly*, no. 5 (spring 1987), 50–60.

James Lull, "Popular Music and Communication: An Introduction," in *Popular Music and Communication*, edited by James Lull. Newbury Park, CA: Sage, 1992), 1–32.

J. Fred MacDonald, *Don't Touch That Dial! Radio Programming in American Life from 1920 to 1960*. Chicago: Nelson-Hall, 1979.

Tom McGrath, *MTV: The Making of a Revolution*. Philadelphia: Running Press, 1996.

Keith Negus, "Plugging and Programming: Pop Radio and Record Promotion in Britain and the United States," *Popular Music* XII (January 1993), 57–68.

Mark Newman, *Entrepreneurs of Profit and Pride: From Black Appeal to Radio Soul*. New York: Praeger Books, 1988.

Edward C. Pease and Everette E. Dennis (eds.), *Radio: The Forgotten Medium*. New Brunswick, NJ: Transaction, 1995.

John M. Phelan, *Disenchantment: Meaning and Morality in the Media*. New York: Hastings House, 1980.

Shaun Phillips et al., *M-Cyclopedia: The Official MTV Guide to Music*. New York: Carlton Books, 1997.

John E. Reid, Jr., and Joseph R. Dominick, "A Comparative Analysis of Christian and Mainstream Rock Music Videos," *Popular Music and Society* XVII (fall 1993), 87–97.

Red Robinson and Peggy Hodgins, *Rockbound: Rock 'n' Roll Encounters, 1955 to 1969*. Surrey, British Columbia: Hancock House, 1983.

Jonathan Romney and Adrian Wootton (eds.), *Celluloid Jukebox: Popular Music and the Movies since the 50's*. London: British Film Institute, 1995.

Thomas Ryan, *American Hit Radio: A History of Popular Singles From 1955 to the Present*. Rocklin, CA: Prime, 1995.

Dave Samuelson, " 'And Now for the Kiddies . . .': Ed Sullivan and Rock and Roll, 1954–1971," *Goldmine*, no. 64 (September 1981), 177–9.

Dave Samuelson, "The Ed Sullivan Show and Rock and Roll: Addenda," *Goldmine*, no. 65 (October 1981), 179.

Dave Samuelson, "The Ed Sullivan Show and Rock and Roll: The Readers Respond," *Goldmine*, no. 74 (July 1982), 19.

Barry L. Sherman and Joseph R. Dominck, "Violence and Sex in Music Videos: TV and Rock 'n' Roll," *Journal of Communication* XXXVI (winter 1986), 79–93.

Michael Shore, with Dick Clark, *The History of American Bandstand*. New York: Ballantine, 1985.

Michael Shore (edited by Patricia Romanowski), *Music Video: A Consumer's Guide*. New York: Ballantine Books, 1987.

Wes Smith, *The Pied Pipers of Rock 'n' Roll: Radio DeeJays of the '50s and '60s*, Marietta, GA: Longstreet Press, 1989.

Susan Smulyan, *Selling Radio: The Commercialization of American Broadcasting, 1920–1934*. Washington, D.C.: Smithsonian Institution Press, 1994.

Will Straw, "Music Video in Its Contexts: Popular Music and Post-Modernism in the 1980s," *Popular Music* VII (October 1988), 247–66.

Michael Uslan and Bruce Solomon, *Dick Clark's The First 25 Years of Rock and Roll*. New York: Delacorte Press, 1981.

James R. Walker, "How Viewing of MTV Relates to Exposure to Other Media Violence," *Journalism Quarterly* LXIV (winter 1987), 756–62.

Marc Weingarten, *Station to Station: The History of Rock 'n' Roll on Television*. New York: Pocket Books/Simon & Schuster, 2000.

Edward Jay Whetmore, *Mediamerica: Form, Content, and Consequence of Mass Communication* (3d ed.). Belmont, CA: Wadsworth, 1987.

Adam White, "Mr. Clean," *The History of Rock*, no. 18 (1982), 356–60.

Gilbert A. Williams, *Legendary Pioneers of Black Radio*. Westport, CT: Praeger, 1998.

Music

Alf Bjornberg, " 'Teach You to Rock'? Popular Music in the University Music Department," *Popular Music* XII (January 1993), 69–77.

Richard Bobbitt, *Harmonic Technique in the Rock Idiom: The Theory and Practice of Rock Harmony*. Belmont, CA: Wadsworth, 1976.

Bonna J. Boettcher and Michael Leo McHugh, "Popular Music and the University Curriculum," *Popular Culture in Libraries* IV, no. 2 (1997), 1–10.

Michael Burnett, "Using Pop Music with Middle-School Classes," in *Pop, Rock and Ethnic Music in School*, edited by Graham Vulliamy and Edward Lee. Cambridge: Cambridge University Press, 1982, 24–39.

Graham Collier, *Jazz: A Student's and Teacher's Guide*. Cambridge, MA: Cambridge University Press, 1975.

B. Lee Cooper, "Can Music Students Learn Anything of Value by Investigating Popular Recordings?" *International Journal of Instructional Media* XX, no. 3 (1993), 273–284.

B. Lee Cooper, "Lyrical Commentaries: Learning from Popular Music," *Music Educators Journal* LXXVII (April 1991), 56–59.

Susan D. Crafts, Daniel Cavicchi, and Charles Keil, *My Music*. Hanover, NH: University Press of New England, 1993.

Robert A. Cutietta, "Popular Music: An Ongoing Challenge," *Music Educators Journal* LXXVII (April 1991), 26–29.

Robert A. Cutietta and Thomas Brennan, "Coaching a Pop/Rock Ensemble," *Music Educators Journal* LXXVII (April 1991), 40–45.

Frederick E. Danker, "Blues in the Classroom," *English Journal* LXII (March 1973), 394–401.

Harris Danzinger, "The Role of Popular Music in the Schools," *National Music Council Bulletin* XXX (spring/summer 1970), 16–17.

"Does Popular Music Have Educational Value?" *Music Educators Journal* LXVI (December 1979), 60–65.

Janell R. Duxbury (comp.), *Rockin' the Classics and Classicizin' the Rock: A Selectively Annotated Discography—First Supplement*. Westport, CT: Greenwood, 1991.

Charles B. Fowler, "The Case against Rock: A Reply," *Music Educators Journal* LVII (September 1970), 38–42.

Lawrence Kramer, *Musical Meaning: Toward a Critical History*. Berkeley: University of California Press, 2002.

John Kuzmich, Jr., "Popular Music in Your Program: Growing with the Times," *Music Educators Journal* LXXVII (April 1991), 50–55.

Edward Lee, "Pop and the Teacher: Some Uses and Problems," in *Pop Music in School*, edited by Graham Vulliamy and Edward Lee. Cambridge: Cambridge University Press, 1976, 158–74.

Randolph D. Love, "Design and Teach a Popular Music Class," *Music Educators Journal* LXXVII (April 1991), 46–49.

Thomas MacCluskey, "Rock and Its Elements," *Music Educators Journal* LVI (November 1969), 48–63.

Susan McClary, *Conventional Wisdom: The Content of Musical Form*. Berkeley: University of California Press, 2000.

Edwin McLean, "Understanding Contemporary Music," *American Music Teacher* XXVII (September/October 1977), 17.

Allan F. Moore, *Rock: The Primary Text—Developing a Musicology of Rock*. Buckingham, England: Open University Press, 1993.

Jean-Jacques Nattiez (translated by C. Abbate), *Music and Discourse: Toward a Semiology of Music*. Princeton, NJ: Princeton University Press, 1990.

Keith Negus, *Popular Music in Theory: An Introduction*. Hanover, NH: University Press of New England, 1996.

David Paddy and Arthur J. Michaels, "Blues: A Guide for the Music Teacher," *School Music News* XXXVI (March 1973), 20–22.

Randall G. Pembrook, "Exploring the Musical Side of Pop," *Music Educators Journal* LXXVII (April 1991), 30–34.

Randall G. Pembrook, "Popular Music in Research and in the Classroom," *Update: The Applications of Research in Music Education* IV (fall 1986), 6–10.

Walter Rimler, *Not Fade Away: A Comparison of Jazz Age with Rock Era Pop Song Composers*. Ann Arbor, MI: Pierian Press, 1984.

Emmett R. Sarig, "Ignoring Rock Won't Make It Go Away," *Music Educators Journal* LVI (November 1969), 46–47.

Charles Seeger, *Studies in Musicology, 1935–1975*. Berkeley: University of California Press, 1977.

Piers Spencer, "The Blues: A Practical Project for the Classroom," in *Pop Music in School*, edited by Graham Vulliamy and Edward Lee. Cambridge, England: Cambridge University Press, 1976, 74–96.

Joe Stuessy, "When the Music Teacher Meets Metallica," *Music Educators Journal* LXXX (January 1994), 28–32.

Frederick J. Taylor, "Results of a Survey on Academic Characteristics of Music Business Programs in U.S. Colleges and Universities," *Tracking: Popular Music Studies* III (spring 1991), 7–17.

Dick Thompson, "Plugging into Pop at the Junior High Level," *Music Educators Journal* LXVI (December 1979), 54–59.

Mathias Wexler, "Teaching Music Students to Make Music for Love, Not for a Living," *Chronicle of Higher Education* XLVI (July 28, 2000), B6, B7.

Philosophy and Religion

Henry Carsch, "The Protestant Ethic and the Popular Idol in America: A Case Study," *Social Compass* XV (1968), 45–69.

B. Lee Cooper, "Christmas Songs as American Cultural History: An Update of Holiday Hits, 1991–2001." Audio Presentation at the 24th annual conference of the American Culture Association, March 2002, Toronto, Ontario.

B. Lee Cooper, "Christmas Songs as American Cultural History: Audio Resources for Classroom Investigation, 1940–1990," *Social Education* LIV (October 1990), 374–9.

B. Lee Cooper, " 'Do You Hear What I Hear?' Christmas Recordings as Audio Symbols of Religious Tradition and Social Change in Contemporary America," *International Journal of Instructional Media* XVI, no. 3 (1989), 265–70.

B. Lee Cooper, "Holly Jolly Rock, Rhythm and Blues: Christmas Recordings on Compact Disc," *Rock and Blues News*, no. 7 (December 1999–January 2000), 29–30.

B. Lee Cooper, "Review of *Christmas Carol Reader* by William Studwell," *Popular Music and Society* XXIII (fall 1999), 117–19.

B. Lee Cooper, "Review of *Goldmine Christmas Record Price Guide* by Tim Neely," *Popular Music and Society* XXIV (summer 2000), 153–5.

B. Lee Cooper, "Review of *Merry Christmas Baby: Holiday Music from Bing to Sting* by Dave Marsh and Steve Propes," *Rock and Blues News*, no. 7 (December 1999–January 2000), 42.

B. Lee Cooper, "Review of *Philosophy at 33 1/3 R.P.M.: Themes of Classic Rock Music* by James F. Harris," *Popular Music and Society* XVII (winter 1993), 139–41.

B. Lee Cooper, "Rock Music and Religious Education: A Proposed Synthesis," *Religious Education* LXX (May-June 1975), 289–99.

Earlston E. DeSilva, "The Theology of Black Power and Black Song: James Brown," *Journal of Black Sacred Music* III (fall 1989), 57–67.

James F. Harris, *Philosophy at 33 1/3 R.P.M.: Themes of Classic Rock Music.* La Salle, IL: Open Court Press, 1993.

Robert H. Reid, "Philosophy Teacher Tunes in Students with Rock Music," *The* [Cleveland] *Plain Dealer* (February 20, 1977), 20.

Robert A. Rosenstone, "Mr. Jones, the Professors, and the Freaks (or Every Man His Own Philosopher King): The Philosophical Implications of Rock," *Popular Music and Society* II (fall 1972), 56–61.

William E. Studwell, *The National and Religious Song Reader: Patriotic, Traditional, and Sacred Songs from Around the World.* New York: Harrington Park Press, 1996.

Mark Sullivan, " 'More Popular Than Jesus': The Beatles and the Religious Far Right," *Popular Music* VI (October 1987), 313–26.

Stephen R. Tucker, "Pentecostalism and Popular Culture in the South: A Study of Four Musicians," *Journal of Popular Culture* XVI (winter 1982), 68–80.

Physical Education and Sports Studies

B. Lee Cooper, "Review of *Sports and Recreation Fads* by Frank W. Hoffmann and William G. Bailey," *Journal of Popular Culture* XXVII (spring 1994), 225.

B. Lee Cooper and Donald E. Walker, "Baseball, Popular Music, and Twentieth-Century American History," *Social Studies* LXXXI (May-June 1990), 120–4.

B. Lee Cooper and Donald E. Walker, with assistance from William L. Schurk. "The Decline of Contemporary Baseball Heroes in American Popular Recordings," *Popular Music and Society* XV (summer 1991), 49–58.

David Rowe, *Popular Cultures: Rock Music, Sport, and the Politics of Pleasure.* Thousand Oaks: Sage, 1995.

Donald E. Walker and B. Lee Cooper, "Songs and Baseball," in *Baseball and American Culture.* Jefferson, NC: McFarland, 1995, 202–3.

Political Science

B. Lee Cooper, "Review of *When the Music's Over: The Story of Political Pop* by Robin Denselow," *Notes: Quarterly Journal of the Music Library Association* XLIX (March 1992), 889–90.

Robin Denslow, *When the Music's Over: The Story of Political Pop*. London: Faber and Faber, 1990 (first published 1989).

Steven Doughtery, "From Race Music to Heavy Metal: A Fiery History of Protests," in *Rock Music in America*, edited by Janet Podell. New York: H. W. Wilson, 1987, 143–6.

Mary Ellison, *Lyrical Protests: Black Music's Struggle against Discrimination*. New York: Praeger Books, 1989.

Joe Ferrandino, "Rock Culture and the Development of Social Consciousness," *Radical America* III (November 1969), 11–34.

Reebee Garofalo, *Rockin' Out: Popular Music in the USA*. Boston: Allyn and Bacon, 1997.

Reebee Garofalo (ed.), *Rockin' the Boat: Mass Music and Mass Movements*. Boston: South End Press, 1992.

Peter Garrett, *Political Blues*. Sydney, Australia: Hodder and Stoughton, 1987.

Don J. Hibbard and Carol Kaleialoha, *The Role of Rock: A Guide to the Social and Political Consequences of Rock Music*. Englewood, NJ: Prentice Hall, 1983.

Elizabeth J. Kizer, "Protest Song Lyrics as Rhetoric," *Popular Music and Society* IX (spring 1983), 3–11.

Ralph E. Knupp, "A Time for Every Purpose under Heaven: Rhetorical Dimensions of Protest Music," *Southern Speech Communication Journal* XLVI (summer 1981), 377–89.

George H. Lewis, "Don't Go Down to Waikiki: Social Protest and Popular Music in Hawaii," in *Rockin' the Boat: Mass Music and Mass Movements*, edited by Reebee Garofalo. Boston: South End Press, 1992, 171–83.

George H. Lewis, "Social Protests and Self Awareness in Black Popular Music," *Popular Music and Society* II (summer 1973), 327–33.

James R. McDonald, "Politics Revisited: Metatextual Implications of Rock and Roll Criticism," *Youth and Society* XIX (June 1988), 485–504.

Donald K. Pickens, "The Historical Images in Republican Campaign Songs, 1860–1900," *Journal of Popular Culture* XV (winter 1981), 165–74.

Robert G. Pielke, *You Say You Want a Revolution: Rock Music in American Culture*. Chicago: Nelson-Hall, 1986.

Ray Pratt, *Rhythm and Resistance: Explorations in the Political Uses of Popular Music*. New York: Praeger Books, 1990.

Robert Reid, "Music and Social Problems: A Poster Series," Portland, ME: J. Weston Walch, 1971.

Jerome L. Rodnitzky, *Minstrels of the Dawn: The Folk-Protest Singer as a Cultural Hero*. Chicago: Nelson-Hall, 1976.

Robert A. Rosenstone, "The Times They Are a-Changin': The Music of Protest," in *Old Government/New People: Readings for the New Politics*, edited by Alfred deGrazia, R. Eric Weise, and John Appel. Glenview, IL: Scott Foresman, 1971, 96–110.

Ron Sakolsky and Fred Wei-han Ho (eds.), *Sounding Off! Music as Subversion/Resistance/Revolution*. Brooklyn, NY: Autonomedia, 1995.

Timothy E. Scheurer, "This Land Is Your Land: The Folk-Protest Movement and Other Voices, 1920–1960," in *Born in the U.S.A.* Jackson: University Press of Mississippi, 1991, 138–65.

Laurence I. Seidman, " 'Get on the Raft with Taft' and Other Musical Treats," *Social Education* XL (October 1976), 436–7.

Irwin Silber (ed.), *Songs America Voted By: With the Words and Music That Won and Lost Elections and Influenced the Democratic Process*. Harrisburg, PA: Stackpole Books, 1971.

Jon Wiener, *Professors, Politics, and Pop*. New York: Verso Books, 1991.

Popular Culture Studies

Michael Bérubé, "The 'Elvis Costello Problem' in Teaching Popular Culture," *Chronicle of Higher Education* XLV (August 13, 1999), B4, B5.

Elsa M. Bowman, "The Relationship of Music and Popular Culture in Schooling," *Perspectives of New Music* XXVII (winter 1989), 118–23.

Michael Bracewell, *When Surface Was Depth: Death by Cappuccino and Other Reflections on Music and Culture in the 1990s*. New York: Da Capo Press, 2002.

Ray R. Browne, *Against Academia: The History of the Popular Culture Association/American Culture Association and the Popular Culture Movement, 1967–1988*. Bowling Green, OH: Bowling Green State University Popular Press, 1989.

Ray B. Browne (ed.), *Mission Underway: The History of the Popular Culture Association/American Culture Association and the Popular Culture Movement, 1967–2001*. Bowling Green, OH: Bowling Green State University Popular Press, 2002.

Gary Burns, Jackie Donath, Charles Harpole, Elizabeth Kizer, and Peggy Sullivan, "Popular Culture Studies under Attack at American Universities," *Popular Culture in Libraries* V, no. 2 (1999), 35–53.

John G. Cawelti, *Adventure, Mystery, and Romance: Formula Stories as Art and Popular Culture*. Chicago: University of Chicago Press, 1976.

B. Lee Cooper, "Review of *American Bandstand: Dick Clark and the Making of a Rock 'n' Roll Empire* by John A. Jackson," *Popular Music and Society* XXIV (summer 2000), 149–51.

B. Lee Cooper, "Review of *Dancing in the Dark: Youth, Popular Culture, and the Electronic Media*, by Quentin J. Schultze, Roy M. Anker, James D. Bratt, William D. Romanowski, John W. Worst, and Lambert Zuidervaart," *Michigan Academician* XXIII (summer 1991), 297–8.

B. Lee Cooper, "Review of *The Elvis Catalog: Memorabilia, Icons, and Collectibles Celebrating the King of Rock 'n' Roll* by Lee Cotton," *Popular Music and Society* XIII (fall 1989), 97–98.

B. Lee Cooper, "Review of *Encyclopedia of Pop Culture: An A to Z of Who's Who and What's What from Aerobics and Bubble Gum to Valley of the Dolls and Moon Unit Zappa* by Jane and Michael Stern," *Journal of Popular Culture* XXXIII (fall 1999), 171–2.

B. Lee Cooper, "Review of *Images of Elvis Presley in American Culture, 1977–1997: The Mystery Terrain* by George Plasketes," *Journal of American Culture* XXI (summer 1998), 92–94.

B. Lee Cooper, "Review of *The Monkees—A Manufactured Image: The Ultimate Reference Guide to Monkee Memories and Memorabilia* by Edward Reilly, Maggie McManus, and William Chadwick," *Popular Music and Society* XII (spring 1988), 85–86.

B. Lee Cooper, "Review of *TV Theme Soundtrack Directory and Discography with Cover Versions* by Craig W. Pattillo," *Popular Music and Society* XIV (winter 1990), 115–16.

B. Lee Cooper, "Review of *Wanted Dead or Alive: The American West in Popular Culture* by Richard Aquila," *Journal of American Culture* XXI (summer 1998), 94–95.

B. Lee Cooper, "Sultry Songs as High Humor," *Popular Music and Society* XVII (spring 1993), 71–85.

B. Lee Cooper, "Terror Translated into Comedy: The Popular Music Metamorphosis of Film and Television Horror, 1956–1991," *Journal of American Culture* XX (fall 1997), 31–42.

B. Lee Cooper and William L. Schurk, "Smokin' Songs: Examining Tobacco Use as an American Cultural Phenomenon through Contemporary Lyrics," *International Journal of Instructional Media* XXI, no. 3 (1994), 261–8.

Michael Dunne, *Metapop: Self-Referentiality in Contemporary American Popular Culture*. Jackson: University Press of Mississippi, 1992.

Ken Emerson, *Doo-dah! Stephen Foster and the Rise of American Popular Culture*. New York: Simon & Schuster, 1997.

Paul Farber, Eugene F. Provenzo, Jr., and Gunilla Holm (eds.), *Schooling in the Light of Popular Culture*. Albany: State University of New York Press, 1994.

Herbert J. Gans, *Popular Culture and High Culture: An Analysis and Evaluation of Taste*. New York: Basic Books, 1974.

Mark Gordon and Jack Nachbar (comps.), *Currents of Warm Life: Popular Culture in American Higher Education*. Bowling Green, OH: Bowling Green University Popular Press, 1980.

Lawrence Grossberg, *Dancing in Spite of Myself: Essays on Popular Culture*. Durham, NC: Duke University Press, 1997.

Frank W. Hoffmann and William G. Bailey, *Arts and Entertainment Fads*. Binghamton, NY: Haworth Press, 1990.

Michael Kammen, "The Study of Popular Culture Has Acquired Legitimacy, but Still Lacks Cohesion," *Chronicle of Higher Education* XLV (July 3, 1998), B4.

E. Ann Kaplan, *Rocking Around the Clock: Music Television, Post Modernism, and Consumer Culture*. New York: Methuen Press, 1987.

Connie Kirchberg and Marc Hendrickx, *Elvis Presley, Richard Nixon, and the American Dream*. Jefferson, NC: McFarland, 1999.

Rob Kroes, *If You've Seen One, You've Seen the Mall: Europeans and American Mass Culture*. Urbana: University of Illinois Press, 1996.

Martin W. LaForse and James A. Drake, *Popular Culture and American Life: Selected Topics in the Study of American Popular Culture*. Chicago: Nelson-Hall, 1981.

John Shelton Lawrence, "A Critical Analysis of Roger B. Rollin's 'Against Evaluation,' " *Journal of Popular Culture* XII (summer 1978), 99–112.

Lawrence W. Levine, *Highbrow/Lowbrow: The Emergence of Cultural Hierarchy in America*. Cambridge: Harvard University Press, 1988.

George Lipsitz, "Listening to Learn and Learning to Listen: Popular Culture, Cultural Theory, and American Studies," *American Quarterly* XLII (December 1990), 615–36.

George Lipsitz, *Time Passages: Collective Memory and American Popular Culture*. Minneapolis: University of Minnesota Press, 1990.

Greil Marcus, *Double Trouble: Bill Clinton and Elvis Presley in a Land of No Alternatives*. New York: John Macrae Books/Henry Holt, 2000.

Angela McRobbie (ed.), *Zoot Suits and Second-Hand Dresses: An Anthology of Fashion and Music*. Boston: Unwin Hyman, 1989.

Hughson Mooney, "Commercial 'Country' Music in the 1970s: Some Social and Historical Perspectives," *Popular Music and Society* VII (1980), 208–13.

Hughson Mooney, "Just before Rock: Pop Music 1950–1953 Reconsidered," *Popular Music and Society* III, no. 2 (1974), 65–108.

Hughson Mooney, "Popular Music before Ragtime, 1840–1890: Some Implications for the Study of American Culture," *Popular Music and Society* V (1977), 43–60.

Hughson Mooney, "Twilight of the Age of Aquarius? Popular Music in the 1970s," *Popular Music and Society* VII (1980), 182–98.

Russel Nye, *The Unembarrassed Muse: The Popular Arts in America*. New York: Dial Press, 1970.

Charles Panati, *Panati's Parade of Fads, Follies, and Manias: The Origins of Our Most Cherished Obsessions*. New York: HarperCollins, 1991.

Richard Pells, *Not Like Us: How Europeans Have Loved, Hated, and Transformed American Culture since World War II*. New York: Basic Books, 1997.

Richard A. Peterson and Russell David, Jr., "The Fertile Crescent of Country Music," *Journal of Country Music* VI (spring 1975), 19–27.

Richard A. Peterson, "The Production of Cultural Change: The Case of Contemporary Country Music," *Social Research* XLV (summer 1978), 292–314.

George Plasketes, *Images of Elvis Presley in American Culture, 1977–1997*. New York: Haworth Press, 1997.

Neil Postman, *Amusing Ourselves to Death: Public Discourse in the Age of Show Business*. New York: Viking Books, 1985.

Robert Prechter, "Popular Culture and the Stock Market," *The Elliott Wave Theorist* (August 22, 1985), 1–20.

Steve Redhead, with Derek Wynne and Justin O'Connor (eds.), *The Clubcultures Reader: Readings in Popular Cultural Studies*. Malden, MA: Blackwell, 1997.

Matthew Rettenmund, *Totally Awesome 80s: A Lexicon of the Music, Videos, Movies, TV Shows, Stars, and Trends of That Decadent Decade*. New York: St. Martin's Griffin, 1996.

Roger B. Rollin, "Against Evaluation: The Role of the Critic of Popular Culture," *Journal of Popular Culture* XI (fall 1975), 355–65.

Roger Rollin (ed.), *The Americanization of the Global Village: Essays in Comparative Popular Culture*. Bowling Green, OH: Bowling Green State University Popular Press, 1989.

Roger B. Rollin, "Son of 'Against Evaluation': A Reply to John Shelton Lawrence," *Journal of Popular Culture* XII (summer 1978), 113–17.

Jack Santino, *New Old-Fashioned Ways: Holidays and Popular Culture*. Knoxville: University of Tennessee Press, 1996.

Thomas Schatz, *Hollywood Genres: Formulas, Filmmaking, and the Studio System*. Philadelphia: Temple University Press, 1981.

Fred E. H. Schroeder (ed.), *5000 Years of Popular Culture*. Bowling Green, OH: Bowling Green State University Popular Press, 1980.

Quentin J. Schultze, Roy M. Anker, James D. Bratt, William D. Romanowski, John W. Worst, and Lambert Zuidervaart, *Dancing in the Dark: Youth, Popular Culture, and the Electronic Media*. Grand Rapids, MI: William B. Eerdmans, 1991.

Susan S. Tamke, "Oral History and Popular Culture: A Method for the Study of the Experience of Culture," *Journal of Popular Culture* XI (summer 1977), 267–79.

Steve Waksman, *Instruments of Desire: The Electric Guitar and the Shaping of Musical Experience*. Cambridge: Harvard University Press, 1999.

William Woodward, "America as a Culture (I): Some Emerging Lines of Analysis," *Journal of American Culture* XI (spring 1988), 1–15.

William Woodward, "America as a Culture (II): A Fourfold Heritage," *Journal of American Culture* XI (spring 1988), 17–32.

William Woodward, "History and Popular Culture . . . and Vice Versa," *Popular Culture Association Newsletter* XVI (February 1989), 1–3.

Psychology

B. Lee Cooper, "What Kind of Fool Am I? Audio Imagery, Personal Identity, and Social Relationships," *International Journal of Instructional Media* XXIV, no. 3 (1997), 253–67.

Evan Davis, "The Psychological Characteristics of Beatle Mania," *Journal of the History of Ideas* XXX (April-June 1969), 273–80.

Robert B. LeLieuvre, " 'Goodnight Saigon': Music, Fiction, Poetry, and Film in Readjustment Group Counseling," *Professional Psychology: Research and Practice* XXIX (January 1998), 74–78.

June Price, "The Beatles' Arrival: Mania in the Media," *Goldmine*, no. 224 (February 24, 1989), 8, 93.

A. J. W. Taylor, "Beatlemania—A Study of Adolescent Enthusiasm," *British Journal of Social and Clinical Psychology* V (September 1966), 81–88.

Science and Technology

Stanley R. Alten, *Audio in Media: The Recording Studio*. Belmont, CA: Wadsworth, 1996.

Tony Bacon (ed.), *Classic Guitars of the '50s: The Electric Guitar and the Musical Revolution of the '50s*. San Francisco: Miller Freeman Books, 1996.

Tony Bacon and Paul Day, *The Fender Book: A Complete History of Fender Electric Guitars*. San Francisco: GPI Books/Miller Freeman Books, 1992.

Tony Bacon and Paul Day, *The Gretsch Book: A Complete History of Gretsch Electric Guitars*. San Francisco: GPI Books/Miller Freeman Books, 1996.

Tony Bacon and Paul Day, *The Rickenbacker Book: A Complete History of Rickenbacker Electric Guitars*. San Francisco: GPI Books/Miller Freeman Books, 1994.

Tony Bacon and Barry Moorhouse, *The Bass Book: A Complete Illustrated History of Bass Guitars*. San Francisco: GPI Books/Miller Freeman Books, 1999.

Anthony Baines, *The Oxford Companion to Musical Instruments*. New York: Oxford University Press, 1992.

Richard Barbieri, "Prime Time for the Telephone," *Channels* V (May/June 1985), 54–55.

Ken Barnes, "Heavy Phones: Calling Up the Telephone Songs," *Radio and Records*, no. 568 (January 25, 1985), 46.

John Blair and Stephen J. McParland, *The Illustrated Discography of Hot Rod Music, 1961–1965*. Ann Arbor, MI: Popular Culture, Ink., 1990.

Bob Brozman, with John Dopyera, Jr., Richard R. Smith, and Gary Atkinson, *The History and Artistry of National Resonator Instruments*. Fullerton, CA: Centerstream, 1993.

Michael Bull, *Sounding Out the City: Personal Stereos and the Management of Everyday Life*. New York: Berg, 2000.

Richard Buskin, *Insidetracks: A First-Hand History of Popular Music from the World's Greatest Record Producers and Engineers*. New York: Spike/Avon Books, 1999.

Walter Carter, *Gibson Guitars: 100 Years of an American Icon*. Los Angeles: General, 1994.

Walter Carter, *The Martin Book: A Complete Illustrated History of Martin Guitars*. London: Balafon Books, 1995.

Michael Chanan, *Repeated Takes: A Short History of Recording and Its Effects on Music*. London: Verso, 1995.

B. Lee Cooper, " 'Cruisin' and Playin' the Radio': Exploring Images of the American Automobile through Popular Music," *International Journal of Instructional Media* VII (1979–80), 327–34.

B. Lee Cooper, "Information Services, Popular Culture, and the Librarian: Promoting a Contemporary Learning Perspective," *Drexel Library Quarterly* XVI (July 1980), 24–42.

B. Lee Cooper, "Review of *The Illustrated Discography of Hot Rod Music, 1961–1965* by John Blair and Stephen J. McParland," *Popular Music and Society* XV (spring 1991), 114–15.

B. Lee Cooper, "Review of *Recorded Music in American Life: The Phonograph and Popular Memory, 1890–1945* by William Howland Kenney," Notes: *The Quarterly Journal of the Music Library Association* (March 2000), 733–4.

B. Lee Cooper, "Review of *Television Theme Recordings: A Discography* by Steve Gelfand," *Popular Music* VII (January 1988), 116–17.

B. Lee Cooper, "Shifting Images of Transportation Technology and American Society in Railroad Songs, 1920–1980," *International Journal of Instructional Media* X (1982–83), 131–45.

B. Lee Cooper, "Squeezing Sugar from the Phone: Rock, Blues, and Pop Telephone Songs," *Rock and Blues News*, no. 4 (May-June 1999), 26–28.

B. Lee Cooper, "A Telephone Song Discography," *Popular Music and Society* XXI, no. 4 (winter 1997), 111–22.

B. Lee Cooper, Patty Falk, and William L. Schurk, "From Piccolo Pete to the Piano Man: Music Instruments Referenced in Sound Recordings," *International Journal of Instructional Media* XXVIII, no. 3 (2001), 319–326.

B. Lee Cooper and Verdan D. Traylor, "Liberal Education and Technology in Small Colleges: Popular Music and the Computer," *International Journal of Instructional Media* VII (1979–80), 25–35.

Michael G. Corenthal, *Cohen on the Telephone: A History of Jewish Recorded Humor and Popular Music, 1892–1942*. Milwaukee, WI: Yesterday's Memories, 1984.

Michael G. Corenthal, *The Iconography of Recorded Sound, 1885–1986: One Hundred Years of Commercial Entertainment and Collecting Opportunity*. Milwaukee, WI: Yesterday's Memories, 1986.

A. Costandina Titus and Jerry L. Simich, "From 'Atomic Bomb Baby' to 'Nuclear Funeral': Atomic Music Comes of Age, 1945–1990," *Popular Music and Society* XIV (winter 1990), 11–37.

Ralph Denyer, *The Guitar Handbook* (rev. ed.). New York: Knopf, 1997.

Evan Eisenberg, *The Recording Angel: Music, Records, and Culture from Aristotle to Zappa*. New York: McGraw-Hill, 1987.

Tom Evans and Mary Anne Evans, *Guitars: Music, History, Construction, and Players from Renaissance to Rock*. New York: Facts on File, 1977.

Joe Goldman, *1991 International Steel Guitar Discography*. San Francisco: J. Goldman, 1990.

Fred Goodman, "Future Shocks: How the New Technologies Will Change the Music Business Forever," *Musician*, no. 182 (December 1993), 32–49.

George Gruhn and Walter Carter, *Acoustic Guitars and Other Fretted Instruments: A Photographic History*. San Francisco: Miller Freeman Books, 1993.

George Gruhn and Walter Carter, *Electric Guitars and Basses: A Photographic History*. San Francisco: Miller Freeman Books, 1994.

John Harvith and Susan Harvith (eds.), *Edison, Musicians, and the Phonograph: A Historical Guide*. Westport, CT: Greenwood, 1987.

Jake Jacobson (photographer), *Heart and Hands: Musical Instrument Makers of America*. Telluride: Northlight of Colorado, 1999.

Steve Jones, "The Intro and the Outro: Technology and Popular Music Practice," *Popular Music and Society* XIV (spring 1990), 1–6.

Steve Jones, *Rock Formation: Music, Technology, and Mass Communication.* Newbury Park, CA: Sage, 1992.

Steve Jones, "Technology and the Future of Popular Music," *Popular Music and Society* XIV (spring 1990), 19–23.

Anahid Kassabian, *Hearing Film: Tracking Identifications in Contemporary Hollywood Film Music.* New York: Routledge, 2001.

William Howland Kenney, *Recorded Music in American Life: The Phonograph and Popular Memory, 1890–1945.* New York: Oxford University Press, 1999.

Allan Kozinn, Pete Welding, Dan Forte, and Gene Santoro, *The Guitar: The History, the Music, the Players.* New York: William Morrow, 1984.

Nina E. Lerman, Ruth Oldenziel, and Arwen P. Mohun (eds.), *Gender and Technology: A Reader.* Baltimore: Johns Hopkins University Press, 2003.

René T. A. Lysloff and Leslie C. Gay, Jr. (eds.), *Music and Technoculture.* Middleton, CT: Wesleyan University Press, 2003.

George Martin (ed.), *Making Music: The Guide to Writing, Performing, and Recording.* London: Pan Books, 1983.

Rebecca McSwain, "The Power of the Electric Guitar," *Popular Music and Society* XIX (winter 1995), 21–40.

Andrew Millard, *America on Record: A History of Recorded Sound.* Cambridge: Cambridge University Press, 1995.

John Morrish, *The Fender Amp Book.* San Francisco: GPI Books/Miller Freeman Books, 1995.

David Morton, *Off the Record: The Technology and Culture of Sound Recording in America.* New Brunswick, NJ: Rutgers University Press, 2000.

Charles Shaar Murray, "Electrifying Music," *The History of Rock*, no. 4 (1982), 78–80.

Iris Newson (ed.), *Wonderful Inventions: Motion Pictures, Broadcasting, and Recorded Sound at the Library of Congress.* Washington, D.C.: Library of Congress, 1985.

Geoff Nicholls, *The Drum Book: A History of the Rock Drum Kit.* San Francisco: Miller Freeman Books, 1997.

Michael Norman and Ben Dickey, *The Complete Synthesizer Handbook.* London: Zomba Books, 1984.

Brian Priestly, Dave Gelly, Paul Trynka, and Tony Bacon, *The Sax and Brass Book: Saxophones, Trumpets, and Trombones in Jazz, Rock and Pop*. San Francisco, CA: Miller Freeman Books, 1998.

April Reilly, "The Impact of Technology on Rhythm n' Blues," *The Black Perspective in Music* I (fall 1973), 136–46.

Stanley Sadie (ed.), *The New Grove Dictionary of Musical Instruments*. London: Macmillan, 1984.

James R. Smart and Jon W. Newsom, *"A Wonderful Invention": A Brief History of the Phonograph from Tinfoil to the LP*. Washington, D.C.: Library of Congress, 1977.

Richard R. Smith, *Rickenbacker Guitar: The History*. Fullerton, CA: Centerstream, 1988.

Brian Southall, *Abbey Road: The Story of the World's Most Famous Recording Studio*. Cambridge: Patrick Stephens, 1982.

Warren C. Swindell, "Technology and the Music Industry," *OneTwoThreeFour*, no. 9 (autumn 1990), 61–72.

Paul Trynka (ed.), *Rock Hardware: 40 Years of Rock Instrumentation*. San Francisco: Miller Freeman Books, 1996.

Timothy Warner, *Pop Music—Technology and Creativity*. Burlington, VT: Ashgate, 2003.

Steve Waksman, *Instruments of Desire: The Electric Guitar and the Shaping of Musical Experience*. Cambridge: Harvard University Press, 1999.

Tom Wheeler, *American Guitars: An Illustrated History* (rev. and updated ed.). New York: HarperCollins, 1992.

Tom Wheeler, "Rare Bird: The Origin of the Stratocaster," *Guitar Player* XIII (October 1979), 12–18.

Charles Wolfe, "Nuclear Country: The Atomic Bomb in Country Music," *Journal of Country Music* VI (January 1978), 4–22.

Martin Zehr, "Abbey Road Revisited: Touring the Abbey Road Studios," *Goldmine*, no. 96 (March 30, 1984), 96–98.

Social Studies

B. Lee Cooper, "Images of the Future in Popular Music: Lyrical Comments on Tomorrow' in *Ideas for Teaching Gifted Students: Social Studies (Secondary)*, edited by Jackie Mallis. Austin, TX: Multi Media Arts, 1979, 97–108.

B. Lee Cooper, "A Popular Music Perspective: Challenging Sexism in the Social Studies Classroom," *Social Studies* LXXI (March/April 1980), 71–76.

B. Lee Cooper, "Popular Music in the Social Studies Classroom: Audio Resources for Teachers" in *How to Do It,* series 2, no. 13. Washington, D.C.: National Council for the Social Studies, 1981, 1–8

B. Lee Cooper, "Searching for Personal Identity in the Social Studies: Male and Female Perspectives in Contemporary Lyrics," *International Journal of Instructional Media* VI (1978–79), 351–60.

B. Lee Cooper, "Social Change, Popular Music and the Teacher," in *Ideas for Teaching Gifted Students: Social Studies (Secondary)*, edited by Jackie Mallis. Austin, TX: Multi Media Arts, 1979, 9–19.

B. Lee Cooper, "Social Concerns, Political Protest, and Popular Music," *Social Studies* LXXIX (March/April 1988), 53–60.

B. Lee Cooper and Larry S. Haverkos, "The Image of American Society in Popular Music: A Search for Identity and Values," *Social Studies* LXIV (December 1973), 319–22.

B. Lee Cooper and Larry S. Haverkos, "Using Popular Music in Social Studies Instruction," *Audiovisual Instruction* XVII (November 1972), 86–88.

John Litevich, "Popular Music as a Learning Tool in the Social Studies." Clinton, CT: Project Share/J. Litevich, 1983.

Samuel D. Miller and Manny Brand, "Music of Other Cultures in the Classroom," *Social Studies* LXXIV (March/April 1983), 62–64.

Sharon I. Ritt, "Using Music to Teach Reading Skills in Social Studies," *Reading Teacher* XXVII (March 1974), 596–601.

Sociology and Anthropology

Jane A. Ahekvist, "Music and Cultural Analysis in the Classroom," *Teaching Sociology* XXVII (1999), 126–44.

Howard S. Becker, *Outsiders: Studies in the Sociology of Deviance.* New York: Free Press of Glencoe, 1963.

Donald Allpoort Bird, Stephen C. Holder, and Diane Sears, "Walrus Is Greek for Corpse: Rumor and the Death of Paul McCartney," *Journal of Popular Culture* X (summer 1976), 110–21.

Gary Burns, "Of Our Elaborate Plans, the End," *Popular Music and Society* XI (winter 1987), 47–60.

George Carpozi, Jr., *John Lennon: Death of a Dream*. New York: Manor Books, 1980.

Alan Clayson, *Death Discs: An Account of Fatality in the Popular Song*. London: Sanctuary, 1997.

B. Lee Cooper, "Awarding an "A" Grade to Heavy Metal: A Review Essay [*Running with the Devil* by Robert Walser and *Heavy Metal* by Deena Weinstein]," *Popular Music and Society* XVII (fall 1993), 99–102.

B. Lee Cooper, "Bear Cats, Chipmunks, and Slip-in Mules: The Answer Song in Contemporary American Recordings, 1950–1985," *Popular Music and Society* XII (fall 1988), 57–77.

B. Lee Cooper, "Review of *Anti-Rock: The Opposition to Rock 'n' Roll* by Linda Martin and Kerry Segrave," *Popular Music and Society* XIII (fall 1989), 93–94.

B. Lee Cooper, "Review of *Living in the Rock 'n' Roll Mystery: Reading, Context, Self, and Others as Clues* by H. L. Goodall, Jr.," *Popular Culture in Libraries* I, no. 1 (1993), 158–60.

B. Lee Cooper, "Review of *Performing Rites: On the Value of Popular Music* by Simon Frith," *Journal of American Culture* XXI (fall 1998), 103–4.

B. Lee Cooper, "Review of *Rhythm and Noise: An Aesthetics of Rock* by Theodore Gracyk," *Popular Music and Society* XXIII (fall 1999), 125–6.

B. Lee Cooper, "Review of *Sound Effects: Youth, Leisure, and the Politics of Rock 'n' Roll* by Simon Frith," *Popular Music and Society* XI, no. 2 (1983), 92–94.

B. Lee Cooper, "From Johnny Ace to Frank Zappa: Debating the Meaning of Death in Rock Music—A Review Essay [*The Death of Rock 'n' Roll* by Jeff Pike]," *Popular Culture in Libraries* III, no. 1 (1995), 51–75.

B. Lee Cooper, "Human Relations, Communication Technology, and Popular Music: Audio Images of Telephone Use in the United States, 1950–1985," *International Journal of Instructional Media* XIII, no. 1 (1986), 75–82.

B. Lee Cooper, "The Image of the Outsider in Contemporary Lyrics," *Journal of Popular Culture* XII (summer 1978), 168–78.

B. Lee Cooper, "Marriage" in *Rock Music in American Popular Culture II: More Rock 'n' Roll Resources*, by B. Lee Cooper and Wayne S. Haney. New York: Haworth Press, 1997, 183–203.

B. Lee Cooper, "Review of *Work's Many Voices*, vol. I and II (*JEMF* 110/111) Compiled by Archie Green," *Popular Music and Society* XII (spring 1988), 77–79.

B. Lee Cooper, "Sex, Songs, and Censorship: A Thematic Taxonomy of Popular Recordings for Music Librarians and Sound Recording Archivists," *Popular Culture in Libraries* II, no. 4 (1994), 11–47.

B. Lee Cooper, "Sultry Songs as High Humor," *Popular Music and Society* XXVII (spring 1993), 71–85.

B. Lee Cooper, "What Kind of Fool Am I? Audio Imagery, Personal Identity, and Social Relationships," *International Journal of Instructional Media* XXIV, no. 3 (1997), 253–67.

B. Lee Cooper, "Wise Men Never Try: A Discography of Fool Songs, 1945–1995," *Popular Music and Society* XXI (summer 1997), 115–31.

B. Lee Cooper and William L. Schurk, "From 'I Saw Mommy Kissing Santa Claus' to "Another Brick in the Wall': Popular Recordings Featuring Pre-Teen Performers, Traditional Childhood Stories, and Contemporary Pre-Adolescent Perspectives, 1945–1985," *International Journal of Instructional Media* XVI, no. 1 (1989), 83–90.

Nikki Corvette, *Rock 'n' Roll Heaven: The Death and Lives of Musical Legends from the Big Bopper to Kurt Cobain*. New York: Boulevard Books, 1997.

Karl Dalls, "They Died Young," *The History of Rock*, no. 10 (1982), 194–5.

Donald M. Davis, "Rock 'n' Roll and Death: Nihilism in Music Videos," *Feedback* XXVII (fall 1986), 9–13.

R. Serge Denisoff, " 'Teen Angel': Resistance, Rebellion, and Death—Revisited," *Journal of Popular Culture* XVI (spring 1983), 116–22.

R. Serge Denisoff and John Bridges, "The Sociology of Popular Music: A Review," *Popular Music and Society* XI (1983), 51–62.

R. Serge Denisoff and Mark H. Levine, "The One Dimensional Approach to Popular Music: A Research Note," *Journal of Popular Culture* IV (spring 1971), 911–19.

Dr. Demento, "Summertime Blues from Percy Faith to Alice Cooper: A History of the Summer Song," *Waxpaper* III, no. 5 (June 2, 1978), 18–19, 28.

George E. Dickinson, Michael R. Leming, and Alan C. Mermann (eds.), *Dying, Death, and Bereavement* (2d ed.). Guilford, CT: Dushkin, 1994.

Robert Duncan, *Only the Good Die Young: The Rock 'n' Roll Book of the Dead*. New York: Harmony Books, 1986.

Fritz Eichenberg, *Dance of Death: A Graphic Commentary on the Danse Macabre through the Centuries*. New York: Abbeville Press, 1983.

Mary Ellison, "Consciousness of Poverty in Black Music," *Popular Music and Society* X (summer 1985), 17–46.

Howard Elterman, "Using Popular Music to Teach Sociology," *Teaching Sociology* XI (1983), 529–38.

Thomas G. Endress, "A Dramatic Analysis of Family Themes in the Top 100 Country Songs of 1992," *Popular Music and Society* XVII (winter 1993), 29–46.

Fred Fogo, *I Read the News Today: The Social Drama of John Lennon's Death.* Lanham, MD: Littlefield Adams Quality Paperbacks, 1994.

Aaron A. Fox, "The Jukebox of History: Narratives of Loss and Desire in the Discourse of Country Music," *Popular Music* XI (January 1992), 53–72.

Alex S. Freedman, "Country Music and the Theme of Poverty," *Midsouth Folklore* IV (1976), 95–98.

Simon Frith, *Performing Rites: On the Value of Popular Music.* Cambridge: Harvard University Press, 1996.

Simon Frith, *Sound Effects: Youth, Leisure, and the Politics of Rock 'n' Roll.* New York: Pantheon Books, 1981.

Simon Frith (ed.), *World Music, Politics, and Social Change: Papers from the International Association for the Study of Popular Music.* Manchester, England: Manchester University Press, 1989.

Simon Frith and Andrew Goodwin (eds.), *On Record: Rock, Pop, and the Written Word.* New York: Pantheon Books, 1990.

John G. Fuller, *Are the Kids All Right? The Rock Generation and Its Hidden Death Wish.* New York: Times Books, 1981.

H. L. Goodall, Jr., *Living in the Rock 'n' Roll Mystery: Reading Context, Self, and Others as Clues.* Carbondale: Southern Illinois University Press, 1991.

Archie Green (ed.), *Songs about Work: Essays in Occupational Culture for Richard A. Reuss.* Bloomington: Indiana University Press, 1993.

Elizabeth Greene, "Deena Weinstein, Sociology Professor and Heavy-Metal-Music Fiend," *Chronicle of Higher Education* XXXV (June 14, 1989), A3.

Peter Grendysa, "Chuck Willis' Two-Sided 'Epitaph' Still Haunts Studio Musicians Today," *Record Collector's Monthly* (January 1984), 1, 5.

Line Grenier and Jocelyne Guilbault, "Authority Revisited: The 'Other' in Anthropology and Popular Music Studies," *Ethnomusicology* XXXIV (fall 1990), 381–98.

Bill Griggs, "Last Songs," *Rockin' 50s,* no. 28 (February 1991), 24.

Jack Harrell, "The Poetics of Destruction: Death Metal Rock," *Popular Music and Society* XVIII (spring 1994), 91–103.

Philip Jacobs, *Rock 'n' Roll Heaven* London: Apple Press, 1990.

Gary J. Katz, *Death by Rock and Roll: The Untimely Deaths of the Legends of Rock*. Secaucus, NJ: Citadel Press, 1995.

Bob Kinder, "Mark Dinning: 'Teen Angel' Revisited," *Record Exchanger*, no. 30 (1982), 26–27.

Curt Krafft, "Till Death Do Us Part," *Story Untold* I, no. 1 (1977), 36–37.

Elisabeth Kubler-Ross, *On Death and Dying*. New York: Macmillan, 1969.

George H. Lewis, "Traps, Troubles, and Social Issues: Country Music in the Social Science Classroom," *Popular Music and Society* XXIII (winter 1999), 61–82.

Katie Letcher Lyle, *Scalded to Death by the Steam: Authentic Stories of Railroad Disasters and Ballads That Were Written about Them*. Chapel Hill, NC: Algonquin Books, 1991.

Jamie Malanowski, "Jailhouse Rock," *Spin* II (October 1986), 62–67.

Greil Marcus, *Dead Elvis: A Chronicle of Cultural Obsession*. New York: Doubleday/Anchor Books, 1991.

Peter Martin, *Sounds and Society: Themes in the Sociology of Music*. New York: St. Martin's Press, 1995.

James R. McDonald, "Rock and Roll and the Working Class," in *America's Musical Pulse: Popular Music in Twentieth-Century Society*, edited by Kenneth J. Bindas. Westport, CT: Praeger Books, 1992, 83–90.

David A. Milberg, "Saluting Summer: Pop Music's Second Most Favorite Time of the Year," *DISCoveries* LXII (July 1993), 31–35.

Jessica Mitford, *The American Way of Death*. New York: Simon & Schuster, 1963.

Raymond A. Moody, Jr., *Elvis after Life: Unusual Psychic Experiences Surrounding the Death of a Superstar*. Atlanta, GA: Peachtree Books, 1987.

Jon Newlin, "Those Great Old Death Songs," *Wavelength*, no. 33 (July 1983), 19–20.

Robert Niemei, "JFK as Jesus: The Politics of Myth in Phil Ochs' 'Crucifixion'," *Journal of American Culture* XVI (winter 1993), 35–40.

R. Gary Patterson, *Hellhounds on Their Trail: Tales from the Rock 'n' Roll Graveyard*. Nashville, TN: Dowling Press, 1998.

R. Gary Patterson, *The Walrus Was Paul: The Great Beatle Death Clues*. New York: Fireside/Simon & Schuster, 1998.

Robert G. Pielke, *You Say You Want a Revolution: Rock Music in American Culture*. Chicago: Nelson-Hall, 1986.

Jeff Pike, *The Death of Rock 'n' Roll: Untimely Demises, Morbid Preoccupations, and Premature Forecasts of Doom in Pop Music*. Boston: Farber and Farber, 1993.

Bruce L. Plopper and M. Ernest Ness, "Death as Portrayed to Adolescents through Top 40 Rock and Roll Music," *Adolescence* XXVIII, no. 112 (winter 1993), 793–807.

Andru Reeve, "Exclusive! 'Paul Is Dead'," *DISCoveries*, no. 69 (February 1994), 22–26.

Andru J. Reeve, *Turn Me On, Dead Man: The Complete Story of the Paul McCartney Death Hoax*. Ann Arbor, MI: Popular Culture, Ink., 1994.

Monika Reute and David Walczak, *Songware II: Using Popular Music in Teaching Sociology*. Washington, D.C.: American Sociological Association Teaching Resources Center, 1993.

Shari Roman, "Death as a Career Move," *Exposure* III (July 1990), 82–83.

Michael Roos, "Fixin' to Die: The Death Theme in the Music of Bob Dylan," *Popular Music and Society* VIII, nos. 3 and 4 (1982), 103–16.

Cynthia Rose, "Raves from the Grave: The Eternal Appeal of Rock's Death Songs," *History of Rock*, no. 29 (1982), 574–5.

Mark Rowland, "Roger, Roy, Marvin, and John: Requiems for Heavyweights," *Musician*, no. 147 (January 1991), 87–88.

Bob Seymore, *The End: The Death of Jim Morrison*. London: Omnibus Press, 1991.

John Shepherd, *Music as Social Text*. Cambridge, England: Polity Press, 1991.

John Shepherd, Phil Virden, Graham Vulliamy, and Trevor Wishart, *Whose Music? A Sociology of Musical Languages*. New Brunswick, NJ: Transaction, 1980.

Quinton Skinner, *Casualties of Rock*. New York: Pocket Books, 2001.

Robert Somma (ed.), *No One Waved Good-Bye: A Casualty Report on Rock and Roll*. New York: Outerbridge & Dienstfrey, 1971.

John Strausbaugh, *E: Reflections on the Birth of the Elvis Faith*. New York: Blast Books, 1995.

Nick Talevski, *Tombstone Blues: The Encyclopedia of Rock Obituaries*. New York: Omnibus Press, 1999.

Jeff Tamarkin, "Pop Music Suicide Victims," *Goldmine*, no. 360 (May 13, 1994), 10, 12.

Rogan Taylor, *The Death and Resurrection Show*. London: Blond Press, 1985.

Charles C. Thompson II and James P. Cole, *The Death of Elvis: What Really Happened*. New York: Delacorte Press, 1991.

Dave Thompson, *Better to Burn Out: The Cult of Death in Rock 'n' Roll*. New York: Thunder's Mouth Press, 1999.

John C. Thrush and George S. Paulus, "The Concept of Death in Popular Music: A Social Psychological Perspective," *Popular Music and Society* VI (1979), 219–28.

Nick Tosches, "Death in Hi-Fi or First Tastes of Tombstone," *Waxpaper* XXX, no. 2 (March 3, 1978), 18–19, 39.

Kenneth D. Tunnell, "Blood Marks the Spot Where Poor Ellen Was Found: Violent Crime in Bluegrass Music," *Popular Music and Society* XV (fall 1991), 95–115.

Deloris Von Nordheim, "Vision of Death in Rock Music and Musicians," *Popular Music and Society* XVII (summer 1993), 21–31.

David Walczak, Janet Merrill Alger, and Monika Reuter, *Songware: Using Popular Music in Teaching Sociology*. Washington, D.C.: American Sociological Association teaching Resources Center, 1989.

John Foster West, *Lift Up Your Head Tom Dooley: The True Story of the Appalachian Murder That Inspired One of America's Popular Ballads*. Asheboro, NC: Down Home Press, 1993.

Peter Wicke (translated by Rachel Fogg), *Rock Music: Culture, Aesthetics, and Sociology*. Cambridge: Cambridge University Press, 1990 (first published 1987).

Mason Wiley, "It's a Wonderful Death: Our Magnificent Obsession with All-Star Stiffs," *Exposure* III (July 1990), 60–67.

Speech and Oral Interpretation

John D. Bloodworth, "Communication in the Youth Counter Culture: Music as Expression," *Central States Speech Journal* XXVI (winter 1975), 304–9.

Mark W. Booth, "The Art of Words in Songs," *Quarterly Journal of Speech* LXII (October 1976), 242–9.

B. Lee Cooper, "Answer Songs: Comedy, Parody, and Social Commentary," *Rock and Blues News*, no. 8 (February-March 2000), 29–31.

James R. Irvine and Walter G. Kirkpatrick, "The Musical Form in Rhetorical Exchange: Theoretical Considerations," *Quarterly Journal of Speech* LVIII (October 1972), 272–84.

Ralph E. Knupp, "A Time for Every Purpose under Heaven: Rhetorical Dimensions of Protest Music," *Southern Speech Communication Journal* XLVI (summer 1981), 377–89.

Stephen Kosokoff and Carl W. Carmichael, "The Rhetoric of Protest: Song, Speech, and Attitude Change," *Southern Speech Journal* XXXV (spring 1970), 295–302.

Gerald G. LeCoat, "Music and the Three Appeals of Classical Rhetoric," *Quarterly Journal of Speech* LXII (April 1976), 157–66.

G.P. Morhmann and F. Eugene Scott, "Popular Music and World War II: The Rhetoric of Continuation," *Quarterly Journal of Speech* LXII (February 1976), 145–56.

Cheryl I. Thomas, "Look What They've Done to My Song, Ma: The Persuasiveness of Song," *Southern Speech Communication Journal* XXX (spring 1974), 260–68.

Donald W. Turner, "I Ain't Marchin' Anymore: The Rhetorical Potential of Anti-War Song Lyrics during the Vietnam Conflict for the Left." Unpublished Ph.D. dissertation, Pennsylvania State University, 1982.

Urban Studies

Johnnie Allan (comp.), *Memories: A Pictorial History of Southern Louisiana Music, 1910–1990* (2 vols.). Lafayette, LA: Jaofel, 1995.

Kent H. Benjamin, "The Austin Music Scene (A Slight Return)," *Goldmine*, no. 475 (October 9, 1998), 36–42.

Rodger Brown, *Party Out of Bounds: The B-52's, R.E.M., and The Kids Who Rocked Athens, Georgia*. New York: NAL/Dutton Books, 1991.

Gary Burns, "Bosstown: Another Look at the 'Boston Sound' of 1968," *Goldmine*, no. 311 (June 26, 1992), 16–34.

Joe Carr and Alan Munde, *Prairie Nights to Neon Lights: The Story of Country Music in West Texas*. Lubbock: Texas Tech University Press, 1995.

Iain Chambers, *Urban Rhythms: Pop Music and Popular Culture*. New York: St. Martin's Press, 1985.

B. Lee Cooper, "Audio Images of the City," *Social Studies* LXXII (May-June 1981), 130–6.

B. Lee Cooper, "Music and the Metropolis: Lyrical Images of Life in American Cities, 1950–1980," *Teaching History: A Journal of Methods* VI (fall 1981), 72–84.

B. Lee Cooper, "Review of *Rhythm Oil: A Journey through the Music of the American South* by Stanley Booth," *Popular Music and Society* XVI (summer 1992), 120–1.

Mark Costello and David Foster Wallace, *Signifying Rappers: Rap and Race in the Urban Present*. New York: Ecco Press, 1990.

Brian Cross, *It's Not about a Salary: Rap, Race, and Resistance in Los Angeles*. New York: Verso Books, 1993.

James R. Curtis and Richard F. Rose, "The Miami Sound: A Contemporary Latin Form of Place-Specific Music," *Journal of Cultural Geography* IV (fall-winter 1987), 110–18.

Wayne W. Daniel, *Pickin' on Peachtree: A History of Country Music in Atlanta, Georgia*. Champaign-Urbana: University of Illinois Press, 1990.

John T. Davis, *Austin City Limits: 25 Years of American Music*. New York: Billboard Books, 2000.

Anthony DeCurtis and James Henke, with Holly George-Warren (eds.), *The Rolling Stone Illustrated History of Rock and Roll* (2d ed.). New York: Random House/Rolling Stone Press, 1992.

Dave Dexter Jr., "Music Cities, U.S.A.," *Billboard* LXXXI (December 27, 1969), 44–48.

James Dickerson, *Goin' Back to Memphis: A Century of Blues, Rock 'n' Roll, and Glorious Soul*. New York: Schirmer Books, 1996.

Dr. Demento, "Big Apple Dreamin': New York in Song From 'Coney Island Baby' to "Nights on Broadway'," *Waxpaper* II, no. 9 (August 26, 1977), 23–25.

Dr. Demento, "How Nashville Cornered Country," *Waxpaper* II, no. 12 (January 6, 1978), 16–19.

James N. Doukas, *The Electric Tibet: The Rise and Fall of the San Francisco Rock Scene*. North Hollywood, CA: Dominion, 1969.

Clifford Endres, *Austin City Limits: The Story behind Television's Most Popular Country Music Program*. Austin: University of Texas Press, 1987.

Lee Friedlander, *The Jazz People of New Orleans*. London: Jonathan Cape, 1992.

Gillian G. Gaar, "Memphis Guide: The City with the Blues in Its Soul, Where Rock Learned to Roll," *DISCoveries*, no. 100 (September 1996), 30–33.

Daniel Gabriel, "Land of 10,000 Dances: Rockin' and Rollin' in the Twin Cities, Mid-'60s Style," *Goldmine*, no. 94 (March 2, 1984), 59, 134–5, 137–40.

Charlie Gillett, *The Sound of the City: The Rise of Rock and Roll* (2d ed.). New York: Da Capo Press, 1996.

Ralph J. Gleason, *The Jefferson Airplane and the San Francisco Sound*. New York: Ballantine Books, 1969.

Robert Gordon, *It Came from Memphis*. Boston: Faber and Faber, 1995.

Alan Govenar, *Meeting the Blues: The Rise of the Texas Sound*. Dallas, TX: Taylor, 1988.

Alan Govenar and Benny Joseph, *The Early Years of Rhythm 'n' Blues: Focus on Houston*. Houston, TX: Rice University Press, 1990.

Floyd M. Henderson, "The Image of New York City in American Popular Music of 1890–1970," *New York Folklore Quarterly* XXX (December 1974), 267–78.

Judy M. Henderson, *African-American Music in Minnesota: From Spirituals to Rap*. St. Paul: Minnesota Historical Society Press, 1994.

Lee Hildebrand and Michelle Vignes, *Bay Area Blues*. Rohnert Park, CA: Pomegranate Artbooks, 1993.

Barney Hoskyns, *Waiting for the Sun: Strange Days, Weird Scenes, and the Sound of Los Angeles*. New York: St. Martin's Griffin, 1999.

Clark Humphrey, *Loser: The Real Seattle Music Story*. Portland, OR: Feral House, 1995.

Steve James, "Blues from the Big State . . . Then and Now: Texas (A Short Time Line)," *Blues Revue*, no. 30 (August/September 1997), 12–15.

William Howland Kenney, *Chicago Jazz: A Cultural History, 1904–1930*. New York: Oxford University Press, 1993.

Rick Koster, *Texas Music*. New York: St. Martin's Press, 1998.

John Lomax III, *Nashville: Music City U.S.A.* New York: Harry N. Abrams, 1985.

Hugh Maclean and Vernon Joynson (comps.), *An American Rock History—Part Three: Chicago and Illinois*. Telford, England: Borderline Productions, 1992.

Bob Margolin, "Austin in the '70s," *Blues Revue*, no. 3 (August/September 1997), 68–70.

Gil Margulis, "Detroit '60s Rock Scene: Motor City Mayhem," *Goldmine*, no. 192 (December 4, 1987), 30, 33–34.

Jack McDonough, *San Francisco Rock: The Illustrated History of San Francisco Rock Music*. San Francisco: Chronicle Books, 1985.

Margaret McKee and Fred Chisenhall, *Beale Black and Blue: Life and Music on Black America's Main Street*. Baton Rouge: Louisiana State University Press, 1981.

Leroy Ostransky, *Jazz City: The Impact of Our Cities on the Development of Jazz*. Englewood Cliffs, NJ: Prentice Hall, 1978.

Nathan W. Pearson Jr., *Goin' to Kansas City*. Urbana: University of Illinois Press, 1987.

Jim Pettigrew, "From Rhythm 'n' Blues to Disco: A Broad Overview of Atlanta Music Since 1945," *Atlanta Historical Bulletin* XXI (summer 1977), 114–38.

Robert Pruter, "A Historical Overview of Soul Music in Chicago," *Black Music Research Bulletin* XII, no. 2 (fall 1990), 1–4.

Rick Richards, "More than Motown: The Other Side of Detroit R & B," *DISCoveries*, no. 100 (September 1996), 48–51.

Cecilia Ridgeway and John Roberts, "Urban Popular Music and Interaction: A Semantic Relationship," *Ethnomusicology* XX (May 1976), 233–51.

Mike Rowe, *Chicago Blues: The City and the Music*. New York: Da Capo Press, 1981.

Mike Rowe, *Chicago Breakdown*. New York: Drake, 1975.

Ross Russell, *Jazz Style in Kansas City and the Southwest*. Berkeley: University of California Press, 1971.

Barry Shank, *Dissonant Identities: The Rock 'n' Roll Scene in Austin, Texas*. Hanover, NH: University Press of New England, 1994.

Darby Slick, *Don't You Want Somebody to Love: Reflections on the San Francisco Sound*. Berkeley, CA: Snow Lion Graphics Books, 1991.

Tracy Thomes and Walt Bodine, *Right Here in River City: A Portrait of Kansas City*. Garden City, NY: Doubleday, 1976.

Chuck Thompson, "Country Music Is Why God Made Oklahoma," *DISCoveries*, V (June 1992), 42–45.

Steven C. Tracy, *Going to Cincinnati: A History of the Blues in the Queen City*. Champaign: University of Illinois Press, 1993.

Brett Williams, "The South in the City," *Journal of Popular Culture* XVI (winter 1982), 30–41.

Larry Willoughby, *Texas Rhythm/Texas Rhyme: A Pictorial History of Texas Music*. Austin: Texas Monthly Press, 1984.

Brenda and Bill Woods, *Louisville's Own: An Illustrated Encyclopedia of Louisville Area Recorded Pop Music From 1953 to 1983*. Louisville, KY: De Forrest Books, 1983.

Women's Studies

Mavis Bayton, *Frock Rock: Women Performing Popular Music*. New York: Oxford University Press, 1998.

Audrey Becker, "New Lyrics by Women: A Feminist Alternative," *Journal of Popular Culture* XXIV (summer 1990), 1–22.

Alan Betrock, *Girl Groups: The Story of a Sound*. New York: Delilah Books, 1982.

Donald Bogle, *Brown Sugar: Eighty Years of America's Black Female Superstars*. New York: Da Capo Press, 1980.

Anna Strong Bourgeois, *Blueswomen: Profiles of 37 Early Performers with an Anthology of Lyrics, 1920–1945*. Jefferson, NC: McFarland, 1996.

Mary A. Bufwack and Robert K. Oermann, *Finding Her Voice: The Saga of Women in Country Music*. New York: Crown, 1993.

Lori Burns and Melisse LaFrance, *Disruptive Divas: Feminism, Identity, and Popular Music*. New York: Routledge, 2002.

Joyce Cheney, Marcia Deihl, and Deborah Silverstein, *All Our Lives: A Women's Songbook*. Baltimore: Diana Press, 1976.

Susan C. Cook and Judy S. Tsou (eds.), *Cecilia Reclaimed: Feminist Perspectives on Gender and Music*. Champaign: University of Illinois Press, 1994.

B. Lee Cooper, "From Lady Day to Lady Di: Images of Women in Contemporary Recordings, 1938–1998," *International Journal of Instructional Media* XXVI, no. 3 (1999), 353–8.

B. Lee Cooper, "Images of Women in Popular Song Lyrics: A Bibliography," *Popular Music and Society* XXII (winter 1998), 79–89.

B. Lee Cooper, "Review of *Leading Ladies: The Best of the Great Ladies of Song* from Reader's Digest Music," *Popular Music and Society* XXI (winter 1997), 136–44.

B. Lee Cooper, "Review of *The Rolling Stone Women in Rock Collection*," *Rock and Blues News*, no. 2 (February-March 1999), 45–46.

B. Lee Cooper, "Review of *She's a Rebel: The History of Women in Rock and Roll* by Gillian G. Gaar," *Journal of American Culture* XVII (spring 1994), 99–100.

B. Lee Cooper, "The Traditional and Beyond: Resources for Teaching Women's Studies," *Audiovisual Instruction* XXII (December 1977), 14–18ff.

B. Lee Cooper, "Women's Studies and Popular Music Stereotypes," *Popular Music and Society* XXIII (winter 1999), 31–43.

B. Lee Cooper, "Women's Studies and Popular Music: Using Audio Resources in Social Studies Instruction," *The History and Social Science Teacher* XIV (fall 1978), 29–40.

Sarah Cooper (ed.), *Girls! Girls! Girls! Essays on Women and Music*. New York: New York University Press, 1996.

Angela Y. Davis, *Blues Legacies and Black Feminism: Gertrude "Ma" Rainey, Bessie Smith, and Billie Holiday*. New York: Pantheon Books, 1998.

Nicola Dibben, "Representations of Femininity in Popular Music," *Popular Music* XVIII (October 1999), 331–55.

James Dickerson, *Women on Top: The Quiet Revolution That's Rocking the American Music Industry*. New York: Billboard Books, 1998.

Liz Evans, *Women, Sex, and Rock 'n' Roll: In Their Own Words*. San Francisco: Pandora/HarperCollins, 1994.

Gillian G. Gaar, *She's a Rebel: The History of Women in Rock 'n' Roll*. Seattle, WA: Seal Press, 1992.

Leslie Gourse, *Madame Jazz: Contemporary Women Instrumentalists*. New York: Oxford University Press, 1995.

Charlotte Greig, *Will You Still Love Me Tomorrow? Girl Groups from the '50s On*. London: Virago Press, 1989.

Donald V. S. Harley, "Singin' the Blues: Women in Song," *Social Education* LVI (January 1992), 66.

Dapne Duval Harrison, *Black Pearls: Blues Queens of the 1920s*. New Brunswick, NJ: Rutgers University Press, 1988.

Don L. Hixon and Don A. Hennessee, *Women in Music: An Encyclopedic Bibliography* (2d ed.). Metuchen, NJ: Scarecrow Press, 1993.

Colleen Hyden and N. Jane McCandless, "Men and Women as Portrayed in the Lyrics of Contemporary Music," *Popular Music and Society* IX (summer 1983), 19–26.

Hettie Jones, *Big Star Fallin' Mama: Five Women in Black Music*. New York: Viking Press, 1974.

Ellen Koskoff (ed.), *Women and Music in Cross-Cultural Perspective*. Champaign-Urbana: University of Illinois Press, 1989.

Ross Laird (comp.), *Moanin' Low: A Discography of Female Popular Vocal Recordings, 1920–1933*. Westport, CT: Greenwood, 1996.

Lisa A. Lewis, *Gender Politics and MTV: Voicing the Difference*. Philadelphia: Temple University Press, 1990.

Jessica Lustig (ed.), *Angry Women in Rock—Volume One*. New York: Juno Books, 1996.

Dave Marsh (ed.), *Women of Motown: An Oral History*. New York: Avon Books, 1998.

Susan McLary, *Feminine Endings: Music, Gender, and Sexuality*. Minneapolis: University of Minnesota Press, 1991.

Wilfrid Mellers, *Angels of the Night: Popular Female Singers of Our Time*. New York: Basil Blackwell, 1986.

Kenneth E. Morris, "Sometimes It's Hard to Be a Woman: Reinterpreting a Country Music Classic," *Popular Music and Society* XVI (spring 1992), 1–11.

Neil Nehring, *Popular Music, Gender, and Postmodernism: Anger Is an Energy*. Thousand Oaks, CA: Sage, 1997.

Karl William Neuenfeldt, "Sun, Sea, Sex, and Senoritas: 'Shorthand' Images of Ethnicity, Ethos, and Gender in Country Songs Set in the Circum-Caribbean," *Popular Music and Society* XV (summer 1991), 1–21.

Karen O'Brien, *Hymn to Her: Women Musicians Talk*. London: Virago Press, 1995.

Lucy O'Brien, *She Bop: The Definitive History of Women in Rock, Pop, and Soul*. New York: Penguin Books, 1995.

Barbara O'Dair (ed.), *Trouble Girls: The Rolling Stone Book of Women in Rock*. New York: Random House, 1997.

Katherine Orloff, *Rock 'n' Roll Lady*. Freeport, NY: Nash, 1974.

Aida Pavletich, *Sirens of Song: The Popular Female Vocalist in America*. New York: Da Capo Press, 1980.

John Pidgeon, "Venus in Blue Jeans?" *The History of Rock*, no. 16 (1982), 310–12.

Sally Placksin, *American Women in Jazz, 1900 to the Present: Their Words, Lives, and Music*. New York: Seaview Books, 1982.

Amy Raphael, *Grrrls: Women Rewrite Rock*. Ogden, UT: Griffin Books, 1996.

Simon Reynolds and Joy Press, *The Sex Revolts: Gender, Rebellion, and Rock 'n' Roll*. Cambridge, MA: Harvard University Press, 1995.

Robin Roberts, *Ladies First: Women in Music Videos*. Jackson: University Press of Mississippi, 1996.

Jerry L. Rodnitzky, *Feminist Phoenix: The Rise and Fall of a Feminist Counterculture*. Westport, CT: Praeger, 1999.

Timothy E. Scheurer, "Goddesses and Golddiggers: Images of Women in Popular Music of the 1930s," *Journal of Popular Culture* XXIV (summer 1990), 23–35.

Tim Schlattmann, "From Disco Divas to the Material Girls: Who's Ruling the Charts?" *Popular Music and Society* XV (winter 1991), 1–14.

Greg Shaw, "Leaders of the Pack: Teen Dreams and Tragedy in Girl Group Rock," *History of Rock*, no. 29 (1982), 566–69.

Liz Thomson (ed.), *New Women in Rock*. New York: Delilah Books, 1982.

Alan Wells, "Women on the Pop Charts: A Comparison of Britain and the United States, 1960–1988," *Popular Music and Society* XV (spring 1991), 25–32.

Hilda E. Wenner and Elizabeth Freilicher (comps.), *Here's to the Women: 100 Songs for and about American Women*. Syracuse, NY: Syracuse University Press, 1987.

Sheila Whiteley (ed.), *Sexing the Groove: Popular Music and Gender*. New York: Routledge, 1997.

Marc Woodworth (ed.), *Solo: Women Singer-Songwriters in Their Own Words*. New York: Delta Books, 1998.

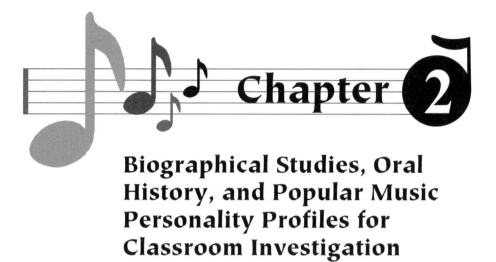

Chapter 2

Biographical Studies, Oral History, and Popular Music Personality Profiles for Classroom Investigation

Biographical pursuits present invaluable teaching techniques and learning opportunities, yet substantive writing about the lives and careers of rock stars is rare. Hagiography is common, as are unauthorized exposes. This chapter provides an introduction to resources available for profiling the professional activities and personal backgrounds of a variety of influential popular music performers. First, a brief list of oral history suggestions and biographical study techniques are provided. Second, an extensive assembly of music encyclopedias and biographical directories is compiled. Finally, an illustrative cross-section of more than ninety popular music artists—ranging from Johnny Ace, Louis Armstrong, and Joan Baez to Stevie Wonder, Frank Zappa, and ZZ Top—are recommended for possible student investigation. The latter section is intended to be descriptive rather than exhaustive. It does not include Boyz II Men, Garth Brooks, Mariah Carey, Mary Chapin Carpenter, Kurt Cobain, Eddie Cochran, Miles Davis, Duke Ellington, Jennifer Lopez, Judas Priest, Tupac Shakur, and a thousand other recording artists who might be fertile figures for biographical examination. It does, however, begin to suggest the extensive variety of personalities from blues, country, folk, jazz, pop, rock, and soul realms that have already been researched. The biographies, interviews, record reviews, and scholarly studies on the numerous artists featured here can serve as models for new student investigations into the lives, lyrics, and careers of Aerosmith, Sheryl Crow,

Destiny's Child, Melissa Ethridge, Guns n' Roses, Whitney Houston, Iron Maiden, k.d. lang, Selena, Barry White, and Neil Young.

Educational Perspectives on Investigating Record Artist Profiles

George O. Carney, "T for Texas, T for Tennessee: The Origins of American Country Music Notables," *Journal of Geography* LXXVIII (November 1979), 218–25.

B. Lee Cooper, "Biographical Studies," in *Rock Music in American Popular Culture: Rock 'n' Roll Resources*, by B. Lee Cooper and Wayne S. Haney. New York: Haworth Press, 1995, 27–43.

B. Lee Cooper, "Constructing Popular Culture Biographies: History Instruction through Literary and Audio Resources," *International Journal of Instructional Media* V (1977–78), 357–69.

B. Lee Cooper, "Contemporary Singers as Subjects for Biographical Study," *Library-College Experimenter* V (May 1979), 13–28.

B. Lee Cooper, "Les McCann, Elvis Presley, Linda Ronstadt, and Buddy Holly: Focusing on the Lives of Contemporary Singers," *Social Education* XLIV (March 1980), 217–21.

B. Lee Cooper, "Review of *Billy Murray: The Phonograph Industry's First Great Recording Artist* by Frank Hoffmann, Dick Carty, and Quentin Riggs," *Journal of American Culture* XXIII (winter 2000), 109–10.

B. Lee Cooper, "Review of *Dangerous Dances—The Authorized Biography* by Nick Tosches, with Daryl Hall and John Oates," *Popular Music and Society* XI, no. 4 (winter 1987), 101–3.

B. Lee Cooper, "Review of *Tattooed on Their Tongues* by Colin Escott," *Popular Music and Society* XXI, no. 4 (winter 1997), 149–50.

Noel Coppage, "Semisecular Dylan," *Stereo Review* 46 (December 1981), 82.

R. Serge Denisoff and John Bridges, "Popular Music: Who Are the Recording Artists?" *Journal of Communication* XXXII (winter 1982), 132–42.

Stan Denski, " 'Inarticulate Speech of the Heart': Limits and Insights in the Popular Interview Literature," *Popular Music and Society* 15 (fall 1991), 11–30.

Frank Ferriano, "Did He Write That? America's Great Unknown Songwriter Harold Arlan," *Tracking: Popular Music Studies* III (winter 1990), 8–17.

Jon Fitzgerald, "Songwriters in the U.S. Top Forty, 1963–1966," *Popular Music and Society* XXI (winter 1997), 85–110.

Jon Fitzgerald, "When the Brill Building Met Lennon-McCartney: Continuity and Change in the Early Evolution of the Mainstream Pop Song," *Popular Music and Society* XIX (spring 1995), 59–77.

Bill Flanagan, "Songwriter Heaven: Rock and Pop Composers Swap Tall Tales at the Bottom Line," *Musician*, no. 169 (November 1992), 78–83.

Simon Frith, "Rock Biography: Essay Review," in *Popular Music 3: Producers and Markets*, edited by Richard Middleton and David Horn. Cambridge: Cambridge University Press, 1983, 271–7.

Stephen B. Groce, "On the Outside Looking In: Professional Socialization and the Process of Becoming a Songwriter," *Popular Music and Society* XV (spring 1991), 33–44.

Roy Hemming and David Hadju, *Discovering Great Singers of Classic Pop: A New Listener's Guide to the Sounds and Lives of Top Performers and Their Recordings, Movies, and Videos*. New York: Newmarket Press, 1991.

Thomas S. Hischak, *Word Crazy: Broadway Lyricists from Cohan to Sondheim*. Westport, CT: Greenwood, 1991.

Frank Hoffmann (comp.), *The Literature of Rock, 1954–1978*. Metuchen, NJ: Scarecrow Press, 1981.

Frank Hoffmann and B. Lee Cooper (comps.), *The Literature of Rock II, 1979–1983*. Metuchen, NJ: Scarecrow Press, 1986.

Frank Hoffmann and B. Lee Cooper (comps.), *The Literature of Rock III, 1984–1990*. Metuchen, NJ: Scarecrow Press, 1995.

William G. Hyland, *The Song Is Ended: Songwriters and American Music, 1900–1950*. New York: Oxford University Press, 1995.

Arthur L. Iger, *Music of the Golden Age, 1900–1950 and Beyond: A Guide to Popular Composers and Lyricists*. Westport, CT: Greenwood, 1998.

Dick Jacobs and Harriet Jacobs, *Who Wrote That Song?* (2d ed., updated and expanded). Cincinnati, OH: Writer's Digest Books, 1994.

Wayne Jancik and Tad Lathrop, *Cult Rockers: 150 of the Most Controversial, Distinctive, Offbeat, Intriguing, Outrageous, and Championed Rock Musicians of All Time*. New York: Fireside Books, 1995.

David A. Jasen, *Tin Pan Alley: The Composers, the Performers, and Their Times—The Golden Age of American Popular Music From 1886 to 1956*. New York: Donald I. Fine, 1988.

David A. Jasen and Gene Jones, *Spreadin' Rhythm Around: Black Popular Songwriters, 1880–1930*. New York: Schirmer Books, 1998.

Kenneth Aaron Kantor, *The Jews of Tin Pan Alley: The Jewish Contribution to American Popular Music, 1830–1940*. New York: KTAU, 1982.

Gene Lees, *Singers and the Song*. New York: Oxford University Press, 1987.

Brady J. Leyser, with additional research by Pol Gosset (comp.), *Rock Stars/Pop Stars: A Comprehensive Bibliography, 1955–1994*. Westport, CT: Greenwood, 1994.

Greil Marcus, "Review of *Elvis* by Albert Goldman," *Journal of Country Music* IX, no. 2 (1982), 116–20.

Jack McDonough, "Review Essay on Jackson Browne," *Popular Music and Society*, IV (1975), 242–50.

Rick Mitz, "Who Writes All Those Rock Lyrics?" *Stereo Review* 38 (February 1977), 60–63.

Terence J. O'Grady, "Review of *The Lives of John Lennon* by Albert Goldman," *American Music* VII (fall 1989), 341–5.

Edward Pessen, "The Great Songwriters of Tin Pan Alley's Golden Age: A Social, Occupational, and Aesthetic Inquiry," *American Music* III (summer 1985), 180–97.

Bruce Pollock, *In Their Own Words: Twenty Successful Song Writers Tell How They Write Their Songs*. New York: Collier Books, 1975.

John Potter, "The Singer, Not the Song: Women Singers as Composer-Poets," *Popular Music* XIII (May 1994), 191–9.

Walter Rimler, *Not Fade Away: A Comparison of Jazz Age with Rock Era Pop Song Composers*. Ann Arbor, MI: Pierian Press, 1984.

Wayne Russell, "Brother Acts: Brother, Can You Spare a Tune?" *Goldmine*, no. 207 (July 1, 1988), 20, 78.

Robert Santelli, *The Big Book of the Blues: A Biographical Encyclopedia*. New York: Penguin Books, 1993.

Bob Sarlin, *Turn It Up (I Can't Hear the Words): The Best of the New Singer/Songwriters*. New York: Simon & Schuster, 1973.

Tony Staveacre, *The Songwriters*. London: BBC, 1980.

Doug Stewart, "Now Playing in Academe: The King of Rock 'n' Roll," *Smithsonian* XXVI, no. 8 (November 1995), 56–67.

Mike Swann, *How Many Roads? History and Guide of American Singer Songwriters.* Lewes, England: E. Sussex Book Guild, 1989.

Paul Zollo, *Songwriters on Songwriting* (expanded ed.). New York: Da Capo Press, 1997.

Music Encyclopedias and Biographical Directories as Teaching Resources

Bob Allen (ed.), *The Blackwell Guide to Recorded Country Music.* Cambridge, MA: Blackwell, 1994.

American Society of Composers, Authors, and Publishers (compiled by Jaques Cattell Press), *ASCAP Biographical Dictionary* (4th ed.). New York: Bowker Press, 1981.

Christine Amber, *The HarperCollins Dictionary of Music* (2d ed.). New York: HarperCollins, 1991 (first published 1987).

Robert Anderson and Gail North (comps.), *Gospel Music Encyclopedia.* New York: Sterling, 1979.

Richard Aquila, *That Old-Time Rock and Roll: A Chronicle of an Era, 1954–1963.* Urbana: University of Illinois Press, 2000 (first published 1989).

Kristin Baggelaar and Donald Milton (comps.), *Folk Music: More than a Song.* New York: Thomas Y. Crowell, 1976.

Glenn A. Baker and Stuart Coupe, *The New Music.* New York: Harmony Books, 1980.

Whitney Balliett, *American Singers: Twenty-Seven Portraits in Songs* (expanded ed.). New York: Oxford University Press, 1988.

Michael Bane, *Who's Who in Rock.* New York: Facts on File, 1981.

Russell D. Barnard (ed.), *The Comprehensive Country Music Encyclopedia.* New York: Country Music Magazine Press/Times Books/Random House, 1994.

Steve Barrow and Peter Dalton (edited by Orla Duane), *Reggae: The Rough Guide* (2d ed.). London: Rough Guides, 2001.

Alan Betrock, *Girl Groups: The Story of a Sound.* New York: Delilah Books, 1982.

David Bianco (comp.), *Who's New Wave in Music: An Illustrated Encyclopedia, 1976–1982 (The First Wave).* Ann Arbor, MI: Pierian Press, 1985.

Patti Jean Birosik, *The New Age Music Guide: Profiles and Recordings of 500 Top New Age Musicians*. New York: MacMillan/Collier Books, 1989.

Vladimir Bogdanov, Chris Woodstra, and Stephan Thomas Erlewine (eds.), *All Music Guide: The Definitive Guide to Popular Music* (4th ed.). San Francisco, CA: Backbeat Books, 2001.

Vladimir Bogdanov, Chris Woodstra, Stephen Thomas Erlewine, and John Bush (eds.), *All Music Guide to Electronica: The Definitive Guide to Electronic Music*. San Francisco: Backbeat Books, 2001.

Ray Bonds (ed.), *The Harmony Illustrated Encyclopedia of Rock* (3d ed.). New York: Harmony Books, 1982.

Ray Bonds (ed.), *Illustrated Encyclopedia of Black Music*. New York: Harmony Books, 1982.

Caryl Brahms and Ned Sherrin, *Song by Song: The Lives and Work of 14 Great Lyric Writers*. Bolton, England: Ross Anderson, 1984.

Luann Brennan (ed.), *Contemporary Musicians—Volume 22: Profiles of the People in Music*. Detroit, MI: Gale Group, 1998.

Luann Brennan (ed.), *Contemporary Musicians—Volume 23: Profiles of the People in Music*. Detroit, MI: Gale Group, 1999.

Luann Brennan (ed.), *Contemporary Musicians—Volume 24: Profiles of the People in Music*. Detroit, MI: Gale Group, 1999.

Simon Broughton, Mark Ellingham, and Richard Trilla, with Orla Duane and Vanessa Dowell (eds.), *World Music—Volume One: Africa, Europe, and the Middle East—The Rough Guide*. London: Penguin Books/Rough Guides, 1999.

Simon Broughton and Mark Ellingham, with James McConnachie and Orla Duane (eds.), *World Music—Volume Two: Latin and North America, Caribbean, India, Asia, and Pacific*. London: Penguin Books/Rough Guides, 2000.

Len Brown and Gary Friedrich (comps.), *Encyclopedia of Country and Western Music*. New York: Tower Books, 1971.

Len Brown and Gary Friedrich (comps.), *Encyclopedia of Rock 'n' Roll*. New York: Tower, 1970.

Pete Brown and H. P. Newquist, *Legends of Rock Guitar: The Essential Reference of Rock's Greatest Guitarists*. Milwaukee, WI: Hal Leonard, 1997.

Ray B. Browne and Pat Browne (eds.), *The Guide to United States Popular Culture*. Bowling Green, OH: Bowling Green State University Popular Press, 2001.

Jonathan Buckley, Orla Duane, Mark Ellingham, and Al Spice (eds.), *Rock: The Rough Guide* (2d ed.). London: Rough Guides, 1999.

Arthur Butterfield, *Encyclopedia of Country Music*. New York: Gallery Books, 1985.

Alan Cackett with Alec Foege, *The Harmony Illustrated Encyclopedia of Country Music* (3d ed.). New York: Crown, 1994

Richard Carlin, *The Big Book of Country Music: A Biographical Encyclopedia*. New York: Penguin Books, 1995.

Joseph R. Carlton (comp.), *Carlton's Complete Reference Book of Music*. Studio City, CA: Carlton, 1980.

Ian Carr, Digby Fairweather, and Brian Priestly (eds.), *Jazz—The Rough Guide* (2d ed.). London: Rough Guides, 2000.

Patrick Carr (ed.), *The Illustrated History of Country Music*. Garden City, NY: Country Music Magazine Press/Doubleday, 1979.

Brian Case et al., *The Illustrated History of Jazz* (rev. ed.). London: Salamander Press, 1986.

Bryan Chalker, *Country Music*. Secaucus, NJ: Chartwell Books, 1976.

Chris Charlesworth, *A—Z of Rock Guitarists*. New York: Proteus Press, 1982.

Marti Smiley Childs and Jeff March, *Echoes of the Sixties: Intimate Profiles of 43 of the Musical Composers and Performers Who Influenced an Entire Generation*. New York: Billboard Books/Watson-Guptill, 1999.

John Chilton (comp.), *Who's Who in Jazz: Storyville to Swing Street*. New York: Da Capo Press, 1985.

Robert Christgau, *Grown Up All Wrong: 75 Great Rock and Pop Artists from Vaudeville to Techno*. Cambridge: Harvard University Press, 1998.

Bob Cianci, *Great Rock Drummers of the Sixties*. Milwaukee, WI: Third Earth/Hal Leonard, 1989.

Charles E. Claghorn (comp.), *Biographical Dictionary of Jazz*. Englewood Cliffs, NJ: Prentice Hall, 1983.

Donald Clarke (ed.), *The Penguin Encyclopedia of Popular Music* (2d ed.). New York: Penguin Putnam, 1998.

Alan Clayson, *Call Up the Groups! The Golden Age of British Beat, 1962–1967*. Poole, England: Blandford Press, 1986.

John Clemente, *Girl Groups: Fabulous Females That Rocked the World*. Iola, WI: Krause, 2000.

Mike Clifford, *The Harmony Illustrated Encyclopedia of Rock* (5th ed.). New York: Crown, 1986.

Warren E. Colbert, *Who Wrote That Song? Or Who in the Hell Is J. Fred Coots? An Informal Survey of American Popular Songs and Their Composers.* New York: Revisionist Press, 1975.

Stuart Colman, *They Kept on Rockin': The Giants of Rock 'n' Roll.* Poole, Dorset, England: Blandford Press, 1982.

B. Lee Cooper, "Review of *Contemporary Musicians* (vols. 1–6), edited by Micahel L. LaBlanc," *MI Academician* XXIV (summer 1992), 599–600.

B. Lee Cooper, "Review of *Contemporary Musicians* (vols. 6 and 8), edited by Michael L. LaBlanc and Julia M. Rubiner," *Popular Music and Society* XVII, no. 3 (fall 1993), 104–6.

B. Lee Cooper, "Review of *Contemporary Musicians* (vols. 21–24), edited by Stacy A. McConnell and Luann Brennan," *Popular Music and Society* XXIV, no. 1 (spring 2000), 122–4.

Lee Cotten, *Shake, Rattle, and Roll—The Golden Age of American Rock 'n' Roll: Volume One, 1952–1955.* Ann Arbor, MI: Pierian Press, 1989.

Lee Cotten, *Reelin' and Rockin'— The Golden Age of American Rock 'n' Roll: Volume Two, 1956–1959.* Ann Arbor, MI: Popular Culture, 1995.

Lee Cotten, *Twist and Shout— The Golden Age of American Rock 'n' Roll: Volume Three, 1960–1963.* Sacramento, CA: High Sierra Books, 2002.

Stuart Coupe and Glenn A. Baker, *The New Rock 'n' Roll: The A–Z of Rock in the '80s.* New York: St. Martin's Press, 1983.

John Cowley and Paul Oliver (eds.), *The New Blackwell Guide to Recorded Blues.* Cambridge, MA: Blackwell, 1996.

Warren Craig, *The Great Songwriters of Hollywood.* San Diego, CA: Barnes Press, 1980.

Warren Craig (comp.), *Sweet and Lowdown: America's Popular Song Writers.* Metuchen, NJ: Scarecrow Press, 1978.

Colin Cross, with Paul Kendall and Mick Farren (comps.), *Encyclopedia of British Beat Groups and Solo Artists of the Sixties.* London: Omnibus Press, 1980.

Bruce Crowther and Mike Pinfold, *The Jazz Singers: From Ragtime to the New Wave.* Poole, England: Blandford Press, 1986.

David Dachs, *American Pop.* New York: Scholastic Book Services, 1969.

David Dachs, *Encyclopedia of Pop/Rock*. New York: Scholastic Book Services, 1972.

David Dachs, *Inside Pop: America's Top Ten Groups*. New York: Scholastic Book Services, 1968.

David Dachs, *Inside Pop 2*. New York: Scholastic Book Services, 1970.

David Dachs (comp.), *100 Pop/Rock Stars*. New York: Scholastic Book Services, 1980.

David Dalton and Lenny Kaye, *Rock 100: The Greatest Stars of Rock's Golden Age*. New York: Cooper Square Press/Rowman and Littlefield, 1999 (first published 1977).

Andrew David (comp.), *Country Music Stars: People at the Top of the Charts*. Northbrook, IL: Quality Books, 1980.

Andrew David (comp.), *Rock Stars: People at the Top of the Charts*. Northbrook, IL: Quality Books, 1979.

Anthony DeCurtis and James Henke, with Holly George-Warren (eds.), *The Rolling Stone Illustrated History of Rock and Roll* (fully revised and updated). New York: Random House, 1992.

Chip Deffaa, *Blue Rhythms: Six Lives in Rhythm and Blues*. Urbana: University of Illinois Press, 1996.

Dominique-Rene de Lerma and Marsha J. Reisser (comps.), *Black Music and Musicians in the New Grove Dictionary of American Music and the New Harvard Dictionary of Music*. Chicago: Center for Black Music Research, 1989.

Fred Dellar, Alan Cackett, Roy Thompson, and Douglas B. Green, *The Harmony Illustrated Encyclopedia of Country Music*. London: Salamander Books, 1986.

Didier C. Deutsch (ed.), *MusicHound Soundtracks: The Essential Album Guide to Film, Television, and Stage Music*. Detroit, MI: Visible Ink Press, 2000.

Dave DiMartino, *Singer-Songwriters: Pop Music's Performer—Composers, from A to Zevon*. New York: Billboard Books, 1994.

Bob Doerschuk (ed.), *Rock Keyboard*. New York: Quill/A Keyboard Book, 1985.

Editors of Country Music Magazine (comps.), *The Comprehensive Country Music Encyclopedia*. New York: Times Books/Random House, 1994.

Editors of Flip Magazine (comp.), *Flip's Groovy Guide to the Groups!* New York: Signet/New American Library, 1968.

Editors of Goldmine Magazine (comps.), *Goldmine Classic Rock Digest: 25 Years of Rock 'n' Roll*. Iola, WI: Krause, 1998.

Editors of Goldmine Magazine (comps.), *Goldmine Roots of Rock Digest*. Iola, WI: Krause, 1999.

Editors of Guitar Player Magazine (comps.), *The Guitar Player Book* (3d ed.). New York: Grove Press, 1983.

Editors of Rolling Stone (comps.), *The Rolling Stone Interviews*. New York: Paperback Library, 1971.

Walli Elmlark and Timothy Green Beckley, *Rock Raps of the 70's*. New York: Drake, 1972.

Howard Elson, *Early Rockers*. New York: Proteus Books, 1982.

Michael Erlewine, Vladimir Bogdanov, Chris Woodstra, and Stephen Thomas Erlewine (eds.), *All Music Guide: The Experts' Guide to the Best CDs, Albums and Tapes* (3d ed.). San Francisco: Miller Freeman Books, 1997.

Michael Erlewine, Vladimir Bogdanov, Chris Woodstra, and Cub Koda (eds.), *All Music Guide to the Blues* (2d ed.). San Francisco: Miller Freeman Books, 1999.

Michael Erlewine, Vladimir Bogdanov, Chris Woodstra, and Stephen Thomas Erlewine (eds.), *All Music Guide to Country: The Experts' Guide to the Best Recordings in Country Music*. San Francisco: Miller Freeman Books, 1997.

Michael Erlewine, Vladimir Bogdanov, Chris Woodstra, and Scott Yanow (eds.), *All Music Guide to Jazz* (3d ed.). San Francisco: Miller Freeman Books, 1998.

Michael Erlewine, Vladimir Bogdanov, and Chris Woodstra (eds.), *All Music Guide to Rock*. San Francisco: Miller Freeman Books, 1995.

Michael Erlewine, Vladimir Bogdanov, Chris Woodstra, Stephen Thomas Erlewine, and Richie Unterberger (eds.), *All Music Guide to Rock: The Experts' Guide to the Best Rock, Pop, Soul, R&B, and Rap* (2d ed.). San Francisco: Miller Freeman Books, 1997.

Michael Erlewine and Scott Bultman (eds.), *All Music Guide*. San Francisco: Miller Freeman Books, 1992.

Michael Erlewine with Chris Woodstra and Vladimir Bogdanov (eds.), *All Music Guide: The Best CDs, Albums, and Tapes* (2d ed.). San Francisco: Miller Freeman Books, 1994.

Colin Escott (ed.), *All Roots Lead to Rock: Legends of Early Rock 'n' Roll*. New York: Schirmer Books, 1999.

Colin Escott, *Tattooed on Their Tongues: A Journey through the Backrooms of American Music*. New York: Schirmer Books, 1996.

David Ewen, *American Songwriters: 144 Biographies of America's Greatest Popular Composers and Lyricists* (expanded ed.). New York: Wilson Press, 1986.

David Ewen, *Great Men of American Popular Song*. Englewood Cliffs, NJ: Prentice Hall, 1970.

Leonard Feather, *The Book of Jazz: A Guide to the Entire Field*. New York: Horizon Books, 1965.

Leonard Feather, *The Encyclopedia of Jazz in the Sixties*. New York: Horizon Books, 1967.

Leonard Feather, *The New Edition of the Encyclopedia of Jazz*. New York: Horizon Press, 1960.

Leonard Feather, *The Pleasures of Jazz: Leading Performers on Their Lives, Their Music, Their Contemporaries*. New York: Horizon Press, 1976.

Leonard Feather and Ira Gitler, *The Biographical Encyclopedia of Jazz*. New York: Oxford University Press, 1999.

Leonard Feather and Ira Gitler (comps.), *The Encyclopedia of Jazz in the Seventies*. New York: Horizon Press, 1976.

Bill Flanagan, *Written in My Soul: Conversations with Rock's Great Songwriters*. Chicago: Contemporary Books, 1987.

Ben Fong-Torres (ed.), *The Rolling Stone Interviews—Volume II*. New York: Warner Paperback Library, 1973.

Pete Frame, John Tobler, Ed Hanel, Roger St. Pierre, Chris Trengove, John Beecher, Clive Richardson, Gary Cooper, Marsha Hanlon, and Linda Sandahl, *The Harmony Illustrated Encyclopedia of Rock* (6th ed.). New York: Harmony Books, 1989.

Vic Fredericks (ed.), *Who's Who in Rock 'n' Roll*. New York: Frederick Fell, 1958.

David Freeland, *Ladies of Soul*. Jackson: University Press of Mississippi, 2001.

David Fricke, John Morthland, John Swenson, and Mark Mehler (comps.), "Who's Who—Artists," in *Contemporary Music Almanac 1980/81*, compiled by Ronald Zalkind. New York: Schirmer Books, 1980, 157–349.

Goldie Friede, Robin Titone, and Sue Weiner, *The Beatles A to Z: The Complete Illustrated Beatle Encyclopedia*. New York: Methuen Books, 1980.

Gillian G. Gaar, *She's a Rebel: The History of Women in Rock and Roll*. Seattle, WA: Seal Press, 1992.

Steve Gaines, *Who's Who in Rock 'n' Roll*. New York: Popular Library, 1975.

Paul Gambaccini, *Masters of Rock*. London: Omnibus Press, 1982.

Paul Gambaccini, *Track Records: Profiles of 22 Rock Stars*. North Pomfret, VT: David and Charles, 1986.

Peter Gammond, *The Oxford Companion to Popular Music*. New York: Oxford University Press, 1991.

Kurt Ganzl, *The Encyclopedia of Musical Theatre—Three Volumes* (2d ed.). New York: Schirmer Books, 2001.

Linnell Gentry (comp.), *A History and Encyclopedia of Country, Western, and Gospel Music* (2d ed.). Nashville, TN: Clairmont, 1969.

Holly George-Warren and Patricia Romanowski (eds.), *The Rolling Stone Encyclopedia of Rock and Roll: Revised and Updated for the 21st Century* (3d ed.). New York: Fireside/Rolling Stone Press, 2001.

Chris Gill, *Guitar Legends: The Definitive Guide to the World's Greatest Guitar Players*. London: Studio Editions, 1995.

Charlie Gillett (ed.), *Rock File 1*. London: New English Library, 1972.

Charlie Gillett (ed.), *Rock File 2*. St. Albans, England: Panther Press, 1974.

Charlie Gillett and Simon Frith (eds.), *Rock File 3*. St. Albans, England: Panther Press, 1975.

Charlie Gillett and Simon Frith (eds.), *Rock File 4*. St. Albans, England: Panther Press, 1976.

Charlie Gillett and Simon Frith (eds.), *Rock File 5*. St. Albans, England: Panther Press, 1978.

Dave Given, *The Dave Given Rock 'n' Roll Stars Handbook: Rhythm and Blues Artists and Groups*. Smithtown, NY: Exposition Press, 1980.

Tim Gracyk, with Frank Hoffmann, *Popular American Recording Pioneers, 1895–1925*. New York: Haworth Press, 2000.

Gary Graff, Josh Freedom du Lac, and Jim McFarlin (eds.), *MusicHound R&B: The Essential Album Guide*. Detroit, MI: Visible Ink Press, 1998.

Gary Graff (ed.), *MusicHound Rock: The Essential Album Guide*. Detroit, MI: Visible Ink Press, 1996.

Gary Graff and Daniel Durchholz (eds.), *MusicHound Rock: The Essential Album Guide*. Detroit, MI: Visible Ink Press, 1999.

Andy Gray, *Great Pop Stars*. London: Hamlyn, 1974.

Hugh Gregory, *A Century of Pop: A Hundred Years of Music That Changed the World*. Chicago: a cappella Books/Chicago Review Press, 1998.

Hugh Gregory, *1000 Great Guitarists*. San Francisco: Miller Freeman Books, 1994.

Hugh Gregory, *Soul Music A–Z* (rev. ed.). New York: Da Capo Press, 1995 (first published 1991).

Charlotte Greig, *Will You Still Love Me Tomorrow? Girl Groups from the '50s on*. London: Virago Press, 1989.

Anthony J. Gribin and Matthew M. Schiff, *The Complete Book of Doo-Wop*. Iola, WI: Krause, 2000.

Bill Griggs, *A "Who's Who" of West Texas Rock 'n' Roll Music*. Lubbock, TX: William F. Griggs/Rockin' 50s Magazine, 1994.

Peter Guralnick, *Feel Like Going Home: Portraits in Blues and Rock 'n' Roll*. Boston: Back Bay Books/Little, Brown, 1999 (first published 1971).

Peter Guralnick, *Lost Highway: Journeys and Arrivals of American Musicians*. Boston: Back Bay Books/ Little, Brown, 1999 (first published 1979).

Peter Guralnick, *Sweet Soul Music: Rhythm and Blues and the Southern Dream of Freedom*. Boston: Back Bay Books/Little, Brown, 1999 (first published 1986).

Neil Haislop, Tad Lathrop, and Harry Sumrall, *Giants of Country Music: Classic Sounds and Stars, from the Heart of Nashville to the Top of the Charts*. New York: Billboard Books, 1995.

Jeff Hannusch, *I Hear You Knockin': The Sound of New Orleans Rhythm and Blues*. Ville Platte, LA: Swallow, 1985.

Jeff Hannusch, *The Soul of New Orleans: A Legacy of Rhythm and Blues*. Ville Platte, LA: Swallow, 2001.

Barry Hansen, *Rhino's Cruise through the Blues*. San Francisco: Miller Freeman Books, 2000.

Phil Hardy and Dave Laing, *The Da Capo Companion to 20th-Century Popular Music*. New York: Da Capo Press, 1995 (first published 1990).

Phil Hardy and Dave Laing (comps.), *Encyclopedia of Rock, 1955–1975*. London: Aquarius Books, 1977.

Phil Hardy and Dave Laing, with additional material by Stephen Barnard and Don Perretta, *Encyclopedia of Rock*. New York: Schirmer Books, 1988 (first published 1987).

Phil Hardy and Dave Laing, *The Faber Companion to 20th-Century Music*. London: Faber and Faber, 1990.

Sheldon Harris (comp.), *Blues Who's Who: A Biographical Dictionary of Blues Singers*. New Rochelle, NY: Arlington House, 1979.

Nigel Harrison, *Songwriters: A Biographical Dictionary with Discographies*. Jefferson, NC: McFarland, 1998.

Lucinda Hawksley (ed.), *The Billboard Illustrated Encyclopedia of Rock*. New York: Billboard Books, 1998.

Michael Heatley (ed.), *The Ultimate Encyclopedia of Rock: The World's Most Comprehensive Illustrated Rock Reference*. New York: HarperCollins, 1993.

Michael Heatley (ed.), *Virgin Encyclopedia of Rock*. London: Virgin Books, 1996.

Brock Helander, *Baker's Dictionary of Rock and Roll* (2d ed.). New York: MacMillan, 1996.

Brock Helander (comp.), *The Rock Who's Who: A Biographical Dictionary and Critical Discography—Including Rhythm-and-Blues, Soul, Rockabilly, Folk, Country, Easy Listening, Punk, and New Wave*. New York: Schirmer Books, 1982.

Brock Helander, *The Rockin' '50s: The People Who Made the Music*. New York: Schirmer Books, 1998.

Brock Helander, *The Rockin' '60s: The People Who Made the Music*. New York: Schirmer Books, 1999.

Roy Hemming and David Hadju, *Discovering Great Singers of Classic Pop: A New Listener's Guide to the Sounds and Lives of Top Performers and Their Recordings, Movies, and Videos*. New York: Newmarket Press, 1991.

Peter Herbst (ed.), *The Rolling Stone Interviews: Talking with the Legends of Rock and Roll, 1967–1980*. New York: St. Martin's Press/Rolling Stone Press, 1981.

Gerard Herzhaft (translated by Brigette Debord), *Encyclopedia of the Blues*. Fayetteville: University of Arkansas Press, 1992.

Lee Hildebrand, *Stars of Soul and Rhythm and Blues: Top Recording Artists and Showstopping Performers, from Memphis and Motown to Now*. New York: Billboard Books, 1994.

Thomas S. Hischak, *The American Musical Film Song Encyclopedia*. Westport, CT: Greenwood, 1999.

Morris B. Holbrook, "Rereading the Encyclopedias of Jazz: Analyses of Data on the Tastes of Readers, Critics, and Musicians from 1955 to 1970," *Popular Music and Society* XVII (winter 1993), 83–104.

Sid Holt (ed.), *The Rolling Stone Interviews: The 1980s.* New York: St. Martin's Press/Rolling Stone Press, 1989.

Steve Holtje and Nancy Ann Lee (eds.), *MusicHound Jazz: The Essential Album Guide.* Detroit, MI: Visible Ink Press, 1998.

Phil Hood (ed.), *Artists of American Folk Music: The Legends of Traditional Folk, the Stars of the Sixties, and Virtuosi of the Acoustic Music.* New York: Quill/William Morrow, 1986.

Barney Hoskyns, *From a Whisper to a Scream.* London: Fontana Books, 1991.

Martha Hume, *You're So Cold I'm Turning Blue: Martha Hume's Guide to the Greatest in Country Music.* New York: Penguin Books, 1982.

Alan Isaacs and Elizabeth Martin (eds.), *Dictionary of Music.* New York: Facts on File, 1983.

Edward Jablonski, *The Encyclopedia of American Music.* Garden City, NY: Doubleday, 1981.

Arthur Jacobs, *Dictionary of Musical Performers.* London: Penguin Books, 1991.

Wayne Jancik and Tad Lathrop, *Cult Rockers: 150 of the Most Controversial, Distinctive, Offbeat, Intriguing, Outrageous, and Championed Rock Musicians of all Time.* New York: Fireside Books, 1995.

Tony Jasper and Derek Oliver, *The International Encyclopedia of Hard Rock and Heavy Metal* (3d ed., rev.). London: Sidgwick and Jackson, 1991.

Tony Jasper, Derek Oliver, Steve Hammond, and Dave Reynolds, *The International Encyclopedia of Hard Rock and Heavy Metal.* New York: Facts on File, 1983.

Neil Jeffries (ed.), *Kerrang! Directory of Heavy Metal: The Indispensable Guide to Rock Warriors and Headbangin' Heroes.* London: Virgin Books, 1993.

Wayne Jones, *Rockin', Rollin', and Rappin'.* Fraser, MI: Goldmine Press, 1980.

Steve Kahn, *Tops in Pops, Plus a Rock 'n' Roll Roundup.* New York: MacFadden Books, 1961.

Helmut Kallmann and Gilles Potuin (eds.), *Encyclopedia of Music in Canada* (2d ed.). Toronto: University of Toronto Press, 1992.

Michael Kennedy, *The Oxford Dictionary of Music* (rev. ed.). New York: Oxford University Press, 1997.

Barry Kernfeld (ed.), *The Blackwell Guide to Recorded Jazz*. Cambridge, MA: Basil Blackwell, 1991.

Barry Kernfeld (ed.), *The New Grove Dictionary of Jazz* (2 vols.). New York: Grove's Dictionaries of Music, 1990.

Brent E. Kick, *The Ultimate Musician's Reference Handbook: The Most Complete Guide to Who's Who in Popular Music*. Anaheim Hills, CA: Centerstream, 1996.

Kit Kiefer (ed.), *They Called It Rock: The Goldmine Oral History of Rock 'n' Roll, 1950–1970*. Iola, WI: Krause, 1991.

Rich Kienzle, *Great Guitarists: The Most Influential Players in Blues, Country Music, Jazz, and Rock*. New York: Facts on File, 1985.

Kenn Kingsbury (comp.), *Kingsbury's Who's Who in Country and Western Music*. Culver City, CA: Black Stallion Country Press, 1981.

Paul Kingsbury and the Country Music Foundation (eds.), *Country: The Music and the Musicians—from the Beginnings to the '90s* (rev. ed.). New York: Abbeville, 1994.

Paul Kingsbury (ed.), *The Encyclopedia of Country Music: The Ultimate Guide to the Music*. New York: Oxford University Press, 1998.

Paul Kingsbury, *The Grand Ole Opry History of Country Music: 70 Years of the Songs, the Stars, and the Stories*. New York: Villard/Random House, 1995.

Roger D. Kinkle, *The Complete Encyclopedia of Popular Music and Jazz, 1900–1950: Volume One—Music Year by Year, 1900–1950*. New Rochelle, NY: Arlington House, 1974.

Roger D. Kinkle, *The Complete Encyclopedia of Popular Music and Jazz, 1900–1950: Volume Two—Biographies, A—K*. New Rochelle, NY: Arlington House, 1974.

Roger D. Kinkle, *The Complete Encyclopedia of Popular Music and Jazz, 1900–1950: Volume Three—Biographies, L—Z*. New Rochelle, NY: Arlington House, 1974.

Roger D. Kinkle, *The Complete Encyclopedia of Popular Music and Jazz, 1900–1950: Volume Four—Indexes and Appendices*. New Rochelle, NY: Arlington House, 1974.

Hans Jurgen Klitsch with assistance from Mike Korbik (comps.), *Great Bands/Small Labels*. Mulheim, Germany: Gorilla Beat, 1979.

Steve Knopper (ed.), *MusicHound Lounge: The Essential Album Guide to Martini Music and Easy Listening*. Detroit, MI: Visible Ink Press, 1998.

Steve Knopper (ed.), *MusicHound Swing! The Essential Album Guide*. Detroit, MI: Visible Ink Press, 1999.

Jeff Kreiter, *45 rpm Vocal Group Record Guide: A Reference and Price Guide to Vocal Group Harmony Records, 1949–1999* (7th ed.). Bridgeport, OH: J. Kreiter, 2000.

Laura Kuhn (comp.), *Baker's Student Encyclopedia of Music* (3 vols.). New York: Schirmer Books, 1999.

Michael L. LaBlanc (ed.), *Contemporary Musicians—Volume One: Profiles of the People in Music*. Detroit, MI: Gale Research, 1989.

Michael L. LaBlanc (ed.), *Contemporary Musicians—Volume Two: Profiles of the People in Music*. Detroit, MI: Gale Research, 1990.

Michael L. LaBlanc (ed.), *Contemporary Musicians—Volume Three: Profiles of the People in Music*. Detroit, MI: Gale Research, 1990.

Michael L. LaBlanc (ed.), *Contemporary Musicians—Volume Four: Profiles of the People in Music*. Detroit, MI: Gale Research, 1991.

Michael L. LaBlanc (ed.), *Contemporary Musicians—Volume Five: Profiles of the People in Music*. Detroit, MI: Gale Research, 1991.

Michael L. LaBlanc (ed.), *Contemporary Musicians—Volume Six: Profiles of the People in Music*. Detroit, MI: Gale Research, 1992.

Michael L. LaBlanc (ed.), *Contemporary Musicians—Volume Seven: Profiles of the People in Music*. Detroit, MI: Gale Research, 1992.

Colin Larkin (ed.), *The Guinness Encyclopedia of Popular Music* (4 vols.). Enfield, England: Guinness, 1993.

Colin Larkin (ed.), *The Guinness Who's Who of Blues Music*. Enfield, England: Guinness, 1993.

Colin Larkin (ed.), *The Guinness Who's Who of Country Music*. Enfield, England: Guinness, 1993.

Colin Larkin (ed.), *The Guinness Who's Who of Fifties Music*. Enfield, England: Guinness, 1993.

Colin Larkin (ed.), *The Guinness Who's Who of Folk Music*. Enfield, England: Guinness, 1993.

Colin Larkin (ed.), *The Guinness Who's Who of Reggae*. Enfield, England: Guinness, 1994.

Colin Larkin (ed.), *The Guinness Who's Who of Seventies Music*. Enfield, England: Guinness, 1993.

Colin Larkin (ed.), *The Guinness Who's Who of Soul*. Enfield, England: Guinness, 1993.

Colin Larkin (ed.), *The Guinness Who's Who of Stage Musicals*. Enfield, England: Guinness, 1994.

Colin Larkin (ed.), *The Virgin Encyclopedia of Indie and New Wave*. London: Virgin Books, 1998.

Colin Larkin (ed.), *The Virgin Encyclopedia of Popular Music* (concise ed.). London: Virgin Books, 1997.

Colin Larkin (ed.), *The Virgin Encyclopedia of Sixties Music* (concise ed.). London: Virgin Books, 1997.

Colin Larkin (ed.), *The Virgin Encyclopedia of Seventies Music* (concise ed.). London: Virgin Books, 1997.

Colin Larkin (ed.), *The Virgin Encyclopedia of Eighties Music* (concise ed.). London: Virgin Books, 1997.

Ray McKinley Lawless, *Folksingers and Folksongs in America: A Handbook of Biography, Bibliography, and Discography*. Westport, CT: Greenwood, 1981 (first published 1965).

Barry Lazell, *Guinness Book of Rock Stars*. Enfield, England: Guinness, 1989.

Barry Lazell with Dafydd Rees and Luke Crampton (eds.), *Rock Movers and Shakers: An A to Z of the People Who Made Rock Happen*. New York: Billboard Books, 1989.

Alan Leibowitz (comp.), "Personalities and Vocalists," in *The Record Collector's Handbook*. New York: Everest House, 1980, 104–119.

Robert Lissauer, *Lissauer's Encyclopedia of Popular Music in America: 1888 to the Present* (3 vols.). New York: Facts on File, 1996.

Nick Logan and Bob Woffinden (comps.), *The Illustrated New Musical Express Encyclopedia of Rock*. London: Salamander Books, 1977.

Nick Logan and Bob Woffinden (comps.), *The Harmony Illustrated Encyclopedia of Rock* (3d ed.). New York: Harmony Books, 1982.

Stephen Longstreet, *Jazz from A—Z: A Graphic Dictionary*. London: Turnaround, 1990.

Michael Lydon, *Rock Folk: Portraits from the Rock 'n' Roll Pantheon*. New York: Dial Press, 1971.

Michael Lydon and Ellen Mandel, *Boogie Lightning: How Music Became Electric*. New York: Da Capo Press, 1980.

Brian Mansfield and Gary Graff (eds.), *MusicHound Country: The Essential Album Guide*. Detroit, MI: Visible Ink Press, 1997.

Pearce Marchbank and [Barry] Miles (comp.), *The Illustrated Rock Almanac*. New York: Paddington Press/Grosset and Dunlap, 1977.

Rick Marschall, *The Encyclopedia of Country and Western Music*. New York: Exeter Books, 1985.

Ritchie Marsh and Sam Johnson, *Encyclopedia of Rock/Pop Stars*. New York: Gallery Books, 1985.

Chris May and Tim Phillips (comps.), *British Beat*. London: Scion Books, 1974.

Barry McCloud, and contributing writers, *Definitive Country: The Ultimate Encyclopedia of Country Music and Its Performers*. New York: Perigee Books, 1995.

Stacy A. McConnell (ed.), *Contemporary Musicians—Volume 21: Profiles of the People in Music*. Detroit, MI: Gale Group, 1998.

Adam McGovern (ed.), *MusicHound World: The Essential Album Guide*. Detroit, MI: Visible Ink Press, 2000.

Noel McGrath (comp.), *Noel McGrath's Australian Encyclopedia of Rock*. Collingwood V ictoria, Australia: Outback Press, 1978.

Don Menn (ed.), *Secrets from the Masters: Conversations with Forty Great Guitar Players*. San Francisco: GPI Books/Miller Freeman Books, 1992.

Ruth Midgley (ed.), *Musical Instruments of the World: An Illustrated Encyclopedia by the Diagram Group*. New York: Sterling, 1997.

Bill Milkowski, *Rockers, Jazzbos, and Visionaries*. New York: Billboard Books, 1998.

Bob Millard, *Country Music's What's What: The Fan's Guide to the People, Places, and Things of Today's Country Music*. New York: HarperCollins, 1995.

Jim Miller (ed.), *The Rolling Stone Illustrated History of Rock and Roll*. New York: Random House/Rolling Stone Press, 1976.

Jim Miller (ed.), *The Rolling Stone Illustrated History of Rock and Roll* (2d ed.). New York: Random House/Rolling Stone Press, 1980.

Thurston Moore (ed.), *The Country Music Who's Who*. Denver, CO: Heather, 1960.

Brian Morton, *The Blackwell Guide to Recorded Contemporary Music*. Cambridge, MA: Blackwell, 1996.

Ed Naha (comp.), *Lillian Roxon's Rock Encyclopedia* (rev. ed.). New York: Grosset and Dunlap, 1978.

Norm N. Nite (comp.), *Rock On: The Illustrated Encyclopedia of Rock 'n' Roll—The Solid Gold Years*. New York: Thomas Y. Crowell, 1974.

Norm N. Nite (comp.), *Rock On Almanac: The First Four Decades of Rock 'n' Roll—A Chronology*. New York: Harper & Row, 1989.

Norm N. Nite, with Ralph M. Newman (comps.), *Rock On—The Illustrated Encyclopedia of Rock 'n' Roll: Volume Two—The Years of Change, 1964–1978* (updated ed.). New York: Harper & Row, 1984.

Norm N. Nite, with Ralph M. Newman (comps.), *Rock On—The Illustrated Encyclopedia of Rock 'n' Roll: Volume Three—The Video Revolution, 1978—Present* (updated ed.). New York: Harper & Row, 1985.

Peter L. Noble, *Future Pop: Music for the Eighties*. New York: Delilah Books, 1983.

Philip Norman, *The Road Goes on Forever: Portraits from a Journey through Contemporary Music*. New York: Fireside Book, 1992.

Jas Obrecht (ed.), *Blues Guitar: The Men Who Made the Music*. San Francisco: Guitar Player International Books, 1990.

Jas Obrecht (ed.), *Masters of Heavy Metal*. New York: Quill/Guitar Player Books, 1984.

Jas Obrecht (ed.), *Rollin' and Tumblin': The Postwar Blues Guitarists*. San Francisco: Miller Freeman Books, 2000.

Paul Oliver, Max Harrison, and William Bolcom, *The New Grove Gospel, Blues, and Jazz, with Spirituals and Ragtime*. New York: W. W. Norton, 1986.

Eric Olsen, Paul Verna, and Carlo Wolff, *The Encyclopedia of Record Producers*. New York: Billboard Books, 1999.

Jim O'Neal and Amy Van Singel, *The Voice of the Blues: Classic Interviews from Living Blues Magazine*. New York: Routledge, 2002.

Katherine Orloff, *Rock 'n Roll Woman*. Los Angeles, CA: Nash Publishing, 1974.

Steve Otfinski, *The Golden Age of Rock Instrumentals*. New York: Billboard Books, 1997.

Trisha Palmer (ed.), *The Illustrated Encyclopedia of Country Music*. New York: Harmony Books, 1977.

Jon Pareles and Patricia Romanowski (eds.), *The Rolling Stone Encyclopedia of Rock and Roll*. New York: Rolling Stone Press/Summit Books, 1983.

James Robert Parish and Michael R. Pitts, *Hollywood Songsters: A Biographical Dictionary*. New York: Garland, 1991.

Jeremy Pascall, *The Illustrated History of Rock Music*. New York: Galahad Books, 1978.

Jeremy Pascall and Bob Burt, *The Stars and Superstars of Black Music*. Secaucus, NJ: Chartwell Books, 1977.

Tom Pendergast and Sara Pendergast (eds.), *St. James Encyclopedia of Popular Culture* (5 vols.). Detroit, MI: St. James Press, 2000.

Gavin Petrie (ed.), *Black Music*. London: Hamlyn, 1974.

Gavin Petrie (comp.), *Rock Life*. New York: Hamlyn, 1974.

Michael Pitts and Frank Hoffmann, with the assistance of Dick Carty and Jim Bedoian, *The Rise of the Crooners: Gene Austin, Russ Columbo, Bing Crosby, Nick Lucas, Johnny Marvin, and Rudy Vallee*. Lanham, MD: Scarecrow Press, 2002.

Henry Pleasants, *The Great American Popular Singers*. New York: Simon & Schuster, 1974.

Steve Propes and Galen Gart, *L.A. R&B Vocal Groups, 1945–1965*. Milford, NH: Big Nickel, 2001.

Harvey Rachlin (comp.), *The Encyclopedia of the Music Business*. New York: Harper & Row, 1981.

Henry Rasof, *The Folk, Country, and Bluegrass Musician's Catalogue*. New York: St. Martin's Press, 1982.

Dafydd Rees (comp.), *Star File: The Ultimate Rock Reference*. London: W. H. Allen, 1977.

Dafydd Rees and Luke Crampton (comps.), *Encyclopedia of Rock Stars*. New York: DK, 1996.

Dafydd Rees and Luke Crampton (comps.), *Guinness Book of Rock Stars* (2d ed.). Enfield, England: Guinness, 1991.

Dafydd Rees and Luke Crampton (comps.), *VH1 Music First Rock Stars Encyclopedia* (rev. ed.). New York: DK, 1999.

Tony Rees (comp.), *Rare Rock: A Collector's Guide*. Poole, England: Blandford Press, 1985.

Tad Richards and Melvin B. Shestack (comps.), *The New Country Music Encyclopedia*. New York: Fireside Books/Simon & Schuster, 1993.

Ira A. Robbins (ed.), *The Trouser Press Guide to '90s Rock: The All-New Fifth Edition of the Trouser Press Record Guide*. New York: Fireside Books/Simon & Schuster, 1997.

Rock Guitarists. Saratoga, NY: Guitar Player, 1974.

Rock Guitarists—Volume Two. Saratoga, NY: Guitar Player, 1978.

Paul Roland (ed.), *Jazz Singers: The Great Song Stylists in Their Own Words*. New York: Billboard Books, 2000 (first published 1999).

Patricia Romanowski and Holly George-Warren, with Jon Pareles (eds.), *The New Rolling Stone Encyclopedia of Rock and Roll* (rev. ed.). New York: Fireside/Rolling Stone Press, 1995.

Mitch Rosalsky, *Encyclopedia of Rhythm and Blues and Doo-Wop Vocal Groups*. Lanham, MD: Scarecrow Press, 2000.

Arlen Roth, *Masters of the Telecaster*. Miami, FL: Belwin Mills/Warner Brothers, 1996.

Lillian Roxon, *Lillian Roxon's Rock Encyclopedia*. New York: Universal Library/Grosset and Dunlap, 1969.

David Rubin, *Inside the Blues, 1942–1982: Four Decades of the Greatest Blues Guitarists*. Milwaukee, WI: Hal Leonard, 1995.

Julia M. Rubiner (ed.), *Contemporary Musicians—Volume Eight: Profiles of the People in Music*. Detroit, MI: Gale Research, 1993.

Julia M. Rubiner (ed.), *Contemporary Musicians—Volume Nine: Profiles of the People in Music*. Detroit, MI: Gale research, 1993.

Leland Rucker (ed.), *MusicHound Blues: The Essential Album Guide*. Detroit, MI: Visible Ink Press, 1998.

Tony Russell (ed.), *Encyclopedia of Rock*. London: Crescent Books, 1983.

Stanley Sadie (ed.), *The New Grove Dictionary of Music and Musicians—20 Volumes*. London: Macmillan, 1980.

James Sallis, *The Guitar Players: One Instrument and Its Masters in American Music*. New York: William Morrow, 1982.

Larry Sandberg and Dick Weissman, *The Folk Music Sourcebook*. Dobbs Ferry, NY: Da Capo Press, 1989.

Robert Santelli, *The Big Book of the Blues: A Biographical Encyclopedia*. New York: Penguin Books, 1993.

Robert Santelli, *Sixties Rock: A Listener's Guide*. Chicago: Contemporary Books, 1985.

Roni Sarig, *The Secret History of Rock: The Most Influential Bands You've Never Heard*. New York: Billboard Books, 1998.

John Schaefer, *New Sounds: A Listener's Guide to New Music*. New York: Harper & Row, 1987.

Nicholas Schaffner, *The British Invasion: From the First Wave to the New Wave*. New York: McGraw-Hill, 1982.

Tony Scherman (ed.), *The Rock Musician—15 Years of Interviews: The Best of Musician Magazine*. New York: St. Martin's Press, 1994.

Tom Schnabel, *Stolen Moments: Conversations with Contemporary Musicians*. Los Angeles: Acrobat Books, 1988.

Frank Scott et al. (comps.), *Blues and Gospel Catalog, 1987–1988*. El Cerrito, CA: Down Home Music, 1988.

Frank Scott et al., *Country Music Catalog, 1985–1986*. El Cerrito, CA: Down Home Music, 1985.

Frank Scott and the Staff of Down Home Music, *The Down Home Guide to the Blues*. Pennington, NJ: A Cappella Books, 1991.

Frank Scott, Al Ennis, and the Staff of Roots and Rhythm. *The Roots and Rhythm Guide to Rock*. Chicago: A Capella Books, 1993.

Harry Shapiro, *A–Z of Rock Drummers*. New York: Proteus Books, 1982.

Nat Shapiro (comp.), *An Encyclopedia of Quotations about Music*. Garden City, NY: Doubleday, 1978.

Melvin Shestack (comp.), *The Country Music Encyclopedia*. New York: Thomas Y. Crowell, 1974.

Caroline Silver, *The Pop Makers—British Rock 'n' Roll: The Sound, the Scene, the Action*. New York: Scholastic Book Services, 1966.

Jerry Silverman, *Folk Song Encyclopedia* (2 vols.). New York: Chappell Music, 1975.

George T. Simon and Friends (comps.), *The Best of the Music Makers*. Garden City, NY: Doubleday, 1979.

Jeff Simpson (ed.), *Radio One's Classic Interviews: 25 Rock Greats in Their Own Words*. London: BBC Books, 1992.

Nicolas Slonimsky (edited by Richard Kassel), *Baker's Dictionary of Music*. New York: Schirmer Books, 1997.

Nicolas Slonimsky (edited by Richard Kostelanetz), *The Portable Baker's Biographical Dictionary of Musicians*. New York: Schirmer Books, 1995.

Bradley Smith, *The Billboard Guide to Progressive Music*. New York: Billboard Books, 1997.

Eileen Southern (comp.), *Biographical Dictionary of Afro-American and African Musicians*. Westport, CT: Greenwood, 1982.

Irwin Stambler and Grelun Landon (comps.), *Encyclopedia of Folk, Country, and Western Music*. New York: St. Martin's Press, 1969.

Irwin Stambler and Grelun Landon (comps.), *The Encyclopedia of Folk, Country, and Western Music* (2d ed.). New York: St. Martin's Press, 1983.

Irwin Stambler and Grelun Landon (comps.), *Country Music: The Encyclopedia* (3d ed.). New York: St. Martin's Press, 1998.

Irwin Stambler (comp.), *Encyclopedia of Popular Music*. New York: St. Martin's Press, 1965.

Irwin Stambler (comp.), *Encyclopedia of Pop, Rock, and Soul*. New York: St. Martin's Press, 1974.

Irwin Stambler, *The Encyclopedia of Pop, Rock and Soul* (rev. ed.). New York: St. Martin's Press, 1989.

Jane and Michael Stern, *Encyclopedia of Pop Culture: An A to Z of Who's Who and What's What, from Aerobics to Bubble Gum to Valley of the Dolls and Moon Unit Zappa*. New York: HarperCollins, 1992.

Steve J. Stoll, *Who's Who in Soul*. Washington, D.C.: Unicorn International, 1969.

Denise Sullivan, *Rip It Up! Rock and Roll Rulebreakers*. San Francisco: Backbeat Books, 2001.

Harry Sumrall, *Pioneers of Rock and Roll: 100 Artists Who Changed the Face of Rock*. New York: Billboard Books, 1994.

John Swenson (ed.), *The Rolling Stone Jazz Record Guide*. New York: Random House/Rolling Stone Press, 1985.

John Swenson (ed.), *The Rolling Stone Jazz and Blues Album Guide*. New York: Random House, 1999.

Nick Talevski, *Tombstone Blues: The Encyclopedia of Rock Obituaries*. New York: Omnibus Press, 1999.

Nick Talevski, *The Unofficial Encyclopedia of the Rock and Roll Hall of Fame*. Westport, CT: Greenwood, 1998.

Ralph Tee, *Soul Music: Who's Who*. Rocklin, CA: Prima, 1992.

Liz Thomson (ed.), *New Women in Rock*. New York: Delilah/Putnam Books, 1982.

Art Tipaldi, *Children of the Blues: 49 Musicians Shaping a New Blues Tradition*. San Francisco: Backbeat Books, 2002.

Jeff Todd Titon and Bob Carlin (eds.), *American Musical Traditions—Volume One: Native American Music*. New York: Schirmer Reference, 2002.

Jeff Todd Titon and Bob Carlin (eds.), *American Musical Traditions—Volume Two: African American Music*. New York: Schirmer Reference, 2002.

Jeff Todd Titon and Bob Carlin (eds.), *American Musical Traditions—Volume Three: British Isles Music*. New York: Schirmer Reference, 2002.

Jeff Todd Titon and Bob Carlin (eds.), *American Musical Traditions—Volume Four: European American Music*. New York: Schirmer Reference, 2002.

Jeff Todd Titon and Bob Carlin (eds.), *American Musical Traditions—Volume Five: Latino American and Asian American Music*. New York: Schirmer Reference, 2002.

John Tobler, *Guitar Heroes*. New York: St. Martin's Press, 1978.

John Tobler (ed.), *NME Who's Who in Rock and Roll*. London: Hamlyn Books, 1991.

John Tobler and Pete Frame, *Rock 'n' Roll: The First 25 Years*. New York: Exeter Books, 1980.

Nick Tosches, *Unsung Heroes of Rock 'n' Roll: The Birth of Rock in the Wild Years Before Elvis* (rev. ed.). New York: Harmony Books, 1991.

Eric Townley, *Tell Your Story: A Dictionary of Jazz and Blues Recordings, 1917–1950*. Chigwell, England: Storyville Books, 1976.

Eric Townley, *Tell Your Story—Volume Two: Dictionary of Mainstream Jazz and Blues Recordings, 1951–1975*. Chigwell, England: Storyville Books, 1987.

Sheila Tracy (comp.), *Who's Who in Popular Music in Britain*. Kingswood, England: World's Work, 1984.

Artemy Troitsky, *Tusovka: Who's Who in the New Soviet Rock Culture*. London: Omnibus Press, 1990.

Paul Trynka, *Portrait of the Blues: America's Blues Musicians in Their Own Words*. New York: Da Capo Press, 1997.

Don Tyler, *Hit Parade, 1920–1955: An Encyclopedia of the Top Songs of the Jazz, Depression, Swing, and Sing Eras*. New York: Quill/William Morrow, 1985.

Sean Tyler (ed.), *International Who's Who in Music—Volume Two: Popular Music*. Cambridge, England: Melrose Press/International Who's Who in Music, 1996.

Richie Unterberger, *Music USA—The Rough Guide: A Coast-to-Coast Tour of American Music—The Artists, the Venues, the Stories, and the Essential Recordings*. London: Rough Guides, 1999.

Richie Unterberger, *Unknown Legends of Rock 'n' Roll: Psychedelic Unknowns, Mad Geniuses, Punk Pioneers, Lo-Fi Mavericks, and More*. San Francisco: Miller Freeman Books, 1998.

Richie Unterberger, *Urban Spaceman and Wayfaring Strangers: Overlooked Innovators and Eccentric Visionaries of '60s Rock*. San Francisco: Miller Freeman Books, 2000.

Michael Uslan and Bruce Solomon, *Dick Clark's The First 25 Years of Rock and Roll*. New York: Dell, 1981.

Andrew Vaughan, *Who's Who in New Country Music*. New York: St. Martin's Press, 1990.

Lee Vinson, *Encyclopedia of Rock*. New York: Drake, 1976.

Leo Walker, *The Big Band Almanac*. Pasadena, CA: Ward Ritchie Press, 1978.

David Walters, *The Children of Nuggets: The Definitive Guide to "Psychedelic Sixties" Punk Rock on Compilation Albums*. Ann Arbor, MI: Popular Culture, Ink., 1990.

Neal Walters and Brian Mansfield (eds.), *MusicHound Folk: The Essential Album Guide*. Detroit, MI: Visible Ink Press, 1998.

Jay Warner, *The Da Capo Book of American Singing Groups: A History, 1940–1990*. New York: Da Capo Press, 2000 (first published 1992).

Max Weinberg with Robert Santelli, *The Big Beat: Conversations with Rock's Great Drummers*. New York: Billboard Books, 1991.

Pete Welding and Toby Byron (eds.), *Bluesland: Portraits of Twelve Major American Blues Masters*. New York: Dutton/Penguin Books, 1991.

Henk N. Werkhoven, *The International Guide to New Age Music: A Comprehensive Guide to the Vast and Varied Artists and Recordings of New Age Music*. New York: Billboard Books, 1998.

Mark White, *"You Must Remember This": Popular Songwriters, 1900–1980*. New York: Scribner's, 1985.

Timothy White, *Music to My Ears: The Billboard Essays—Profiles of Popular Music in the '90s*. New York: Henry Holt, 1996.

Timothy White, *Rock Lives: Profiles and Interviews*. New York: Henry Holt, 1990.

Timothy White, *Rock Stars*. New York: Stewart, Tabori, and Chang, 1984.

Alec Wilder (edited by James T. Maher), *American Popular Song: The Great Innovators, 1900–1950*. New York: Oxford University Press, 1972.

Max Wilk, *They're Playing Our Song: From Jerome Kern to Stephen Sondheim*. New York: Atheneum, 1973.

Charles R. Wilson and William Ferris (eds.), *Encyclopedia of Southern Culture*. Chapel Hill: University of North Carolina Press, 1989.

Charles K. Wolfe and James E. Akenson (eds.), *Country Music Annual 2002*. Lexington: University Press of Kentucky, 2002.

Robbie Woliver, *Bringing It All Back Home: 25 Years of American Music at Folk City*. New York: Pantheon Books, 1986.

Graham Wood, *An A—Z of Rock and Roll*. London: Studio Vista, 1971.

John Wooley, Thomas Conner, and Mark Brown, *Forever Lounge: A Laid-Back Price Guide to the Languid Sounds of Lounge Music*. Norfolk, Virginia: Antique Trader/Landmark Specialty Books, 1999.

Richard Wooton, *The Illustrated Country Almanac: A Day by Day History of Country Music*. New York: Dial Press, 1982.

Ron Wynn, with Michael Erlewine and Vladimir Bogdanov (eds.), *All Music Guide to Jazz: The Best CDs, Albums, and Tapes*. San Francisco: Miller Freeman Books, 1994.

William York (comp.), *Who's Who in Rock: An A–Z of Groups, Performers, Session Men, Engineers*. New York: Omnibus Press, 1979.

William York (comp.), *Who's Who in Rock Music* (rev. ed.). New York: Scribner's, 1982.

Alan Young, *Woke Me Up This Morning: Black Gospel Singers and the Gospel Life*. Jackson: University Press of Mississippi, 1997.

Ronald Zalkind (comp.), *Contemporary Music Almanac 1980/81*. New York: Schirmer Books, 1980.

114 \ 2—Biographical Studies, Oral History, and Popular Music

Influential Popular Music Performers and Composers for Student Examination

Johnny Ace

B. Lee Cooper, "From Johnny Ace to Frank Zappa: Debating the Meaning of Death in Rock Music," *Popular Culture in Libraries* III, no. 1 (1995), 51–75.

B. Lee Cooper, "Review of *The Late Great Johnny Ace and the Transition from R&B to Rock 'n' Roll* by James M. Salem," *Rock and Blues News*, no. 6 (October-November 1999), 41.

Lee Cotten, "Johnny Ace," in *Shake, Rattle, and Roll—The Golden Age of American Rock 'n' Roll: Volume One, 1952–1955.* Ann Arbor, MI: Pierian Press, 1989, 61–62.

Robert Duncan, "Johnny Ace: The Games People Play," in *Only the Good Die Young: The Rock 'n' Roll Book of the Dead.* New York: Harmony Books, 1986, 11–15.

Colin Escott, "Johnny Ace: The First Rock 'n' Roll Casualty," *Goldmine*, no. 165 (November 21, 1986), 16–17.

Peter Grendysa, "Johnny Ace: The 'Ace' of Duke," *Goldmine*, no. 187 (September 25, 1987), 28, 91.

Joe Pecoraro, "John Marshall Alexander (1929–1954)," *Record Exchanger*, no. 14 (April 1973), 19.

James M. Salem, "Death and the Rhythm-and-Bluesman: The Life and Recordings of Johnny Ace," *American Music* XI (fall 1993), 316–67.

James M. Salem, "Johnny Ace: A Case Study in the Diffusion and Transformation of Minority Culture," *Prospects: An Annual of American Cultural Studies* XVII (1992), 211–41.

Jim Salem, "Johnny Ace: His Death and How It Played in America," *Goldmine*, no. 266 (October 5, 1990), 34, 38, 146.

James M. Salem, *The Late Great Johnny Ace and the Transition to Rock 'n' Roll.* Urbana: University of Illinois Press, 1999.

Nick Tosches, "Johnny Ace: Number One with a Bullet," in *Unsung Heroes of Rock 'n' Roll in the Birth of Rock 'n' Roll in the Dark and Wild Years Before Elvis.* New York: Scribner's, 1984, 133–8.

Louis Armstrong

Almost Slim, "The Year Satchmo Was King," *Wavelength*, no. 28 (February 1983), 16–19.

Louis Armstrong, *Louis Armstrong: A Self-Portrait*. New York: Eakins Press, 1971.

Louis Armstrong, *Satchmo: My Life in New Orleans*. New York: Da Capo Press, 1986 (first published 1954).

Louis Armstrong, *Swing That Music*. London: Longmans, Green, 1937.

James Lincoln Collier, *Louis Armstrong*. New York: Oxford University Press, 1983.

Leonard Feather, *From Satchmo to Miles*. New York: Stein and Day, 1972.

Gary Giddins, *Satchmo*. New York: Dolphin/Doubleday Books, 1988.

Jorgen Grunnet Jepsen (comp.), *A Discography of Louis Armstrong* (3 vols.). Copenhagen: Knudsen, 1968.

Max Jones and John Chilton. *Louis: The Louis Armstrong Story, 1900–1971*. Boston: Little, Brown, 1971.

Albert J. McCarthy, *Louis Armstrong*. New York: Barnes, 1961.

Mike Pinfold, *Louis Armstrong: His Life and Times*. New York: Universe Books, 1987.

William Ruhlmann, "Louis Armstrong: 'Pops' the Pop Star," *Goldmine*, no. 551 (September 7, 2001), 14–19.

Phil Schaap, *Louis Armstrong Festival Discography*. New York: WKCR, 1982.

Stephen M. Stroff, "Louis Armstrong: A Select Discography," *Goldmine*, no. 73 (June 1982), 11–13, 15.

Hans Westerberg, *Boy from New Orleans: Louis "Satchmo" Armstrong on Records, Films, Radio, and Television*. Copenhagen: Jazz Media, 1981.

Joan Baez

Joan Baez, *And a Voice to Sing With: A Memoir*. New York: Summit Books, 1987.

Joan Baez, *Daybreak*. New York: Avon Books, 1968.

Bil Carpenter, "The Voice and Vision of Folk Music: Joan Baez," *Goldmine*, no. 430 (January 17, 1997), 18–44, 178.

David A. DeTurk and A. Poulin. "Joan Baez: An Interview," in *The American Folk Scene: Dimensions of the Folksong Revival.* New York: Dell, 1967, 231–49.

DuBois, Fletcher Ranney. *A Troubadour as Teacher, The Concert as Classroom? Joan Baez—Advocate of Nonviolence and Motivator of the Young: A Study in the Biographical Method.* Frankfurt: Haag and Herchen, 1985.

"Folk Singing: Sibyl with Guitar" *Time* LXXX (November 23, 1962), 54–60.

Charles J. Fuss, *Joan Baez: A Bio-Bibliography.* Westport, CT: Greenwood, 1996.

Charles J. Fuss, "Joan Baez: An American Artist," *Goldmine*, no. 237 (Aug. 25, 1989), 98–105.

John Grissim, Jr., "Joan Baez," in *The Rolling Stone Rock 'n' Roll Reader*, edited by Ben Fong-Torres. New York: Bantam Books, 1974, 1–8.

Nat Hentoff, "The *Playboy* Interview: Joan Baez," *Playboy* XVII (July 1970), 54–62ff.

Jerome Rodnitzky, "A Pacifist St. Joan: The Odyssey of Joan Baez," in *Heroes of Popular Culture*, edited by Ray B. Browne, Marshall Fishwick, and Michael T. Marsden. Bowling Green, OH: Bowling Green State University Popular Press, 1972, 138–56.

Joan Swanekamp (ed.), *Diamonds and Rust: A Bibliography and Discography on Joan Baez.* Ann Arbor, MI: Pierian Press, 1980.

The Beach Boys

Kingsley Abbott (ed.), *Back to the Beach: A Brian Wilson and the Beach Boys Reader.* London: Helter Skelter, 1999 (first published 1997).

Kevin J. Butch, "The Beach Boys: Music, Myths, and Memories (1961–1989)," *DISCoveries* II (October 1989), 20–27.

B. Lee Cooper, "Review of *The Beach Boys* (rev. ed.) by David Leaf," *Popular Music and Society* XI, no. 2 (summer 1987), 111–14.

Brad Elliott, *Surf's Up! The Beach Boys on Record, 1961–1981.* Ann Arbor, MI: Pierian Press, 1982.

Steven Gaines, *Heroes and Villains: The True Story of the Beach Boys.* New York: New American Library, 1986.

Bruce Golden, *The Beach Boys: Southern California Pastoral.* San Bernardino, CA: Borgo Press, 1976.

David Leaf, *The Beach Boys and the California Myth*. Philadelphia: Running Press Book, 1985.

David Leaf, *The Beach Boys: Spirit of America*. New York: Putnam, 1986.

Jim Miller, "The Beach Boys," in *The Rolling Stone Illustrated History of Rock and Roll*. New York: Random House/Rolling Stone Press, 1976, 158–63.

Ralph M. Newman and Jeff Tamarkin. "The Beach Boys from the Beginning: An Interview," *Time Barrier Express*, no. 24 (April-May 1979), 33–52.

John Tobler, *The Beach Boys*. New York: Phoebus Books, 1977.

Timothy White, "From Surfing to Psychedelia: The Beach Boys and the Birth of the L.A. Rock 'n' Roll Industry," *Musician*, no. 194 (December 1994), 40–52, 101.

Timothy White, *The Nearest Faraway Place: Brian Wilson, the Beach Boys, and the Southern California Experience*. New York: Henry Holt, 1994.

Paul Williams, *Brian Wilson and the Beach Boys: How Deep Is the Ocean? Essays and Conversations*. New York: Omnibus Press, 1997.

Brian Wilson, with Todd Gold. *Wouldn't It Be Nice: My Own Story*. New York: HarperCollins, 1991.

The Beatles

Alan Aldridge (ed.), *The Beatles Illustrated Lyrics*. New York: Black Dog and Leventhal, 1999 (first published 1969).

Harry Castleman and Walter J. Podrazik (comps.), *All Together Now: The First Complete Beatles Discography, 1961–1975*. New York: Ballantine, 1975.

Harry Castleman and Walter J. Podrazik. *The Beatles Again?* Ann Arbor, MI: Pierian Press, 1977.

Harry Castleman and Walter J. Podrazik. *The End of the Beatles? Sequel to the "Beatles Again" and "All Together Now: The First Complete Beatles Discography."* Ann Arbor, MI: Pierian Press, 1985.

B. Lee Cooper, "Review of *The Beatles: Untold Tales* by Howard A. DeWitt," *Popular Music and Society* (winter 1987), 100–1.

Laura E. Cooper and B. Lee Cooper. "The Pendulum of Cultural Imperialism: Popular Music Interchanges between the United States and Britain, 1943–1967," *Journal of Popular Culture* XXVII (winter 1993), 61–78.

Howard A. DeWitt, *The Beatles: Untold Tales*. Fremont, CA: Horizon Books, 1985.

Bill Harry, *Paperback Writers: The History of the Beatles in Print*. London: Virgin Books, 1984.

Mark Hertsgaard, *A Day in the Life: The Music and Artistry of the Beatles*. New York: Delacorte Press, 1995.

Ian Inglis (ed.), *The Beatles, Popular Music, and Society: A Thousand Voices*. New York: St. Martin's Press, 2000.

Lewisohn, Mark. *The Complete Beatles Chronicle: The Only Definitive Guide to the Beatles' Entire Career*. London: Hamlyn Books/Octopus 2000 (first published 1992).

Ian MacDonald, *Revolution in the Head: The Beatles' Records and the Sixties*. New York: Henry Holt, 1994.

Greil Marcus, "The Beatles," in *The Rolling Stone Illustrated History of Rock and Roll* (rev. ed.), edited by Anthony DeCurtis and James Henke, with Holly George-Warren. New York: Random House/Rolling Stone Press, 1992, 209–22.

William McKeen, *The Beatles: A Bio-Bibliography*. Westport, CT: Greenwood, 1989.

Charles P. Neises (ed.), *The Beatles Reader: A Selection of Contemporary Views, News and Reviews of the Beatles in Their Heyday*. Ann Arbor, MI: Pierian Press, 1984.

Philip Norman, *Shout! The Beatles in Their Generation*. New York: Simon & Schuster (Fireside Book), 1981.

Terence J. O'Grady, *The Beatles: A Musical Evolution*. Boston: Twayne, 1983.

Gareth L. Pawlowski, *How They Became the Beatles: A Definitive History of the Early Years, 1960–1964*. New York: E. P. Dutton, 1989.

Walter J. Podrazik, *Strange Days: The Music of John, Paul, George, and Ringo Twenty Years On*. Ann Arbor, MI: Pierian Press, 1988.

David Pritchard and Alan Lysaght. *The Beatles: An Oral History*. New York: Hyperion Books, 1998.

Nicholas Schaffner, *The Boys from Liverpool: John, Paul, George, and Ringo*. New York: Methuen, 1980.

Carol D. Terry (comp.), *Here, There, and Everywhere: The First International Beatles Bibliography, 1962–1982*. Ann Arbor, MI: Pierian Press, 1998.

Turner, Steve. *A Hard Day's Write: The Stories behind Every Beatles Song*. New York: HarperCollins, 1999 (first published 1994).

Chuck Berry

Chuck Berry, *Chuck Berry: The Autobiography*. New York: Harmony Books, 1987.

Bob Blumenthal, "Chuck Berry: Berryland," in *Bluesland: Portraits of Twelve Major American Blues Masters*, edited by Pete Welding and Toby Byron. New York: Dutton/Penguin Books, 1991, 238–49.

Robert Christgau, "Chuck Berry," in *The Rolling Stone Illustrated History of Rock and Roll* (rev. ed.), edited by Anthony DeCurtis and James Henke, with Holly George-Warren. New York: Random House/Rolling Stone Press, 1992, 60–66.

B. Lee Cooper, "Chuck Berry and the American Motor Car," *Music World*, no. 86 (June 1981), 18–23.

B. Lee Cooper, "Review of *Chuck Berry: Rock 'n' Roll Music* (2d ed.) by Howard A. DeWitt," *The Sonneck Society Newsletter* XII (summer 1986), 69–70.

Howard A. DeWitt, *Chuck Berry: Rock 'n' Roll Music* (2d ed.). Ann Arbor, MI: Pierian Press, 1985.

Peter Doggett, "Chuck Berry: The Chess Years," *Record Collector*, no. 150 (February 1992), 90–95.

John Etheredge, "Chuck Berry: A Conversation with Mr. Rock 'n' Roll," *Goldmine*, no. 90 (November 1983), 6–8, 12–13, 15ff.

Cub Koda, "Chuck Berry: And the Joint Was Rockin'," *Goldmine*, no. 297 (December 31, 1991), 8–22.

Yasue Kuwahara, "I'm So Glad I'm Living in the U.S.A.: Chuck Berry's America," *Popular Music and Society* XIII (winter 1989), 17–34.

Michael Lydon, "Chuck Berry," in *Rock Folk: Portraits from the Rock 'n' Roll Pantheon*. New York: Dial Press, 1971, 1–23.

Charles Shaar Murray, "Chuck Berry," *The History of Rock*, no. 4 (1982), 64–68.

Ralph M. Newman, "The Chuck Berry Story: Long Lives Rock and Roll," *Time Barrier Express*, no. 27 (April-May 1980), 34–46.

Krista Reese, *Chuck Berry: Mr. Rock 'n' Roll*. London: Proteus Books, 1982.

Timothy D. Taylor, "His Name Was in Lights: Chuck Berry's 'Johnny B. Goode'," *Popular Music* XI (January 1992), 27–40.

Tom Wheeler, "Chuck Berry: The Interview," *Guitar Player* XXII (March 1988), 56–63.

Tom Wheeler, "Chuck Berry: The Story," *Guitar Player* XXII (March 1988), 50–54.

Timothy White, "Chuck Berry," in *Rock Lives: Profiles and Interviews.* New York: Henry Holt, 1990, 21–26.

David Bowie

Kevin Cann, *David Bowie: A Chronology.* New York: Fireside Books/Simon & Schuster, 1984.

Roy Carr, and Charles Shaar Murray. *Bowie: An Illustrated Record.* New York: Avon Books, 1981.

Chris Charlesworth, *David Bowie: A Profile.* New York: Proteus Books, 1985.

Henry Edwards and Tony Zanetta. *Stardust: The David Bowie Story.* New York: McGraw-Hill, 1986.

David Jeffrey Fletcher (comp.), *David Robert Jones Bowie: The Discography of a Generalist, 1962–1979* (3d ed.). Chicago: F. Ferguson, 1979.

Chet Flippo (author) and Denis O'Regan (photographer). *David Bowie's Serious Moonlight: The World Tour.* Garden City, NY: Dolphin/Doubleday, 1984.

Peter Gillman and Leni Gillman. *Alias David Bowie: A Biography.* London: Hodder and Stoughton, 1986.

Peter Goddard and Philip Kamin. *David Bowie: The Man Who Came Out of the Cool.* New York: Beaufort Books, 1983.

Stuart Hoggard (comp.), *David Bowie: An Illustrated Discography.* London: Omnibus Press, 1980.

Jerry Hopkins, *Bowie.* New York: Macmillan, 1985.

Thomas Kamp (comp.), *David Bowie—The Wild-Eyed Boy, 1964–1984: A Comprehensive Reference and World-Wide Discography Guide.* Phoenix, AZ: O'Sullivan and Woodside, 1985.

Arthur King, "David Bowie: The Ziggy Stardust Years—A Complete Guide to Bowie's Recording Career Between 1970 and 1974," *Record Collector*, no. 90 (February 1987), 3–8.

Kate Lynch, *David Bowie: A Rock 'n' Roll Odyssey.* New York: Proteus Books, 1984.

Robert Matthew-Walker, *David Bowie: Theatre of Music*. Boston: Merrimack Books, 1986.

Charles Shaar Murray, "Let's Talk: A Conversation with David Bowie," *Rolling Stone*, no. 433 (October 25, 1984), 14–18, 74.

Kenneth Pitt, *Bowie: The Pitt Report*. New York: Omnibus Press, 1985.

Dave Thompson, *David Bowie: Moonage Daydream*. London: Plexus Books, 1987.

Elizabeth Thompson and David Gutman (eds.), *The Bowie Companion*. New York: Da Capo Press, 1996 (first published 1993).

Tony Zanetta and Henry Edwards. *Stardust: The David Bowie Story*. New York: McGraw-Hill, 1986.

James Brown

Geoff Brown, *James Brown: A Biography*. London: Omnibus Press, 1996.

James Brown, with Bruce Tucker. *James Brown: The Godfather of Soul*. New York: Macmillan Books, 1986.

Jason Chervokas, "Make It Funky! James Brown: How the Godfather of Soul Became the Father of Funk," *Goldmine*, no. 287 (May 26, 1995), 18–32, 72.

Guralnick, Peter. "Papa's Got a Brand New Bag," in *Sweet Soul Music: Rhythm and Blues and the Southern Dream of Freedom*. New York: Harper & Row, 1986, 220–45.

Robert Palmer, "James Brown," in *The Rolling Stone Illustrated History of Rock 'n' Roll* (rev. ed.), edited by Anthony DeCurtis and James Henke, with Holly George-Warren. New York: Random House/Rolling Stone Press, 1992), 163–70.

Steve Propes, "James Brown: The Godfather of Soul's First Decade," *DISCoveries*, no. 60 (May 1993), 16–19.

Cynthia Rose, *Living in America: The Soul Saga of James Brown*. London: Serpent's Tail Press, 1990.

Roger St. Pierre, "The Blues and Soul Hall of Fame: no. 22—James Brown," *Blues & Soul*, no. 590 (July 9–22, 1991), 26–29.

Steve Scott, "James Brown: Godfather of Soul," *Record Collector*, no. 40 (December 1982), 13–20.

Mel Watkins, "The Lyrics of James Brown," in *Amistad 2*, edited by John A. Williams and Charles F. Harris. New York: Vintage Books, 1971, 109–15.

Cliff White, "The Roots of James Brown—Part One," *Now Dig This*, no. 122 (May 1993), 19–21.

Cliff White, "The Roots of James Brown—Part Two," *Now Dig This*, no. 123 (June 1993), 27–28.

Cliff White, "The Roots of James Brown—Part Three," *Now Dig This*, no. 125 (August 1993), 25–26.

Timothy White, "James! The Power of Positive Badness," *Musician*, no. 90 (April 1986), 50–61.

Johnny Cash

George Carpozi, Jr., *The Johnny Cash Story*. New York: Pyramid Books, 1970.

Johnny Cash, *The Man in Black*. Grand Rapids, MI: Zondervan Press, 1975.

Howard Cockburn, "The Man in Black: The Ultimate Johnny Cash Collection!" *Now Dig This*, no. 92 (November 1990), 17–21.

Frederick E. Danker, "Country Music and the Mass Media: The Johnny Cash Television Show," *Popular Music and Society* II (winter 1973), 124–44.

Danker, Frederick E. "The Repertory and Style of a Country Singer: Johnny Cash," *Journal of American Folklore* LXXXV (October-December 1972), 309–29.

Danker, Frederick E. "The World According to Johnny Cash: Lyrical Themes in His Music," in *You Wrote My Life: Lyrical Themes in Country Music*, edited by Melton McLauren and Richard Peterson. New York: Gordon and Breach, 1992, 131–54.

Peter Doggett, "Johnny Cash," *Record Collector*, no. 58 (June 1984), 3–8.

Colin Escott with Martin Hawkins, "Johnny Cash: Hillbilly Heads Uptown," in *Good Rockin' Tonight: Sun Records and the Birth of Rock 'n' Roll*. San Francisco: Pandora/HarperCollins, 1991, 95–109.

Bill Flanagan, "Johnny Cash, American," *Musician*, no. 115 (May 1988), 96–112.

John Lomax III, "Portrait of Johnny Cash: From Rockabilly Rebel to Country King," *Country Style*, no. 69 (August 1981), 58–62.

Teresa Ortega, "My Name Is Sue! How Do You Do? Johnny Cash as a Lesbian Icon," in *Readin' Country Music: Steel Guitars, Opry Stars, and Honky Tonk Bars*, edited by Cecilia Techi. Durham, NC: Duke University Press, 1995, 259–72.

John L. Smith, (comp.), *The Johnny Cash Record Catalog*. Westport, CT: Greenwood, 1994.

Christopher S. Wren, *Winners Got Scars Too: The Life and Legends of Johnny Cash*. New York: Ballantine Books, 1974.

Ray Charles

Chris Albertson, "Ray Charles," *Stereo Review* LI (February 1986), 55–59.

"The Blues and Soul Hall of Fame: no. 18—Ray Charles," *Blues and Soul*, no. 586 (May 14–27, 1991), 23–25.

Stanley Booth, "Ray Charles Tells the Truth," *Pulse* CLXVI (December 1997), 34–40, 132.

Ray Charles and David Ritz. *Brother Ray: Ray Charles' Own Story*. New York Warner, 1979.

B. Lee Cooper, "Review of *Ray Charles—Genius and Soul: The 50th Anniversary Collection*," *Popular Music and Society* XXI (winter 1997), 134–6.

Peter Doggett, "Ray Charles," *Record Collector*, no. 45 (May 1983), 40–46.

Jivin' Johnny Etheredge, "Ray Charles: A Performer of Nearly Mythical Stature," *Goldmine*, no. 134 (September 13, 1985), 12, 14, 16, 18.

Peter Guralnick, "Ray Charles," in *The Rolling Stone Illustrated History of Rock and Roll* (rev. ed.), edited by Anthony DeCurtis and James Henke, with Holly George-Warren. New York: Random House/Rolling Stone Press, 1992, 130–4.

Robin Katz, "Brother Ray," *The History of Rock*, no. 17 (1982), 323–9.

Michael Lydon, *Ray Charles: Man and Music*. New York: Riverhead Books, 1998.

Sharon B. Mathis and Susan B. Weber. *Ray Charles*. New York: Thomas Y. Crowell, 1973.

Moonoogian, George A. " 'Young Genius': The Early Ray Charles," *Goldmine*, no. 45 (February 1980), 10–11.

"Playboy Interview: Ray Charles," *Playboy* XVII (March 1970), 67–82.

Pete Welding, "Ray Charles—Senior Diplomat of Soul," *Downbeat* XLIV (May 5, 1977), 12–15, 46.

Timothy White, "Ray Charles," in *Rock Lives: Profiles and Interviews*. New York: Henry Holt, 1990, 27–31.

Cher

Mark Bego, *Cher!*. New York: Pocket Books, 1986.

Bil Carpenter, "The Serious Side of Cher," *Goldmine*, no. 308 (May 15, 1992), 16–28, 168.

Peter Doggett, "Cher," *Record Collector*, no. 106 (June 1988), 48–52.

Nigel Goodall, *Cher in Her Own Words*. London: Omnibus Books, 1992.

Lynn Hirschberg, "Cher Wants to Be Taken Seriously," *Rolling Stone*, no. 418 (March 29, 1984), 23–28.

Brian Hogg, "Sonny and Cher," *Record Collector*, no. 42 (February 1983), 30–36.

Ward Lamb, "Cher: Three Decades of Hits while Dealing with Gypsies, Tramps, and Thieves," *Goldmine*, no. 507 (December 31, 1999), 38–44, 88.

Vicki Pellegrino, *Cher!* New York: Ballentine Books, 1975.

Lawrence J. Quirk, *Totally Uninhibited: The Life and Wild Times of Cher*. New York: William Morrow, 1991.

J. Randy Taraborelli, *Cher: A Biography*. New York: St. Martin's Press, 1987.

Rick Wilson, "Cher: The Vinyl Definitive," *Goldmine*, no. 69 (February 1982), 12–15.

Eric Clapton

Ray Coleman, *Clapton! An Authorized Biography*. New York: Warner Books, 1985.

Dan Forte, "The Eric Clapton Story," *Guitar Player* XIX (July 1985), 10–16, 147–9.

Peter Guralnick, "Eric Clapton at the Passion Threshold," *Musician*, no. 136 (February 1990), 44–56.

James Henke, "Eric Clapton: The Rolling Stone Interview," *Rolling Stone*, no. 615 (October 17, 1991), 42–49, 106.

Edward J. Lozano (ed.), *Eric Clapton: A Life in the Blues*. New York: Amsco, 1995.

John Pidgeon, *Eric Clapton*. North Pomfret, VT: David and Charles, 1986.

Marc Roberty, *Eric Clapton: The Complete Recording Sessions, 1963–1992*. New York: St. Martin's Press, 1993.

Marc Roberty, *Slowhand: The Life and Music of Eric Clapton*. New York: Crown, 1993.

Michael Schumacher, *Crossroads: The Life and Music of Eric Clapton*. New York: Hyperion Books, 1995.

Harry Shapiro, *Eric Clapton: Lost in the Blues*. New York: Da Capo Press, 1993 (first published 1992).

Dave Thompson, "The Second Coming of a Reluctant God: Eric Clapton's Mid-70s Comeback," *Goldmine*, no. 473 (September 11, 1998), 16–20, 114–22.

Steve Turner, *Conversations with Eric Clapton*. London: Abacus (Sphere Books), 1976.

Patsy Cline

Mark Bego, *I Fall to Pieces: The Music and the Life of Patsy Cline*. Holbrook, MA: Adams, 1995.

Doug Hall, *The Real Patsy Cline*. Kingston, Ontario: Quarry Press, 1998.

Cindy Hazen and Mike Freeman. *Love Always, Patsy: Patsy Cline's Letters to a Friend*. New York: Berkley Books, 1999.

Joli Jensen, "Patsy Cline, Musical Negotiation, and the Nashville Sound," in *All That Glitters: Country Music in America*, edited by George H. Lewis. Bowling Green, OH: Bowling Green State University Popular Press, 1993, 38–50.

Joli Jensen, "Patsy Cline's Recording Career: The Search for a Sound," *Journal of Country Music* IX, no. 2 (1982), 34–46.

Margaret Jones, *Patsy: The Life and Times of Patsy Cline*. New York: HarperCollins, 1994.

Bob Millard, "Patsy Cline: Owen Bradley Remembers," *Goldmine*, no. 192 (December 4, 1987), 20, 25, 137.

Ellis Nassour, *Honky Tonk Angel: The Intimate Story of Patsy Cline*. New York: St. Martin's Press, 1993 (first published 1981).

Robert K. Oermann, "Honky Tonk Angels: Kitty Wells and Patsy Cline," in *Country: The Music and the Musicians*, edited by Paul Kingsbury and Alan Axelrod. New York: Abbeville Press, 1988, 314–41.

Don Roy, (comp.), "The Patsy Cline Discography," *Journal of Country Music* IX, no. 2 (1982), 47–115.

George Vecsey and Leonore Fleischer. *Sweet Dreams*. New York: St. Martin's Press, 1985.

The Coasters

"The Coasters," *The Golden Age*, no. 18 (1988), 12–20.

Stuart Colman, "The Coasters: That Is Rock 'n' Roll," in *They Kept on Rockin': The Giants of Rock 'n' Roll*. Dorset, England: Blandford Press, 1982, 95–97.

B. Lee Cooper, "The Coasters—What Was the Secret of Their Success? A Review Essay," *Popular Music and Society* XVII, no. 2 (summer 1993), 115–19.

Bill Dahl, "Review of *50 Coastin' Classics* (Rhino CD R2–71090) by The Coasters," *Goldmine*, no. 330 (March 19, 1993), 44.

Peter Doggett, "The Coasters," *Record Collector*, no. 26 (October 1981), 13–18.

Marv Goldberg and Mike Redmond. "The Cornell Gunter Story," *Record Exchanger*, no. 13 (June 1973), 4–10.

Bill Griggs, "Spotlight on Carl Gardner and The Coasters," *Rockin' 50s*, no. 58 (June/July 2001), 10–15.

Philip Hardy and Dave Laing. "The Coasters," in *The Faber Companion to 20th-Century Popular Music*. London: Faber and Faber, 1990, 152–3.

Bill Millar, "At Smokey Joe's Café," *The History of Rock*, no. 15 (1982), 294–7.

Bill Millar, *The Coasters*. London: Star Book (W. H. Allen), 1974.

Stambler, Irwin. "The Coasters," in *The Encyclopedia of Pop, Rock, and Soul* (rev. ed.). New York: St. Martin's Press, 1989, 134–5.

Chris Woodford, "Who Are the True Coasters?" *Now Dig This*, no. 108 (March 1992), 5–7.

Nat King Cole

Maria Cole and Louie Robinson. *Nat King Cole: An Intimate Biography*. New York: William Morrow, 1971.

Peter Doggett, "Nat King Cole," *Record Collector*, no. 66 (February 1985), 21–28.

Daniel Mark Epstein, *Nat King Cole*. New York: Farrar, Straus & Giroux, 1999.

Charles Garrod and Bill Korst. *Nat King Cole: His Voice and Piano*. Zephyrhills, FL: Joyce Record Club, 1987.

Leslie Gourse, *Unforgettable: The Life and Mystique of Nat King Cole*. London: New English Library, 1991.

George Hall (comp.), *The Nat "King" Cole Trio*. Whittier, CA: Jazz Discographies, 1965.

James Haskins and Kathleen Benson. *Nat "King" Cole*. London: Robson Books, 1991.

Roy Hemming and David Hadju. "Nat King Cole," in *Discovering Great Singers of Classic Pop*. New York: Oxford University Press, 1981, 165–8.

Jerry Osborne, "Nat King Cole: Unforgettable," *DISCoveries* III (March 1990), 22–23.

Marianne Ruuth, *Nat King Cole: Singer and Jazz Pianist*. Los Angeles: Holloway House, 1992.

Klaus Teubig (comp.), *Straighten Up and Fly Right: A Chronology and Discography of Nat "King" Cole*. Westport, CT: Greenwood, 1994.

Nick Tosches, "Nat King Cole: Beyond Pink Cadillacs," in *Unsung Heroes of Rock 'n' Roll in the Dark and Wild Years before Elvis* (New York: Scribner's, 1984), 26–32.

Sam Cooke

Clive Anderson, "Twistin' the Night Away," *The History of Rock*, no. 17 (1982), 333–5.

Ray Funk, "Sar Records: Sam Cooke's Soul Label," *Goldmine*, no. 211 (Aug. 26, 1988), 86–88.

Paul Gambaccini, "Sam Cooke," in *Masters of Rock*. London: Omnibus Press, 1982, 27–33.

Peter Guralnick, "Prologue to Soul: Sam Cooke, Ray Charles, and the Business of Music," in *Sweet Soul Music: Rhythm and Blues and the Southern Dream of Freedom*. New York: Harper & Row, 1986, 21–75.

Gerri Hirshey, "Lady, You Shot Me," in *Nowhere to Run: The Story of Soul Music*. New York: Times Books, 1984, 99–116.

Joe McEwen, "Sam Cooke," in *The Rolling Stone Illustrated History of Rock and Roll* (rev. ed.), edited by Anthony DeCurtis and James Henke, with Holly George-Warren. New York: Random House/Rolling Stone Press, 1992, 135–8.

Joe McEwen, Joe. *Sam Cooke: The Man Who Invented Soul*. New York: Chappell Music, 1977.

Pete Nickols, "Sam Cooke: Soul Stirrer," *Now Dig This*, no. 27 (June 1985), 30–31.

Joanne Palmer, "Sam Cooke: Still Strong 30 Years after 'You Send Me' Hits #1," *Goldmine*, no. 168 (January 2, 1987), 8–12.

Roger St. Pierre, "The Blues and Soul Hall of Fame: no. 20—Sam Cooke," *Blues and Soul*, no. 588 (June 11–24, 1991), 36–37.

Steve Scott, "Sam Cooke," *Record Collector*, no. 44 (April 1983), 35–40.

Timothy White, "Sam Cooke," in *Rock Lives: Profiles and Interviews*. New York: Henry Holt, 1990, 52–55.

Daniel Wolff, with S. R. Crain, Clifton White, and G. David Tenenbaum. *You Send Me: The Life and Times of Sam Cooke*. New York: William Morrow, 1995.

Elvis Costello

Peter Doggett, "Elvis Costello: A Complete Guide to His British and American Releases, Promos, and Rarities," *Record Collector*, no. 49 (September 1983), 20–23.

Peter Doggett, "Elvis Costello Rarities," *Record Collector*, no. 91 (March 1987), 27–30.

Bill Flanagan, "The Last Elvis Costello Interview," *Musician*, no. 89 (March 1986), 36–54.

David Gouldstone, *Elvis Costello: A Man out of Time*. London: Sidgwick and Jackson, 1989.

Richard Jackson, "Elvis Costello," *Record Collector*, no. 16 (December 1980), 21–26.

Greil Marcus, "Elvis Costello Explains Himself: The Rolling Stone Interview," *Rolling Stone*, no. 377 (September 2, 1982), 12–17, 56.

Geoff Parkyn, *Elvis Costello: An Illustrated Discography*. London: Omnibus Books, 1984.

James E. Perone, *Elvis Costello: A Bio-Bibliography*. Westport, CT: Greenwood, 1998.

Krista Reese, *Elvis Costello: A Completely False Biography Based on Rumor, Innuendo, and Lies*. New York: Proteus Books, 1981.

Mark Rowland, "Elvis Costello Is Love and War," *Musician*, no. 125 (March 1989), 62–79, 98.

Mick St. Michael, *Elvis Costello: An Illustrated Biography*. London: Omnibus Books, 1986.

Jeff Tamarkin, "Elvis Costello: I'm Not Angry Anymore," *Goldmine*, no. 91 (December 1983), 6–8, 14, 16, 18, 22.

Bing Crosby

Ken Barnes, *The Crosby Years*. New York: St. Martin's Press, 1980.

John Bassett, Leslie Gaylor, and Bert Bishop (comps.), *The Bing Crosby Mini-Discography, 1926–1974* (2d ed.). Cwmbran, Wales: International Crosby Circle, 1974.

Bing Crosby, as told to Pete Martin. *Call Me Lucky*. New York: Simon & Schuster, 1953.

Gary Giddins, "Bing for the Millions," in *Riding on a Blue Note: Jazz and American Pop*. New York: Oxford University Press, 1981, 14–21.

Roy Hemming and David Hadju. "Bing Crosby," in *Discovering Great Singers of Classic Pop*. New York: Newmarket Press, 1991, 44–53.

Timothy A. Morgereth (comp.), *Bing Crosby: A Discography, Radio Program List, and Filmography*. Jefferson, NC: McFarland, 1987.

Sheldon O'Connell, with Gord Atkinson. *Bing: A Voice for All Seasons*. Tralee, Ireland: Kerryman Books, 1984.

J. Roger Osterholm, *Bing Crosby: A Bio-Bibliography*. Westport, CT: Greenwood, 1994.

William Ruhlmann, "Swingin' (on a) Star: The Road to Bing Crosby," *Goldmine*, no. 350 (December 24, 1993), 14–44ff.

Bob Thomas, *The One and Only Bing*. New York: Grosset and Dunlap, 1977.

Donald Shepherd and Robert F. Slatzer. *Bing Crosby: The Hollow Man*. New York: St. Martin's Press, 1981.

Laurence J. Zwisohn, *Bing Crosby: A Lifetime of Music*. Los Angeles: Palm Tree Library, 1978.

Bobby Darin

Jeff Bleiel, "Bobby Darin," *DISCoveries*, no. 67 (December 1993), 30–34.

Jeff Bleiel, *That's All: Bobby Darin on Record, Stage, and Screen*. Ann Arbor, MI: Popular Culture, Ink., 1993.

Al DiOrio, *Borrowed Time: The 37 Years of Bobby Darin*. Philadelphia: Running Press, 1986.

Peter Jones, "The Bobby Darin Story," *Record Collector*, no. 23 (August 1981), 24–30.

Art Klinger, "Spotlight on Bobby Darin," *Rockin' 50s*, no. 36 (June 1992), 8–15.

Richard J. Lorenzo, "Bobby Darin: Doing His Own Thing and Other Things," *Goldmine*, no. 227 (April 7, 1989), 18–20.

John Pidgeon, "Dream Lover," *The History of Rock*, no. 18 (1982), 344–7.

Steve Roeser, "Bobby Darin: Beyond the Sea, beyond the Music," *Goldmine*, no. 398 (October 27, 1995), 18–48.

Bryan Smith, "Bobby Darin," *Record Collector*, no. 149 (Jan. 1992), 122–8.

Allen J. Weiner, "Bobby Darin: The Available Recordings," *Goldmine*, no. 227 (April 7, 1989), 22–25.

Bo Diddley

Billy Atwell III, "Bo Diddley: The Originator Still Rockin' and Rollin'," *Blues Revue*, no. 25 (October/November 1996), 36–38.

Geoff Barker and Barry Holley, "Diddley Daddy's Day," *Now Dig This*, no. 101 (August 1991), 11.

Rick Coleman, "Bo Diddley," *Wavelength*, no. 20 (June 1982), 21–23.

Bill DeYoung, "Bo Diddley: Still Rockin'," *Goldmine*, no. 433 (February 28, 1997), 12–13, 22.

Paul-Henri Goulet, "Spotlight on Bo Diddley," *Rockin' 50s*, no. 35 (April 1992), 8–14.

George Groom-White, *Bo Diddley: The Living Legend*. London: Plexus Books, 1993.

Jeff Hannusch, "Bo Diddley Is a Gunslinger," *Guitar Player* XVIII (June 1984), 62–70.

Scott Isler, "Bo Diddley—The Chess Box," *Musician*, no. 147 (January 1991), 90.

Frank Krutnik, "Bo Diddley," *Record Collector*, no. 46 (June 1983), 15–20.

Howard Mandel, "Bo Diddley: Still Boppin'," *Guitar World* XVIII (July 1984), 45–50.

Bob Naylor, "Bo Diddley Is a . . . Boxed Set," *Now Dig This*, no. 129 (December 1993), 5–8.

Robert Pruter, "Let's Put Some Harmonies in There: Bo Diddley the Doo-Wopper," *Goldmine*, no. 332 (April 16, 1993), 24–28, 48.

George R. White (comp.), *The Complete Bo Diddley Sessions*. Bradford, England: George R. White, 1993.

Valerie Wilmer, "You Can Snatch Anything You Want from Me, But I Still Got My Soul: Bo Diddley Interview," *Blues Unlimited*, Nos. 135/136 (July-September 1979), 31–33.

Fats Domino

Clive Anderson, "The Fat Man," *The History of Rock*, no. 8 (1982), 144–7.

Jason Berry, Jonathan Foose, and Tad Jones. "Antoine Domino: The Fat Man," in *Up from the Cradle of Jazz: New Orleans Music since World War II*. Athens: University of Georgia Press, 1986, 29–39.

Rick Coleman, "Fats Domino and the New Orleans Rock Revolution," *DISCoveries*, no. 67 (Dec. 1993), 22–28.

Rick Coleman, "42 Things You Probably Don't Know about Fats Domino," *Wavelength*, no. 79 (May 1987), 22–23.

Rick Coleman, "Happy Birthday, Fats! 70 Reasons Why You Gotta Love the Fat Man," *Rock and Blues News*, no. 1 (December 1998/January 1999), 15–18.

Rick Coleman, "The Imperial Fats Domino," *Goldmine*, no. 282 (May 17, 1991), 8–12.

Stuart Colman, "Fats Domino: 'They Call Me the Fat Man'," in *They Kept on Rockin': The Giants of Rock 'n' Roll*. Dorset, England: Blandford Press, 1982, 42–52.

B. Lee Cooper, "The Fats Domino Decades, 1950–1969," *R.P.M.*, no. 5 (May 1984), 56–58, 71.

B. Lee Cooper, "Review of 'That's Fats': A Tribute to Fats Domino," *Popular Music and Society* XX (fall 1996), 129–30.

Howard Elson, "Fats Domino," in *Early Rockers*. New York: Proteus Books, 1982, 36–43.

Mike Gordon, "Fats Domino," *Record Collector*, no. 15 (Nov. 1980), 24–27.

Peter Guralnick, "Fats Domino," in *The Rolling Stone Illustrated History of Rock and Roll* (rev. ed.), edited by Anthony DeCurtis and James Henke, with Holly George-Warren. New York: Random House/ Rolling Stone Press, 1992, 48–51.

Paul Harris, "Hey! Fat Man," *Blues and Rhythm*, no. 66 (Jan. 1992), 4–8.

Roger St. Pierre, "The Blues and Soul Hall of Fame: no. 28—Fats Domino," *Blues and Soul*, no. 596 (October 1–14, 1991), 22–24.

The Doors

Chuck Crisafulli, *Moonlight Drive: The Stories behind Every Doors Song*. Miami Springs, FL: Music Book Services/Carlton Books, 1995.

David Dalton, *Mojo Risin': Jim Morrison, the Last Holy Fool*. London: Sidgwick and Jackson, 1991.

John Densmore, *Riders on the Storm: My Life with Jim Morrison and the Doors*. London: Bloomsbury Books, 1991.

Brian Hogg, "The Doors," *Record Collector*, no. 35 (July 1982), 14–20.

Brian Hogg, "The Doors," *Record Collector*, no. 105 (May 1988), 58–62.

Jerry Hopkins, *The Lizard King: The Essential Jim Morrison*. New York: Scribner's, 1992.

Jerry Hopkins and Danny Sugerman. *No One Gets out of Here Alive*. New York: Warner, 1980.

Mike Jahn, *Jim Morrison and the Doors: An Unauthorized Book*. New York: Grosset and Dunlap, 1969.

Dylan Jones, *Jim Morrison: Dark Star*. New York: Viking Studio, 1991.

Yasue Kuwahara, "Apocalypse Now! Jim Morrison's Vision of America," *Popular Music and Society* XVI (summer 1992), 55–66.

Tony Magistrale, "Wild Child: Jim Morrison's Poetic Journeys," *Journal of Popular Culture* XXVI (winter 1992), 133–44.

Ray Manzarek, *Light My Fire: My Life with the Doors*. New York: G. P. Putnam, 1998.

James Riordan and Jerry Prochnicky. *Break on Through: The Life and Death of Jim Morrison*. New York: William Morrow, 1991.

Ken Sharp, "The Doors: Wild Dionysian Screamers," *Goldmine*, no. 512 (March 10, 2000), 88–94.

Danny Sugerman, *The Doors: The Illustrated History*. New York: William Morrow, 1983.

The Drifters

Tony Allan with Faye Treadwell. *Save the Last Dance for Me: The Musical Legacy of the Drifters, 1953–1993*. Ann Arbor, MI: Popular Culture, Ink., 1993.

Chris Beachley, with assistance from Mike Redmond and Marv Goldberg. "The 'new' Drifters—A Total Reorganization, 1959–1971: Part 2 of the Drifters Story," *It Will Stand* I, no. 6 (1979), 4–7.

Chris Beachley and Marv Goldberg. "The Drifters—Let Their Music Play: Part 3," *It Will Stand*, no. 7 (1979), 4–8.

Robert Christgau, "The Drifters in History," in *Any Old Way You Choose It: Rock and Other Pop Music, 1967–1973*. Baltimore: Penguin Books, 1973, 158–63.

B. Lee Cooper, "The Drifters: From Gospel Glory to Rock Royalty," *Popular Music and Society* XVII (winter 1993), 125–8.

B. Lee Cooper, "Review of *Save the Last Dance for Me: The Musical Legacy of the Drifters, 1953–1993* by Tony Allan, with Faye Treadwell and *Rockin' and Driftin': The Drifters Box*," *Popular Music and Society* XXIV (spring 2000), 129–34.

Jim Davis and Chris Beachley. "The Early Drifters (1953–1959) and the Bill Pinkney Story," *It Will Stand*, I, no. 5 (1979), 4–7.

Paul Gambaccini, "The Drifters," in *Masters of Rock*. London: Omnibus Press, 1982, 142–50.

Marv Goldberg, "The Drifters: The Early Years," *DISCoveries*, no. 155 (April 2001), 39–45.

Marv Goldberg and Mike Redmond. "Starring the Original Drifters," *Record Exchanger* IV, no. 2 (December 1974), 4–25.

Peter Grendysa, "Liner Notes for *the Drifters, 1953–1958: Let the Boogie Woogie Roll (Atlantic CD 7–81927–2)*." New York: Atlantic Records, 1988.

Frank Krutnik, "The Drifters," *Record Collector*, no. 39 (November 1982), 50–56.

Bill Millar, *The Drifters: The Rise and Fall of the Black Vocal Group*. New York: Collier Books, 1971.

Bill Millar, "Under the Boardwalk," *The History of Rock*, no. 15 (1982), 290–3.

Jay Warner, "The Drifters (1953–1979)," in *The Billboard Book of American Singing Groups: A History, 1940–1990*. New York: Billboard Books, 1992, 159–67.

Bob Dylan

Robert H. Bell, "Double Dylan," *Popular Music and Society* XXIV (summer 2000), 109–26.

Carl Benson (ed.), *The Bob Dylan Companion: Four Decades of Commentary*. New York: Schirmer Books, 1998.

Betsy Bowden, *Performed Literature: Words and Music by Bob Dylan*. Bloomington: Indiana University Press, 1982.

Aidan Day, *Jokerman: Reading the Lyrics of Bob Dylan*. Cambridge, England: Basil Blackwell, 1988.

Tim Dowley and Barry Dunnage. *Bob Dylan: From a Hard Rain to a Slow Train*. New York: Hippocrene Books, 1982.

Michael Gray, *Song and Dance Man: The Art of Bob Dylan* (rev. ed.). New York: St. Martin's Press, 1981.

Michael Gray and John Baldie (eds.), *All across the Telegraph: A Bob Dylan Handbook*. London: Sidgwick and Jackson, 1987.

Clinton Heylin, *Bob Dylan: The Recording Sessions, 1960–1994*. New York: St. Martin's Griffin, 1995.

Clinton Heylin, *Dylan: Behind the Shades—A Biography*. New York: Summit Books/Simon & Schuster, 1991.

Michael Krogsgaard, *Positively Bob Dylan: A Thirty-Year Discography, Concert, and Recording Session Guide, 1960–1991*. Ann Arbor, MI: Popular Culture, Ink., 1991.

Craig McGregor (ed.), *Bob Dylan—The Early Years: A Retrospective*. New York: Da Capo Press, 1990.

Elizabeth Thompson and David Gutman (eds.). *The Dylan Companion* (updated and expanded ed.). New York: Da Capo Press, 2001.

Paul Williams, *Bob Dylan: Performing Artist—The Early Years, 1960–1973*. Navato, CA: Underwood-Miller, 1991.

Paul Williams, *Bob Dylan: Performing Artist—The Middle Years, 1974–1986*. Novato, CA: Underwood-Miller, 1992.

Paul Williams, *Bob Dylan: Watching the River Flow—Observations on His Art-in-Progress, 1966–1995*. London: Omnibus Press, 1996.

The Everly Brothers

Peter Aarts and Martin Alberts. *For Everly Yours: A Guide for Everly Brothers Album Collecting*. Gouda, Holland: Everly Brothers International, 1992.

Jay Berman, "Spotlight on the Everly Brothers," *Rockin' 50s*, no. 3 (December 1986), 9–17.

Dave "Daddy Cool" Booth (edited by Colin Escott), "The Everly Brothers," *Goldmine*, no. 94 (March 2, 1984), 14–15, 18, 24, 28ff.

B. Lee Cooper, "Review of *Ike's Boys: The Story of the Everly Brothers* by Phyllis Karpp," *Popular Music and Society* XIII, no. 2 (summer 1989), 110–11.

Howard A. DeWitt, "The Everly Brothers: From Country Roots to Cadence Hits," *Blue Suede News*, no. 29 (winter 1995), 7–12.

Consuelo Dodge, *The Everly Brothers: Ladies Love Outlaws*. Starke, FL: CIN-DAV, 1991.

Peter Doggett, "The Everly Brothers," *Record Collector*, no. 175 (March 1994), 126–34.

Colin Escott, "The Everly Brothers: Brothers in Arms," *Goldmine*, no. 337 (June 25, 1993), 14–32.

John Hosum (comp.), *Living Legends: The History of the Everly Brothers on Record—An Illustrated Discography*. Seattle, WA: Foreverly Music, 1985.

Phyllis Karpp, *Ike's Boys: The Story of the Everly Brothers*. Ann Arbor, MI: Pierian Press, 1988.

Bob Naylor, "The Everly Brothers: The Cadence Recordings 1957–1960—Part One," *Now Dig This*, no. 97 (April 1991), 10–13.

Bob Naylor, "The Everly Brothers: The Cadence Recordings, 1957–1960—Part Two," *Now Dig This*, no. 98 (May 1991), 12–15.

Joan Savers, *The Everly Brothers Rock 'n' Roll Odyssey*. New York: G. P. Putnam, 1986.

Roger White, *The Everly Brothers: Walk Right Back*. London: Plexus Books, 1998.

Fleetwood Mac

Bob Brunning, *Fleetwood Mac: Behind the Masks*. London: New English Library, 1990.

Roy Carr and Steve Clarke. *Fleetwood Mac: Rumours 'n' Fax*. New York: Harmony Books, 1978.

Steve Clarke, *Fleetwood Mac*. New York: Proteus Books, 1984.

Peter Doggett and Lorne Murdoch. "Fleetwood Mac," *Record Collector*, no. 107 (July 1988), 13–16.

Mick Fleetwood, with Stephen Davis. *Fleetwood Mac: My Life and Adventures with Fleetwood Mac*. London: Sidgwick and Jackson, 1990.

Samuel Graham, *Fleetwood Mac: The Authorized History*. New York: Warner Books, 1978.

Amy Hanson, "Fleetwood Mac: Never Break the Chain," *Goldmine*, no. 492 (November 21, 1997), 17–20, 150–70.

Stuart Penney, "Fleetwood Mac—Part One," *Record Collector*, no. 43 (March 1983), 14–21.

Stuart Penney, "Fleetwood Mac—Part Two," *Record Collector*, no. 44 (April 1983), 24–31.

Timothy White, "Last Tangos/New Beginnings: The Fleetwood Mac Nobody Knows," *Musician*, no. 124 (February 1989), 74–86.

Aretha Franklin

Mark Bego, *Aretha Franklin: The Queen of Soul*. New York: Da Capo Press, 2001 (first published 1989).

B. Lee Cooper, "Review of *Aretha Franklin—Queen of Soul: The Atlantic Recordings*," *Popular Music and Society* XVI (winter 1992), 109–11.

Peter Doggett, "Aretha Franklin," *Record Collector*, no. 96 (August 1987), 44–49.

Aretha Franklin, with David Ritz. *Aretha: From These Roots*. New York: Villard Books, 1999.

Russell Gersten, "Aretha Franklin," in *Rolling Stone Illustrated History of Rock and Roll*, edited by Anthony DeCurtis and James Henke, with Holly George-Warren. New York: Random House/Rolling Stone Press, 1992, 332–8.

Peter Guralnick, "Aretha Arrives," in *Sweet Soul Music: Rhythm and Blues and the Southern Dream of Freedom*. New York: Harper & Row, 1986, 332–52.

Gerri Hirshey, "Aretha Franklin: A Woman's Only Human," in *Nowhere to Run: The Story of Soul Music*. New York: Da Capo Press, 1994, 228–49.

Debbie Kellom, "Aretha Franklin: Heart and Soul Indivisible," *Goldmine*, no. 225 (March 10, 1989), 8–16, 30.

Michael Lydon and Ellen Mandell. "Aretha Franklin," in *Boogie Lightning: How Music Became Electric* (2d ed.). New York: Da Capo Press, 1980, 160–84.

David Nathan, "Aretha Franklin: The Columbia Years (1960–1965)," *Goldmine*, no. 364 (July 8, 1994), 47–50, 166.

David Nathan, "The Blues and Soul Hall of Fame: no. 12—Aretha Franklin," *Blues and Soul*, no. 580 (February 19–March 4, 1991), 21–24.

Richard Robinson, "Aretha Franklin," *Record Collector*, no. 37 (September 1982), 18–24.

Timothy White, "Aretha Franklin," in *Rock Lives: Profiles and Interviews.* New York: Henry Holt, 1990, 194–8.

Alan Freed

Carl Belz, "The Role of the Disk Jockey," in *The Story of Rock* (2d ed.). New York: Harper & Row, 1972, 49–52.

B. Lee Cooper, "Review of *Big Beat Heat: Alan Freed and the Early Years of Rock and Roll* by John A. Jackson," in *Rock Music in American Popular Culture II: More Rock 'n' Roll Resources* by B. Lee Cooper and Wayne S. Haney. New York: Hawthorn Press, 1997, 168–9.

Julie Fanslow, "Alan Freed—Mr. Rock 'n' Roll Remembered," *The* [Cleveland] *Plain Dealer* (September 6, 1985), "Friday!" section, 3, 14.

Bill Griggs and Kaptin Ignatz. "Alan Freed's Moondog Coronation Ball," *Rockin' 50s*, no. 35 (April 1992), 6–7.

John A. Jackson, *Big Beat Heat: Alan Freed and the Early Years of Rock and Roll*. New York: Schirmer Books, 1991.

John Jackson, "Spotlight on Alan Freed," *Rockin' 50s*, no. 1 (August 1986), 8–15.

Bill Millar, "Mr. Rock 'n' Roll," *The History of Rock*, no. 11 (1982), 215–17.

Keith Rathburn, "Alan Freed's Defense Plea," *Scene* XVII (March 20–26, 1986), 11.

Keith Rathburn, "The Moondog Coronation Ball: Happy Birthday, Rock 'n' Roll," *Scene* XVII (March 20–26, 1986), 9.

Mike Richard, "Banned in Boston!" *Goldmine*, no. 41 (October 1979), 125–6.

Jeffrey L. Rutledge, "Alan Freed: The Fall From Grace of a Forgotten Hero," *Goldmine*, no. 118 (February 1, 1985), 22–54, 57.

Jane Scott, "When 'Moon Dog' Howled in Cleveland," *The* [Cleveland] *Plain Dealer* (September 6, 1985), "Friday!" section, 3.

Arnold Shaw, "Rock 'n' Roll's Superpromoter," in *The Rockin' '50s*. New York: Hawthorn Books, 1974, 104–11.

Wes Smith, "The Moon Dog," in *The Pied Pipers of Rock 'n' Roll: Radio Dee-Jays of the '50s and '60s*. Marietta, GA: Longstreet Press, 1989, 163–219.

Marvin Gaye

David Bianco, "Marvin Gaye," in *Heat Wave: The Motown Fact Book*. Ann Arbor, MI: Pierian Press, 1988, 27–33.

"The Blues and Soul Hall of Fame: no. 1—Marvin Gaye," *Blues and Soul*, no. 569 (September 11–24, 1990), 12–15.

Bill Dahl, "Marvin Gaye: Trouble Man," *Goldmine*, no. 232 (June 16, 1989), 8–10, 16, 20, 78.

Sharon Davis, *I Heard It through the Grapevine: Marvin Gaye—The Biography*. Edinburgh, England: Mainstream, 1991.

Peter Doggett, "Marvin Gaye," *Record Collector*, no. 20 (April 1981), 36–42.

Peter Doggett, "Marvin Gaye," *Record Collector*, no. 78 (February 1986), 38–44.

Ben Fong-Torres and Kurt Loder. "From Sideman to Superstar: The Story of Motown's Sexiest Singer," *Rolling Stone*, no. 421 (May 10, 1984), 14–15, 59–61.

Michael Goldberg, "Trouble Man: Marvin Gaye, 1939–1984,"*Rolling Stone*, no. 421 (May 10, 1984), 13, 16.

Orea Jones, "The Theology of 'Sexual Healing': Marvin Gaye," *Journal of Black Sacred Music* III (fall 1989), 68–74.

Dave Marsh, "Wonderful One: Marvin Gaye (1939–1984)," in *Fortunate Son*. New York: Random House, 1985, 307–12.

David Ritz, *Divided Soul: The Life of Marvin Gaye*. New York: Da Capo Press, 1991 (first published 1985).

Grateful Dead

David G. Dodd and Robert G. Weiner (comps.), *The Grateful Dead and the Deadheads: An Annotated Bibliography*. Westport, CT: Greenwood, 1997.

David Gans and Peter Simon, *Playing in the Band: An Oral and Visual Portrait of the Grateful Dead*. New York: St. Martin's Press, 1985.

Fred Goodman, "The End of the Road?" *Rolling Stone*, no. 585 (August 23, 1990), 21–26, 147.

Fred Goodman, "The Rolling Stone Interview: Jerry Garcia," *Rolling Stone*, no. 566 (November 30, 1989), 66–74, 118.

Blair Jackson, *Grateful Dead: The Music Never Stopped*. New York: Delilah Books, 1983.

Stephen Peters, *What a Long, Strange Trip: The Stories behind Every Grateful Dead Song, 1965–1995*. New York: Thunder's Mouth Press, 1999.

Nancy Reist, "Counting Stars by Candlelight: An Analysis of the Mythic Appeal of the Grateful Dead," *Journal of Popular Culture* XXX (spring 1997), 183–209.

William Ruhlmann, *The History of the Grateful Dead*. London: Bison Books, 1990.

Steve Sutherland, "Grateful Dead: Bone Idols," *Melody Maker* (October 27, 1990), 50–51.

Robert G. Weiner (ed.), *Perspectives on the Grateful Dead: Critical Writings*. Westport, CT: Greenwood, 1999.

Al Green

Stanley Booth, "Psalms vs. Soul," *Musician*, no. 89 (March 1986), 30–33.

Stanley Booth, "Psalmist of Soul: Al Green," in *Rhythm Oil: A Journey through the Music of the American South*. New York: Pantheon Books, 1991, 150–8.

Bart Bull, "Amazing Grace," *Spin* III (June 1987), 62–66, 76.

Robert Christgau, "Al Green," in *The Rolling Stone Illustrated History of Rock and Roll* (rev. ed.), edited by Jim Miller. New York: Random House/Rolling Stone Press, 1980, 360–3.

Bill Dahl, "Al Green: The Hit Records Years," *Goldmine*, no. 476 (October 23, 1998), 120–8.

Al Green, with Davin Seay, *Take Me to the River*. New York: HarperCollins, 2000.

Geoffrey Himes, "Al Green: Sanctity and Sexuality on a Higher Plane," *Musician*, no. 54 (April 1983), 26–34, 110.

Brian Hogg, "Al Green," *Record Collector*, no. 51 (November 1983), 36–39.

Wayne Jancik, "Al Green: 'It's You I Want, but It's Him That I Need'," *Goldmine*, no. 184 (August 14, 1987), 108, 110.

Roger St. Pierre, "The Blues and Soul Hall of Fame: no. 14—Al Green," *Blues and Soul*, no. 582 (March 19—April 1, 1991), 26–28.

Alton B. Pollard III, "The Last Soul Singer in America: Al Green," *Journal of Black Sacred Music* III (fall 1989), 85–97.

Woody Guthrie

Woody Guthrie, *Bound for Glory*. New York: E. P. Dutton, 1968 (first published 1943).

Woody Guthrie (edited by Dave Marsh and Harold Leventhal), *Pastures of Plenty: A Self-Portrait*. New York: HarperCollins, 1990.

Joe Klein, *Woody Guthrie: A Life*. New York: Delta Books, 1999 (first published 1980).

Jim Longhi, *Woody, Cisco, and Me: Seamen Three in the Merchant Marine*. Urbana: University of Illinois Press, 1997.

Richard Reuss (comp.), *A Woody Guthrie Bibliography, 1912–1967*. New York: Guthrie Children's Trust Fund, 1968.

Ed Robbin, *Woody Guthrie and Me: An Intimate Reminiscence*. Berkeley, CA: Lancaster-Miller, 1979.

Robert Santelli and Emily Davidson (eds.), *Hard Travelin': The Life and Legacy of Woody Guthrie*. Hanover, NH: Wesleyan University Press/University Press of New England, 1999.

Bill Haley

Stuart Colman, "Bill Haley: Father of Rock 'n' Roll," in *They Kept on Rockin': The Giants of Rock 'n' Roll*. Poole, England: Blandford Press, 1982, 12–28.

Peter Doggett, "Bill Haley and the Comets," *Record Collector*, no. 139 (March 1991), 42–46.

Howard Elson, "Bill Haley," in *Early Rockers*. New York: Proteus Books, 1982, 52–59.

Colin Escott, "Bill Haley: Indisputably—The First," *Goldmine*, no. 280 (April 19, 1991), 12–18.

Rob Finnis, "The Haley Story," *The History of Rock*, no. 2 (1982), 24–28.

John W. Haley and John Von Hoelle. *Sound and Glory: The Incredible Story of Bill Haley, the Father of Rock and Roll, and the Music That Shook the World.* Wilmington, DE: Dyne-American, 1990.

Adrina Gilbert, "Rock around the Clock," *The History of Rock*, no. 2 (1982), 21–23.

Denise Gregoire, "Spotlight on Bill Haley," *Rockin' 50s*, no. 4 (February 1987), 8–15.

Spencer Leigh, "Bill Haley and His Comets," *Record Collector*, no. 176 (April 1994), 33–38.

John Swenson, *Bill Haley: The Daddy of Rock and Roll.* New York: Stein and Day, 1983.

Nick Tosches, "Young Bill Haley: The Lounge Act That Transcendeth All Knowing," in *Unsung Heroes of Rock 'n' Roll: The Birth of Rock in the Wild Years Before Elvis* (rev. ed.). New York: Harmony Books, 1991, 103–8.

George Harrison

Alan Clayson, *The Quiet One: A Life of George Harrison.* London: Sidgwick and Jackson, 1990.

Peter Doggett, "George Harrison's Solo Rarities," *Record Collector*, no. 32 (April 1982), 4–12.

Bill Flanagan, "George Harrison: The Dark Horse Candidate," *Musician*, no. 167 (September 1992), 40–48.

Geoffrey Giuliano, *Dark Horse: The Secret Life of George Harrison.* New York: E. P. Dutton, 1990.

Ross Michaels, *George Harrison: Yesterday and Today.* New York: Flash Books, 1977.

Walter Rimler, "George Harrison: Fall from Grace," in *Not Fade Away: A Comparison of Jazz Age with Rock-Era Pop Song Composers.* Ann Arbor, MI: Pierian Press, 1984, 157–61.

Mark Rowland, "The Quiet Wilbury," *Musician*, no. 137 (March 1990), 30–36, 97.

Dave Thompson, "The Music of George Harrison: An Album-by-Album Guide," *Goldmine*, no. 561 (January 25, 2002), 14–19.

Timothy White, "Far East Man: George Harrison and the Road to 'Live in Japan'—An In-Depth Interview," *Goldmine*, no. 322 (November 27, 1992), 12–20, 220.

Timothy White, "George Harrison Reconsidered," *Musician*, no. 109 (November 1987), 50–67.

Jimi Hendrix

Johnny Black, *Jimi Hendrix: The Ultimate Experience*. New York: Thunder's Mouth Press, 1999.

Tony Brown, *Jimi Hendrix: A Visual Documentary—His Life, Loves, and Music*. London: Omnibus Books, 1992.

Monika Dannemann, *The Inner World of Jimi Hendrix*. New York: St. Martin's Press, 1995.

Peter Doggett, "Jimi Hendrix," *Record Collector*, no. 50 (Oct. 1983), 12–16.

Gillian G. Gaar, "In from the Storm—Jimi Hendrix: His Legacy and the City of Seattle," *Goldmine*, no. 441 (June 20, 1997), 16–19, 50–56ff.

Caesar Glabbeek and Douglas J. Noble. *Jimi Hendrix: The Man, the Music, the Memorabilia*. New York: Thunder's Mouth Press, 1996.

Martin I. Green and Bill Sienkiewicz. *Voodoo Child: The Illustrated Legend of Jimi Hendrix*. New York: Penguin Studio, 1995.

David Henderson, *'Scuse Me while I Kiss the Sky: The Life of Jimi Hendrix*. London: Plexus Books, 1990.

Jerry Hopkins, *Hit and Run: The Jimi Hendrix Story*. New York: Perigee Books, 1983.

Scott Isler, " 'I Had All These Ideas and Sounds in my Brain': Jimi Hendrix in His Own Words," *Musician*, no. 157 (Nov. 1991), 32–46.

John McDermott, with Billy Cox and Eddie Kramer. *Jimi Hendrix Sessions: The Complete Studio Recording Sessions, 1963–1970*. Boston: Little, Brown, 1995.

Mitch Mitchell, with John Platt. *Jimi Hendrix: Inside the Experience*. New York: Harmony Books, 1990.

Charles Shaar Murray, *Crosstown Traffic: Jimi Hendrix and Post-War Pop*. London: Faber and Faber, 1989.

Mark Paytress, "Jimi Hendrix," *Record Collector*, no. 171 (November 1993), 62–67.

Noel Redding and Carol Apelleby. *Are You Experienced? The Inside Story of the Jimi Hendrix Experience*. London: Fourth Estate, 1990.

Harry Shapiro and Caesar Glenbeek. *Jimi Hendrix: Electric Gypsy*. New York: St. Martin's Press, 1990.

Dave Thompson, "Who Was Jimi Hendrix?" *Goldmine*, no. 448 (September 26, 1997), 32–56, 178.

Steve Waksman, "Black Sound, Black Body: Jimi Hendrix, the Electric Guitar, and the Meanings of Blackness," *Popular Music and Society* XXIII (spring 1999), 75–113.

Buddy Holly

Ellis Amburn, *Buddy Holly: A Biography*. New York: St. Martin's Press, 1995.

Richard Aquila, " 'Not Fade Away': Buddy Holly and the Making of an American Legend," *Journal of Popular Culture* XV (spring 1982), 75–80.

John Beecher, "The Buddy Holly Story," *The History of Rock*, no. 10 (1982), 184–9.

William J. Bush, "Buddy Holly: The Legend and Legacy," *Guitar Player* XVI (June 1982), 64–66, 74–108.

Alan Clark, *Buddy Holly (1936–1959)/The Crickets—Number One*. West Covina, CA: Alan Lungstrum/National Rock and Roll Archives, 1989.

B. Lee Cooper, "Buddy Holly," in *Rock Music in American Popular Culture: Rock 'n' Roll Resources* by B. Lee Cooper and Wayne S. Haney. New York: Haworth Press, 1995, 251–68.

B. Lee Cooper, "Review of *Rave On: The Biography of Buddy Holly* by Philip Norman," *Journal of Popular Culture* XXXIII, no. 4 (spring 2000), 156–7.

John Goldrosen and John Beecher. *Remembering Buddy: The Definitive Biography of Buddy Holly*. New York: Penguin Books, 1986.

Bill Griggs, " 'American Pie': Was It a Tribute to Buddy Holly? Was It a Protest Song?" *Rockin' 50s*, no. 20 (October 1989), 22–23.

Bill Griggs and Jim Black (comps.). *Buddy Holly: A Collector's Guide*. Shebygan, WI: Red Wax, 1983.

Bill Griggs, *The Words and Music of Buddy Holly: His Songs and Interviews*. Lubbock, TX: B. Griggs/Rockin' 50s Magazine, 1995.

Alan Mann, *The A–Z of Buddy Holly*. London: Aurum Press, 1996.

Phil Norman. *Rave On: The Biography of Buddy Holly*. New York: Simon & Schuster, 1996.

Richard Peters, *The Legend That Is Buddy Holly.* New York: Barnes and Noble Books, 1990.

John Tobler, *The Buddy Holly Story.* London: Plexus, 1979.

Michael Jackson

Christopher Anderson, *Michael Jackson Unauthorized.* New York: Simon & Schuster, 1994.

Mark Bego, *On the Road with Michael Jackson.* New York: Pinnacle Books, 1984.

Geoff Brown, *The Music of Michael Jackson and the Jackson Family.* London: Omnibus Press, 1996.

B. Lee Cooper, "Review of *Sequins and Shades: The Michael Jackson Reference Guide* by Carol D. Terry," *Michigan Academician* XXII (summer 1990), 303–4.

Nelson George and Mark Rowland, with additional material from Vic Garbarini. "Michael Jackson's Perfect Universe: The Education and Execution of Total Victory," *Musician*, no. 69 (July 1984), 44–56.

Todd Gold, *Michael Jackson: The Man in the Mirror.* London: Sidgwick and Jackson, 1989.

Michael Jackson, *Moonwalk.* Garden City, NY: Doubleday, 1988.

Richard Jackson,. "Michael Jackson," *Record Collector*, no. 99 (November 1987), 17–20.

Dave Marsh, *Trapped: Michael Jackson and the Crossover Dream.* New York: Bantam Books, 1985.

J. Randy Taraborrelli, *Michael Jackson: The Magic and the Madness.* New York: Birch Lane Press, 1991.

Carol D. Terry (comp.), *Sequins and Shades: The Michael Jackson Reference Guide.* Ann Arbor, MI: Pierian Press, 1987.

Waylon Jennings

Bob Allen, *Waylon and Willie.* New York: Quick Fox, 1979.

Montgomery Blaine, "Waylon Jennings: The Wolf Has Survived," *Song Hits*, no. 248 (October 1986), 48–49.

Patrick Carr, "Waylon Jennings: 'I Couldn't Go Pop with a Mouthful of Firecrackers'," *Country Music* I (April 1973), 42–46.

Noel Coppage, "Crossing Over with Waylon Jennings," *Stereo Review* XXXVII (October 1976), 104–6.

Albert Cunniff, *Waylon Jennings*. New York: Zebra Books, 1985.

R. Serge Denisoff, *Waylon: A Biography*. Knoxville: University of Tennessee Press, 1983.

R. Serge Denisoff, "Waylon Jennings 'The Last Tour': A New Journalism Approach," *Journal of Popular Culture*, 13 (spring 1980), 663–71.

Rush Evans, "Outlaw Music His Way: Remembering Waylon Jennings," *DIS-Coveries*, no. 167 (April 2002), 44–45.

Bob Garbutt, "Waylon Jennings: The Road to Nashville," *Goldmine*, no. 43 (December 1979), 20–22.

Peter Guralnick, "Waylon Jennings: The Pleasures of Life in a Hillbilly Band," in *Lost Highway: Journeys and Arrivals of American Musicians*. Boston: David R. Godine, 1979, 204–16.

John L. Smith, *Waylon Jennings: Recording History and Complete Discography, 1959–1972*. Des Moines, IA: J. L. Smith, 1972.

John L. Smith, " 'I Ain't No Ordinary Dude'—A Bio-Discography of Waylon Jennings," *Journal of Country Music* VI (summer 1975), 45–95.

Billy Joel

Christopher Connelly, "Billy Joel: Not as Bad as You Think," *Rolling Stone*, no. 381 (October 28, 1982), 28–30, 77.

Anthony DeCurtis, "Billy Joel," in *The Rolling Stone Interviews: The 1980s*, edited by Sid Holt. New York: St. Martin's Press/Rolling Stone Press, 1989, 221–8.

Peter Gambaccini, *Billy Joel: A Personal File*. New York: Quick Fox, 1979.

Debbie Geller and Tom Hibbert. *Billy Joel: An Illustrated Biography*. London: Virgin Books, 1985.

Stephen Holden, "Billy Joel's Brutally Frank, Aurally Ambitious Pop Masterpiece," *Rolling Stone*, no. 380 (October 14, 1982), 71–72.

Mark Lewisohn, "Billy Joel," *Record Collector*, no. 70 (June 1985), 13–16.

Dave Marsh, "Billy Joel: The Miracle of 52nd Street," *Rolling Stone*, no. 280 (December 14, 1978), 70–74.

Michael McKenzie, *Billy Joel*. New York: Ballentine Books, 1984.

Peter Reilly, "Billy Joel's 'Glass Houses': Beyond Category," *Stereo Review*, 44 (June 1980), 75–76.

William Ruhlmann, "Billy Joel: Keeping the Faith," *Goldmine*, no. 351 (January 7, 1994), 16–30, 38–52.

David Sheff and Victoria Sheff, "Playboy Interview: Billy Joel," *Playboy* XXIX (May 1982), 71–96.

Jeff Tamarkin, *Billy Joel: From Hicksville to Hitsville*. Port Chester, NY: Cherry Lane Books, 1984.

Timothy White, "Billy Joel," *Musician*, no. 50 (December 1982), 58–70.

Timothy White, "Billy Joel Is Angry," *Rolling Stone*, no. 325 (September 4, 1980), 37–40.

Elton John

Alan Aldridge and Mike Dempsey (eds.). *Bernie Taupin—The One Who Writes the Words for Elton John: Complete Lyrics from 1968 to Goodbye, Yellow Brick Road*. New York: Knopf, 1976.

Claude Bernardin and Tom Stanton. *Rocket Man: Elton John From A–Z*. Westport, CT: Praeger, 1996 (first published 1995).

Rick Carr, "Elton John," *DISCoveries* V (May 1992), 22–28.

Chris Charlesworth, *Elton John—Only the Piano Player: The Illustrated Elton John Story*. New York: Omnibus Press 1984.

Robert Christgau, "Elton John," in *The Rolling Stone Illustrated History of Rock and Roll* (rev. ed.), edited by Anthony DeCurtis and James Henke, with Holly George-Warren. New York: Random House/Rolling Stone Press, 1992, 526–31.

Susan Crimp and Patricia Burstein. *The Many Lives of Elton John*. New York: Birch Lane Press/Carol, 1992.

John DiStefano, *The Complete Elton John Discography*. New Baltimore, MI: East End Lights, 1993.

Peter Doggett, "Elton John," *Record Collector*, no. 37 (September 1982), 26–36.

Alan Finch (comp.), *Elton John: The Illustrated Discography*. London: Omnibus Press, 1981.

Paul Gambaccini, *A Conversation with Elton John and Bernie Taupin*. New York: Flash Books, 1975.

Andy Peebles, *The Elton John Tapes*. New York: St. Martin's Press, 1981.

Philip Norman, *Elton John: The Biography*. New York: Harmony Books, 1991.

"Playboy Interview: Elton John," *Playboy* XXIII (January 1976), 57–70.

William Ruhlmann, "Elton John: The Story of a Cat Named Hercules," *Goldmine*, no. 213 (September 23, 1988), 5–14, 20–21.

Robert Johnson

Stanley Booth, "Standing at the Crossroads," in *Rythm Oil: A Journey through the Music of the American South*. New York: Pantheon Books, 1991, 4–12.

Samuel Charters, *Robert Johnson*. New York: Oak, 1973.

Samuel Charters, "Robert Johnson: A New Consideration,." *Goldmine*, no. 276 (February 22, 1991), 30, 32, 34.

Charles Ford, "Robert Johnson's Rhythm," *Popular Music* XVII (January 1998), 71–93.

Alan Greenberg, *Love in Vain: A Vision of Robert Johnson*. New York: Da Capo Press, 1994 (first published 1983).

Stefan Grossman and Woody Mann, *Roots of Robert Johnson*. Pacific, MT: Mel Bay, 1993.

Peter Guralnick, *Searching for Robert Johnson: The Life and Legend of the 'King of the Delta Singers'*. New York: Dutton/Obelisk, 1989.

Cub Koda, "Robert Johnson: Last Fair Deal Gone Down," *Goldmine*, no. 276 (February 22, 1991), 36, 38, 40.

Peter Lee, "The Death of Robert Johnson," *Guitar Player* XXV (July 1991), 72–76, 142.

Bob Naylor, "Forefathers of Rock—no. 1: Robert Johnson," *Now Dig This*, no. 45 (December 1986), 26–27.

William Ruhlmann, "Talking to Peter Guralnick about *Searching for Robert Johnson*," *Goldmine*, no. 276 (February 22, 1991), 42, 44,46, 120.

Tony Sherman, "The Hellhound's Trail: Following Robert Johnson," *Musician*, no. 147 (January 1991), 31–53.

John D. Wells, "Me and the Devil Blues: A Study of Robert Johnson and the Music of the Rolling Stones," *Popular Music and Society* IX (1983), 17–24.

Lance A. Williams, "Sleuthing the Robert Johnson Mystique," *Blues Revue*, no. 41 (October 1998), 60–61.

Al Young, "Robert Johnson: Towards a Robert Leroy Johnson Memorial Museum," in *Bluesland: Portraits of Twelve Major American Blues Masters*, edited by Pete Welding and Toby Byron. New York: Dutton/Penguin Books, 1991, 68–97.

Janis Joplin

Gary Carey, *Lenny, Janis and Jimi*. New York: Pocket Books, 1975.

Peggy Caserta, *Going Down with Janis*. New York: Dell, 1973.

David Dalton, *Piece of My Heart: A Portrait of Janis Joplin*. New York: Da Capo Press, 1991.

Eric Eberwein, "Big Brother and the Holding Company: An Updated Legacy," *Goldmine*, no. 130 (July 19, 1985), 8, 18.

David Emblidge, "I Feel, Therefore I Am: The Blues-Rock of Janis Joplin," *Southwest Review* LXI (1976), 341–53.

Myra Friedman, *Buried Alive: The Biography of Janis Joplin*. London: Plexus Books, 1984 (first published 1974).

Brian Hogg, "Janis Joplin and Big Brother," *Record Collector*, no. 88 (December 1986), 22–26.

Jon E. Johnson, "Musical Heritage Exhibit Kicks Off with 'Kozmic' Event—Port Arthur Honors Janis Joplin," *DISCoveries*, I (May/June 1988), 14–18.

Deborah Landau, *Janis Joplin: Her Life and Times*. New York: Paperback Library, 1971

Michael Lydon, "Janis Joplin," in *Rock Folk: Portraits from the Rock 'n' Roll Pantheon*. New York: Dial Press, 1971, 85–105.

Steve Roeser, "Do What You Love: The Continuing Story of Big Brother and the Holding Company," *Goldmine*, no. 474 (September 25, 1998), 16–20, 32–54, 106.

Jeff Tamarkin, "Big Brother and the Holding Company: An Interview with David Getz," *R.P.M.*, no. 9 (March 1985), 16–22.

Jeff Tamarkin, "Four Gentlemen . . . and Some Great, Great Broads: Sam Andrew Talks About the Ongoing Legacy of Big Brother and the Holding Company," *DISCoveries*, no. 122 (July 1998), 40–45.

Jeff Tamarkin, "Janis Joplin: Before Big Brother—An Ugly Duckling in Texas," *Goldmine*, no. 173 (March 13, 1987), 24, 102.

Allan Vorda, "Big Brother and the Holding Company," *DISCoveries* III (October 1990), 28–33

Ellen Willis, "Janis Joplin," in *The Rolling Stone Illustrated History of Rock and Roll* (revised ed.), edited by Jim Miller. New York: Random House/Rolling Stone Press, 1980, 275–9.

B. B. King

Stanley Booth, "Blues Boy," in *Rythm Oil: A Journey through the Music of the American South*. New York: Pantheon Books, 1991, 89–105.

B. Lee Cooper, "Review of *The B. B. King Companion: Five Decades of Commentary* by Richard Kostelanetz," *Popular Music and Society* XXIV (summer 2000), 156–7.

B. Lee Cooper, "Review of *'Blues Boy': The Life and Music of B. B. King* by Sebastian Danchin," *Popular Music and Society* XXIV (summer 2000), 166–8.

Sebastian Danchin, *'Blues Boy': The Life and Music of B. B. King*. Jackson: University Press of Mississippi, 1998.

Colin Escott, "An Appreciation of B. B. King: The Fortunate Son," *Goldmine*, no. 359 (April 29, 1994), 14–22.

Peter Gurlanick, "B. B. King," in *Rolling Stone Illustrated History of Rock and Roll* (2d ed.), edited by Anthony DeCurtis and James Henke, with Holly George Warren. New York: Random House/Rolling Stone Press, 1992, 339–42.

Charles Keil, "B. B. King Backstage," in *Urban Blues*. Chicago: University of Chicago Press, 1966, 96–113.

B. B. King, with David Ritz, *Blues All around Me: The Autobiography of B. B. King*. New York: Spike/Avon Books, 1999 (first published 1996).

Richard Kostelanetz (ed.), *The B. B. King Companion: Five Decades of Commentary*. New York: Schirmer Books, 1997.

Michael Lydon, "B. B. King," in *Rock Folk: Portraits from the Rock 'n' Roll Pantheon*. New York: Dial Press, 1971, 46–67.

Jerry Richardson and Rob Bowman, "Conversation with B. B. King: 'King of the Blues'," *The Black Perspective in Music* XVII (1989), 135–52.

Charles Sawyer, *The Arrival of B. B. King: The Authorized Biography*. Garden City, NY: Doubleday, 1980.

Steve Scott, "B. B. King," *Record Collector*, no. 52 (December 1983), 18–21.

David Shirley, *Every Day I Sing the Blues: The Story of B. B. King.* Danbury, CT: Franklin Watts, 1995.

Harold Steinblatt, "Blues Is King" *Guitar World* XII (July 1991), 42–48, 118.

Pete Welding, "B. B. King: From Beale Street to the World," in *Bluesland: Portraits of Twelve Major American Blues Masters,* edited by Pete Welding and Toby Byron. New York: Dutton/Penguin Books, 1991, 176–203.

Freddie King

Chris Beachley, "Takin' Care of Business with . . . Freddie King," *It Will Stand,* nos. 27/28 (1982), 32–33.

Dave 'Daddy Cool' Booth and Colin Escott, "Freddie King: A Profile," *Goldmine,* no. 102 (June 22, 1984), 6–14.

B. Lee Cooper, "Review of *The Best of Freddie King: The Shelter Records Years,*" *Rock and Blues News,* no. 15 (April-May 2001), 42.

"Freddie King: A Growing Legend," *Soul* VII (July 3, 1972), 10.

"He Bridges the Gap between Rock, Blues," *Soul* VIII (September 3, 1973), 11.

Wayne Jancik, "Freddie King: Texas 'Ghetto Blues' Giant," *Goldmine,* no. 173 (March 13, 1987), 26.

M. Jones, "Don't Mess with Freddie," *Melody Maker* XLVI (December 18, 1971), 40.

Mike Leadbitter, "Freddie King," *Blues,* no. 69 (January 1970), 5.

Tim Schuller and Bruce Iglauer, "Freddie King, 1934–1976," *Living Blues,* no. 31 (March/April 1977), 7–11.

Tim Schuller, Bruce Iglauer, Hans Schweitz, and Janne Rosenqvist, "Freddie King," in *The Voice of the Blues,* edited by Jim O'Neal and Amy van Singel. New York: Routledge, 2002, 358–87.

Led Zeppelin

Joe Bosso, "Glory Days," *Guitar World* XII (January 1991), 52–62, 68–81.

J. D. Considine, "In through the Out Door: Jimmy Page and Robert Plant Conquer the World . . . Again," *Musician,* no. 194 (December 1994), 56–68, 101.

Charles Cross and Erik Flannigan, *Led Zeppelin: Heaven and Hell.* New York: Crown, 1991.

Stephen Davis, *Hammer of the Gods: The Led Zeppelin Saga*. New York: Ballantine Books, 1985.

Joe Gore and Andrew Goodwin, "Your Time Is Gonna Come: Talking about Led Zeppelin," *OneTwoThreeFour*, no. 4 (winter 1987), 4–11.

Dave Lewis, "The Essential Led Zeppelin," *Record Collector*, no. 177 (May 1994), 20–28.

Dave Lewis, "Led Zeppelin," *Record Collector*, no. 97 (September 1987), 28–33.

Dave Lewis, *Led Zeppelin: A Celebration*. London: Omnibus Press, 1991.

Jim Miller, "Led Zeppelin," in *Rolling Stone Illustrated History of Rock and Roll* (2d ed.), edited by Anthony DeCurtis and James Henke, with Holly George-Warren. New York: Random House/Rolling Stone Press, 1992, 455–8.

Howard Mylett, *Led Zeppelin: From the Archives*. Portslade, England: Howard Mylett, 1993.

Charles M. Young, "Jimmy Page's True Will," *Musician*, no. 117 (July 1988), 74–84.

Charles M. Young, "Zeppelin to Zen: Robert Plant Digs through His Past to Uncover His Future," *Musician*, no. 113 (March 1988), 76–88, 105–6.

Brenda Lee

"Brenda Lee," *The Golden Age*, no. 11 (August 1987), 7–35.

Lee Cotten, "The Brenda Lee Interview," *Rock and Blues News*, no. 11 (August/September 2000), 4–7.

Lee Cotten, "The Brenda Lee Interview—Part Two," *Rock and Blues News*, no. 12 (October/November 2000), 21–24.

Peter Doggett, "Brenda Lee," *Record Collector*, no. 157 (September 1992), 84.

Bob Garbutt, "Brenda Lee," *Goldmine*, no. 47 (April 1980), 9–11.

Bob Garbutt, "Brenda Lee: The Early Years," *New Kommotion*, no. 18 (winter 1978), 31.

Martin Hawkins, "Little Miss Dynamite," *The History of Rock*, no. 16 (1982), 318–20.

Hill, Randal C. "Brenda Lee: Sweet Somethin's," *Goldmine*, no. 185 (Aug. 28, 1987), 36, 78.

Peter Jones, "The Brenda Lee Story," *Record Collector*, no. 23 (July 1981), 13–18.

Brenda Lee, with Robert K. Oermann and Julie Clay. *Little Miss Dynamite: The Life and Times of Brenda Lee*. New York: Hyperion Books, 2002.

Alanna Nash, "Brenda Lee," in *Behind Closed Doors: Talking with the Legends of Country Music*. New York: Knopf, 1988, 264–89.

Jim Newcombe, "Little Miss Dynamite," *Now Dig This*, no. 52 (July 1987), 24–25.

Roger Nunn, "Little Miss Dynamite," *Now Dig This*, no. 114 (September 1992), 17–21.

Bruce Pollock, "Brenda Lee," in *When Rock was Young: A Nostalgic Review of the Top 40 Era*. New York: Holt, Rinehart, and Winston, 1981, 159–71.

John Smith III, "Spotlight on Brenda Lee," *Rockin' 50s*, no. 5 (April 1987), 9–17.

Sue Van Hecke, "Brenda Lee: Little Miss Dynamite," *Goldmine*, no. 408 (March 15, 1996), 26–56, 203.

Jerry Leiber and Mike Stoller

Dave "Daddy Cool" Booth and Colin Escott, "Jerry Leiber and Mike Stoller: What Is the Secret of Your Success?" *Goldmine*, no. 111 (October 26, 1984), 14–30.

B. Lee Cooper, "Review of *Smokey Joe's Café: The Songs of Leiber and Stoller* and *There's a Riot Goin' on: The Rock 'n' Roll Classics of Leiber and Stoller*." *Popular Music and Society* XXI (winter 1997), 128–31.

Peter Doggett, "Leiber and Stoller: The Great Producers," *Record Collector*, no. 59 (July 1984), 30–36.

Ted Fox, "Leiber and Stoller," in *In the Groove: The Men behind the Music*. New York: St. Martin's Press, 1986, 156–86.

David Fricke, "Leiber and Stoller," *Rolling Stone*, no. 576 (April 19, 1990), 97–100.

Peter Guralnick, "Leiber and Stoller: White Songs for Black Groups," *The History of Rock*, no. 15 (1982), 286–9.

Peter Guralnick, "Some Cats Know: Words and Music by Leiber and Stoller," *Goldmine*, no. 63 (August 1981), 138–9.

Harvey R. Kubernik, "A Yakety Yak with Leiber and Stoller," *Goldmine*, no. 385 (April 28, 1995), 60–67, 124.

Robert Palmer (comp.), *Baby, That Was Rock and Roll: The Legendary Leiber and Stoller*. New York: Harcourt Brace Jovanovich, 1978.

Joe Smith (edited by Mitchell Fink), "Jerry Leiber and Mike Stoller," in *Off the Record: An Oral History of Popular Music*. New York: Warner Books, 1988, 120–4.

John Tobler and Stuart Grundy, "Leiber and Stoller," in *The Record Producers*. New York: St. Martin's Press, 1982, 10–23.

Stuart Winkles, "Leiber and Stoller: The Elvis Connection," *Goldmine*, no. 184 (August 14, 1987), 32, 111.

Chris Woodford, "The Songs of Leiber and Stoller," *Now Dig This*, no. 53 (August 1987), 12–13.

John Lennon

Richard Aquila, "Why We Cried: John Lennon and American Culture," *Popular Music and Society* X, no. 1 (1985), 33–42.

Ray Coleman, *John Winston Lennon—Volume One, 1940–1966*. London: Sidgwick and Jackson, 1984.

Ray Coleman, *John Ono Lennon—Volume Two, 1967–1980*. London: Sidgwick and Jackson, 1984.

Todd Compton, "McCartney or Lennon? Beatle Myths and the Composing of the Lennon-McCartney Songs," *Journal of Popular Culture* XXII (fall 1988), 99–131.

Peter Doggett, "John Lennon," *Record Collector*, no. 134 (October 1990), 3–6.

Paul Du Noyer, *We All Shine On: The Stories behind Every John Lennon Song, 1970–1980*. New York: Carlton Books/HarperCollins, 1997.

Vic Garbarini and Brian Cullman, with Barbara Graustark, *Strawberry Fields Forever: John Lennon Remembered*. New York: Bantam Books, 1980.

Albert Goldman, *The Lives of John Lennon*. New York: William Morrow, 1988.

Geoffrey Giuliano, *Lennon in America, 1971–1980: Based in Part on the Lost Lennon Diaries*. New York: Cooper Square Press/Rowman and Littlefield, 2000.

Geoffrey Giuliano, *Two of Us: John Lennon and Paul McCartney behind the Myth*. New York: Penguin Books, 1999.

John Green, *Dakota Days: The Untold Story of John Lennon's Final Years*. New York: St. Martin's Press, 1983.

Wayne Hampton, *Guerrilla Minstrels: John Lennon, Joe Hill, Woody Guthrie, and Bob Dylan*. Knoxville: University of Tennessee Press, 1986.

Bill Harry, *The Book of Lennon*. New York: Delilah Books, 1984.

Kevin Howlett and Mark Lewisohn, *In My Life: John Lennon Remembered*. London: British Broadcasting Corporation Books, 1990.

Philip Norman, *Days in the Life: John Lennon Remembered*. London: Century Books, 1990.

Jim O'Donnell, *The Day John Met Paul: An Hour-by-Hour Account of How the Beatles Began*. New York: Penguin Books, 1996.

John Robertson, *The Art and Music of John Lennon*. London: Omnibus Press, 1990.

James Sauceda, *The Literary Lennon: A Comedy of Letters—The First Study of All the Major and Minor Writings of John Lennon*. Ann Arbor, MI: Pierian Press, 1984.

David Sheff and G. Barry Golson, "John Lennon: His Final Words on the Beatles' Music," *Playboy* XXVIII (April 1981), 179–99.

John Wenner (ED.), *Lennon Remembers: The Rolling Stone Interview*. San Francisco: Straight Arrow Books, 1971.

Jon Wiener, *Come Together: John Lennon in His Time*. New York: Random House, 1984.

Jerry Lee Lewis

Robert Cain, *Whole Lotta Shakin' Goin' On: Jerry Lee Lewis—The Rock Years, The Country Years, the Triumphs, and the Tragedies*. New York: Dial Press, 1981.

Alan Clark, *Jerry Lee Lewis: The Ball of Fire*. West Covina, CA: Alan Clark Productions, 1980.

B. Lee Cooper, "My Vote's on Jerry Lee . . . ," *Rock and Blues News*, no. 3 (April-May, 1999), 35–37

B. Lee Cooper and James A. Creeth, "Present at the Creation: The Legend of Jerry Lee Lewis on Record, 1956–1963," *Fire-Ball Mail* XXII, no. 6 (May/June 1984), 9–12.

Colin Escott, *Jerry Lee Lewis: The Killer, 1963–1968*. Bremen, Germany: Bear Family Records, 1986.

Colin Escott, *Jerry Lee Lewis: The Killer, 1969–1972*. Bremen, Germany: Bear Family Records, 1986.

Colin Escott, *Jerry Lee Lewis: The Killer, 1973–1977*. Bremen, Germany: Bear Family Records, 1987.

Jimmy Guterman, *Rockin' My Life Away: Listening to Jerry Lee Lewis*. Nashville, TN: Rutledge Hill Press, 1991.

Jerry Lee Lewis and Charles White, *Killer!* London: Century Books, 1993.

Linda Gail Lewis, with Les Pendleton, *The Devil, Me, and Jerry Lee*. Atlanta, GA: Longstreet Press, 1998.

Myra Lewis, with Murray Silver, *Great Balls of Fire! The Uncensored Story of Jerry Lee Lewis*. New York: St. Martin's Press, 1989.

Robert Palmer, *Jerry Lee Lewis Rocks!* New York: Delilah Books, 1981.

Nick Tosches, *Hellfire: The Jerry Lee Lewis Story*. New York: Dell, 1982.

Little Richard

Pete Bowen, "Little Richard—The Specialty Years," *Now Dig This*, no. 80 (November 1989), 4–8.

Stuart Colman, "Little Richard: Back to the Church," in *They Kept on Rockin': The Giants of Rock 'n' Roll*. Poole, Dorset, England: Blandford Press, 1982, 128–131.

B. Lee Cooper, "Review of *The Life and Times of Little Richard: The Quasar of Rock*" by Charles White, *R.P.M.*, no. 10 (July/August 1985), 56–57.

B. Lee Cooper, "Rock 'n' Roll Royalty: Jerry Lee Lewis and Little Richard," *Rock and Blues News*, no. 13 (December 2000-January 2001), 27–28.

Peter Doggett, "Little Richard," *Record Collector*, no. 25 (September 1981), 20–25.

Peter Doggett, "Little Richard," *Record Collector*, no. 69 (May 1985), 32–36.

Howard Elson, "Little Richard," in *Early Rockers*. New York: Proteus Books, 1982, 90–99.

W. T. Lhamon, Jr., "Little Richard as a Folk Performer," *Studies in Popular Culture* VIII, no. 2 (1985), 7–17.

Tony Watson, "Little Richard's Specialty Sessions," *Blues and Rhythm*, no. 50 (March 1990), 24–26.

Michael Watts, "His Majesty," *The History of Rock*, no. 8 (1982), 148–52.

Charles White, *The Life and Times of Little Richard: The Quasar of Rock*. New York: Da Capo Press, 1994.

Langdon Winner, "Little Richard," in *Rolling Stone Illustrated History of Rock and Roll* (2d ed.), edited by Anthony DeCurtis and James Henke, with Holly George-Warren. New York: Random House/Rolling Stone Press, 1992, 52–29.

Madonna

Bruce Baron, "Deca-Dance: Madonna's Sire/Warner Brothers Career, 1982–1992," *Goldmine*, no. 313 (July 24, 1992), 12–30.

Barbara Bradby, "Freedom, Feeling, and Dancing—Madonna's Songs Traverse Girls' Talk: Madonna—The Apparition and the Text," *OneTwoThreeFour*, no. 9 (Autumn 1990), 35–52.

Editors of Rolling Stone, *Madonna—The Rolling Stone Files: The Ultimate Compendium of Interviews, Articles, Facts, and Opinions from the Files of Rolling Stone*. New York: Hyperion Books, 1997.

Allan Metz and Carol Benson (eds.), *The Madonna Companion: Two Decades of Commentary*. New York: Schirmer Books, 1999.

Andrew Morton, *Madonna*. New York: St. Martin's Press, 2001.

Cathy Schwichtenberg (ed.), *The Madonna Connection: Representational Politics, Subcultural Identities, and Cultural Theory*. Boulder, CO: Westview Press, 1993.

J. Randy Taraborrelli, *Madonna: An Intimate Biography*. New York: Simon & Schuster, 2001.

Carol Vernallis, "The Aesthetics of Music Video: An Analysis of Madonna's 'Cherish'," *Popular Music* XVII (May 1998), 153–85.

Bob Marley

Adrian Boot and Chris Salewicz (eds.), *Bob Marley: Songs of Freedom*. New York: Viking Studio Books, 1995.

Laurence Cane-Honeysett, "Bob Marley," *Record Collector*, no. 141 (May 1991), 28–33.

Stephen Davis, *Bob Marley: The Biography*. London: Barker Press, 1983.

Peter Doggett, "Bob Marley," *Record Collector*, no. 38 (October 1982), 49–55.

Stephen King and Richard J. Jensen, "Bob Marley's 'Redemption Song': The Rhetoric of Reggae and Rastafari," *Journal of Popular Culture* XXIX (winter 1995), 17–36.

Observer Station, *Bob Marley: The Illustrated Disco/Biography*. New York: Omnibus Books, 1985.

Dave Thompson, "Bob Marley and the Wailers," *Goldmine*, no. 547 (July 13, 2001), 14–19.

Garth White, *The Development of Jamaican Popular Music, with Special Reference to the Music of Bob Marley: A Bibliography*. Kingston, Jamaica: African-Caribbean Institute of Jamaica, 1982.

Timothy White, "Bob Marley: The King of Reggae Finds His Zion, 1945–1981," *Rolling Stone*, no. 346 (June 25, 1981), 25–27, 86.

Timothy White, *Catch a Fire: The Life of Bob Marley* (rev. ed.). New York: Henry Holt, 1989.

Timothy White, "Days of Dying," *Musician*, no. 132 (October 1989), 30–39, 114.

Timothy White, "The Legend and Legacy of Bob Marley and the Wailers," *Goldmine*, no. 247 (January 12, 1990), 8–22.

Malika Lee Whitney and Dermott Hussey, *Bob Marley: Reggae King of the World*. New York: E. P. Dutton, 1984.

Curtis Mayfield

Michael Alexander, "The Impressions," in *Side-Saddle on the Golden Calf: Social Structure and Popular Culture in America*, edited by George H. Lewis. Pacific Palisades, CA: Goodyear, 1972, 191–6.

B. Lee Cooper, "Review of *Curtis Mayfield and the Impressions: The Anthology, 1961–1977*," *Popular Music and Society* XVII (fall 1993), 112.

Peter Doggett, "Curtis Mayfield," *Record Collector*, no. 95 (July 1987), 29–32.

Peter Doggett, "The Impressions," *Record Collector*, no. 32 (April 1982), 14–22.

Bill Flanagan, "Black History: Speech Meets Curtis Mayfield," *Musician*, no. 176 (June 1993), 60–67.

Michael A. Gonzales, "The Legend of Soul: Long Live Curtis Mayfield!" in *Soul: Black Power, Politics, and Pleasure*, edited by Monique Guillory and Richard C. Green. New York: New York University Press, 1998, 227–35.

Chuck Phillips and Andy Widders-Ellis, "Curtis Mayfield: The Soul of an R & B Genius," *Guitar Player* XXV (August 1991), 52–61, 62.

Steve Propes, "Curtis Mayfield: The August 12th Interview," *Goldmine*, no. 274 (January 25, 1991), 24, 28, 30, 127.

Robert Pruter, "Curtis Mayfield and the Impressions: We're a Winner," *Goldmine*, no. 331 (April 2, 1993), 12–20, 172.

Jeff Tamarkin, "Curtis Mayfield and Jerry Butler Talk about the Impressions," *Goldmine*, no. 85 (June 1983), 30–36.

Jeff Tamarkin, "Curtis Mayfield, 1942–1999," *DISCoveries*, no. 141 (February 2000), 16, 18.

Craig Werner, "A Deeper Shade of Soul," *Goldmine*, no. 442 (July 4, 1997), 16–19, 40–56, 129

Cliff White, "Jerry Butler, Curtis Mayfield, and the Impressions," *Time Barrier Express*, no. 23 (July—August 1977), 28–32.

Paul McCartney

B. Lee Cooper, "Review of *Paul McCartney: From Liverpool to Let It Be* by Howard A. Dewitt," *Blue Suede News*, no. 22 (spring 1993), 14–15.

Howard A. DeWitt, *Paul McCartney: From Liverpool to Let It Be*. Fremont, CA: Horizon Books, 1992.

Peter Doggett, "Paul McCartney's Solo Rarities," *Record Collector*, no. 19 (March 1981), 20–27.

Howard Elson, *McCartney: Songwriter*. London: W. H. Allen, 1986.

Chet Flippo, *Yesterday: The Biography of a Beatle*. Garden City, NY: Doubleday, 1988.

Geoffrey Giuliano, *Blackbird: The Life and Times of Paul McCartney*. London: Smith Gryphon, 1991.

Spencer Leigh, "Paul McCartney and Wings," *Record Collector*, no. 162 (February 1993), 14–25.

Paul McCartney (edited by Adrian Mitchell), *Blackbird Singing: Poems and Lyrics, 1965–1999*. New York: W. W. Norton, 2001.

John Mendelsohn, *Paul McCartney: A Biography in Words and Pictures*. New York: Sire Books/Chappell Music, 1977.

Barry Miles, *Paul McCartney: Many Years from Now*. New York: Henry Holt, 1997.

Jim O'Donnell, *The Day John Met Paul: An Hour-by-Hour Account of How the Beatles Began*. New York: Penguin Books, 1996.

Dennis Polkow, "Paul McCartney Returns to Liverpool," *Musician*, no. 155 (September 1991), 54–64.

Dennis Polkow, "McCartney Settles the Score," *Musician*, no. 156 (October 1991), 56–67.

Walter Rimler, "Paul McCartney: Keeper of the Flame," in *Not Fade Away: A Comparison of Jazz Age with Rock-Era Pop Song Composers*. Ann Arbor, MI: Pierian Press, 1984, 143–53.

Chris Salewicz, *McCartney: The Biography*. New York: St. Martin's Press, 1986.

Dave Thompson, "Paul and Linda McCartney and Wings—First Flights," *DISCoveries*, no. 99 (August 1996), 24–30.

Mark Wallgren, "The Paul McCartney Collection: Hot Hits or Cold Cuts?" *Goldmine*, no. 347 (November 12, 1993), 62–80, 221

Chris Welch, *Paul McCartney: The Definitive Biography*. New York: Proteus Books, 1984.

Clyde McPhatter

Tony Allan and Faye Treadwell. "Drifting Away: The Tragedy of Clyde McPhatter," *DISCoveries*, no. 66 (November 1993), 39–41.

Tony Allan, with Faye Treadwell. *Save the Last Dance for Me: The Musical Legacy of the Drifters, 1953–1993*. Ann Arbor, MI: Popular Culture, Ink., 1993.

"Clyde McPhatter Atlantic Discography," *Big Beat of the 50's*, no. 27 (May 1981), 23–25.

B. Lee Cooper, "Review of *Clyde McPhatter: A Biographical Essay* by Colin Escott," *Popular Music and Society* XIII, no. 2 (summer 1989), 113–15.

Lee Cotten, "Clyde McPhatter and the Drifters," in *Shake, Rattle, and Roll—The Golden Age of American Rock 'n' Roll: Volume One, 1952–1955*. Ann Arbor, MI: Pierian Press, 1989, 133–4.

Peter Doggett, "Clyde McPhatter," *Record Collector*, no. 102 (February 1988), 54–55.

Colin Escott, *Clyde McPhatter: A Biographical Essay*. Vollersode, Germany: Bear Family Books, 1987.

Bob Garbutt, "Clyde McPhatter: The Forgotten Hero," *Goldmine*, no. 85 (June 1983), 22–28.

Bill Millar, "Clyde McPhatter," *The History of Rock*, no. 4 (1982), 74–75.

Pete Nickols, "Clyde McPhatter," *Record Collector*, no. 76 (December 1985), 25–28.

Bruce Sylvester, "Clyde McPhatter: Doo-Wop's Most Thrilling Voice," *Goldmine*, no. 488 (April 9, 1999), 28–34.

Nick Tosches, "Liner Notes for *Clyde McPhatter: Deep Sea Ball* (Atlantic CD 7–82314–2)." New York: Atlantic Recording, 1991.

Richard Weize (comp.), "A Preliminary Clyde McPhatter Discography," in *Clyde McPhatter: A Biographical Essay*, by Colin Escott. Vollersode, West Germany: Bear Family Books, 1987, 80–100.

John Cougar Mellencamp

Bob Guccione, Jr., "Man on Fire," *Spin* III (September 1987), 32–39, 71.

David Harshfield, *Manchild for Real: The Life and Lyrics of John Cougar Mellencamp*. New York: Vantage Books, 1986.

Ellie M. Hisama, "Postcolonialism on the Make: The Music of John Mellencamp, David Bowie, and John Zorn," *Popular Music* XII (May 1993), 91–104.

Tim Homes, *John Cougar Mellencamp*. New York: Ballentine Books, 1986.

Randal C. Hill, "John Cougar Mellencamp: R.O.C.K.I.N.' in the U.S.A.," *Goldmine*, no. 192 (December 4, 1987), 10–12.

J. Kordosh, "John Cougar and the Fooling of America," *Creem* XIV (September 1982), 36–38.

Jim Miller, "One from the Heartland," *Newsweek* 107 (January 6, 1986), 62–63.

Steve Perry, "John Mellencamp's Brutal Honesty," *Musician*, no. 130 (August 1989), 32–42.

Mark Rowland, "John Cougar Mellencamp Comes of Age (sort of)," *Musician*, no. 84 (October 1985), 40–48.

Mark Rowland, "John Cougar: The Complicated Rock Brat," *Musician*, no. 52 (February 1983), 20–34.

Martin Torgoff, *American Fool: The Roots and Improbable Rise of John Cougar Mellencamp*. New York: St. Martin's Press, 1986.

Martin Torgoff and Skeeter Hagler, "Everybody, Come Runnin' to the Jubilee," *Rock Express* XI (September-October 1987), 32–35.

Mel Van Elteren, "Populist Rock in Postmodern Society: John Cougar Mellencamp in Perspective," *Journal of Popular Culture* XXVIII, no. 3 (winter 1994), 95–123.

Joni Mitchell

Noel Coppage, "Joni Mitchell: Innocence on a Spree," *Stereo Review* 36 (April 1976), 64–67.

Cameron Crowe, "Joni Mitchell," *R.S.I.* (1979), 376–91.

Bill Flanagan, "Joni Mitchell Loses Her Cool," *Musician*, no. 86 (December 1985), 64–75.

Bill Flanagan, "Secret Places: Joni Mitchell Builds Shelter from the Rainstorm," *Musician*, no. 115 (May 1988), 64–79.

Leonore Fleischer, *Joni Mitchell*. New York: Flash Books, 1976.

Brian Hinton, *Joni Mitchell: Both Sides Now—The Biography*. London: Sanctuary, 2000 (first published 1996).

Joni Mitchell, *The Complete Poems and Lyrics*. New York: Crown, 1997.

Alanna Nash, "Joni Mitchell," *Stereo Review* 51 (March 1986), 69–71.

Debbie Pead, "Joni Mitchell," *Record Collector*, no. 62 (October 1984), 31–36.

Steve Pond, "Joni Mitchell: Wild Things Run Fast," *Rolling Stone*, no. 383 (Nov. 25, 1982), 27–29, 87.

William Ruhlmann, "Joni Mitchell: From Blue to Indigo," *Goldmine*, no. 380 (February 17, 1995), 16–52, 60.

Chip Stern, "Songs to Aging Children: Joni Mitchell Pulls Your Ear," *Musician*, no. 195 (January/February 1995), 22–31.

Timothy White, "Joni Mitchell," in *Rock Lives: Profiles an Interviews*. New York: Henry Holt, 1990, 328–39.

Monkees

Glenn A. Baker, with Tom Czarnota and Peter Hogan, *Monkee-Mania: The True Story of the Monkees*. New York: St. Martin's Press, 1986.

Carl Cafarelli, "The Monkees: Here They Come—Again," *Goldmine*, no. 298 (December 27, 1991), 9 –14, 120.

Peter Doggett, "The Monkees," *Record Collector*, no. 57 (May 1984), 3–7.

Peter Doggett, "The Monkees," *Record Collector*, no. 86 (October 1986), 17–22.

Peter Doggett, "The Monkees Are Back!" *Record Collector*, no. 101 (January 1988), 36–39.

Micky Dolenz and Mark Bego, *I'm a Believer: My Life of Monkees, Music, and Madness*. New York: Hyperion Books, 1993.

Mark Easter, with Jeff Hahn, "Ladies and Gentlemen, Re-Monkees!" *Goldmine*, no. 423 (October 11, 1996), 50–64.

William J. Fletcher, "The Monkees: On Television, 1966–68," *Goldmine*, no. 158 (August 15, 1986), 18–22, 64.

Gillian G. Gaar, "Davy Jones," *Goldmine*, no. 298 (December 27, 1991), 28–30.

Gillian G. Gaar, "The Monkees," *DISCoveries*, no. 88 (September 1995), 42–46.

Laura Goostree, "The Monkees and the Deconstruction of Television Realism," *Journal of Popular Film* XVI (summer 1988), 50–58.

Brian Hartigan, "Michael Nesmith: The Solo Years," *Goldmine*, no. 95 (March 16, 1984), 6–14.

Brian Hogg, "The Monkees," *Record Collector*, no. 23 (July 1981), 4–12.

Davy Jones and Alan Green, *Mutant Monkees: Meet the Masters of the Multi-Media Manipulation Machine*. Selinsgrove, PA: Click!, 1992.

Michael Lynch, "Goin' Down: The Monkees, 1968–1970 (the Post-Tube Years)," *Goldmine*, no. 423 (October 11, 1996), 38–50.

Edward Reilly, Maggie McManus, and William Chadwick (comps.), *The Monkees—A Manufactured Image: The Ultimate Reference Guide to Monkee Memories and Memorabilia*. Ann Arbor, MI: Pierian Press, 1987.

Jeff Tamarkin, "Michael Nesmith," *Goldmine*, no. 298 (December 27, 1991), 15–20, 118.

Jeff Tamarkin, "Micky Dolenz," *Goldmine*, no. 298 (December 27, 1991), 22–26, 116.

Van Morrison

Jonathan Cott, "Van Morrison: The Rolling Stone Interview," *Rolling Stone*, no. 279 (November 20, 1978), 50–54.

Howard A. DeWitt, "Van Morrison: The Bang Years, 1967–1968," *R.P.M.*, no. 1 (August 1983), 8–10.

Howard A. DeWitt, *Van Morrison: The Mystic's Music*. Fremont, CA: Horizon Books, 1983.

Howard A. DeWitt, "Van Morrison and the Incredible Them," *DISCoveries*, no. 69 (February 1994), 27–31.

Peter Doggett, "Them," *Record Collector*, no. 149 (January 1992), 112–16.

Peter Doggett, "Van Morrison," *Record Collector*, no. 178 (June 1994), 78–82.

Peter Doggett, "Van Morrison, 1969–1974," *Record Collector*, no. 179 (July 1994), 46–49.

Michael Dunne, " 'Tore Down a la Rimbaud': Van Morrison's References and Allusions," *Popular Music and Society* XXIV (winter 2000), 15–29.

Bill Flanagan, "Van Morrison Emerges from the Shadows," *Musician*, no. 75 (January 1985), 30–36.

Brian Hinton, *Celtic Crossroads: The Art of Van Morrison*. London: Sanctuary Publishing, 1997.

Trevor Hodgett, "Them," *Record Collector*, no. 89 (January 1987), 52–57.

Michael Goldberg, "Van Morrison Breaks His Silence (sort of)," *Rolling Stone*, no. 363 (February 18, 1982), 34–35, 43–45.

Paul Lewis, "Roots and Influences: An Interview with Van Morrison," *Now Dig This*, no. 105 (December 1991), 22–26.

Peter Mills, "Into the Mystic: The Aural Poetry of Van Morrison," *Popular Music* XIII, no. 1 (January 1994), 91–103.

Johnny Rogan, "Van Morrison," *Record Collector*, no. 57 (May 1984), 22–24.

Johnny Rogan, V*an Morrison: A Portrait of the Artist*. New York: Proteus Books, 1984.

William Ruhlmann, "Van Morrison: A Look at the Mystic's Career So Far," *Goldmine*, no. 189 (October 23, 1987), 8–12.

John Stewart, "Van Morrison and Them," *Record Collector*, no. 18 (February 1981), 44–47.

Steve Turner, *Van Morrison: Too Late to Stop Now*. New York: Viking Books, 1993.

Rick Nelson

Philip Bashe, *Teenage Idol/Travelin' Man: The Complete Biography of Rick Nelson*. New York, Hyperion Books, 1992.

Mike Callahan, Bud Buschardt, and Steve Goddard, "Rick Nelson," *Goldmine*, no. 51 (August 1980), 17–20.

B. Lee Cooper, "Rick Nelson: A Review Essay," *Popular Music and Society* XIII (winter 1989), 77–82.

Harry Dodds, "Ricky Nelson—The Story of a Teenage Idol: Part One, 1940–1958," *Now Dig This*, no. 45 (December 1986), 18–22.

Harry Dodds, "Ricky Nelson—The Story of a Teenage Idol: Part Two, 1959–1965," *Now Dig This*, no. 46 (January 1987), 10–13.

Harry Dodds, "Ricky Nelson—The Story of a Teenage Idol: Part Three, 1966–1972," *Now Dig This*, no. 47 (February 1987), 8–11.

Harry Dodds, "Ricky Nelson—The Story of a Teenage Idol: Part Four, 1973–1985," *Now Dig This*, no. 48 (March 1987), 25–28.

Ben Givens, "Spotlight on Rick Nelson," *Rockin' 50s*, no. 18 (June 1989), 9–15.

Phil Hardy, "Small-Screen Rocker," *The History of Rock*, no. 16 (1982), 302–5.

Sandie Johnson, "Backstage with the Prince of Rock 'n' Roll," *DISCoveries*, no. 61 (June 1993), 122–5.

Peter Jones, "The Rick Nelson Story," *Record Collector*, no. 14 (October 1980), 44–48.

Spencer Leigh, "Rick Nelson," *Record Collector*, no. 78 (February 1986), 17–23.

Tim Rice, *Rick Nelson: A Travelin' Man*. Preston, England: Rick Nelson International Commemorative Society, 1987.

Joel Selvin, *Ricky Nelson: Idol for a Generation*. Chicago: Contemporary Books, 1990.

John Stafford and Iain Young, *The Ricky Nelson Story: The Hollywood Hillbilly*. Folkestone, England: Finbarr International, 1988.

Jeff Tamarkin, "Rick Nelson: Pioneer Rock 'n' Roll Teen Idol," *Goldmine*, no. 145 (February 14, 1986), 14–16, 76–78.

Willie Nelson

Bob Allen, *Waylon and Willie: The Full Story in Words and Pictures of Waylon Jennings and Willie Nelson*. New York: Jove Press, 1979.

Bob Allen, "Interview: Willie Nelson," *Journal of Country Music* VIII (August 1980), 3–14.

Michael Bane, *Willie: An Unauthorized Biography of Willie Nelson*. New York: Dell, 1984.

Bill DeYoung, "Willie Nelson: Funny How Time Slips Away," *Goldmine*, no. 377 (January 6, 1995), 16–48, 68–74, 135–42.

Chet Flippo, "The Saga of Willie Nelson: From the Night Life to the Good Life," *Rolling Stone*, no. 269 (July 13, 1978), 45–49.

W. A. Kelly Huff, "A Thematic Analysis of Willie Nelson's Song Lyrics," *Popular Music and Society* XVIII (summer 1994), 91–124.

Spencer Leigh, "Willie Nelson," *Record Collector*, no. 84 (August 1986), 20–25.

Susie Nelson, *Heart Worn Memories: A Daughter's Personal Biography of Willie Nelson*. Austin, TX: Eakin Press, 1987.

Willie Nelson, *The Facts of Life and Other Dirty Jokes*. New York: Random House, 2002.

Willie Nelson (edited by Don Cusic), *Willie Nelson Lyrics, 1957–1994*. New York: St. Martin's Press, 1995.

Willie Nelson, with Bud Shrake, *Willie*. New York: Simon & Schuster, 1988.

Lola Scobey, *Willie Nelson: Country Outlaw*. New York: Zebra Books, 1982.

David Standish, "Saint Willie," *Playboy* XXVIII (April 1981), 176, 214–20.

Phil Ochs

John Berendt, "Phil Ochs Ain't Marchin' Anymore," *Esquire* LXXXV (October 1976), 110–12.

David Cohen, *Phil Ochs: A Bio-Bibliography*. Westport, CT: Greenwood, 1999.

Noel Coppage, "Phil Ochs and the Death of Innocence," *Stereo Review* XXXVIII (April 1977), 104.

Eric Eberwein, "Phil Ochs—Toasting a Legend Gone: Michael Ochs on Phil Ochs," *Goldmine*, no. 167 (December 19, 1986), 10–11.

Marc Eliot, *Death of a Rebel—Starring Phil Ochs and a Small Circle of Friends: A Biography*. Garden City, NY: Anchor Press/Doubleday, 1979.

Brian Hogg, "Phil Ochs," *Record Collector*, no. 81 (May 1986), 25–28.

Jon McAuliffe, "Those Fabulous Foreign Pressings," *Music World*, no. 84 (April 1981), 12–15.

Tom Nolan, "God Help the Troubador: Pissing away the Memories with Phil Ochs," *Rolling Stone*, no. 83 (May 27, 1971), 22–23.

David Pichaske, "Phil Ochs," in *The Poetry of Rock: The Golden Years*. Peoria, IL: Ellis Press, 1981, 155–67.

Bruce Pollock, "Phil Ochs," in *In Their Own Words: Twenty Successful Song Writers Tell How They Write Their Songs*. New York: Collier Books, 1975, 46–56.

Roy Orbison

Ellis Amburn, *Dark Star: The Roy Orbison Story*. New York: Lyle Stuart Books/Carol, 1990.

Stephen Barnard, "Only the Lonely," *The History of Rock*, no. 21 (1982), 412–16.

Dave "Daddy Cool" Booth and Colin Escott, "Roy Orbison: A Cadillac and a Diamond Ring," *Goldmine*, no. 118 (February 1, 1985), 6–12.

Alan Clayson, *Only the Lonely: The Roy Orbison Story—10th Anniversary Special Edition*. London: Sanctuary, 1998

Peter Doggett, "Roy Orbison," *Record Collector*, no. 43 (March 1983), 25–32.

Peter Doggett, "Roy Orbison," *Record Collector*, no. 158 (October 1992), 80–82.

Howard Elson, "Roy Orbison," in *Early Rockers*. New York: Proteus Books, 1982, 100–7.

Ken Emerson, "Roy Orbison," in *Rolling Stone Illustrated History of Rock and Roll* (2d ed.), edited by Anthony DeCurtis and James Henke, with Holly George-Warren. New York: Random House/Rolling Stone Press, 1992, 153–7.

Colin Escott, "Roy Orbison: The Early Years," *Goldmine*, no. 229 (May 5, 1989), 16–19.

Colin Escott, "Roy Orbison: The M-G-M Years, 1965–1973," *Goldmine*, no. 229 (May 5, 1989), 20–21.

Colin Escott, with Martin Hawkins, "Roy Orbison: A Cadillac and a Diamond Ring," in *Good Rockin' Tonight: Sun Records and the Birth of Rock 'n' Roll*. New York: St. Martin's Press, 1991, 145–53.

Burt Kaufman, "Spotlight on Roy Orbison," *Rockin' 50s*, no. 31 (August 1991), 8–16.

Carl Perkins

Trevor Cajiao, "Carl Perkins: The Man behind the Music (Part One)," *Now Dig This*, no. 54 (September 1987), 4–7.

Trevor Cajiao, "Carl Perkins: The Man behind the Music (Part Two)," *Now Dig This*, no. 55 (October 1987), 11–12.

Trevor Cajiao, "Carl Perkins: The Man behind the Music (Part Three)," *Now Dig This*, no. 56 (November 1987), 10–11.

Stuart Colman, "Carl Perkins: King of Rockabilly," in *They Kept on Rockin': The Giants of Rock 'n' Roll*. Poole, England: Blandford Press, 1982, 66–72.

Hank Davis, "Carl Perkins: Rock 'n' Roll Pioneer," *Goldmine*, no. 459 (February 27, 1998), 22–23.

Howard Elson, "Carl Perkins," in *Early Rockers*. New York: Proteus Books, 1982, 108–15.

Colin Escott and Martin Hawkins, "Blue Suede Shoes: One Song Rocketed Carl Perkins to Stardom," *History of Rock*, no. 6 (1982), 109–11.

Colin Escott, with Martin Hawkins, "Carl Perkins: Prophet in Blue Suede Shoes," in *Good Rockin' Tonight: Sun Records and the Birth of Rock 'n' Roll*. New York: St. Martin's Press, 1991, 125–43.

Bill Flanagan, "Carl Perkins," in *Written in My Soul: Conversations with Rock's Great Songwriters*. Chicago: Contemporary Books, 1987, 12–22.

Tom Frangione and Ken Michaels, "Carl Perkins: The Beatles Connection," *Goldmine*, no. 477 (November 6, 1998), 68–84.

Lenny Kaye, "The Very Large Legend of Carl Perkins," *Guitar World* III (July 1982), 30–33, 76–77.

Michael Lydon, "Carl Perkins," in *Rock Folk: Portraits from the Rock 'n' Roll Pantheon*. New York: Dial Press, 1971, 24–45.

Ralph M. Newman and Jeff Tamarkin, "Ol' Blue Suede—Then and Now," *Time Barrier Express*, no. 25 (July/August 1979), 25–30.

Carl Perkins, with Ron Rendleman, *Disciple in Blue Suede Shoes*. Grand Rapids, MI: Zondervan, 1978.

Carl Perkins and David McGee, *Go, Cat, Go! The Life and Times of Carl Perkins*. New York: Hyperion Press, 1996.

Steve Scott, "Carl Perkins," *Record Collector*, no. 73 (September 1983), 41–44.

Jan Slevigen, "Carl Perkins: Still Boppin' the Blues," *Now Dig This*, no. 47 (February 1987), 19–22.

Jeff Tamarkin, "Rock 'n' Roll Pioneer, Carl Perkins, 1932–1998," *DISCoveries*, no. 118 (March 1998), 24–26.

Gary Theroux, "Carl Perkins: A Legend in Blue Suede Shoes," *Goldmine*, no. 161 (September 26, 1986), 5–12.

Pink Floyd

David Fricke, "Pink Floyd," *Musician*, no. 50 (December 1982), 48–56.

George Garford, "Pink Floyd," *Record Collector*, no. 23 (July 1981), 34–39.

Barry Miles (comp.), *Pink Floyd: The Illustrated Discography*. New York: Omnibus Books, 1981.

Mark Paytress, "Pink Floyd," *Record Collector*, no. 83 (July 1986), 38–43.

Mark Paytress, "Pink Floyd and Syd Barrett," *Record Collector*, no. 104 (April 1988), 3–8.

Glenn Povey, "Pink Floyd: Furious Madness and Technicolor Dreams," *Goldmine*, no. 195 (January 15, 1988), 8–9, 20.

Glenn Povey, "Pink Floyd: Furious Madness and Technicolor Dreams—Part Two," *Goldmine*, no. 197 (February 12, 1988), 121–5.

Matt Resnicoff, "Roger and Me: The Other Side of the Pink Floyd Story," *Musician*, no. 170 (December 1992), 38–48.

William Ruhlmann, "Pink Floyd: Variations on a Theme of Absence," *Goldmine*, no. 325 (January 5, 1993), 12–22, 169–80.

Nicholas Schaffner, "The Dark Side of Pink Floyd: Music, Magic, and Madness in Psychedelic London," *Musician*, no. 148 (February 1991), 38–51, 95.

Nicholas Schaffner, *Saucerful of Secrets: The Pink Floyd Odyssey*. New York: Crown, 1991.

Roger Waters, *Pink Floyd Lyric Book*. London: Chappell Books, 1982.

Timothy White, "Pink Floyd," in *Rock Lives: Profiles and Interviews*. New York: Henry Holt, 1990, 507–23.

Kevin Whitlock, "Pink Floyd Live!" *Record Collector*, no. 121 (September 1989), 22–26.

Elvis Presley

Howard F. Banney (comp.), *Return to Sender: The First Complete Discography of Elvis Tribute and Novelty Records, 1956–1986*. Ann Arbor, MI: Pierian Press, 1987.

Vernon Chadwick (ed.), *In Search of Elvis: Music, Race, Art, Religion*. Boulder, CO: Westview Press, 1997.

B. Lee Cooper, "Review of *Elvis: The Sun Years—The Story of Elvis Presley in the Fifties* by Howard A. Dewitt," *DISCoveries*, no. 71 (April 1994), 116.

Lee Cotten, *All Shook Up: Elvis Day-by-Day, 1954–1977*. Ann Arbor, MI: Pierian Press, 1985.

Lee Cotten and Howard A. Dewitt, *Jailhouse Rock: The Bootleg Records of Elvis Presley, 1970–1983*. Ann Arbor, MI: Pierian Press, 1983.

R. Serge Denisoff and George Plasketes, *True Disbelievers: The Elvis Contagion*. New Brunswick, NJ: Transaction, 1995.

Howard A. Dewitt, *Elvis—The Sun Years: The Story of Elvis Presley in the Fifties*. Ann Arbor, MI: Popular Culture, Ink., 1993.

Neal Gregory and Janice Gregory, *When Elvis Died: A Chronicle of National and International Reaction to the Passing of an American King*. Washington, D.C.: Communications Press, 1980.

Peter Guralnick, *Careless Love: The Unmaking of Elvis Presley*. Boston: Little, Brown, 1999.

Peter Guralnick, *Last Train to Memphis: The Rise of Elvis Presley*. Boston: Little, Brown, 1994.

Patsy Guy Hammontree, *Elvis Presley: A Bio-Bibliography*. Westport, CT: Greenwood, 1985.

Greil Marcus, *Dead Elvis: A Chronicle of Cultural Obsession*. Garden City, NY: Doubleday, 1991.

Dave Marsh, *Elvis*. New York: Quadrangle/New York Times Books, 1982.

Robert Matthew-Walker, *Heartbreak Hotel: The Life and Music of Elvis Presley*. Chessington, England: Castle Communications, 1995.

Steven Opdyke, *The Printed Elvis: The Complete Guide to Books about the King*. Westport, CT: Greenwood, 1999.

George Plasketes, *Images of Elvis Presley in American Culture, 1977–1997: The Mystery Terrain*. New York: Harrington Park Press, 1997.

Kevin Quain (ed.), *The Elvis Reader: Texts and Sources on the King of Rock 'n' Roll*. New York: St. Martin's Press, 1992.

Gilbert B. Rodman, *Elvis after Elvis: The Posthumous Career of a Living Legend*. New York: Routledge, 1996.

Paul M. Sammon (ed.), *The King Is Dead: Tales of Elvis Postmortem*. New York: Delta Books, 1994.

Wendy Sauers (comp.), *Elvis Presley: A Complete Reference: Biography, Chronology, Concerts Lists, Filmography, Discography, Vital Documents, Bibliography, and Index*. Jefferson, NC: McFarland, 1984.

David E. Stanley, with Frank Coffey, *The Elvis Encyclopedia: The Complete and Definitive Reference Book on the King of Rock and Roll*. Santa Monica, CA: General, 1997.

Jac L. Tharpe (ed.), *Elvis: Images and Fancies*. Jackson: University Press of Mississippi, 1979.

John Townsen, Gordon Minto, and George Richardson, *Elvis U.K.: The Ultimate Guide to Elvis Presley's British Record Releases, 1956–1986*. Poole, England: Blandford Press, 1987.

John A. Whisler (comp.), *Elvis Presley: Reference Guide and Discography*. Metuchen, NJ: The Scarecrow Press, 1981.

Peter O. Whitmer, *The Inner Elvis: A Psychological Biography of Elvis Aron Presley*. New York: Hyperion Books, 1996.

Prince

Kevin Barrett, "Prince and the Time Machine Experienced," *OneTwoThreeFour*, no. 2 (1985), 59–64.

Jon Bream, *Prince: Inside the Purple Reign*. New York: Collier Books/ Macmillan, 1984.

Chris Dawson and Peter Doggett, "Prince," *Record Collector*, no. 84 (August 1986), 8–12.

Peter Doggett, "Prince," *Record Collector*, no. 130 (June 1990), 54–58.

Dave Fudger (ed.), *Prince: In His Own Words*. Port Chester, NY: Cherry Lane Books, 1984.

Dave Hill, *Prince: A Pop Life*. New York: Crown Books, 1989.

Barney Hoskyns, *Prince: Imp of the Perverse*. London: Virgin Books, 1988.

Kurt Loder, "Prince Reigns," *Rolling Stone*, no. 428 (August 16, 1984), 16–21, 46.

Debby Miller, "Prince," *Rolling Stone*, no. 394 (April 28, 1983), 18–23, 73.

Per Nilsen, *Prince: A Documentary*. London: Omnibus Press, 1990.

Steve Perry, "Prince: The Purple Decade," *Musician*, no. 121 (November 1988), 82–99.

Alton B. Pollard III, "Religion, Rock, and Eroticism: Prince," *Journal of Black Sacred Music* III (fall 1989), 133–41.

Timothy White, "Prince," in *Rock Lives: Profiles and Interviews.* New York: Henry Holt, 1990, 768–80.

Richard E. Wimberley, "Prophecy, Eroticism, and Apocalypicism in Popular Music: Prince," *Journal of Black Sacred Music* III (fall 1989), 125–32.

Bonnie Raitt

Mark Bego, *Bonnie Raitt: Just in the Nick of Time.* New York: Birch Lane Press Books, 1995.

Noel Coppage, "Bonnie Raitt," *Stereo Review* XXXVII (October 1976), 74–75.

Debra DeSalvo, "Bonnie Raitt: Devoted to the Blues," *Blues Revue*, no. 25 (October/November 1996), 26–35.

Scott Isler, "Bonnie Raitt: Still Takin' Her Time," *Musician*, no. 96 (October 1986), 48–54.

Daisann McLane, "Bonnie Raitt: Music for the Movement," *Rolling Stone*, no. 311 (February 21, 1980), 25.

Michael Molenda, "The Raitt Stuff," *Guitar Player*, no. 343 (July 1998), 44–106.

Katherine Orloff, "Bonnie Raitt," in *Rock 'n' Roll Woman.* Los Angeles, CA: Nash, 1974, 105–20.

Mark Rowland, "Bonnie Raitt," *Musician*, no. 186 (April 1994), 7.

Mark Rowland, "Bonnie Raitt's Ace of Hearts," *Musician*, no. 153 (July 1991), 32–40, 95.

Sam Sutherland, "Raitt Reckons She Will Shake Fans with 8th LP," *Billboard* XCIV (March 27, 1982), 55–56.

Ken Tucker, "Bonnie Raitt Rocks Again," *Rolling Stone*, no. 370 (May 27, 1982), 45, 50.

Otis Redding

Stanley Booth, "The Memphis Soul Sound," in *Rhythm Oil: A Journey through the Music of the American South.* New York: Pantheon Books, 1991, 69–88.

Rob Bowman, "Otis Redding: R-E-S-P-E-C-T," *Goldmine*, no. 258 (June 15, 1990), 8–13, 102.

Thomas J. Cullen III, "Remembering Otis Redding, 1941–1967," *Blues Revue*, no. 33 (December 1997), 74–76.

Paul Gambaccini, "Otis Redding," in *Masters of Rock*. London: Omnibus Press, 1982, 108–15.

Peter Guralnick, "Otis Redding," in *Sweet Soul Music: Rhythm and Blues and the Southern Dream of Freedom*. New York: Harper & Row, 1986, 133–51.

Gerri Hirshey, "Respect When I Come Home," in *Nowhere to Run: The Story of Soul Music*. New York: Times Books, 1984, 331–47.

Bruce Huston, "Otis Redding Remembered," *Soul Survivor*, no. 8 (winter 1987/88), 4–7.

Jon Landau, "Otis Redding," in *The Rolling Stone Illustrated History of Rock and Roll* (2d ed.), edited by Anthony DeCurtis and James Henke, with Holly George-Warren. New York: Random House/Rolling Stone Press, 1992, 272–6.

Dave Oksanen, "Otis Redding: A Legend in Soul," *Music World*, no. 86 (June 1981, 15–16.

Mark Paytress, "The Definitive Otis Redding," *Record Collector*, no. 173 (January 1994), 111–12.

Brian Reynolds, "Otis Redding," *Record Collector*, no. 67 (March 1985), 31–35.

Roger St. Pierre, "The Blues and Soul Hall of Fame: no. 4—Otis Redding," *Blues and Soul*, no. 572 (October 23–November 5, 1990), 26–28.

Chris Savory, "Otis Redding," *Record Collector*, no. 23 (July 1981), 40–43.

Jane Schiesel, *The Otis Redding Story*. Garden City, NY: Doubleday, 1973.

Bill Stuart, "Otis Redding: Stax Records Survivors on 20th Anniversary of Soulmate's Death," *Nine-o-One Network*, no. 10 (February 1988), 14–15, 34.

Jimmy Reed

John Broven, "Gimme That Harp, Boy!" *The History of Rock*, no. 30 (1982), 594–5.

B. Lee Cooper, "Review of *Charly Blues Masterworks—Volume 17: Jimmy Reed—Bright Lights, Big City* and *Speak the Lyrics to Me, Mama Reed*," *Popular Music and Society* XVII (fall 1993), 114.

Ron Courtney, "The Blues of Jimmy Reed: Boogie in the Dark," *R.P.M.*, no. 3 (December 1983-January 1984), 66–69.

Dan Forte, "Jimmy Reed," in *Blues Guitar: The Men Who Made the Music*, edited by Jas Obrecht. San Francisco: Guitar Player, 1990), 164–9.

Wayne Jancik, "Jimmy Reed: The Primitive Genius," *Goldmine*, no. 189 (October 23, 1987), 39, 43.

Jim O'Neal and Amy O'Neal, "Jimmy Reed," *Living Blues*, no. 25 (May-June 1975), 16–41.

Jim O'Neal and Amy van Singel, "Jimmy Reed," in *The Voice of the Blues*, edited by Jim O'Neal and Amy van Singel. New York: Routledge, 2002, 304–57.

David Whiteis, "Ain't That Lovin' You Baby: The Blues Life of Jimmy Reed," *Goldmine*, no. 344 (October 1, 1993), 26–40, 126.

Johnny Rivers

Cary Baker, "Johnny Rivers Weathers the Summer Rain," *Goldmine*, no. 80 (January 1983), 30–31.

Glenn A. Baker, "Johnny Rivers: The Singer, Not the Song," *Goldmine*, no. 180 (June 19, 1987), 16, 67.

Ken Barnes, "Review of *Blue Suede Shoes* by Johnny Rivers," *Phonograph Record*, III (July 1973), 28.

B. Lee Cooper, "Johnny Rivers and Linda Ronstadt: Rock 'n' Roll Revivalists," *JEMF Quarterly* XVIII, nos. 67/68 (fall 1982/winter 1983), 166–77.

B. Lee Cooper, "Review of *The Memphis Sun Recordings* and *Last Train to Memphis* by Johnny Rivers," *Rock and Blues News*, no. 6 (October-November 1999), 35.

Bill Dahl, "Johnny Rivers—Mr. 'Memphis' Relaunches His Soul City Records Label—And His Career," *Goldmine*, no. 481 (January 1, 1999), 16–33.

Steve Roeser, "Johnny Rivers: The Man Who Made the Whisky," *Goldmine*, no. 290 (September 6, 1991), 8–15.

Joe Smith, "Johnny Rivers," in *Off the Record: An Oral History of Popular Music*. New York: Warner Books, 1988, 225–7.

Marty Robbins

Bob Airlie, "Rockin' in the Country—Part One: The Columbia Rockabilly Sounds of Marty Robbins," *New Kommotion* II (summer 1977), 25–26.

Howard Cockburn, "Rockin' with (Marty) Robbins," *Now Dig This*, no. 102 (September 1991), 12–13.

B. Lee Cooper, "Review of *Marty Robbins: Fast Cars and Country Music* by Barbara J. Pruett," *Journal of American Culture* XVI (summer 1993), 109.

Colin Escott, "Marty Robbins: The Early Years—Rockin' Rollin' Robbins," *Goldmine*, no. 312 (July 10, 1992), 8–12, 189.

Bob Garbutt, "Marty Robbins: Twentieth Century Drifter," *Goldmine*, no. 58 (March 1981), 197–9.

Alanna Nash, "Marty Robbins," in *Behind Closed Doors: Talking with the Legends of Country Music.* New York: Knopf, 1988, 436–454.

Barbara J. Pruett, *Marty Robbins: Fast Cars and Country Music.* Metuchen, NJ: Scarecrow Press, 1990.

"Marty Robbins," *The Golden Age*, no. 2 (November 1986), 29.

Arnold L. Rogers, "Marty Robbins: A 20th Century Drifter," *DISCoveries* II (September 1989), 20–24.

Rolling Stones

Felix Aeppli, *Heart of Stone: The Definitive Rolling Stones Discography, 1962–1983.* Ann Arbor, MI: Pierian Press, 1985.

Felix Aeppli, *Rolling Stones, 1962–1995: The Ultimate Guide to Their Career.* Bromley, England: Record Information Services, 1996.

Steve Appleford, *The Rolling Stones—It's Only Rock and Roll: Song by Song.* New York: Schirmer Books, 1997.

Stephen Barnard, *Rolling Stones: Street Fighting Years.* London: Mallard Press, 1998.

Massimo Bonanno, *The Rolling Stones Chronicle: The First Thirty Years.* New York: Henry Holt, 1990.

Stanley Booth, *Dance with the Devil: The Rolling Stones and Their Times.* New York: Random House, 1986.

Gus Coral, David Hinckley, and Debra Rodman, *The Rolling Stones: Black and White Blues, 1963.* Atlanta, GA: Turner, 1995.

Stephen Davis, *Old Gods almost Dead: The 40-Year Odyssey of the Rolling Stones.* New York: Broadway Books, 2001.

Mary LaVerne Dimmick, *The Rolling Stones: An Annotated Bibliography.* Pittsburgh, PA: University of Pittsburgh, 1979.

Simon Dudfield, *Stoned—Andrew Loog Oldham: The Man Who Made the Rolling Stones*. London: Hodder and Stoughton, 1997.

Editors of Rolling Stone, *The Rolling Stone Files: The Ultimate Compendium of Interviews, Articles, Facts and Opinions from the Files of Rolling Stone*. New York: Hyperion Press, 1995.

Martin Elliott, *The Rolling Stones Complete Recording Sessions, 1963—1989: A Sessionography, Discography, and History of Recordings from the Famous Chart-Toppers to the Infamous Rarities, January 1963–November 1989*. London: Blandford Press, 1990.

Geoffrey Giuliano and Chris Eborn (comps.), *Not Fade Away: The Rolling Stones Collection*. London: Paper Tiger, 1995.

John M. Hellmann, Jr., " 'I'm A Monkey': The Influence of the Black American Blues Argot on the Rolling Stones," *Journal of American Folklore* LXXXVI (October-December 1973), 367–73.

Jools Holland and Dora Loewenstein, *The Rolling Stones: A Life on the Road*. New York: Penguin Studio/Penguin Putnam, 1998.

A. E. Hotchner, *Blown Away: The Rolling Stones and the Death of the Sixties*. New York: Simon & Schuster, 1990.

James Karnbach and Carol Bernson, *It's Only Rock 'n' Roll: The Ultimate Guide to the Rolling Stones*. New York: Facts on File, 1997.

Jessica Holman Whitehead MacPhail (comp.), *Yesterday's Papers: The Rolling Stones in Print, 1963–1984*. Ann Arbor, MI: Pierian Press, 1986.

Philip Norman, *Symphony for the Devil: The Rolling Stones Story*. New York: Linden Press/Simon & Schuster, 1984.

Mark Paytress, *The Complete Guide to the Music of the Rolling Stones*. London: Omnibus Books, 1995.

Alan Stewart and Cathy Sanford, *Time Is on My Side: The Rolling Stones Day-by-Day, 1962–1984*. Ann Arbor, MI: Popular Culture, Ink., 1992.

Bill Wyman, with Richard Havers, *Bill Wyman's Blues Odyssey: A Journey to Music's Heart and Soul*. London: DK, 2001.

Bill Wyman, with Ray Coleman, *Stone Alone: The Story of a Rock 'n' Roll Band*. New York: Da Capo Press, 1997.

Linda Ronstadt

Marianne Biskup, "Linda Ronstadt: The Natural History of the Song Bird," *Goldmine*, no. 104 (July 20, 1984), 6–14.

Vivian Claire, *Linda Ronstadt*. New York: Quick Fox, 1978.

B. Lee Cooper (comp.), "The Linda Ronstadt Rock 'n' Roll Revival System: Selected Examples of Her Hit Tunes, 1967–1979," *JEMF Quarterly*, nos. 67/68 (fall 1982/winter 1983), 176–7.

Noel Coppage, "Linda Ronstadt Linda Ronstadt," *Stereo Review* XXXVII (November 1976), 78–82.

Bill DeYoung, "Walls and Bridges: Talking with Emmylou Harris and Linda Ronstadt," *Goldmine*, no. 500 (September 24, 1999), 46–48.

Bill Flanagan and Roy Leonard, "Linda Ronstadt: Solving the Retro Riddle— The Queen of Cover Rock Re-Ignites the Torch Tune," *Musician*, no. 65 (March 1984), 20–22.

Ben Fong-Torres, "Linda Ronstadt: Heartbreak on Wheels," *Rolling Stone*, no. 182 (March 27, 1975), 34–41, 63–64.

Peter Herbst, "The Rolling Stone Interview: Linda Ronstadt," *Rolling Stone*, no. 276 (October 19, 1978), 50–59.

Aaron Latham, "Snow White in South Africa," *Rolling Stone*, no. 402 (August 18, 1983), 7–13, 58–59.

Annie Leibovitz, "Linda Ronstadt: More Than Just One Look," *Rolling Stone*, no. 314 (April 3, 1980), 10–13.

Katherine Orloff, "Linda Ronstadt," in *Rock 'n' Roll Woman* (Los Angeles, CA: Nash, 1974), 121–38.

[Jerry Osborne], "Who Is Really the Most Popular Female Singer?" *Record Digest* I (March 15, 1978), 3–7.

Linda Sanders, "Diva Linda," *Saturday Review* X (November-December 1984), 26–30.

Jean Vallely and Linda Ronstadt, "Playboy Interview: Linda Ronstadt," *Playboy* XXVII (April 1980), 85–118.

Paul Simon

Chris Charlesworth, *The Complete Guide to the Music of Paul Simon*. London: Omnibus Press, 1997.

Mitchell S. Cohen, *Simon and Garfunkel: A Biography in Words and Pictures*. New York: Sire Books/Chappell Music, 1977.

B. Lee Cooper, "Review of *Still Crazy after All These Years* by Paul Simon," in *Images of American Society in Popular Music: A Guide to Reflective Teaching*. Chicago: Nelson-Hall, 1982, 205–6.

Peter Doggett, "Simon and Garfunkel," *Record Collector*, no. 36 (August 1982), 4–12.

Walter Everett, "Swallowed by a Song: Paul Simon's Crisis of Chromaticism," in *Understanding Rock: Essays in Musical Analysis*, edited by John Covach and Graeme M. Boone. New York: Oxford University Press, 1997, 113–53.

Bill Flanagan, "Paul Simon," in *Written in My Soul: Conversations with Rock's Great Songwriters*. Chicago: Contemporary Books, 1987, 274–87.

Nelson George, "Paul Simon," *Musician*, no. 97 (November 1986), 11–16.

Stephen Holden, "Paul Simon," in *Rolling Stone Illustrated History of Rock and Roll* (2d ed.), edited by Anthony DeCurtis and James Henke, with Holly George-Warren. New York: Random House/Rolling Stone Press, 1992, 318–23.

Patrick Humphries, *Bookends: The Simon and Garfunkel Story*. New York: Proteus, 1982.

Patrick Humphries, *Paul Simon: Still Crazy after All These Years*. Garden City, NY: Doubleday, 1988.

Victoria Kingston, *Simon and Garfunkel: The Biography*. New York: Fromm International, 1998.

Spencer Leigh, *Paul Simon: Now and Then*. Liverpool: Raven Books, 1973.

David Marsh, *Paul Simon*. New York: Music Sales, 1978.

Dave Marsh, "What Do You Do When You're Not a Kid Anymore and You Still Want to Rock and Roll? In 'One-Trick Pony' Paul Simon Looks at the Way Things Might Have Been," *Rolling Stone*, no. 329 (October 30, 1980), 42–45.

Robert Matthew-Walker, *Simon and Garfunkel*. New York: Hippocrene Books, 1984.

Joseph Morella and Patricia Barey, *Simon and Garfunkel: Old Friends*. London: Robert Hale, 1992.

Jesse Nash and George Flowers, "Paul Simon," *Guitar Player* XXV (February 1991), 22–23, 27.

James E. Perone, *Paul Simon: A Bio-Bibliography*. Westport, CT: Greenwood, 2000.

David Pichaske, "Paul Simon," in *Poetry of Rock: The Golden Years*. Peoria, IL: Ellis Press, 1981, 139–53.

"Playboy Interview: Paul Simon," *Playboy* XXXI (February 1984), 49–51, 163–74.

Jon Swenson, *Simon and Garfunkel: A Musical Autobiography*. London: W. H. Allen, 1984.

Timothy White, "Paul Simon: The Luminous Heart of a Dark Horse," *Musician*, no. 65 (March 1984), 60–68.

Timothy White, "The Rhythm Method: Paul Simon's Solo Expeditions," *Goldmine*, no. 305 (April 3, 1992), 8–14.

Frank Sinatra

Richard W. Ackelson, *Frank Sinatra: A Complete Recording History of Techniques, Songs, Composers, Lyricists, Arrangers, Sessions and First-Issue Albums, 1939–1984*. Jefferson, NC: McFarland, 1992.

T. H. Adamowski, "Frank Sinatra: The Subject and His Music," *Journal of Popular Culture* XXXIII, no. 4 (spring 2000), 1–11.

John Collis, *Complete Guide to the Music of Frank Sinatra*. London: Omnibus Press, 1998.

Michael Freedland, *All the Way: A Biography of Frank Sinatra, 1915–1998*. New York: St. Martin's Press, 1997.

Will Friedwald, *Sinatra! The Song Is You—A Singer's Art*. New York: Da Capo Press, 1997 (first published 1995).

Pete Hamill, *Why Sinatra Matters*. Boston: Little, Brown, 1998.

Kitty Kelley, *His Way: The Unauthorized Biography of Frank Sinatra*. New York: Bantam Books, 1986.

Albert I. Lonstein, *The Revised Compleat Sinatra: 1981 Cumulative Supplement*. Ellenville, NY: Sondra M. Lonstein, 1981.

Albert I. Lonstein and Vito R. Marino (comps.), *The Revised Complete Sinatra: Discography, Filmography, Television Appearances, Motion Picture Appearances, Radio Appearances, Concert Appearances, and Stage Appearances*. Ellenville, NY: Sondra M. Lonstein, 1979.

Leonard Mustazza (ed.), *Frank Sinatra and Popular Culture: Essays on an American Icon*. Westport, CT: Praeger, 1998.

Leonard Mustazza, *Ol' Blue Eyes: A Frank Sinatra Encyclopedia*. Westport, CT: Greenwood, 1998.

Leonard Mustazza, *Sinatra: An Annotated Bibliography, 1939–1998*. Westport, CT: Greenwood, 1999.

Luiz Carlos do Nascimento Silva (comp.), *Put Your Dreams Away: A Frank Sinatra Discography*. Westport, CT: Greenwood, 2000.

Ed O'Brien and Scott P. Sayers, Jr., *Sinatra: The Man and His Music—The Recording Artistry of Francis Albert Sinatra, 1939–1992*. Austin, TX: TSD Press, 1992.

Ed O'Brien and Robert Wilson, *Sinatra 101: The 101 Best Recordings and the Stories Behind Them*. New York: Boulevard Books, 1996.

Steven Petkov and Leonard Mustazza (eds.), *The Frank Sinatra Reader*. New York: Oxford University Press, 1995.

Ethlie Ann Vare (ed.), *Legend: Frank Sinatra and the American Dream*. New York: Boulevard Books, 1995.

Bill Zehme, *The Way You Wear Your Hat: Frank Sinatra and the Lost Art of Livin'*. New York: HarperCollins, 1997.

Phil Spector

Michael Aldred, "Phil Spector: Wall to Wall," *Goldmine*, no. 206 (June 17, 1988), 6–16.

Michael Aldred, "Phil Spector: Wall to Wall—Part Two," *Goldmine*, no. 207 (July 1, 1988), 26, 30, 75, 77.

Keith A. Beach, "Phil Spector: An Overview," *Goldmine*, no. 55 (December 1980), 11–15.

Mike Callahan, "Phil Spector—The Pre-Phillies Years," *Goldmine*, no. 46 (March 1980), 141–2.

Mike Callahan, "Phil Spector: The Phillies Years," *Goldmine*, no. 47 (April 1980), 148–9.

Nik Cohn, "Phil Spector," in *The Rolling Stone Illustrated History of Rock and Roll* (rev. ed.), edited by Jim Miller. New York: Random House/Rolling Stone Press, 1980, 148–59.

Peter Doggett, "Phil Spector," *Record Collector*, no. 61 (September 1984), 19–24.

Peter Doggett, "Phil Spector and the Girl Group Sound," *Record Collector*, no. 159 (November 1992), 108–13.

Peter Doggett, "Phil Spector and Phillies Records," *Record Collector*, no. 62 (October 1984), 21–27.

Peter Doggett, "Phil Spector: 1969 to the Present Day," *Record Collector*, no. 63 (November 1984), 22–30.

Rob Finnis, *The Phil Spector Story*. London: Rockon Books, 1975.

John J. Fitzpatrick and James E. Fogerty, *Collecting Phil Spector: The Man, the Legend, the Music*. St. Paul, MN: Spectacle Press, 1991.

Harvey Kubernik, "Phil Spector: From the Girl Groups of the '60s to the Beatles, the Rolling Stones and Beyond, Phil Spector's 'Wall of Sound' Permeates Popular Music," *Goldmine*, no. 563 (February 22, 2002), 14–18.

Chuck Miller, "Ronnie Spector: For Every Kiss You Give Me, I'll Give You Three," *Goldmine*, no. 506 (December 17, 1999), 14–20, 56–58, 92.

Mark Ribowsky, *He's a Rebel: The Truth about Phil Spector—Rock and Roll's Legendary Madman*. New York: E. P. Dutton, 1989.

Ronnie Spector, with Vince Walsron, *Be My Baby: How I Survived Mascara, Miniskirts, and Madness during My Life as a Fabulous Ronette*. New York: Harmony Books, 1991.

Richard Williams, *Out of His Head: The Sound of Phil Spector*. New York: Outerbridge and Lazard, 1972.

Bruce Springsteen

Eric Alterman, *It Ain't No Sin to Be Glad You're Alive: The Promise of Bruce Springsteen*. Boston: Little, Brown, 1999.

H. Eric Branscomb, "Literacy and a Popular Medium: The Lyrics of Bruce Springsteen," *Journal of Popular Culture* XXVII (summer 1993), 29–42.

Daniel Cavicchi, *Tramps Like Us: Music and Meaning among Springsteen Fans*. New York: Oxford University Press, 1998.

Charles R. Cross (ed.), *Backstreets: Springsteen—The Man and His Music*. New York: Harmony Books, 1989.

Jim Cullen, *Born in the U.S.A.: Bruce Springsteen and the American Tradition*. New York: Harper Perennial Books, 1997.

Editors of Rolling Stone, *Bruce Springsteen: The Rolling Stone Files—The Ultimate Compendium of Interviews, Articles, Facts, and Opinions from the Files of Rolling Stone*. New York: Hyperion Books, 1999.

Brad Elliot, *Wild and Innocent: The Recordings of Bruce Springsteen, 1972–1985*. Ann Arbor, MI: Popular Culture, Ink., 1991.

Clinton Heylin and Simon Gee (comps.), *The E Street Shuffle: Springsteen and the E Street Band in Performance, 1971–1988*. Sale, England: Labour of Love Productions, 1989.

Robert Hilburn, *Bruce Springsteen: Born in the U.S. A.* London: Sidgwick and Jackson, 1985.

Julie Lyons and George H. Lewis, "The Price You Pay: The Life and Lyrics of Bruce Springsteen," in *American Popular Music—Volume Two: The Age of Rock*, edited by Timothy E. Scheurer. Bowling Green, OH: Bowling Green State University Popular Press, 1989, 258–67.

Susan Mackey-Kallis and Ian McDermott, "Bruce Springsteen, Ronald Reagan, and the American Dream," *Popular Music and Society* XVI (winter 1992), 1–9.

Dave Marsh, *Born to Run: The Bruce Springsteen Story.* Garden City, NY: Doubleday, 1979.

Dave Marsh, *Glory Days: Bruce Springsteen in the '80s.* New York: Pantheon Press, 1987.

Christopher Phillips, "Loose Ends: Springsteen's Alternative History— Outtakes, Live Tracks, Alternative Tracks, and Rarities," *DISCoveries*, no. 132 (May 1999), 36–42.

Ray Pratt, "Is a Dream a Lie If It Don't Come True, or Is It Something Worse? A Commentary on Political Implications of the Springsteen Phenomenon," *Popular Music and Society* XI, no. 1 (spring 1987), 51–74.

Alan Rauch, "Bruce Springsteen and the Dramatic Monologue," *American Studies* XXIX (spring 1988), 29–49.

Christopher Sandford, *Springsteen Pointblank.* New York: Da Capo Press, 1999.

Deanna D. Sellnow and Timothy L. Sellnow, "The Human Relationship from Idealism to Realism: An Analysis of the Music of Bruce Springsteen," *Popular Music and Society* XIV (fall 1990), 71–88.

Bruce Springsteen, *Songs.* New York: Avon Books, 1998.

Rod Stewart

Paul Gambaccini, "Rod Stewart," in *Masters of Rock.* London: Omnibus Press, 1982, 34–41.

David Gans, "A Candid Interview with Rod Stewart," *The Record*, no. 3 (January 1982), 1.

John Gray, "Rod Stewart," *Record Collector*, no. 116 (April 1989), 44–50.

Tony Jasper, *Rod Stewart.* Secaucus, NJ: Chartwell Books, 1977.

Greil Marcus, "Rod Stewart," in *The Rolling Stone Illustrated History of Rock and Roll* (rev. ed.), edited by Jim Miller. New York: Random House/Rolling Stone Press, 1980, 377–80.

Paul Nelson and Lester Bangs, *Rod Stewart*. New York: Delilah Books, 1981.

Philip Norman, "Rod Stewart: The Familiar Face," in *The Road Goes on Forever: Portraits from a Journey through Contemporary Music*. New York: Fireside Books, 1982, 83–89.

Robert Palmer, "Rod Stewart Says He's Sorry," *Rolling Stone*, no. 365 (March 18, 1982), 50–51, 71–72.

John Pidgeon, *Rod Stewart and the Changing Faces*. St. Albans: Panther Books, 1976.

John Stewart, "Rod Stewart: A Guide to His Solo Rarities, and Records Made with Jeff Beck and the Faces, 1964–1975," *Record Collector*, no. 33 (May 1982), 4–12.

Dave Thompson, "Rod Stewart's Early Years: The Story That Every Picture Tells," *Goldmine*, no. 308 (May 15, 1992), 8.

George Tremlett, *The Rod Stewart Story*. New York: Warner Paperback Library, 19.

Timothy White, "Rod Stewart," in *Rock Lives: Profiles and Interviews*. New York: Henry Holt, 1990, 317–27.

Josef Woodard, "Pictures of an Exhibitionist," *Musician*, no. 72 (October 1984), 52–56.

Barbra Streisand

Shaun Considine, *Barbra Streisand: The Woman, the Myth, the Music*. New York: Delacorte Press, 1985.

Ernest W. Cunningham, *The Ultimate Barbra*. Los Angeles: Renaissance Books, 1998.

Roy Hemming and David Hadju, "Barbra Streisand," in *Discovering Great Singers of Classic Pop*. New York: Newmarket Press, 1991, 206–11.

James Kimbrell, *Barbra—An Actress Who Sings: An Unauthorized Biography*. Boston: Branden, 1989.

Linda Pohly, *The Barbra Streisand Companion: A Guide to Her Vocal Style and Repertoire*. Westport, CT: Greenwood, 2000.

Randall Reise, *Her Name Is Barbra: An Intimate Portrait of the Real Barbra Streisand*. New York: Birch Lane Press, 1993.

William Ruhlmann, "Barbra Streisand: The Way She Is," *Goldmine*, no. 329 (March 5, 1993), 10–34.

James Spada, *Streisand: Her Life*. New York: Crown, 1995.

James Spada with Christopher Nickens, *Streisand: The Woman and the Legend*. Garden City, NY: Doubleday, 1981.

Ethlie Ann Vare (ed.), *Diva: Barbra Streisand and the Making of a Superstar*. New York: Boulevard Books, 1996.

Donald Zec and Anthony Fowles, *Barbra: A Biography of Barbra Streisand*. New York: St. Martin's Press, 1982.

The Supremes

Connie Berman, *Diana Ross: Supreme Lady*. New York: Popular Library, 1978.

Dave Brown, "Diana Ross and the Supremes," *Record Collector*, no. 30 (February 1982), 55–63.

David Brown, "Diana Ross and the Supremes," *Record Collector*, no. 170 (October 1993), 86–93.

David Brown, "Diana Ross," *Record Collector*, no. 172 (December 1993), 58–65.

Geoff Brown, *Diana Ross*. New York: St. Martin's Press, 1981.

Thomas A. Ingrassia, "The Dreams of a Supreme: The 40th Anniversary Interview with Mary Wilson," *Goldmine*, no. 505 (December 3, 1999), 32–44, 46, 53.

Thomas A. Ingrassia, "The Supremes—The Post-Diana Years: Part I—1967 to 1973," *Goldmine*, no. 190 (November 6, 1987), 18–20, 127.

Thomas A. Ingrassia, "The Supremes—The Post-Diana Years: Part II—1973 to 1987," *Goldmine*, no. 201 (April 8, 1988), 109–11.

Diana Ross, *Secrets of a Sparrow: Memoirs of Diana Ross*. New York: Villard Books, 1993.

Marianne Ruuth, *Triumph and Tragedy: The True Story of the Supremes*. Los Angeles: Holloway House, 1986.

J. Randy Taraborrelli, *Call Her Miss Ross: The Unauthorized Biography of Diana Ross*. New York: Carol, 1989.

Tony Turner, with Barbara Aria, *All That Glittered: My Life with the Supremes*. New York: E. P. Dutton, 1991.

Jay Warner, "First Ladies of Motown . . . The Supremes," *DISCoveries*, no. 68 (January 1994), 11–14.

Mary Wilson, *Dreamgirl and Supreme Faith: My Life as a Supreme* (updated ed.). New York: Cooper Square Press/Rowman and Littlefield, 1999 (first published 1986).

Randall Wilson, *Forever Faithful: A Study of Florence Ballard and the Supremes*. San Francisco: Renaissance Sound, 1987.

Tina Turner

Chris Albertson, "Stereo Review Salutes Tina Turner," *Stereo Review*, 50 (October 1985), 59–61.

Sharon Davis, "The Blues and Soul Hall of Fame: no. 10—Ike and Tina Turner," *Blues and Soul*, no. 578 (January 22—February 4, 1991), 21–23.

Sharon Davis, "The Blues and Soul Hall of Fame: no. 25—Tina Turner," *Blues and Soul*, No 593 (August 20—September 2, 1991), 26–29.

Peter Doggett, "Ike and Tina Turner," *Record Collector*, No 64 (December 1984), 11–15.

Laura Fissinger, *Tina Turner*. New York: Ballentine Books, 1985.

Randal C. Hill, "Tina Turner: Guts, Grit and Grammys," *Goldmine*, no. 189 (October 23, 1987), 41–42.

Steven Ivory, *Tina Turner*. New York: Perigee Books, 1985.

Kurt Loder, "Sole Survivor," *Rolling Stone*, no. 432 (October 11, 1984), 18–20, 57–60.

Brant Mewborn, "Tina Turner: Raunchy, Rollin' and Back in the Rock of It," *Rolling Stone*, no. 347 (July 9, 1981), 48–49.

Bart Mills, *Tina*. New York: Warner Books, 1985.

Mark Rowland, "Mega Woman Conquers the World," *Musician*, no. 96 (October 1986), 70–84.

Mark Rowland, "Tina Turner," *Musician*, no. 71 (September 1984), 13–16.

Ike Turner, with Nigel Cawthorne, *Takin' back My Name: The Confessions of Ike Turner*. London: Virgin Books, 1999.

Tina Turner with Kurt Loder, *I, Tina: My Life Story*. New York: William Morrow, 1986.

Chris Welch, *The Tina Turner Experience: The Illustrated Biography*. London: Virgin Books, 1994.

Ron Wynn, *Tina: The Tina Turner Story*. New York: Collier Books/Macmillan, 1985.

U2

Pete Barrett, "U2 on Video and in Print," *Record Collector*, no. 145 (September 1991), 72–75.

Barbara Bradby, "God's Gift to the Suburbs?" *Popular Music* VIII (January 1989), 109–16.

Barbara Bradby and Brian Tordoe, "To Whom do U2 Appeal?" *OneTwoThreeFour*, no. 4 (winter 1987), 34–41.

Peter Doggett, "U2," *Record Collector*, no. 112 (December 1988), 3–6.

Eamon Dunphy, *Unforgettable Fire: Past, Present, and Future—The Definitive Biography of U2*. New York: Warner Books, 1988.

Bill Flanagan, "Bono," in *Written in My Soul: Conversations with Rock's Great Songwriters.* Chicago: Contemporary Books, 1987, 404–16.

Bill Flanagan, "U2: Soul Revelation and the Baptism of Fire," *Musician*, no. 75 (January 1985), 38–43.

Bill Flanagan, "One If by Land, U2 If by Sea: The Adventures of Bono's Bomb Squad," *Musician*, no. 167 (September 1992), 50–70.

Bill Graham, *U2: The Early Days*. New York: Delta Books, 1990.

Jo-Ann Greene, "U2," *Record Collector*, no. 85 (September 1986), 10–12.

John Harvey, "U2: The Early Years," *Record Collector*, no. 127 (March 1990), 3–8.

James Henke, "Blessed Are the Peacemakers," *Rolling Stone*, no. 397 (June 9, 1983), 11–14.

Susan Mackey-Kallis, " 'How Long to Sing This Song?': The Rhetorical Vision of U2's 'Holy' Community," *Popular Music and Society* XIV (fall 1990), 51–58.

Geoff Parkyn, *U2—Touch the Flame: An Illustrated Documentary*. New York: Perigee Books, 1988.

Fred Schruers, "U2," *Musician*, no. 53 (May 1983), 44–50.

Niall Stokes, *U2: Three Chords and the Truth*. New York: Harmony Books, 1989.

Timothy White, "At Play in the Fields of the Lord: Bono Vox on the History of U2," *Goldmine*, no. 270 (November 30, 1990), 8–11, 13.

Gary Young, "U2," *Record Collector*, no. 51 (November 1983), 8–11.

Ritchie Valens

Alan Clark, *Ritchie Valens (1941–1959)—Number Two*. West Covina, CA: Alan Lungstrum/National Rock and Roll Archives, 1989.

Bruce Eder, "Ritchie Valens," *Goldmine*, no. 223 (February 10, 1989), 14–18.

Marcia Farley, "Ritchie Valens," *Cat Tales*, no. 4 (March 1992), 6.

Salvador Guitarez and Beverly Mendheim, "Ritchie Valens: The Spirit Continues," *DISCoveries* III (February 1990), 34–36.

Martin Hawkins, "Ritchie Valens," *The History of Rock*, no. 10 (1982), 196–7.

Beverly A. Mendheim, *Ritchie Valens: The First Latino Rocker*. Tempe, AZ: Bilingual Review Press (Hispanic Research Center at Arizona State University), 1987.

Beverly A. Mendheim, "Ritchie Valens: Remembering 'The 17-Year-Old Recording Sensation'," *Goldmine*, no. 168 (January 2, 1987), 22, 59–60.

Beverly Mendheim, "Spotlight on Ritchie Valens," *Rockin' 50s*, no. 6 (June 1987), 9–16.

Paul Pelletier, "Ritchie Valens," *Record Collector*, no. 76 (December 1985), 54–56.

"Ritchie Valens," *The Golden Age*, no. 13 (October 1987), 4–9.

Chan Romero, "Remembering Ritchie [Valens]," *Now Dig This*, no. 132 (March 1994), 20–21.

Stevie Ray Vaughan

Almost Slim, "Stevie Ray Vaughan," *Goldmine*, no. 228 (April 21, 1989), 10–14.

Kenneth Bays, "Trouble Once More: Stevie Ray's Rhythm Section Forging a New Legacy," *Blues Revue*, no. 64 (January-February 2001), 8–11.

Stephanie Chernikowski, "Stevie Ray and Jimmie Vaughan: A Final Interview," *Guitar Player* XXV (March 1991), 37–40.

B. Lee Cooper, "Review of *Hats Off to Stevie Ray* (1993), *Greatest Hits* (1995), and *A Tribute to Stevie Ray Vaughan* (1996)," *Popular Music and Society* XX, no. 3 (fall 1996), 125–7.

Larry Coryell, "Praying through the Guitar: Stevie Ray Vaughan Interview," *Musician*, no. 134 (December 1989), 70–82.

Dan Forte, "Brothers," *Guitar Player* XXV (March 1991), 26–35.

Dan Forte, "Pride and Joy: Stevie Ray Vaughan, 1954–1990," *Guitar Player* XXV (March 1991), 22–24.

Dan Forte, "Soul to Soul," *Guitar Player* XXV (March 1991), 42–44, 46–49.

Dan Forte, "Stevie Ray Vaughan," *Guitar Player* XVIII (October 1984), 68–76, 135.

David Fricke, "Texas Six String Shoot-Out: Stevie Ray Vaughan—'It's Gotta Be Real'," *Musician*, no. 59 (September 1983), 78–79, 82, 94.

Dennis V. Hickey, "Stevie Ray Vaughan Concert Posters: A Visual History of the Master of the Blues Guitar," *Goldmine*, no. 500 (September 24, 1999), 116, 128.

Jim Kelton, "Stevie [Ray Vaughan] Blows Through," *Blues Revue*, no. 59 (August 2000), 18–21.

Keri Leigh, *Stevie Ray: Soul to Soul*. Dallas, TX: Taylor, 1993.

Joe Nick Patoski and Bill Crawford, "The Coming of Stevie Ray Vaughan: The Early Days of the Texas Guitar Legend," *Musician*, no. 175 (May 1993), 38–49, 52–53.

Joe Nick Patoski and Bill Crawford, *Stevie Ray Vaughan: Caught in the Crossfire*. Boston: Little, Brown, 1993.

Tony Scherman, "Stevie Ray Vaughan, 1954–1990: Lost and Found and Lost Again," *Musician*, no. 145 (November 1990), 66–72.

Alexander Shashko, "Ain't Gone 'n' Give Up on Love: Remembering Stevie Ray Vaughan," *Goldmine*, no. 500 (September 24, 1999), 16–20, 26–34.

Timothy White, "Stevie Ray Vaughan: Talking with the Master," *Musician*, no. 152 (June 1991), 36–46.

Muddy Waters

Don DeMichael, "Father and Son: An Interview with Muddy Waters and Paul Butterfield," *Down Beat* XXXVI (August 7, 1969), 12–13, 32.

Robert Gordon, *Can't Be Satisfied: The Life and Times of Muddy Waters*. Boston: Little, Brown, 2002.

Peter Guralnick, "Muddy Waters: Gone to Main Street," in *Feel Like Goin' Home: Portraits in Blues and Rock 'n' Roll*. New York: Outerbridge and Dienstfrey, 1971, 42–46.

Brian Hogg, "Muddy Waters," *Record Collector*, no. 68 (April 1985), 36–40.

Christine Kreiser, "Muddy Waters: The *Real* Hoochie Coochie Man," *Blues Revue*, no. 76 (June/July 2002), 8–15.

Dave Marsh, "Muddy Waters, 1915–1983: Let's Say He Was a Gentleman," in *Fortunate Son*. New York: Random House, 1985, 74–78.

George A. Moonoogian, "Muddy Waters: The Man, the Music, the Legend," *Record Collector's Monthly*, no. 9 (May 1983), 1, 11.

Chris Morris, "Deep in the Big Muddy: The Master Bluesman Gets His Dues," *Musician*, no. 136 (February 1990), 112–14.

Bob Naylor, "Muddy Waters: The Blues Had a Baby and They Called It Rock 'n' Roll," *Now Dig This*, no. 116 (November 1992), 5–8.

Jim O'Neal and Amy van Singel, "Muddy Waters," in *The Voice of the Blues*, edited by Jim O'Neal and Amy van Singel. New York: Routledge, 2002, 154–201.

Jas Obrecht, "Muddy Waters: Bluesman, 1915–1983," *Guitar Player* XVII (August 1983), 48–57, 67–70.

Paul Oliver, "Muddy Waters—'Hoochie-Coochie Man'," *Jazz Monthly* IV (January 1959), 2–6.

Robert Palmer, "Muddy Waters: The Delta Son Never Sets," *Rolling Stone*, no. 275 (October 5, 1978), 53–56.

Robert Palmer, "Muddy Waters: 1915—1983," *Rolling Stone*, no. 398 (June 23, 1983), 37–40.

Jones Rooney, *Bossmen: Bill Monroe and Muddy Waters*. New York: Dial Press, 1971.

Arlen Roth, "Electric Slide, Muddy Waters Style," *Guitar Player* XVII (August 1983), 72–77.

Sandra B. Tooze, *Muddy Waters: The Mojo Man*. Toronto, Ontario: ECW Press, 1997.

Bob Tremain, "I Feel Like Going Home: Muddy Waters, 1915–1983," *R.P.M.*, no. 1 (August 1983), 6–7.

Pete Welding, "Muddy Waters: Gone to Main Street," in *Bluesland: Portraits of Twelve Major American Blues Masters*, edited by Pete Welding and Toby Bryon. New York: Dutton/Penguin Books, 1991, 130–57.

Tom Wheeler, "(Muddy) Waters/(Johnny) Winter Interview," *Guitar Player* XVII (August 1983), 58–65.

Phil Wight and Fred Rothwell (comps.), *The Complete Muddy Waters*. Cheadle, England: Blues and Rhythm, 1990.

Jerry Wexler

T. Fox, "Jerry Wexler: Navigator of the Atlantic Sound," *Audio* LXIX (May 1985), 52–59.

T. Fox, "Jerry Wexler: Navigator of the Atlantic Sound," *Audio* LXIX (June 1985), 62–71.

Fred Goodman, "Jerry Wexler: Production without Style—on Purpose," *Musician*, no. 181 (November 1993), 56–61.

Arnold Shaw, "Jerry Wexler Interview," in *The Rockin' 50s* (New York: Hawthorn Books, 1974), 78–79.

Richard Skelly, "Jerry Wexler: Mr. Rhythm 'n' Blues," *Goldmine*, no. 353 (February 4, 1994), 36–50, 94, 96.

Joe Smith, "Jerry Wexler," in *Off the Record: An Oral History of Popular Music*. New York: Warner Books, 1988, 80–82.

Wayne Stierle, "Ertegun and Wexler: The First Rock and Roll Songwriters," *DISCoveries* II (July 1989), 100–1.

Dorothy Wade and Justine Picardie, *Music Man: Ahmet Ertegun, Atlantic Records, and the Triumph of Rock 'n' Roll*. New York: W.W. Norton and Company, 1990.

Jerry Wexler and David Ritz, *Rhythm and the Blues: A Life in American Music*. New York: Knopf, 1993.

Jerry Wexler, "What It Is—Is Swamp Music—Is What It Is," *Billboard*, 81 (December 27, 1969), 70.

The Who

Richard Barnes, *The Who: Maximum R & B* (rev. ed.). London: Plexus Books, 1995.

Dougal Butler, with Chris Trengove and Peter Lawrence, *Full Moon: The Amazing Rock and Roll Life of the Late Keith Moon*. New York: William Morrow, 1981.

Chris Charlesworth, *Townshend: A Career Biography*. New York: Proteus Books, 1984.

Ted Dicks (ed.), *A Decade of the Who: An Authorized History in Music, Paintings, Words, and Photographs*. New York: Music Sales, 1977; London: Fabulous Music, 1977.

Peter Doggett, "The Who's U.K. Singles," *Record Collector*, no. 76 (December 1985), 3–10.

Thom Duffy, "I'm a Sensation: You Could Call Me Mr. Townshend, but That's Not How I Think of Myself," *Musician*, no. 177 (July 1993), 34–45.

Bill Flanagan, "Pete Townshend: Between Rock and a Hard Place," *Musician*, no. 95 (September 1986), 78–85, 113–14.

Tony Fletcher, *Moon: The Life and Death of a Rock Legend*. New York: HarperCollins, 2000.

Geoffrey Giuliano, *Behind Blue Eyes: The Life of Pete Townshend*. New York: Dutton/Penguin Books, 1996.

Ed Hanel (comp.), *The Who: An Illustrated Discography*. London: Omnibus Press, 1981.

Dave Marsh, *Before I Get Old: The Story of the Who*. New York: St. Martin's Press, 1983.

Larry David Smith, *Pete Townshend: The Minstrel's Dilemma*. Westport, CT: Praeger, 1999.

Stephen Wolter, and Karen Kimber, *The Who in Print: An Annotated Bibliography, 1965 through 1990*. Jefferson, NC: McFarland, 1992.

Hank Williams

Derek Bull, "Hank Williams," *Record Collector*, no. 125 (January 1990), 79–83.

Jay Caress, *Hank Williams: Country Music's Tragic King*. New York: Stein and Day, 1979.

Howard A. Dewitt, "Hank Williams: The Road to Stardom Runs through the Louisiana Hayride," *Blue Suede News*, no. 22 (spring 1993), 6–8.

Colin Escott, with George Merritt and William MacEwen, *Hank Williams: The Biography*. Boston: Little, Brown, 1995.

Chet Flippo, *Your Cheatin' Heart: A Biography of Hank Williams*. Garden City, NY: Dolphin/Doubleday, 1985.

Tim Jones, with Harold McAlindon and Richard Courtney, *The Essential Hank Williams*. Nashville, TN: Eggman, 1996.

George William Koon, *Hank Williams: A Bio-Bibliography*. Westport, CT: Greenwood, 1983.

Richard Leppert and George Lipsitz, " 'Everybody's Lonesome for Somebody': Age, the Body, and Experience in the Music of Hank Williams," *Popular Music* IX (October 1990), 259–74.

Christopher Metress, "Sing Me a Song about the Ramblin' Man: Visions and Revisions of Hank Williams in Country Music," in *Readin' Country Music: Steel Guitars, Opry Stars, and Honky Tonk Bars*, edited by Cecelia Tichi. Durham, NC: Duke University Press, 1995, 7–27.

Larry Powell, "Hank Williams: Loneliness and Psychological Alienation," *Journal of Country Music* VI (fall 1975), 130–5.

Roger M. Williams, *Sing a Sad Song: The Life of Hank Williams* (2d ed.). Urbana: University of Illinois Press, 1981.

Chris Woodford, "The Legendary Hank Williams—Part One," *Now Dig This*, no. 35 (February 1986), 28–30.

Chris Woodford, "The Legendary Hank Williams—Part Two," *Now Dig This*, no. 36 (March 1986), 18–22.

Chris Woodford, "The Legendary Hank Williams—Part Three," *Now Dig This*, no. 37 (April 1986), 29–31.

Chris Woodford, "The Legendary Hank Williams—Part Four," *Now Dig This*, no. 38 (May 1986), 22–24.

Chris Woodford, "The Legendary Hank Williams—Part Five," *Now Dig This*, no. 39 (June 1986), 24–26.

Jackie Wilson

"The Blues and Soul Hall of Fame: no. 11—Jackie Wilson," *Blues and Soul*, no. 579 (February 5–18, 1991), 21–23.

B. Lee Cooper, "Jackie Wilson—Mr. Excitement? Mr. Musical Diversity? Mr. Song Stylist? Or Mr. Stage Show? A Review Essay," *Popular Music and Society* XVII (summer 1993), 119–22.

Tony Douglas, *Lonely Teardrops: The Jackie Wilson Story*. London: Sanctuary, 1997.

Gary Giddins, "Jolson's Greatest Heir," in *Rhythm-a-Ning: Jazz and Innovation in the 80's*. New York: Oxford University Press, 1985, 146–52.

Bill Griggs, "Spotlight on Jackie Wilson (Part One)," *Rockin' 50s*, no. 26 (October 1990), 8–15.

Bill Griggs, "Spotlight on Jackie Wilson (Part Two)," *Rockin' 50s*, no. 27 (December 1990), 7–13.

Dick Jacobs, as told to Tim Holmes, "Jackie Wilson—Taking It Higher: A Producer Remembers 'Mr. Excitement'," *Musician*, no. 111 (January 1988), 21–26, 97–98.

Kevin Keegan, "Above Jacob's Ladder: A Tribute to Jackie Wilson," *R.P.M.*, no. 4 (February-March 1984), 8–11, 26–27, 59–61.

Kurt Loder, "Jackie Wilson: 1934–1984," *Rolling Stone*, no. 417 (March 15, 1984), 44.

Joe McEwen, "Jackie Wilson," in *Rolling Stone Illustrated History of Rock and Roll* (2d ed.), edited by Anthony DeCurtis and James Henke, with Holly George-Warren. New York: Random House/Rolling Stone Press, 1992, 139–42.

Ralph M. Newman and Alan Kaltman, "Lonely Teardrops: The Story of a Forgotten Man [Jackie Wilson]," *Time Barrier Express* III, no. 24 (April-May 1979), 29–32.

Pete Nickols, "Jackie Wilson," *Record Collector*, no. 56 (April 1984), 15–18.

Robert Pruter, "Jackie Wilson: His Chicago Years," *Goldmine*, no. 192 (December 4, 1987), 30, 34.

Robert Pruter, "Jackie Wilson: The Most Tragic Figure in Rhythm 'n' Blues," *Goldmine*, no. 294 (November 1, 1991), 10–18.

Clive Richardson, "Hot Gospel," *The History of Rock*, no. 17 (1982), 330–2.

Stevie Wonder

Zita Allen, "Stevie Wonder," *Stereo Review* XLIV (May 1980), 56–60.

David Bianco, "Stevie Wonder," in *Heat Wave: The Motown Fact Book*. Ann Arbor, MI: Pierian Press, 1988, 125–31.

David Breskin, "Waiting on the Man: Stevie (Wonder) Comes down from the Mountaintop," *Musician*, no. 64 (February 1984), 52–60, 65.

Sharon Davis, "The Blues and Soul Hall of Fame: no. 7—Stevie Wonder," *Blues and Soul*, no. 575 (December 4–17, 1990), 25–29.

Peter Doggett, "Stevie Wonder's U.K. Singles," *Record Collector*, no. 82 (June 1986), 23–27.

Paul Gambaccini, "Stevie Wonder," in *Masters of Rock*. London: Omnibus Press, 1982, 124–32.

Barry Krutchik, "Stevie Wonder: Jungle Fever and Funk," *Musician*, no. 154 (August 1991), 21–22.

Dave Marsh, "Scoring Blind," in *Fortunate Son.* New York: Random House, 1985, 277–82.

Steve Perry, "Blind Optimism: Stevie Wonder Sees Only the Good," *Musician*, no. 115 (May 1988), 14–20, 112–14.

Trevor Rhodes, "Stevie Wonder," *Record Collector*, no. 13 (September 1980), 38–42.

John Rockwell, "Stevie Wonder," in *Rolling Stone Illustrated History of Rock and Roll* (2d ed.), edited by Anthony DeCurtis and James Henke, with Holly George-Warren. New York: Random House/Rolling Stone Press, 1992, 293–8.

John Swenson, *Stevie Wonder.* New York: Harper & Row, 1986.

Harold Dean Trulear, "The Prophetic Character of Black Secular Music: Stevie Wonder," *Journal of Black Sacred Music* III (fall 1989), 75–84.

Eric Robert Weisman, "The Good Man Singing Well: Stevie Wonder as Noble Lover," *Critical Studies in Mass Communication* II (June 1985), 136–51.

Craig Werner, "Stevie Wonder: Singing in the Key of Life," *Goldmine*, no. 501 (October 8, 1999), 14–20, 28–32.

Timothy White, "Stevie Wonder," in *Rock Lives: Profiles and Interviews.* New York: Henry Holt, 1990, 204–9.

Frank Zappa

Howard A. DeWitt, "Frank Zappa: Child of the 1950s," *Blue Suede News*, no. 26 (spring 1994), 6–10.

"Frank Zappa," *Musician*, no. 184 (February 1994), 18–32.

Michael Gray, *Mother! The Frank Zappa Story* (rev. ed.). London: Plexus Books, 1992.

Richard Kostelanetz (ed.), *The Frank Zappa Companion: Four Decades of Commentary.* New York: Schirmer Books, 1997.

Stuart Penny, "Frank Zappa on CD: 1966–1979," *Record Collector*, no. 165 (May 1993), 88–93.

Stuart Penny, "Frank Zappa on CD: 1979–1988," *Record Collector*, no. 171 (November 1993), 86–90.

Stuart Penny, "Frank Zappa on CD: 1988–1994," *Record Collector*, no. 177 (May 1994), 74–80.

Matt Resnicoff, "Poetic Justice: Frank Zappa Puts Us in Our Place," *Musician*, no. 157 (November 1991), 66–77.

William Ruhlmann, "Frank Zappa, 1940–1993," *Goldmine*, no. 351 (January 7, 1994), 8–12.

William Ruhlmann, "Frank Zappa: The Present Day Composer," *Goldmine*, no. 375 (December 9, 1994), 14–46, 74–84.

Greg Russo, "The Collected History and Improvisations of Frank Zappa," *DISCoveries*, no. 57 (February 1993), 22–34.

Greg Russo, "Frank Zappa (Born 1940–Died 1993)," *DISCoveries*, no. 72 (May 1994), 48–53.

Greg Russo, "Frank Zappa—Part Two," *DISCoveries*, no. 73 (June 1994), 43–51.

Ben Watson, *Frank Zappa: The Negative Dialectics of Poodle Play*. New York: St. Martin's Press, 1995.

ZZ Top

Terry Atkinson, "ZZ Top!" *Waxpaper* IV (February 12, 1979), 21–22.

David Blayney, *Sharp-Dressed Men: ZZ Top Behind the Scenes—From Blues to Boogie to Beards*. New York: Hyperion Books, 1994.

Dante Bonutto, "Top Hats and Tales . . ." *Kerrang!* no. 39 (April 7–20, 1983), 4–9.

Stanley Booth, "Bring Billy Gibbons His Burden," *Musician*, no. 119 (September 1988), 70–78.

J. D. Considine, "Texas Six String Shoot-Out: Billy Gibbons—'It's Gotta Have Crunch'," *Musician*, no. 59 (September 1983), 78–80, 92.

Deborah Frost, *ZZ Top: Bad and Worldwide*. New York: Collier Books, 1985.

Randal C. Hill, "ZZ Top: Tres Hombres Pre-MTV," *Goldmine*, no. 173 (March 13, 1987), 26, 102.

Cub Koda, "ZZ Top: Twenty Years of Texas Cool," *Goldmine*, no. 293 (October 18, 1991), 8–16, 122.

Kurt Loder, "ZZ Top: The Boys Just Want to Have Fun," *Rolling Stone*, no. 419 (April 12, 1984), 19–20, 63–64.

Bill Milkowski, "Billy Gibbons Blazes His Way to the Top," *Guitar World* V (May 1984), 28–34.

Jeff Nesin, "Whopping and Bopping with ZZ Top," *Creem* XV (September 1983), 46–47, 68–69.

Jas Obrecht, "Billy Gibbons," *Texas Guitar* III (winter 1987), 6–17.

Jas Obrecht, "High-Tech Boogieman," *Texas Guitar* III (winter 1987), 19–25.

Jas Obrecht, "ZZ Top, Bill Gibbons—Bad and Nationwide," *Guitar Player* XV (February 1981), 64–66.

Harold Steinblatt and Brad Tolinski, "Doubleback," *Guitar World* XII (March 1991), 36–46, 60, 89.

Dave Thompson, "ZZ Top," *Record Collector*, no. 103 (March 1988), 42–48.

Timothy White, "How Tres Hombres Discovered the Electric Blues," *Musician*, no. 119 (September 1988), 74–80, 121.

Timothy White, "ZZ Top: The Ongoing Legend of Texan Rock's Rough Boys," *Musician*, no. 87 (January 1986), 54–65.

Chapter 3

Popular Music Styles and Dance Trends as Topics for Classroom Discussion and Student Research Projects

Music styles and dance trends offer a variety of potential topics for student investigation. The '90s lyrical hostility in rap can be compared and contrasted with the more moderate '60s social criticism contained in folk and folk-rock. The Louisiana regional lifestyles of Cajun and zydeco music can be examined against the cultural heritages found in Kentucky bluegrass and Minnesota polka music. For geographers, the roots of music in specific places—jazz in New Orleans, blues in Memphis, Motown sound in Detroit, beach music in Myrtle Beach, and grunge in Seattle—beckon for classroom discussion. The origination and revival of dance trends such as swing or music styles like rockabilly are also worth reviewing from economic, sociological, and psychological perspectives. The impact of American adaptations of international rhythms such as calypso, reggae, and salsa by U.S. recording artists such as Harry Belafonte, Stevie Wonder, and Paul Simon offers opportunities to assess the evolution of musical styles. The following pages offer resources for teaching, research, and discussion.

197

General Observations and Overviews on Segmentation of Music

Garth Alper, "Making Sense out of Postmodern Music?" *Popular Music and Society*, no. 4 (winter 2000), 1–14.

Amiri Baraka and Amini Baraka, *The Music: Reflections on Jazz and Blues*. New York: William Morrow, 1987.

Harris M. Berger, *Metal, Rock, and Jazz: Perception and the Phenomenology of Musical Experience*. Hanover, NH: Wesleyan University Press/University Press of New England, 1999.

Billy Bergman and Richard Horn, *Experimental Pop: Frontiers of the Rock Era*. Poole, England: Blandford Press, 1985.

St. George Bryan, "Rock 'n' Roll Dictionary," *Wavelength*, no. 65 (April 1986), 20.

Richard Carlin and Bob Carlin, *Southern Exposure: The Story of Southern Music in Pictures and Words*. New York: Billboard Books/Watson-Guptill, 2000.

Katherine Charlton, *Rock Music Styles: A History* (3d ed.). Boston: McGraw-Hill, 1998.

Ricardo Cooney, Kathleen Lavey, Don Ramsey, and Tom Schmitz, "A Definitive Approach," *Lansing* [Michigan] *State Journal* (January 2, 1992), 4–5.

B. Lee Cooper, "Review of *The Golden Age of American Rock 'n' Roll: Hot 100 Hits From 1954–1963* (Six Volumes)," *Popular Music and Society* XXI (winter 1997), 131–2.

B. Lee Cooper, "Review of *Rockin' the Classics and Classicizin' the Rock: A Selectively Annotated Discography* by Janell R. Duxbury," *Popular Music and Society* XI (fall 1987), 118–20.

B. Lee Cooper, "Review of *Rockin' the Classics and Classicizin' the Rock: A Selectively Annotated Discography—First Supplement* by Janell R. Duxbury," *Popular Music and Society* XVI (summer 1992), 116–17.

B. Lee Cooper, "Review of *The Seventh Stream: The Emergence of RocknRoll in American Popular Music* by Phillip H. Ennis," *Popular Music and Society* XVII (winter 1993), 136–7.

Philip H. Ennis, *The Seventh Stream: The Emergence of RocknRoll in American Popular Music*. Hanover, NH: Wesleyan University Press, 1992.

Mark C. Gridley, "Clarifying Labels: Jazz, Rock, Funk, and Jazz–Rock," *Popular Music and Society* XI, no. 2 (1983), 27–34.

Craig Heller, *From Metal to Mozart: The Rock and Roll Guide to Classical Music*. San Francisco: Chronicle Books, 1994.

Nat Hentoff, "Blues, Rock, Jazz, Country: The Endless River of Our Music," *Words and Music* II (May 1972), 20–25.

Charles Keil, " 'Ethnic' Music Traditions in the USA (Black Music; Country Music; Others; All)," *Popular Music* XIII (May 1994), 175–8.

Chuck Mancuso, *Popular Music and the Underground: Foundations of Jazz, Blues, Country, and Rock, 1900–1950*. Dubuque, IA: Kendall/Hunt, 1996.

Richard A. Peterson, "Popular Music Is Plural," *Popular Music and Society* XXI (spring 1997), 53–58.

Ellen Sander and Tom Clark, "A Rock Taxonomy," in Ellen Sander, *Trips: Rock Life in the Sixties*. New York: Scribner's, 1973, 162–258.

Robert Santelli, Holly George-Warren, and Jim Brown (eds.), *American Roots Music*. New York: Harry N. Abrams, 2001.

Jeff Todd Titon and Bob Carlin (eds.), *American Musical Traditions—Volume One: Native American Music*. New York: Schirmer Reference, 2002.

Jeff Todd Titon and Bob Carlin (eds.), *American Musical Traditions—Volume Two: African American Music*. New York: Schirmer Reference, 2002.

Jeff Todd Titon and Bob Carlin (eds.), *American Musical Traditions—Volume Three: British Isles Music*. New York: Schirmer Reference, 2002.

Jeff Todd Titon and Bob Carlin (eds.), *American Musical Traditions—Volume Four: European American Music*. New York: Schirmer Reference, 2002.

Jeff Todd Titon and Bob Carlin (eds.), *American Musical Traditions—Volume Five: Latino American and Asian American Music*. New York: Schirmer Reference, 2002.

Major Styles and Trends

Blues

Houston A. Baker, Jr., *Blues, Ideology, and Afro-American Literature: A Vernacular Theory*. Chicago: University of Chicago Press, 1985.

William Barlow, *"Looking up at Down": The Emergence of the Blues Culture*. Philadelphia: Temple University Press, 1989.

Bruce Bastin, *Crying for the Carolines*. London: Studio Vista, 1971.

Bruce Bastin, *Red River Blues: The Blues Tradition in the Southeast*. Champaign: University of Illinois Press, 1986.

Bob Brunning, *Blues in Britain: The History—1950s to the Present*. London: Blandford Press, 1995.

Samuel Charters, *The Legacy of the Blues: Art and Lives of Twelve Great Bluesmen*. New York: Da Capo Press, 1975.

Lawrence Cohn, *Nothing but the Blues: The Music and the Musicians*. New York: Abbeville Press, 1993.

B. Lee Cooper, "Review of *All Music Guide to the Blues* by Michael Erlewine et al. and *MusicHound Blues: The Essential Album Guide* by Leland Rucker," *Popular Music and Society* XXIV (spring 2000), 121–2.

B. Lee Cooper, "Review of *Chess Blues*," *Popular Music and Society* XVIII (fall 1994), 99–100.

B. Lee Cooper, "Review of *Every Woman's Blues: The Best of the New Generation*," *Rock and Blues News*, no. 4 (May-June 1999), 43.

John Cowley and Paul Oliver (eds.), *The New Blackwell Guide to Recorded Blues*. Cambridge, MA: Blackwell, 1996.

Francis Davis, *The History of the Blues: The Roots, the Music, and the People From Charley Patton to Robert Cray*. New York: Hyperion Books, 1995.

David Dicaire, *Blues Singers*. Jefferson, NC: McFarland, 1999.

Robert M. W. Dixon, John Godrich, and Howard W. Rye (comps.), *Blues and Gospel Records, 1890–1943* (4th ed.). New York: Oxford University Press, 1997.

Michael Erlewine, Vladimir Bogdanov, Chris Woodstra, and Cub Koda (eds.), *All Music Guide to the Blues* (2d ed.). San Francisco: Miller Freeman Books, 1999.

David Evans, *Big Road Blues: Tradition and Creativity in the Folk Blues*. Berkeley: University of California Press, 1982.

William Ferris, *Blues from the Delta*. Garden City, NY: Anchor Books/Doubleday, 1979.

Julio Finn, *The Bluesman: The Musical Heritage of Black Men and Women in the Americas*. Brooklyn, New York: Interlink, 1992 (first published 1986).

James Fraher (ed.), *The Blues Is a Feeling: Voices and Visions of African-American Blues Musicians*. Mount Horeb, WI: Midwest Tradition, 1998.

Paul Garon, *Blues and the Poetic Spirit*. New York: Da Capo Press, 1975.

Alan Govenar, *Meeting the Blues: The Rise of the Texas Sound*. New York: Da Capo Press, 1995.

Stephen Green, *Really the Blues*. San Francisco: Woodford, 1996.

Bob Groom, *The Blues Revival*. London: Studio Vista, 1971.

Peter Guralnick, *Listener's Guide to the Blues*. New York: Facts on File, 1982.

Barry Hansen, *Rhino's Cruise through the Blues*. San Francisco: Miller Freeman Books, 2000.

Sheldon Harris (comp.), *Blues Who's Who: A Biographical Dictionary of Blues Singers*. New Rochelle, NY: Arlington House, 1979.

Gérard Herzhaft (translated by Brigitte Debord), *Encyclopedia of the Blues* (2d ed.). Fayetteville: University of Arkansas Press, 1997.

Laurence J. Hyman and Stephen Green, *Going to Chicago: A Year on the Chicago Blues Scene*. San Francisco: Woodford, 1990.

LeRoi Jones (aka Imamu Amiri Baraka), *Blues People: Negro Music in White America*. New York: William Morrow, 1963.

Charles Keil, *Urban Blues*. Chicago: University of Chicago Press, 1966.

Colin Larkin (ed.), *The Guinness Who's Who of Blues Music*. Enfield, England: Guinness Books, 1993.

Mike Leadbitter and Neil Slaven, *Blues Records, 1943–1970: A Selective Discography—Volume One: A–K*. London: Record Information Services, 1987.

Mike Leadbitter, Leslie Fancourt, and Paul Pelletier (comps.), *Blues Records, 1943–1970—Volume Two: L to Z*. Milford, NH: Big Nickel Publications, 1994.

Mike Leadbitter, *Crowley, Louisiana Blues: The Story of J. D. Miller and His Blues Artists—With a Guide to Their Music*. Bexhill-on-Sea, England: Blues Unlimited, 1968.

Mike Leadbitter, *Delta Country Blues*. Bexhill-on-Sea, England: Blues Unlimited, 1968.

Mike Leadbitter and Eddie Shuler, *From the Bayou*. Bexhill-on-Sea, England: Blues Unlimited, 1969.

Mike Leadbitter (ed.), *Nothing but the Blues*. London: Hanover Books, 1971.

Alan Lomax, *The Land Where the Blues Began*. New York: Pantheon Books, 1993.

Lynn Ellis McCutcheon, *Rhythm and Blues: An Experience and Adventure in Its Origin and Development*. Arlington, VA: Beatty, 1971.

Margaret McKee and Fred Chisenhall, *Beale Black and Blue: Life and Music on Black America's Main Street*. Baton Rouge: Louisiana State University Press, 1981.

Jeffrey Melnick, *A Right to Sing the Blues: African Americans, Jews, and American Popular Song*. Cambridge: Harvard University Press, 1999.

Richard Middleton, *Pop Music and the Blues: A Study of the Relationship and Its Significance*. London: Victor Gollancz, 1972.

Albert Murray, *The Hero and the Blues*. Columbia: University of Missouri Press, 1973.

Albert Murray, *Stomping the Blues*. New York: Da Capo Press, 2000.

Giles Oakley, *The Devil's Music: A History of the Blues*. New York: Da Capo Press, 1997 (first published 1978).

Jas Obrecht (ed.), *Rollin' and Tumblin': The Postwar Blues Guitarists*. San Francisco: Miller Freeman Books, 2000.

Paul Oliver, *Aspects of the Blues Tradition*. New York: Oak, 1970.

Paul Oliver (ed.), *The Blackwell Guide to Blues Records*. Cambridge, MA: Basil Blackwell, 1989.

Paul Oliver, *Blues Fell This Morning: Meaning in the Blues*. Cambridge: Cambridge University Press, 1990.

Paul Oliver, *Blues Off the Record: The Thirty Years of Blues Commentary*. Tunbridge Wells, England: Baton Press, 1984.

Paul Oliver, *Conversation with the Blues*. New York: Horizon Press, 1982.

Paul Oliver, *Screening the Blues*. London: Cassell, 1968.

Paul Oliver, *Songsters and Saints: Vocal Traditions on Race Records*. Cambridge: Cambridge University Press, 1984.

Paul Oliver, *The Story of the Blues*. Radnor, PA: Chilton Books, 1969.

Paul Oliver, Tony Russell, Robert M. W. Dixon, John Godrich, and Howard Rye, *Yonder Come the Blues: The Evolution of a Genre*. Cambridge: Cambridge University Press, 2001.

Bengt Olsson, *Memphis Blues*. London: Studio Vista, 1970.

Harry Oster (comp.), *Living Country Blues*. New York: Minerva Press, 1975.

Robert Palmer, *Deep Blues*. New York: Viking Press, 1981.

Dave Rubin, *Inside the Blues, 1942–1982: Four Decades of the Greatest Electric Blues Guitarists*. Milwaukee, WI: Hal Leonard, 1995.

Leland Rucker (ed.), *MusicHound: The Essential Album Guide*. Detroit, MI: Visible Ink Press, 1998.

Tony Russell, *Blacks, Whites and Blues*. New York: Stein and Day, 1970.

Tony Russell, *The Blues: From Robert Johnson to Robert Cray*. New York: Schirmer Books, 1997.

Robert Santelli, *The Big Book of the Blues: A Biographical Encyclopedia*. New York: Penguin Books, 1993.

Frank Scott and the Staff of Down Home Music (comps.), *The Down Home Guide to the Blues*. Chicago: A Cappella Books, 1991.

Keith Shadwick, *Blues: Keeping the Faith*. Edison, NJ: Chartwell Books, 1998.

Austin Sonnier, Jr., *A Guide to the Blues: History, Who's Who, Research Sources*. Westport, CT: Greenwood, 1994.

Jon Michael Spencer, *Blues and Evil*. Knoxville: University of Tennessee Press, 1993.

Art Tipaldi, *Children of the Blues: 49 Musicians Shaping a New Blues Tradition*. San Francisco: Backbeat Books, 2002.

Jeff Todd Titon, *Early Downhome Blues: A Musical and Cultural Analysis*. Urbana: University of Illinois Press, 1977.

Steven C. Tracy, *Langston Hughes and the Blues*. Urbana: University of Illinois Press, 1988.

Paul Trynka, *Portrait of the Blues: America's Blues Musicians in Their Own Words*. New York: Da Capo Press, 1997.

Ortiz M. Walton, *Music—Black, White, and Blue: A Sociological Survey of the Use and Misuse of Afro-American Music*. New York: William Morrow, 1972.

Gayle Dean Wardlow, *Chasin' That Devil Music: Searching for the Blues*. San Francisco: Miller Freeman Books, 1998.

Pete Welding and Toby Byron (eds.), *Bluesland: Portraits of Twelve Major American Blues Masters*. New York: Dutton/Penguin Books, 1991.

Bill Wyman, with Richard Havers, *Bill Wyman's Blues Odyssey: A Journey to Music's Heart and Soul*. New York: DK, 2001.

Country

Russel D. Barnard (ed.), *The Comprehensive Country Music Encyclopedia*. New York: Country Music Magazine Press Book/Times Books/Random House, 1994.

Charles T. Brown, *Music U.S.A.: America's Country and Western Tradition*. Englewood Cliffs, NJ: Prentice Hall, 1986.

Alan Cackett with Alec Foege, *The Harmony Illustrated Encyclopedia of Country Music* (3d ed.). New York: Crown, 1994.

Richard Carlin, *The Big Book of Country Music: A Biographical Encyclopedia*. New York: Penguin Books, 1995.

Barbara Ching, *Wrong's What I Do Best: Hard Country Music and Contemporary Culture*. New York: Oxford University Press, 2001.

B. Lee Cooper, "Review of *All That Glitters: Country Music in America* by George H. Lewis," *American Culture Association Newsletter* (spring 1994), 3–4.

B. Lee Cooper, "Review of *The Nashville Sound* by Joli Jensen and *Creating Country Music* by Richard A. Peterson," *Popular Music and Society* XXIII (spring 1999), 118–20.

Nicholas Dawidoff, *In the Country of Country: People and Places in American Music*. New York: Pantheon Books, 1997.

Fred Deller, Alan Cackett, Roy Thompson, and Douglas B. Green, *The Harmony Illustrated Encyclopedia of Country Music*. London: Salamander Books, 1986.

Peter Doggett, *Are You Ready for Country: Elvis, Dylan, Parsons and the Roots of Country Rock*. New York: Penguin Books, 2000.

Curtis W. Ellison, *Country Music Culture: From Hard Times to Heaven*. Jackson: University Press of Mississippi, 1995.

Ralph Emery, with Patsi Bale Cox, *The View From Nashville: On the Record With Country Music's Greatest Stars*. New York: William Morrow, 1998.

Michael Erlewine, Vladimir Bogdanov, Chris Woodstra, and Stephen Thomas Erlewine, *All Music Guide to Country: The Experts' Guide to the Best Recordings in Country Music*. San Francisco: Miller Freeman Books, 1997.

Bruce Feiler, *Dreaming Out Loud: Garth Brooks, Wynonna Judd, Wade Hayes and the Changing Face of Nashville*. New York: Spike/Avon Books, 1999.

Cary Ginell and Kevin Coffey, *Discography of Western Swing and Hot String Bands, 1928–1942*. Westport, CT: Greenwood, 2001.

David Goodman, *Modern Twang: An Alternative Country Music Guide and Directory.* Nashville, TN: Dowling Press, 1999.

Douglas B. Green, *Country Roots: The Origins of Country Music.* New York: Hawthorne Books, 1976.

John Grissim, *Country Music: White Man's Blues.* New York: Paper Back Library, 1970.

Chet Hagan, *The Great Country Music Book.* New York: Pocket Books, 1983.

Neil Haislop, Tad Lathrop, and Harry Sumrall, *Giants of Country Music: Classic Sounds and Stars, From the Heart of Nashville to the Top of the Charts.* New York: Billboard Books, 1995.

Gerald W. Haslam, *Workin' Man Blues: Country Music in California.* Berkeley: University of California Press, 1999.

Paul Hemphill, *The Nashville Sound: Bright Lights and Country Music.* New York: Simon and Schuster, 1970.

Dorothy Horstman, *Sing Your Heart Out, Country Boy.* New York: E. P. Dutton, 1975.

Dorothy Horstman (comp.), *Sing Your Heart Out, Country Boy: Classic Country Songs and Their Inside Stories, by the Men and Women Who Wrote Them* (3d ed.). Nashville, TN: Vanderbilt University Press/Country Music Foundation Press, 1995.

Barney Hoskyns, *Say It One More Time for the Broken-Hearted: The Country Side of Southern Soul.* London: Bloomsbury Books, 1998.

Kathleen Hudson, *Telling Stories, Writing Songs: An Album of Texas Songwriters.* Austin: University of Texas Press, 2001.

Joli Jensen, *The Nashville Sound: Authenticity, Commercialization, and Country Music.* Nashville, TN: Vanderbilt University Press, 1998.

Paul Kingsbury (ed.), *The Encyclopedia of Country Music: The Ultimate Guide to the Music.* New York: Oxford University Press, 1998.

Colin Larkin (ed.), *The Guinness Who's Who of Country Music.* Enfield, England: Guinness Books, 1993.

Jennifer Lawler, *Songs of Life: The Meaning of Country Music.* St. Paul, MN: Pogo Press, 1996.

Laurence Leamer, *Three Chords and The Truth: Behind the Scenes with Those Who Make and Shape Country Music.* New York: Harper Paperbacks, 1997.

George H. Lewis (ed.), *All That Glitters: Country Music in America.* Bowling Green, OH: Bowling Green State University Popular Press, 1993.

Horace Logan, with Bill Sloan, *Elvis, Hank, and Me: Making Musical History on the Louisiana Hayride.* New York: St. Martin's Press, 1998.

Bill C. Malone, *Country Music U.S.A: A Fifty-Year History.* Austin: University of Texas Press, 1968.

Bill C. Malone, *Country Music U.S.A.* (rev. ed.). Austin: University of Texas Press, 1985.

Bill C. Malone, *Don't Get above Your Raisin': Country Music and the Southern Working Class.* Urbana: University of Illinois Press, 2002.

Bill C. Malone, *Singing Cowboys and Musical Mountaineers: Southern Culture and the Roots of Country Music.* Athens: University of Georgia Press, 1993.

Bill Malone and Judith McCulloh (eds.), *Stars of Country Music: Uncle Dave Mason to Johnny Rodriguez.* Urbana: University of Illinois Press, 1975.

Brian Mansfield and Gary Graff (eds.), *MusicHound Country: The Essential Album Guide.* Detroit, MI: Visible Ink Press, 1997.

Barry McCloud and contributing writers, *Definitive Country: The Ultimate Encyclopedia of Country Music and Its Performers.* New York: Perigee Books, 1995.

Melton McLaurin and Richard Peterson (eds.), *You Wrote My Life: Lyrical Themes in Country Music.* New York: Gordon and Breach, 1992.

Bob Millard, *Country Music: 70 Years of America's Favorite Music.* New York: Harper Perennial Books, 1993.

John Morthland, *The Best of Country Music: A Critical and Historical Guide to the 750 Greatest Albums.* Garden City, NY: Dolphin/Doubleday, 1984.

Robert K. Oermann, *America's Music: The Roots of Country.* Atlanta, GA: Turner, 1996.

Robert K. Oermann, *A Century of Country: An Illustrated History of Country Music.* New York: TV Books, 1999.

Robert K. Oermann, with Douglas Green, *The Listener's Guide to Country Music.* New York: Facts on File, 1983.

Robert K. Oermann, *The Roots of Country: The Legend of Country.* Atlanta, GA: Turner, 1995.

Richard A. Peterson, *Creating Country Music: Fabricating Authenticity.* Chicago: University of Chicago Press, 1997.

Steven D. Price, *Take Me Home: The Rise of Country and Western Music*. New York: Praeger, 1974.

Tad Richards and Melvin B. Shestack (comps.), *The New Country Music Encyclopedia*. New York: Fireside Books/Simon & Schuster, 1993.

Jimmie N. Rogers, *The Country Music Message: All about Lovin' and Livin'*. Englewood Cliffs, NJ: Prentice Hall, 1983.

Jimmie N. Rogers, *The Country Music Message: Revisited*. Fayetteville: University of Arkansas Press, 1989.

Tony Russell (comp.), *The Complete Country Music Discography, 1922–1942*. Nashville, TN: Country Music Foundation Press, 1997.

Irwin Stambler and Grelun Landon, *Country Music: The Encyclopedia* (3d ed.). New York: St. Martin's Press, 1998.

Cecelia Tichi, *High Lonesome: The American Culture of Country Music*. Chapel Hill: University of North Carolina Press, 1994.

Cecelia Tichi (ed.), *Readin' Country Music: Steel Guitars, Opry Stars, and Honky Tonk Bars*. Durham, NC: Duke University Press, 1995.

Nick Tosches, *Country: Living Legends and Dying Metaphors in America's Biggest Music* (rev. ed.). New York: Scribner's, 1985.

Joel Whitburn (comp.), *Top Country Singles, 1944–2001*. Menomonee Falls, WI: Record Research, 2002.

Charles K. Wolfe, *A Good-Natured Riot: The Birth of the Grand Ole Opry*. Nashville, TN: Vanderbilt University Press/Country Music Foundation, 1999.

Charles K. Wolfe and James E. Akenson (eds.), *Country Music Annual 2000*. Lexington: University Press of Kentucky, 2000.

Kurt Wolff, *Country Music: The Rough Guide*. London: Rough Guides, 2000.

Folk

Kristin Baggelaar and Donald Milton (comps.), *Folk Music: More than a Song*. New York: Thomas Y. Crowell, 1976.

Philip V. Bohlman, *The Study of Folk Music in the Modern World*. Bloomington: Indiana University Press, 1988.

Robert Cantwell, *When We Were Good: The Folk Revival*. Cambridge: Harvard University Press, 1996.

R. Serge Denisoff, *Great Day Coming: Folk Music and the American Left*. Baltimore: Penguin Books, 1971.

David A. DeTurk and A. Poulin, Jr. (eds.), *The American Folk Scene: Dimensions of the Folksong Revival*. New York: Dell, 1967.

William Ferris and Mary L. Hart, *Folk Music and Modern Sound*. Jackson: University of Mississippi Center for the Study of Southern Culture, 1982.

Samuel L. Forucci, *A Folk Song History of America: America through Its Songs*. Englewood Cliffs, NJ: Prentice Hall, 1984.

Phil Hood (ed.), *Artists of American Folk Music: The Legends of Traditional Folk, the Stars of the Sixties, and the Virtuosi of New Acoustic Music*. New York: Quill Books/Guitar Player, 1986.

Dave Laing, Karl Dallas, Robin Denselow, and Robert Shelton, *The Electric Muse: The Story of Folk into Rock*. London: Methuen Press, 1975.

Colin Larkin (ed.), *The Guinness Who's Who of Folk Music*. Enfield, England: Guinness Books, 1993.

Sarah Lifton, *The Listener's Guide to Folk Music*. New York: Facts on File, 1983.

Alan Lomax, *Folk Song Style and Culture*. New Brunswick, NJ: Transaction, 1978.

Terry E. Miller, *Folk Music in America: A Reference Guide*. New York: Garland, 1986.

Neil V. Rosenberg (ed.), *Transforming Tradition: Folk Music Revivals Examined*. Urbana: University of Illinois Press, 1993.

Larry Sandberg and Dick Weissman, *The Folk Music Sourcebook*. Dobbs Ferry, NY: Da Capo Press, 1989.

John Anthony Scott, *The Ballad of America: The History of the United States in Song and Story*. Carbondale: Southern Illinois University Press, 1983.

Neal Walters and Brian Mansfield (eds.), *MusicHound Folk: The Essential Album Guide*. Detroit, MI: Visible Ink Press, 1998.

Jazz

Daniel Allen (comp.), *Bibliography of Discographies—Volume 2: Jazz*. New York: R. R. Bowker, 1981.

Whitney Balliett, *Collected Works: A Journal of Jazz, 1954–2001*. New York: St. Martin's Griffin, 2002.

Whitney Balliett, *Night Creature: A Journal of Jazz, 1975–1980*. New York: Oxford University Press, 1981.

Joachim Berendt, *The Jazz Book: From New Orleans to Rock to Free Jazz* (4th ed.). Westport, CT: Lawrence Hill, 1981.

Stan Britt, *Jazz Guitarists*. New York: Sterling, 1986.

David Butler, *Jazz Noir: Listening to Music from Phantom Lady to the Last Seduction*. Westport, CT: Praeger, 2002.

Ian Carr, Digby Fairweather, and Brian Priestly (eds.), *Jazz—The Rough Guide: The Essential Companion to Artists and Albums*. London: Rough Guides, 1998.

Peter Clayton and Peter Gammond, *The Guinness Jazz Companion*. New York: Sterling Books, 1989.

James Lincoln Collier, *Jazz: The American Theme Song*. New York: Oxford University Press, 1993.

Richard Cook and Brian Morton, *The Penguin Guide to Jazz on CD* (5th ed.). New York: Penguin Putnam, 2000.

Mervyn Cooke, *The Chronicle of Jazz*. New York: Abbeville Press, 1998.

B. Lee Cooper, "Review of *The Creation of Jazz: Music, Race, and Culture in Urban America* by Burton W. Peretti and *Chicago Jazz: A Cultural History, 1904–1930* by William Howland Kenney," *Popular Culture in Libraries* II, no. 4 (1994), 107–9.

Julie Coryell and Laura Friedman, *Jazz-Rock Fusion: The People—The Music*. New York: Delacorte Press, 1978.

Bruce Crowther and Mike Pinfold, *Singing Jazz: The Singers and Their Styles*. San Francisco: Miller Freeman Books, 1997.

Francis Davis, *In the Moment: Jazz in the 1980s*. New York: Oxford University Press, 1986.

Roger Dean, *New Structures in Jazz and Improvised Music: From the 1960s into the 1980s*. New York: Taylor and Francis, 1991.

Dr. Demento, "Jazz vs. Pop: The Cold War Thaws Out," *Waxpaper* IV (February 12, 1979), 18–19.

J. B. Durant, *A Student's Guide to American Jazz and Popular Music: Outlines, Recordings, and Historical Commentary*. Scottsdale, AZ: J. B. Durant, 1984.

Michael Erlewine, Vladimir Bodganov, Chris Woodstra, and Scott Yanow (eds.), *All Music Guide to Jazz* (3d ed.). San Francisco: Miller Freeman Books, 1998.

Leonard Feather, *The Jazz Years: Earwitness to an Era*. New York: Quartet Books, 1986.

Leonard Feather, *Passion for Jazz*. New York: Da Capo Press, 1990.

Leonard Feather and Ira Gitler, *The Biographical Encyclopedia of Jazz*. New York: Oxford University Press, 1999.

Will Friedwald, *Jazz Singing: America's Great Voices from Bessie Smith to Bebop and Beyond*. New York: Da Capo Press, 1996.

Dave Gelly, *The Giants of Jazz*. New York: Schirmer Books, 1987.

Charley Gerard, *Jazz in Black and White: Race, Culture, and Identity in the Jazz Community*. Westport, CT: Praeger Books, 1998.

Gary Giddins, *Riding on a Blue Note: Jazz and American Pop*. New York: Oxford University Press, 1981.

Gary Giddins, *Visions of Jazz: The First Century*. New York: Oxford University Press, 1999.

Ira Gitler, *Swing to Bop: An Oral History of the Transition in Jazz in the 1940s*. New York: Oxford University Press, 1985.

Ted Gioia, *The History of Jazz*. New York: Oxford University Press, 1997.

Robert Gordon, *Jazz West Coast: The Los Angeles Jazz Scene of the 1950s*. New York: Quartet Books, 1986.

Leslie Gourse, *Louis' Children: American Jazz Singers*. New York: Quill Books, 1984.

Mark Gridley, *How to Teach Jazz History*. Manhattan, KS: National Association of Jazz Educators, 1984.

Mark C. Gridley, *Jazz Styles: History and Analysis* (2d ed.). Englewood Cliffs, NJ: Prentice Hall, 1985.

Max Harrison, Charles Fox, and Eric Thackers (comps.), *The Essential Jazz Records—Volume 1: Ragtime to Swing*. Westport, CT: Greenwood, 1984.

John Edward Hasse (ed.), *Jazz: The First Century*. New York: William Morrow/HarperCollins, 2000.

Nat Hentoff and Albert J. McCarthy (eds.), *Jazz: New Perspectives on the History of Jazz by Twelve of the World's Foremost Jazz Critics and Scholars*. New York: Da Capo Press, 1975.

Mary Lee Hester, *Going to Kansas City*. Sherman, TN: Early Bird Press, 1980.

Steve Holtje and Nancy Ann Lee (eds.), *MusicHound Jazz: The Essential Album Guide*. Detroit, MI: Visible Ink Press, 1998.

Jorgen Grunnet Jepson (comp.), *Jazz Records, 1942–68: A Discography in Ten Volumes*. Copenhagen: Knudsen, 1963–1970.

Rick Kennedy, *Jelly Roll, Bix, and Hoagy: Gennett Studios and the Birth of Recorded Jazz*. Bloomington: Indiana University Press, 1994.

Barry Kernfeld (ed.), *The Blackwell Guide to Recorded Jazz*. Cambridge, MA: Basil Blackwell, 1991.

Barry Kernfeld (ed.), *The New Grove Dictionary of Jazz* (2 vols.). New York: Grove's Dictionaries of Music, 1990.

Barry Kernfeld (ed.), *The New Grove Dictionary of Jazz*. New York: St. Martin's Press, 1994.

Bill Kirchner (ed.), *The Oxford Companion to Jazz*. New York: Oxford University Press, 2000.

Gene Lees, *Cats of Any Color: Jazz, Black and White*. New York: Oxford University Press, 1994.

Gene Lees, *Meet Me at Jim and Andy's: Jazz Musicians and Their World*. Oxford, England: Oxford University Press, 1989.

Neil Leonard, *Jazz: Myth and Religion*. New York: Oxford University Press, 1987.

Neil Leonard, *Jazz and White Americans: The Acceptance of a New Art Form*. Chicago: University of Chicago Press, 1962.

Stephen Longstreet, *Storyville to Harlem: Fifty Years in the Jazz Scene*. New Brunswick, NJ: Rutgers University Press, 1986.

James McCalla, *Jazz: A Listener's Guide*. Englewood Cliffs, NJ: Prentice Hall, 1982.

Albert McCarthy, Max Harrison, Alun Morgan, and Paul Oliver, *Jazz on Record: A Critical Guide to the First 50 Years, 1917–1967*. New York: Oak, 1968.

Lloyd Miller and James K. Skipper, Jr., "Sounds of Black Protest in Avant-Garde Jazz," in R. Serge Denisoff and Richard A. Peterson (eds.), *The Sounds of Social Change: Studies in Popular Culture*. Chicago: Rand McNally, 1972, 26–37.

Norman Mongan, *The History of the Guitar in Jazz*. New York: Oak, 1983.

Dan Morgenstern (text) and Ole Brask (photos), *Jazz People*. Englewood Cliffs, NJ: Prentice Hall, 1976.

Ronald L. Morris, *Wait until Dark: Jazz and the Underworld, 1880–1940*. Bowling Green, OH: Bowling Green University Popular Press, 1980.

Charles Nanry, with Edward Berger, *The Jazz Text*. New York: Van Nostrand Reinhold, 1979.

Stuart Nicholson, *Jazz: The Modern Resurgence*. London: Sidgwick and Jackson, 1990.

Kathy J. Ogren, *The Jazz Revolution: Twenties America and the Meaning of Jazz*. Oxford: Oxford University Press, 1990.

Robert G. O'Meally (ed.), *The Jazz Cadence of American Culture*. New York: Columbia University Press, 1998.

Leroy Ostransky, *Jazz City: The Impact of Our Cities on the Development of Jazz*. Englewood Cliffs, NJ: Prentice Hall, 1978.

Jon Panish, *The Color of Jazz: Race and Representation in Postwar American Culture*. Jackson: University Press of Mississippi, 1997.

Burton W. Peretti, *The Creation of Jazz: Music, Race, and Culture in Urban America*. Urbana: University of Illinois Press, 1992.

Burton W. Peretti, *Jazz in American Culture*. Chicago: I. R. December, 1997.

Brian Priestley, *Jazz on Record: A History*. New York: Billboard Books, 1991.

Paul Roland (ed.), *Jazz Singers: The Great Song Stylists in Their Own Words*. New York: Billboard Books, 2000.

Al Rose, *Storyville, New Orleans*. Tuscaloosa: University of Alabama Press, 1974.

Al Rose and Edmond Souchon (comps.), *New Orleans Jazz: A Family Album* (3d ed.). Baton Rouge: Louisiana State University Press, 1984.

David H. Rosenthal, *Hard Bop: Jazz and Black Music, 1955–1965*. New York: Oxford University Press, 1992.

Ross Russell, *Jazz Style in Kansas City and the Southwest*. Berkeley: University of California Press, 1971.

Brian Rust, *My Kind of Jazz*. London: Hamish Hamilton, 1990.

James Sallis (ed.), *The Guitar in Jazz: An Anthology*. Lincoln: University of Nebraska Press, 1996.

Gene Santoro, *Dancing in Your Head: Jazz, Blues, Rock, and Beyond*. New York: Oxford University Press, 1994.

William J. Schaefer, *Brass Bands and New Orleans Jazz*. Baton Rouge: Louisiana State University Press, 1977.

Nat Shapiro and Nat Hentoff (eds.), *Hear Me Talkin' to Ya: The Story of Jazz as Told by the Men Who Made It*. New York: Dover, 1955.

Arnold Shaw, *52nd Street: The Street of Jazz*. New York: Da Capo Press, 1977.

Arnold Shaw, *The Jazz Age: Popular Music in the 1920s*. New York: Oxford University Press, 1987.

Marshall Stearns, *The Story of Jazz* (rev. ed.). London: Oxford University Press, 1970.

John Swenson (ed.), *The Rolling Stone Jazz Record Guide*. New York: Random House/Rolling Stone Press, 1985.

John Swenson (ed.), *The Rolling Stone Jazz and Blues Album Guide*. New York: Random House, 1999.

Billy Taylor, *Jazz Piano: A Jazz History*. Dubuque, IA: Brown, 1983.

Dean Tudor and Nancy Tudor (comps.), *Jazz: American Popular Music on Elpee*. Littleton, CO: Libraries Unlimited, 1979.

Frederick Turner, *Remembering Song: Encounters with the New Orleans Jazz Tradition*. New York: Viking Press, 1982.

Michael Ullman, *Jazz Lives: Portraits in Words and Music*. New York: Perigee Books, 1982.

Geoffrey C. Ward and Ken Burns, *Jazz: A History of America's Music*. New York: Alfred A. Knopf, 2000.

Dicky Wells and Stanley Dance, *The Night People: Reminiscences of a Jazz Man*. Boston: Crescendo Books, 1971.

Martin Williams, *Jazz Changes*. New York: Oxford University Press, 1991.

Martin Williams, *Jazz in Its Time*. Oxford: Oxford University Press, 1989.

Martin Williams, *Jazz Masters in Transition, 1957–1969*. New York: McMillan, 1970.

Martin Williams, *The Jazz Tradition* (rev. ed.). New York: Oxford University Press, 1983.

Ron Wynn, with Michael Erlewine and Vladimir Bogdanov (eds.), *All Music Guide to Jazz: The Best CDs, Albums, and Tapes*. San Francisco: Miller Freeman Books, 1994.

Rock

Stephen Barnard, *Rock: An Illustrated History*. London: MacDonald Orbis, 1986.

Vladimir Bogdanov, Chris Woodstra, and Stephen Thomas Erlewine (eds.), *All Music Guide to Rock: The Definitive Guide to Rock, Pop, and Soul* (3d ed.). San Francisco: Backbeat Books, 2002.

Charles Brown, *The Art of Rock and Roll*. Englewood Cliffs, NJ: Prentice Hall, 1992.

Charles T. Brown, *The Rock and Roll Story: From the Sounds of Rebellion to an American Art Form*. Englewood Cliffs, NJ: Prentice Hall, 1983.

Jonathan Buckley and Mark Ellingham (eds.), *The Rough Guide to Rock*. New York: Rough Guides/Penguin Books USA, 1996.

Jonathan Buckley, Orla Duane, Mark Ellingham, and Al Spice (eds.), *Rock: The Rough Guide* (2d ed.). London: Rough Guides, 1999.

Katherine Charlton, *Rock Music Styles: A History*. Dubuque, IA: William C. Brown, 1990.

B. Lee Cooper, "Review of *The Classic Rock and Roll Reader: Rock Music from Its Beginnings to the Mid-1970's* by William E. Studwell and D. F. Lonergan," *Popular Music and Society* XXIV (winter 2000), 124–5.

B. Lee Cooper, "Review of *White Boy Singin' the Blues: The Black Roots of White Rock* by Michael Bane," *Popular Music and Society* XVIII (fall 1994), 86–88.

Maury Dean, *The Rock Revolution*. Detroit, MI: Edmore Books, 1966.

Fred Dellar, *Rock Discography*. London: Omnibus Press, 1983.

Alain Dister (translated from French by Toula Ballas), *The Age of Rock: Smash Hits and Superstars*. New York: Harry N. Abrams, 1993.

Philip Dodd, *The Book of Rock*. New York: Thunder's Mouth Press, 2001.

Robert Duncan, *The Noise: Notes from a Rock 'n' Roll Era*. New York: Ticknor and Fields, 1984.

Michael Erlewine, Vladimir Bogdanov, Chris Woodstra, Stephen Thomas Erlewine, and Richie Unterberger (eds.), *All Music Guide to Rock: The Experts' Guide to the Best Rock, Pop, Soul, R & B, and Rap* (2d ed.). San Francisco: Miller Freeman Books, 1997.

Paul David Friedlander, *Rock and Roll Is Here to Stay*. New York: Schirmer Books, 1991.

John Gabree, *The World of Rock*. Greenwich, CT: Fawcett, 1968.

Glen Gass, *A History of Rock Music*. New York: McGraw-Hill Books, 1995.

Gary Graff and Daniel Durchholz (eds.), *MusicHound Rock: The Essential Album Guide*. Detroit, MI: Visible Ink Press, 1999.

Jerry Hopkins, *The Rock Story*. New York: Signet Books, 1970.

Mike Jahn, *Rock: From Elvis Presley to the Rolling Stones*. New York: Quadrangle Books, 1973.

Jeff Kitts, Brad Tolinski, and Harold Steinblatt (eds.), *Guitar World Presents Classic Rock*. Milwaukee, WI: Guitar World Magazine/Hal Leonard, 1999.

J. Marks, *Rock and Other Four Letter Words: Music of the Electric Generation*. New York: Bantam Books, 1968.

David McCarthy, *The Golden Age of Rock and Pop*. London: Apple Press, 1990.

Geoff Nicholas, *Big Noises: Rock Guitar in the 1990s*. London: Quartet Books, 1991.

Philippe Paraire (translated by Sara Newbery), *50 Years of Rock Music*. Edinburgh, Scotland: Chambers Encyclopedic Guides, 1992.

Robert Santelli, *Sixties Rock: A Listener's Guide*. Chicago: Contemporary Books, 1985.

William J. Schafer, *Rock Music: Where It's Been, What It Means, Where It's Going*. Minneapolis, MN: Augsburg, 1972.

Frank Scott, Al Ennis, and the Staff of Roots and Rhythm, *The Roots and Rhythm Guide to Rock*. Chicago: A Cappella Books, 1993.

Arnold Shaw, *Rock Revolution*. New York: Crowell-Collier Press, 1969.

Martin C. Strong (comp.), *The Great Rock Discography* (5th ed.). Edinburgh, Scotland: Mojo Books, 2001.

Joe Stuessy, *Rock and Roll: Its History and Stylistic Development*. Englewood Cliffs, NJ: Prentice Hall, 1990.

Soul

B. Lee Cooper, "Review of *Atlantic Sisters of Soul*," *Popular Music and Society* XVII (summer 1993), 135.

B. Lee Cooper, "Review of *The Blackwell Guide to Soul Recordings* by Robert Pruter," *Popular Music and Society* XVIII (fall 1994), 83–84.

B. Lee Cooper, "Review of *Chicago Soul* by Robert Pruter," *Popular Culture in Libraries* I, no. 1 (1993), 146–8.

B. Lee Cooper, "Review of *Queen of Soul: The Atlantic Recordings by Aretha Franklin*," *Blue Suede News*, no. 22 (spring 1993), p. 30.

B. Lee Cooper, "Review of *Soul Music A–Z* by Hugh Gregory and *Soul Music Who's Who* by Ralph Tee," *Popular Culture in Libraries* II, no. 1 (1994), 103–4.

B. Lee Cooper, "Stax Style: Simple Songs and Soulful Singers," *Rock and Blues News*, no. 15 (April-May 2001), 46.

David Freeland, *Ladies of Soul*. Jackson: University Press of Mississippi, 2001.

Hugh Gregory, *Soul Music A–Z* (rev. ed.). New York: Da Capo Press, 1995 (first published 1991).

Monique Guillory and Richard C. Green (eds.), *Soul: Black Power, Politics, and Pleasure*. New York: New York University Press, 1998.

Peter Guralnick, *Sweet Soul Music: Rhythm and Blues and the Southern Dream of Freedom*. New York: Harper & Row, 1986.

Jeff Hannusch, *The Soul of New Orleans: A Legacy of Rhythm and Blues*. Ville Platte, LA: Swallow, 2001.

Lee Hildebrand, *Stars of Soul and Rhythm and Blues: Top Recording Artists and Showstopping Performers, From Memphis and Motown to Now*. New York: Billboard Books, 1994.

Gerri Hirshey, *Nowhere to Run: The Story of Soul Music*. New York: Da Capo Press, 1994 (first published 1984).

Ian Hoare, Tony Cummings, Clive Anderson, and Simon Frith, *The Soul Book*. New York: Dell, 1976.

Colin Larkin (ed.), *The Guinness Who's Who of Soul*. Enfield, England: Guinness Books, 1993.

Rochelle Larkin, *Soul Music!* New York: Lancer Books, 1970.

Portia K. Maultsby, "Soul Music: Its Sociological and Political Significance in American Popular Culture," *Journal of Popular Culture* XVII (fall 1983), 51–65.

A. Grace Mims, "Soul: The Black Man and His Music," *Negro History Bulletin* XXXIII (October 1970), 141–6.

David Nathan, *The Soulful Divas*. New York: Billboard Books, 1999.

Mark Anthony Neal, *Soul Babies: Black Popular Culture and the Post-Soul Aesthetic*. New York: Routledge, 2002.

Robert Pruter (ed.), *The Blackwell Guide to Soul Recordings*. Oxford, England: Basil Blackwell, 1993.

Robert Pruter, *Chicago Soul*. Champaign-Urbana: University of Illinois Press, 1991.

Arnold Shaw, *The World of Soul*. New York: Paperback Library, 1971.

Ralph Tee, *Soul Music: Who's Who*. Rocklin, CA: Prima, 1992.

Craig Werner, *A Change Is Gonna Come: Music, Race, and the Soul of America*. New York: Plume/Penguin Putnam, 1999.

Other Styles and Trends

Alternative Rock

Alan Cross, *20th Century Rock and Roll: Alternative Rock*. Burlington, Ontario: Collector's Guide, 1999.

Alan di Perna, "Has Success Spoiled Alternative Rock?" *Musician*, no. 183 (January 1994), 52–58.

Jeff Kitts, Brad Tolinski, and Harold Steinblatt (eds.), *Guitar World Presents Alternative Rock*. Milwaukee, WI: Hal Leonard, 1999.

Holly Kruse, "Subcultural Identity in the Alternative Music Culture," *Popular Music* XII (January 1993), 33–41.

Michael Lavine and Pat Blashill, *Noise from the Underground: A Secret History of Alternative Rock*. New York: Fireside/Simon & Schuster, 1996.

Randi Reisfeld, *This Is the Sound! The Best of Alternative Rock*. New York: Aladdin Books, 1996.

Scott Schinder and the Editors of Rolling Stone Press, *Rolling Stone's Alt-Rock-a-Rama: An Outrageous Compendium of Facts, Fiction, Trivia, and Critiques on Alternative Rock*. New York: Dell, 1996.

Dave Thompson, *Alternative Rock: The Essential Listening Companion*. San Francisco: Miller Freeman Books, 2000.

Eric Weisbard, with Craig Marks (eds.), *Spin Alternative Record Guide*. New York: Vintage Books, 1995.

Art Rock

Steve Pond, "The Waxpaper Chronicles—Volume One: Art-Rock," *Waxpaper* II (July 29, 1977), 1–4.

Beach Music

"Beach Music—The All-Time Top 50," *It Will Stand*, no. 20, (1982), 22.

Chris Beachley, "Beach Music," *DISCoveries* I (November 1988), 106.

Chris Beachley, "Beach Music," *DISCoveries* I (December 1988), 82–83.

Chris Beachley, "Beach Music: What Is It and Where Did It Come From?" *DISCoveries* I (May/June 1988), 103.

Chris Beachley, "Beach Music," *DISCoveries* II (October 1989), 152.

Ben Funderburk, "Welcome Back . . . Beach Music," *Wavelength* I (August 1981), 6–7.

John Sippel, " 'Beach Music's' Wave of Success," *Billboard* XCIII (July 25, 1981), 4ff.

Big Band Era

Malcolm F. Bell (comp.), *Theme Songs of the Dance Band Era*. Memphis, TN: KWD, 1981.

B. Lee Cooper, "Review of *Swing Time! The Fabulous Big Band Era, 1925–1955*," *Popular Music and Society* XVII (fall 1993), 118–19.

Dave Dexter Jr., "Big Band Era, 1935–1945: Six Brass, Five Reeds, Rhythm," *Billboard* LXXXI (December 27, 1969), 60–61.

Lewis A. Erenberg, *Swingin' the Dream: Big Band Jazz and the Rebirth of American Culture*. Chicago: University of Chicago Press, 1998.

Paul L. Leslie and James K. Skipper, "Big Bands and Big Band Music: Embedded Popular Culture," *Popular Music and Society* XVII (spring 1993), 23–36.

Albert J. McCarthy, *The Dance Band Era: The Dancing Decades from Ragtime to Swing, 1910–1950*. Radnor: Chilton Book, 1982.

Gunther Schuller, *The Swing Era: The Development of Jazz, 1930–1945*. New York: Oxford University Press, 1989.

George T. Simon, *The Big Bands* (rev. ed.). New York: Macmillan, 1974.

George T. Simon, *The Big Bands* (4th ed.). New York: Schirmer Books, 1981.

George T. Simon, *Simon Says: The Sights and Sounds of the Swing Era, 1935–1955*. New Rochelle, NY: Arlington House, 1971.

David W. Stowe, *Swing Changes: Big Band Jazz in New Deal America*. Cambridge: Harvard University Press, 1994.

Leo Walker, *The Big Band Almanac*. Pasadena, CA: Ward Ritchie Press, 1978.

Bernie Woods, *When the Music Stopped: The Big Band Era Remembered*. New York: Barricade Books, 1995.

Big Band Rock

Mike Bourne, "Big Band Rock and Other Brassy Beasties," *Downbeat* XXXVIII (February 4, 1971), 16–17.

Blue-Eyed Soul

Billj Barol, with Donna Foote and Lynda Wright, "That Sweet Soul Sound," *Newsweek* CVII (March 24, 1986), 70–71.

B. Lee Cooper, "Review of *The Commitments* Soundtrack," *Popular Music and Society* XX (fall 1996), 123–5.

Claude Hall, "R & B Stations Open Airplay Gates to 'Blue-Eyed Soulists'," *Billboard* LXXVII (October 9, 1965), 1ff.

Pete Nickols, "Southern Soul—Nashville, Shreveport, Houston, and Jackson: An Introduction to Classic Sixties Deep Soul Music," *Record Collector*, no. 105 (May 1988), 27–31.

Richard Pack, Bruce Huston, Thomas J. Cullen, and Doug Wright, "A–Z of Blue–Eyed Soul," *Soul Survivor*, no. 8 (winter 1987/1988), 12–15, 20.

Arnold Shaw, "Of Chitlins, Blue-Eyed Soul, and Black Capitalists," in *The World of Soul*. New York: Paperback Library, 1971, 331–8.

Bluegrass

Bob Artis, *Bluegrass*. New York: Hawthorn Books, 1975.

Robert Cantwell, *Bluegrass Breakdown: The Making of the Old Southern Sound*. Urbana: University of Illinois Press, 1984.

Bob Doyle, "Bluegrass and the Custom Record: My Point of View," *Popular Music and Society* VI (fall 1979), 331–3.

Carl Fleischhauer and Neil V. Rosenberg, *Bluegrass Odyssey: A Documentary in Pictures and Words, 1966–1986*. Urbana: University of Illinois Press, 2001.

Fred Hill, *Grass Roots: An Illustrated History of Bluegrass and Mountain Music*. Rutland, VT: Academy Books, 1980.

Neil V. Rosenberg (comp.), *Bill Monroe and His Bluegrass Boys: An Illustrated Discography*. Nashville, TN: Country Music Foundation Press, 1974.

Neil V. Rosenberg, *Bluegrass: A History*. Urbana: University of Illinois Press, 1985.

Neil V. Rosenberg, "From Sound to Style: The Emergence of Bluegrass," *Journal of American Folklore* LXXX (April-June 1967), 143–50.

Neil V. Rosenberg, "Image and Stereotype: Bluegrass Sound Tracks," *American Music* I (fall 1983), 1–22.

John Rumble, "Cultural Dimensions of the Bluegrass Boom, 1979–1975," *Journal of Country Music* VI (fall 1975), 109–21.

L. Mayne Smith, "An Introduction to Bluegrass," *Journal of American Folklore*, LXXVIII (July-September 1965), 245–57.

Stephen Sweet, "Bluegrass Music and Its Misguided Representation of Appalachia," *Popular Music and Society* XX (fall 1996), 37–51.

Dean Tudor and Nancy Tudor, *Grass Roots Music*. Littleton, CO: Libraries Unlimited, 1979.

Boogie-Woogie

Peter Silvester, *A Left Hand Like God: The Story of Boogie-Woogie*. New York: Omnibus Books, 1988.

Bossa Nova

Suzel Ana Reily, "Tom Jobin and the Bossa Nova Era," *Popular Music* XV (January 1996), 1–16.

Chris McGowan and Ricardo Pessanha, *The Billboard Book of Brazilian Music: Samba, Bossa Nova, and the Popular Sounds of Brazil*. New York: Billboard Books, 1991.

British Pop Music (pre-Beatles)

Stephen Barnard, *On the Radio: Music Radio in Britain*. Milton Keynes, England: Open University Press, 1989.

Dick Bradley, *Understanding Rock 'n' Roll: Popular Music in Britain, 1955–1964*. Buckingham, England: Open University Press, 1992.

Iain Chambers, *Urban Rhythms*. London: Macmillan, 1985.

Alan Clayson, *Beat Merchants: The Origins, History, Impact, and Rock Legacy of the 1960s British Pop Groups*. London: Blandford Books, 1996.

Alan Clayson, *Call Up the Groups! The Golden Age of British Beat, 1962–1967*. Poole, England: Blandford Press, 1986.

Michael Bryan Kelly, *The Beatle Myth: The British Invasion of American Popular Music, 1956–1969*. Jefferson, NC: McFarland, 1991.

Chris May and Tim Phillips (comps.), *British Beat*. London: Socion Books, 1974.

Dave McAleer, *The Fab British Rock 'n' Roll Invasion of 1964*. New York: St. Martin's Press, 1994.

Dave McAleer, *Hit Parade Heroes: British Beat before the Beatles*. London: Hamlyn Books, 1993.

Sheila Tracy (comp.), *Who's Who in Popular Music in Britain*. Kingswood, England: World's Work, 1984.

Bubblegum

Ken Barnes, "The Waxpaper Chronicles—Volume Two: Bubblegum," *Waxpaper* II (August 26, 1977), 1–4.

John M. Borack, "A Hook with a Smile Will Last Us Awhile: 30 Yummy Bubblegum Obscurities," *Goldmine*, no. 437 (April 25, 1997), 26–30.

"Bubblegum Is Here to Stay," *Melody Maker* XLVI (November 20, 1971), 13.

Carl Cafarelli, "An Informal History of Bubblegum Music," *Goldmine*, no. 437 (April 25, 1997), 16–19, 32, 38, 60, 66–76.

Jo-Ann Greene, "Bubblegum Music," *Record Collector*, no. 74 (October 1985), 54–57.

Cajun Music

Barry Jean Ancelet, *The Makers of Cajun Music*. Austin: University of Texas Press, 1984.

Shane K. Bernard, "Cajun and Creole Rhythm 'n' Blues: South Louisiana's Swamp Pop Music," *Goldmine*, no. 419 (August 16, 1996), 54–90.

Shane K. Bernard, *Swamp Pop: Cajun and Creole Rhythm and Blues*. Jackson: University Press of Mississippi, 1996.

John Broven, *South to Louisiana: The Music of the Cajun Bayous*. Gretna, LA: Pelican, 1983.

S. L. Del Sesto, "Let the Good Times Roll: Cajun Music and Zydeco in South Louisiana," *Jazz Report* IX (1976), 1–5.

Philip Gould, *Cajun Music and Zydeco*. Baton Rouge: Louisiana State University Press, 1992.

Mark Mattern, "Cajun Music, Cultural Revival: Theorizing Political Action in Popular Music," *Popular Music and Society* XXII (summer 1998), 31–48.

Doug Newcomb, "Outsiders' Guide to Acadiana," *Wavelength*, no. 82 (August 1987), 15–18.

Ben Sandmel, "Born on a Bayou: Cajun Music Gamely Survives and Prospers," *Musician*, no. 82 (August 1985), 36–40.

Ann Allen Savoy, *Cajun Music: A Reflection of a People—Volume One*. Eunice, LA: Bluebird Press, 1984.

Calypso

Patrick Castagne, "This Is Calypso," *Music Journal* XV (January 1958), 32–33ff.

John Cowley, *Carnival, Canboulay, and Calypso: Traditions in the Making*. Cambridge: Press Syndicate of the University of Cambridge, 1996.

Daniel J. Crowley, "Toward a Definition of Calypso," *Ethnomusicology* III (May 1959), 57–66.

Renu Juneja, "We Kind of Music," *Popular Music and Society* XIII (spring 1989), 37–52.

Cynthia Mahabir, "The Rise of Calypso Feminism: Gender and Musical Politics in the Calypso," *Popular Music* XX (October 2001), 409–30.

Polly E. McLean, "Calypso and Revolution in Grenada," *Popular Music and Society* X (winter 1986), 87–99.

Glenn O'Brien, "Calypso," *Spin*, no. 2 (June 1985), 42–45.

Raymond Quevedo, *Attila's Kaiso: A Short History of Trinidad Calypso*. St. Augustine, Trinidad, and Tobago: Department of Extra-Mural Studies at the University of the West Indies, 1983.

Humphrey A. Regis, "Calypso, Reggae, and Cultural Imperialism by Reexportation," *Popular Music and Society* XII (spring 1988), 63–73.

Keith Q. Warner, "Calypso, Reggae, and Rastafarianism: Authentic Caribbean Voices," *Popular Music and Society* XII (spring 1988), 53–62.

Keith Warner, *The Trinidad Calypso*. London: Heinemann Educational, 1982.

Chicano Rock

Galen Gart, "The Latino Connection: R & B Music's 'Flip Side'," *Goldmine*, no. 164 (November 7, 1986), 26, 71.

Steven Loza, *Barrio Rhythm: Mexican American Music in Los Angeles*. Urbana: University of Illinois Press, 1993.

Bill Millar, "Down Mexico Way—Chicano Rock (Part One): Ritchie Valens, Sam the Sham, Sunny and the Sunglows, and More," *Let It Rock*, no. 33 (September 1975), 16–17.

Chuy Varela, "The Eastside Sound," *DISCoveries*, no. 146 (July 2000), 42–46.

Contemporary Christian Music

Jay R. Howard and John M. Streck, *Apostles of Rock: The Splintered World of Contemporary Christian Music*. Lexington: University of Kentucky Press, 1999.

Jay R. Howard and John M. Streck, "The Splintered Art World of Contemporary Christian Music," *Popular Music* XV (January 1996), 37–53.

Country Rock

Michael Bane, *The Outlaws: Revolution in Country Music*. Garden City, NY: Doubleday, 1978.

Peter Doggett, *Are You Ready for Country: Elvis, Dylan, Parsons and the Roots of Country Rock*. New York: Penguin Putnam, 2001.

John Einarson, *Desperados: The Origins of Country Rock and the Roots of New Country*. Milford, CT: Quarry Press, 1998.

Jan Reid, *The Improbable Rise of Redneck Rock*. Austin, TX: Heidelberg, 1974.

Disco

Andy Blackford, *Disco Dancing Tonite*. London: Octopus Books, 1979.

"Dancing Madness," *Rolling Stone*, no. 194 (August 28, 1975), 42–64.

Henry Edwards, "The Street People Have Taken over the Discotheques!" *High Fidelity* XXV (July 1975), 56–58.

Albert H. Goldman, *Disco*. New York: Hawthorn Books, 1978.

Barbara Graustark, with Janet Huck, Peggy Clausen, and Ronald Henkoff, "Disco Takes Over," *Newsweek* XCIII (April 2, 1979), 56–64.

Amy Hanson, "More, More, More! A Brief History of Disco," *Goldmine*, no. 450 (October 24, 1997), 70–80, 150–4.

The Hullabaloo Discotheque Dance Book. New York: Scholastic Book Services, 1967.

James Klein, "The Disco of Our Discontents: The Layered Look in Popular Music," *The Cresset* XLIII (March 1980), 22–23.

Richard A. Peterson, "Disco!" *The Chronicle Review* XVII (October 2, 1978), R-26-27.

Robert E. Sickels, "1970s Disco Daze: Paul Thomas Anderson's *Boogie Nights* and the Last Golden Age of Irresponsibility," *Journal of Popular Culture* XXXV (spring 2002), 49–60.

Clifford Terry, "What Is This Thing Called Disco?" *Stereo Review* XXXVII (September 1976), 74–77.

Jack Villari and Kathleen Sims Villari, *The Official Guide to Disco Dance Steps*. Northbrook, IL: Quality Books, 1978.

Al Wagenaar, "The Disco Debate Drags On," *Goldmine*, no. 39 (August 1979), 36–37.

Doo-Wop

Bob Becker, "Signs of the Times," *Record Exchanger* V (1978), 15–17.

Ashley Brown, "The Alchemists," *The History of Rock*, no. 15 (1982), 281–3.

Ashley Brown, "From Star to Superstar," *The History of Rock*, no. 24 (1982), 461–3.

Geoff Brown, "Black Voices," *The History of Rock*, no. 4 (1982), 61–63.

Geoff Brown, "Doo–Wop," *The History of Rock*, no. 4 (1982), 69–73.

B. Lee Cooper, "Review of *Best of Doo Wop Ballads*, *Best of Doo-Wop Uptempo*, *Acappella* by the Persuasions, and *Modern Acappella*," *Popular Music and Society* XVII (fall 1993), 115–16.

B. Lee Cooper, "Review of *The Doo-Wop Box*, Compiled by Bob Hyde and Walter DeVenne," *Popular Music and Society* XVIII (fall 1994), 89–90.

B. Lee Cooper, "Review of *DooWop: The Chicago Scene* by Robert Pruter," *Popular Music and Society* XX (summer 1996), 244–5.

B. Lee Cooper, "Review of *Doo-Wop: The Forgotten Third of Rock 'n' Roll* by Anthony J. Gribin and Matthew M. Schiff," *Popular Music and Society* XVI (winter 1992), 85–86.

B. Lee Cooper, "Review of *Group Collector's Record Guide* by Jeff Kreiter," *Popular Music and Society* XIV (winter 1990), 116–17.

B. Lee Cooper, "Review of *Voices of America—Vocal Harmony Groups: Then and Now* compiled by Tony Gribin and Matt Schiff," *Popular Music and Society* XXI (winter 1997), 127–8.

Tony D'Ambrosia, "Anatomy of a Street Corner Group: An Interview with Tony Centeno," *Record Exchanger* IV (1974), 24–25.

Jim Dawson, "Music City: Home of Northern California Doo-Wop," *Goldmine*, no. 183 (July 31, 1987), 83–84.

"Doo–Wop," *Record Collector*, no. 162 (February 1993), 145–7.

Frank Driggs, "Uptown Saturday Nights" *Audio* LXIX (June 1985), 14–16.

Edward Engel, *White and Still All Right! A Collection of "White Group" Histories of the 50s and Early 60s—Volume One*. Scarsdale, NY: Crackerjack Press, 1977.

Peter Grendysa, "The Story Behind "The Glory of Love": R & B Classic Spans a Borrowed Bridge," *Record Collector's Monthly*, no. 7 (March 1983), 1, 10–11.

Anthony J. Gribin and Matthew M. Schiff, *The Complete Book of Doo-Wop*. Iola, WI: Krause, 2000.

Anthony J. Gribin and Matthew M. Schiff, *Doo-Wop: The Forgotten Third of Rock 'n' Roll*. Iola, WI: Krause, 1992.

Phil Groia, *They All Sang on the Corner: New York City's Rhythm and Blues Vocal Groups of the 1950s*. Setauket, NY: Edmond, 1974.

Wayne Jancik, " 'Gloria and Linda Lu': The Men and Stories behind the Songs," *Goldmine*, no. 156 (July 1986), 62.

Jeff Kreiter, *45 RPM Vocal Group Record Guide: A Reference and Price Guide to Vocal Group Harmony Records, 1949–1999* (7th ed.). Bridgeport, OH: J. Kreiter, 2000.

Paul Lepri, *The New Haven Sound, 1946–1976*. New Haven, CT: United Printing Services, 1977.

Jean–Charles Marion, "Ten Classic Ballads: Excellence in Performance and Production," *Record Exchanger* III (1973), 14, 25.

Jean-Charles Marion, "Ten Up-Tempo Classics," *Record Exchanger* III (1973), 24.

Lynn McCutcheon, "Unsung Heroes Who Also Sang," *Negro History Bulletin* XXXV (January 1973), 9–11.

Seamus McGarvey, "New York Rock 'n' Roll and Doo-Wop—Paul Winley and Winley Records Interviewed," *Now Dig This*, no. 75 (June 1989), 27–31.

Bill Millar, "Still White and Alright: Part Two of Echoes' Survey of Off-White Doo Wop from Rock 'n' Roll's Dark Ages," *Let It Rock*, no. 29 (May 1975), 14–15.

George A. Moonoogian, "Wax–Fax," *Music World*, no. 83 (March 1981), 20, 54.

George A. Moonoogian, "Wax Fax," *Music World*, no. 86 (June 1981), 9–11.

Allan Moore, "Patterns of Harmony," *Popular Music* XI (June 1992), 73–106.

Pete Nickols, "Doo-Wop," *Record Collector*, no. 87 (November 1986), 24–27.

Pete Nickols, "Doo-Wop," *Record Collector*, no. 88 (December 1986), 45–49.

Steve Propes and Galen Gart, *L.A. R & B Vocal Groups, 1945–1965*. Milford, NH: Big Nickel, 2001.

Robert Pruter, "A Brief Look at Chicago Teen Sopranos," *Goldmine*, no. 137 (October 25, 1985), 83.

Robert Pruter, *Doo Wop: The Chicago Scene*. Urbana: University of Illinois Press, 1996.

Robert Pruter, "The Great Debate: R & B Harmony vs. Modern Harmony," *Goldmine*, no. 53 (October 1980), 173.

Jim Raper, "Doo-Wop on 45 R.P.M.," *Now Dig This*, no. 109 (April 1992), 10, 32.

Jim Raper, "Doo-Woppin'," *Now Dig This*, no. 119 (February 1993), 32.

Jim Raper, "Doo-Woppin'," *Now Dig This*, no. 137 (August 1994), 28.

Mike Redmond, "Crying in the Chapel," *Record Exchanger* IV (1975), 26–27.

Mike Redmond and Marv Goldberg, "The Doo-Wah Sound: Black Pop Groups of the 1950's," *Yesterday's Memories* I, no. 1 (1975), 22–24, 26.

Mitch Rosalsky, *Encyclopedia of Rhythm and Blues and Doo-Wop Vocal Groups*. Lanham, MD: Scarecrow Press, 2000.

Jack Sbarbori, "Black Harmony Today," *Goldmine*, no. 39 (August 1979), 13–17.

Don Shewey, "A Thinking Man's Homage to Doo-Wop," *Rolling Stone*, no. 409 (November 24, 1983), 67–69.

Joe (Moonglow) Sicurella, "Collecting Young Male Tenor-Lead Groups," *Goldmine*, no. 127 (June 7, 1985), 87.

Wane Stierle, "Remember Yesterday Tomorrow," *Record Exchanger*, no. 31 (1983), 30.

Jeff Tamarkin, "Acappella in the '80s: It's Not Just Doo-Wop Anymore," *Goldmine*, no. 210 (August 13, 1988), 22, 79.

Jeff Tamarkin, "New Jersey: The New Home of Doo-Wop," *Goldmine*, no. 75 (August 1982), 27–28.

Art Turco, "Al Frazier and His Groups," *Record Exchanger*, no. 28 (1979), 4–11.

Art Turco, "Interview: Bobby Robinson," *Record Exchanger* II (1972), 4–17.

Art Turco, "Interview: Bobby Robinson," *Record Exchanger* III (1972), 4–13.

Jay Warner, *The Billboard Book of American Singing Groups: A History, 1940–1990*. New York: Billboard Books, 1992.

Jay Warner, *The Da Capo Book of American Singing Groups: A History, 1940–1990*. New York: Da Capo Press, 2000.

Easy Listening and Lounge Music

Irwin Chusid, "Martinis, Mood Music, and Va Va Voom," *Goldmine*, no. 373 (November 11, 1994), 22–27.

Dylan Jones, *Ultra Lounge: The Lexicon of Easy Listening*. New York: Universe, 1997.

Steve Knopper (ed.), *MusicHound Lounge: The Essential Album Guide to Martini Music and Easy Listening*. Detroit, MI: Visible Ink Press, 1998.

Joseph Lanza, "Cocktail Music: Stirred but Not Shaken Too Much," *DISCoveries*, no. 89 (October 1995), 40–42.

John Wooley, Thomas Conner, and Mark Brown, *Forever Lounge: A Laid-Back Price Guide to the Languid Sounds of Lounge Music*. Norfolk, VA: Antique Trader/Landmark Specialty Books, 1999.

Ethnic Music

Richard K. Spottswood (comp.), *Ethnic Music on Records: A Discography of Ethnic Recordings Produced in the United States, 1893 to 1942* (7 vols.). Urbana: University of Illinois Press, 1990.

Folk Rock

Eugene G. Bluestein, "Folk Tradition, Individual Talent: A Note on the Poetry of Rock," *Massachusetts Review* XI (spring 1970), 373–84.

R. Serge Denisoff, "Folk–Rock: Folk Music, Protest, or Commercialism?" *Journal of Popular Culture* III (fall 1969), 214–30.

Jerome L. Rodnitzky, *Minstrels of the Dawn: The Folk-Protest Singer as a Cultural Hero*. Chicago: Nelson–Hall, 1976.

Gene Sculatti, "The Waxpaper Chronicles—Volume Nine: Folk Rock," *Waxpaper* XXX (August 11, 1978), 1–6.

Jacques Vassal, *Electric Children: Roots and Branches of Modern Folkrock*. New York: Taplinger, 1976.

Funk

Michael Rozek, "What Is Funk?" *High Fidelity* XXVIII (October 1978), 160–2.

Rickey Vincent, *Funk: The Music, the People, and the Rhythm of the One*. New York: St. Martin's Griffin, 1996.

Garage Bands

John M. Borack, "25 Garage Rock Nuggets," *Goldmine*, no. 487 (March 26, 1999), 38.

Timothy Gassen, *Echoes in Time: The Garage and Psychedelic Explosion, 1980–1990*. Telford, England: Borderline Productions, 1991.

Michael Hicks, *Sixties Rock: Garage, Psychedelic, and Other Satisfactions*. Champaign: University of Illinois Press, 1999.

Greg Shaw, "Notes from the Garage: Iowa Discography—Part 1," *R.P.M.*, no. 11 (October/November 1985), 44–45.

Jeff Tamarkin, "Garage Sale!" *Goldmine*, no. 120 (March 1, 1985), 18–21.

James Thompson, "Detroit's Play-It-Extra-Loud Rock 'n' Roll Scene: Garage Bands Thrived in the Motor City in the Mid-60s," *Goldmine*, no. 511 (February 25, 2000), 26–36.

Glam Rock

Chris Nickson, "Glam Rock," *DISCoveries*, no. 130 (March 1999), 34–43.

Mark Paytress, "Glam Rock: Putting on the Style," *Record Collector*, no. 160 (December 1992), 32–35.

Dave Thomas, "Glam Rock," *Record Collector*, no. 81 (May 1986), 52–54.

Dave Thompson, "Are You Ready for Glam?" *Goldmine*, no. 325 (January 5, 1993), 42–47, 128.

Gospel Music

Clive Anderson, "Gospel," *The History of Rock*, no. 8 (1982), 158–60.

Robert Anderson and Gail North (comps.), *Gospel Music Encyclopedia*. New York: Sterling, 1979.

Lois S. Blackwell, *The Wings of the Dove: The Story of Gospel Music in America*. Norfolk, VA: B. Donning Press, 1978.

Horace Clarence Boyer, *How Sweet the Sound: The Golden Age of Gospel*. Washington, D.C.: Elliott and Clark, 1995.

Horace Clarence Boyer, *The Golden Age of Gospel*. Champaign-Urbana: University of Illinois Press, 2000.

Viv Broughton, *Black Gospel: An Illustrated History of the Gospel Sound*. Poole, England: Blandford Press, 1985.

Jesse Burt and Duane Allen, *The History of Gospel Music*. Nashville, TN: Abingdon Press, 1971.

David Crawford, "Gospel Songs in Court: From Rural Music to Urban Industry in the 1950s," *Journal of Popular Culture* XI (winter 1977), 551–67.

Don Cusic, *The Sound of Light: A History of Gospel Music*. Bowling Green, OH: Bowling Green State University Popular Press, 1991.

Hank Davis, "Detroit Gospel Quartets: A Regional Phenomenon," *Goldmine*, no. 191 (November 20, 1987), 12, 24.

Hank Davis, "Introduction to Collectible Black Gospel Quartets," *Goldmine*, no. 143 (January 17, 1986), 59–62.

Robert M. W. Dixon and John Godrich, *Blues and Gospel Records, 1902–1943*. (rev. ed.). Chigwell, England: Storyville, 1982.

James C. Downey, "Revivalism, the Gospel Songs, and Social Reform," *Ethnomusicology* IX (May 1965), 115–25.

Dena J. Epstein, *Sinful Tunes and Spirituals*. Urbana: University of Illinois Press, 1977.

James R. Goff, Jr., *Close Harmony: A History of Southern Gospel*. Chapel Hill: University of North Carolina Press, 2002.

Michael W. Harris, *The Rise of Gospel Blues: The Music of Thomas Andrew Dorsey in the Urban Church*. New York: Oxford University Press, 1992.

Cedric J. Hayes and Robert Laughton (comps.), *Gospel Records, 1943–1969: A Black Music Discography* (2 vols.). Milford, NH: Big Nickel, 1993.

Anthony Heilbut, *The Gospel Sound: Good News and Bad Times* (rev. and updated ed.). New York: Limelight Editions, 1985 (first published 1971).

Irene V. Jackson (comp.), *Afro-American Religious Music: A Bibliography and Catalogue of Gospel Music*. Westport, CT: Greenwood, 1979.

John H. Lovell, Jr., *Black Song: The Forge and the Flame—The Story of How the Afro-American Spiritual Was Hammered Out*. New York: Macmillan, 1972.

Bernice Johnson Reagon, *If You Don't Go, Don't Hinder Me: The African American Sacred Song Tradition*. Lincoln: University of Nebraska Press, 2001.

Bernice Johnson Reagon (ed.), *We'll Understand It Better By and By: Pioneering African American Gospel Composers*. Washington, D.C.: Smithsonian Institution Press, 1992.

Gwendolin Sims Warren, *Ev'ry Time I Feel the Spirit: 101 Best-Loved Psalms, Gospel Hymns, and Spiritual Songs of the African-American Church*. New York: Henry Holt, 1997.

Charles K. Wolfe, "Frank Smith, Andrew Jenkins, and Early Commercial Gospel Music," *American Music* I (spring 1983), 49–59.

Charles Wolfe (ed.), *Gospel Ship: Studies in White Gospel Music*. Urbana: University of Illinois Press, 1980.

Alan Young, *Woke Me Up This Morning: Black Gospel Singers and the Gospel Life*. Jackson: University Press of Mississippi, 1997.

Gothic Music

Joshua Gunn, "Gothic Music and the Inevitability of Genre," *Popular Music and Society* XXIII (spring 1999), 31–50.

Grunge Rock

Thomas C. Shevory, "Bleached Resistance: The Politics of Grunge," *Popular Music and Society* XIX (summer 1995), 23–48.

Heavy Metal

Bill Altman, "The Waxpaper Chronicles—Volume Five: Heavy Metal," *Waxpaper* III (February 3, 1978), 1–4.

Jeffrey Jensen Arnett, *Metal Heads: Heavy Metal Music and Adolescent Alienation*. Boulder, CO: Westview Press, 1996.

Philip Bashe, *Heavy Metal Thunder: The Music, Its History, and Its Heroes*. Garden City, NY: Dolphin/Doubleday, 1985.

Andy Boot, "The New Wave of British Heavy Metal," *Record Collector*, no. 114 (February 1989), 66–69.

J. D. Considine, "Good, Bad and Ugly: A Field Guide to Heavy Metal for Confused Consumers, Outraged Critics, and Wimpy New Wavers," *Musician*, no. 71 (September 1984), 52–53.

B. Lee Cooper, "Awarding an "A" Grade to Heavy Metal Music: A Review Essay," *Providence Forum* XIV, no. 3 (spring 1994), 9.

B. Lee Cooper, "Review of *Headbangers: The Worldwide Megabook of Heavy Metal Bands* by Mark Hale," *Popular Music and Society* XVII (spring 1993), 119–21.

Malcolm Dome, *Harsh Metal*. London: Omnibus Press, 1990.

Bruce K. Friesen and Jonathon S. Epstein, "Rock 'n' Roll Ain't Noise Pollution: Artistic Conventions and Tensions in the Major Subgenres of Heavy Metal Music," *Popular Music and Society* XVIII (fall 1994), 1–17.

Robert L. Gross, "Heavy Metal Music: A New Subculture in American Society," *Journal of Popular Culture* XXIV (summer 1990), 119–30.

Mark Hale, *Headbangers: The Worldwide Megabook of Heavy Metal Bands*. Ann Arbor, MI: Popular Culture, Ink., 1993.

Ross Halfin and Pete Makowski, *Heavy Metal: The Power Age*. New York: Delilah Books, 1982.

Brian Harrigan and Malcolm Dome (comps.), *Encyclopedia Metallica: The Bible of Heavy Metal*. London: Omnibus Press, 1986 (first published 1980).

Brian Harrigan (comp.), *H M • A—Z: The Definitive Encyclopedia of Heavy Metal From AC/DC through Led Zeppelin to ZZ Top*. London: Bobcat Books, 1981.

Tony Jasper and Derek Oliver, *The International Encyclopedia of Hard Rock and Heavy Metal* (3d rev. ed.). London: Sidgwick and Jackson, 1991 (first published 1983).

Neil Jeffries (ed.), *Kerrang! Directory of Heavy Metal: The Indispensable Guide to Rock Warriors and Headbangin' Heroes*. London: Virgin Books, 1993.

Chuck Klosterman, *Fargo Rock City: A Heavy Metal Odyssey in Rural North Dakota*. New York: Scribner, 2001.

Joel McIver, *Extreme Metal*. New York: Omnibus Press, 2000.

Don Mennie, "Heavy Metal Underground Spurns Rock Establishment," *Record Collector's Monthly*, no. 17 (February 1984), 3, 8.

Jas Obrecht (ed.), *Masters of Heavy Metal*. New York: Quill/Guitar Player Books, 1984.

Martin Popoff, *Goldmine Heavy Metal Record Price Guide*. Iola, WI: Krause, 1999.

Bryan Reesman, "25 Heavy-Duty Metal Albums," *Goldmine*, no. 488 (April 9, 1999), 32, 36.

Ira Robbins, "Heavy Metal: Down but Not Out," *Trouser Press* IV (September 1977), 20–23.

Steve Rosen, "Heavy Metal Roundtable," *Guitar World* V (January 1984), 29–34, 53, 60.

Will Straw, "Characterizing Rock Music Cultures: The Case of Heavy Metal," *Canadian University Music Review*, no. 5 (1984), 104–23.

Martin C. Strong, *The Great Metal Discography: Complete Discographies Listing Every Track Recorded by More than 800 Groups*. Edinburgh, Scotland: Canongate Books, 1998.

M.C. Strong (comp.), *The Great Metal Discography: From Hard Rock to Hardcore* (2d ed.). Edinburgh, Scotland: Mojo Press, 2001.

John Swenson, "The Roots of Heavy Metal," *Guitar World* V (January 1984), 16, 40.

Robert Walser, "Eruptions: Heavy Metal Appropriations of Classical Virtuosity," *Popular Music* XI (October 1992), 263–308.

Robert Walser, *Running with the Devil: Power, Gender, and Madness in Heavy Metal Music*. Hanover, NH: University Press of New England, 1993.

Deena Weinstein, *Heavy Metal: A Cultural Sociology*. New York: Lexington Books/Macmillan, 1991.

Charles M. Young, "Heavy Metal: In Defense of Dirtbags and Worthless Pups," *Musician*, no. 71 (September 1984), 40–44.

Hip–Hop Music

Greg Dimitriadis, "Hip Hop: From Live Performance to Mediated Narrative," *Popular Music* XV (May 1996), 179–94.

S. H. Fernando, Jr., *The New Beats: Exploring the Music, Culture, and Attitudes of Hip-Hop.* New York: Anchor Books/Bantam Doubleday Dell, 1994.

Nelson George, *Hip Hop America.* New York: Penguin Putnam, 1998.

Steven Hager, *Hip Hop: The Illustrated History of Break Dancing, Rap Music, and Graffiti.* New York: St. Martin's Press, 1984.

Ralph Heibutzki, "Time Enough for the Old School: The Hip Hop Revolution, 1970–1990," *Goldmine*, no. 413 (May 24, 1996), 20–69, 214, 228, 246–7ff.

Alan Light (ed.), *The Vibe History of Hip Hop.* New York: Three Rivers Press, 1999.

Carci McConnell, "Market Research Study on Hip-Hop Generation Misses Mark," *Lansing* [Michigan] *State Journal* (June 22, 1992), 1 B.

Alex Ogg, with David Upshal, *The Hip Hop Years: A History of Rap.* New York: Fromm International, 2001.

Russell A. Potter, *Spectacular Vernaculars: Hip-Hop and the Politics of Postmodernism.* Albany: State University of New York Press, 1995.

William Shaw, *Westside: The Coast-to-Coast Explosion of Hip Hop.* New York: Cooper Square Press/Rowman and Littlefield, 2000.

Instrumental Groups

B. Lee Cooper, "Review of *The Golden Age of Rock Instrumentals* by Steve Otfinoski," *Popular Music and Society* XXIV (summer 2000), 168–70.

B. Lee Cooper, "Review of *Guitar Player Magazine Presents Legends of Guitar–Rock: The '50s* (2 vols.)," *Popular Music and Society* XVIII (fall 1994), 100–1.

B. Lee Cooper, "Review of *Instrumental Gems of the '60s*," *Popular Music and Society* XX (fall 1996), 127–8.

B. Lee Cooper, "Review of *Nothin' but Instrumentals: A Compendium of Rock Instrumentals* by Don Riswick," *Popular Music and Society* XII (fall 1988), 107–8.

Trev Faull, "British Instrumental Groups of the Sixties," *Record Collector*, no. 67 (March 1985), 38–41.

Trev Faull, "British Instrumental Groups of the Sixties," *Record Collector*, no. 72 (August 1985), 48–50.

Rich Hagensen (comp.), *Strictly Instrumental*. New Westminster, British Columbia: R. Hagensen, 1986.

Rich Hagensen, *Strictly Instrumental: The Canadian Scene—A Discography of Canadian Instrumental Bands*. Burnaby, British Columbia: R. Hagensen, 1991.

Jean-Charles Marion, "Instrumentally Speaking," *Record Exchanger* III (1972), 17–20.

Steve Otfinoski, *The Golden Age of Rock Instrumentals*. New York: Billboard Books, 1997.

Charles Reinhart, "Beatles without Words: A Discography of Beatle Instrumentals," *Goldmine*, no. 267 (October 19, 1990), 46–48, 111.

Don Riswick (comp.), *Nothin' but Instrumentals: A Compendium of Rock Instrumentals*. Virginia Beach, VA: D. Riswick, 1985.

Joseph Sasfy, "Where Have All the Instrumentals Gone?" *Goldmine*, no. 86 (July 1983), 134–6.

H. Schoenfeld, "Instrumentals' Hot Market; Riding the 1964 Gravy Groove," *Variety* CCXXXVI (September 30, 1964), 51.

Jah/Jamaican Music

Sebastian Clarke, *JAH Music: The Evolution of the Popular Jamaican Song*. London: Heinemann Educational Press, 1980.

Michael Thomas and Adrian Boot, *JAH Revenge: Babylon Revisited*. London: EEL Pie, 1982.

Jazz Rock

Julie Coryell and Laura Friedman, *Jazz-Rock Fusion: The People/The Music*. Milwaukee, WI: Hal Leonard, 2000.

Robert Hurwitz, "Jazz-Rock: Musical Artistry or Lucrative Cop-Out?" *High Fidelity* XXV (September 1975), 54–55, 62–64.

Stuart Nicholson, *Jazz Rock: A History*. New York: Schirmer Books, 1998.

Muzak

Stephen H. Barnes, *Muzak—The Hidden Messages in Music: A Social Psychology of Culture*. Lewiston, NY: Edwin Mellen Press, 1988.

Al Di Meola, "Why Has Music Become Wallpaper?" *Musician*, no. 165 (July 1992), 33–34, 42.

Kim Foltz, "A Farewell to Mantovani," *Newsweek* CV (January 7, 1985), 44.

Stanley Green, "Music to Hear but Not to Listen To" *Saturday Review* XL (September 28, 1957), 55–56, 118.

Nick Groom, "The Condition of Muzak," *Popular Music and Society* XX (fall 1996), 1–17.

Jerry Herron, "Muzak: A Personal View; or, A Superstructure Mystery in Five Pieces," *Journal of American Culture* IV (winter 1981), 116–31.

Joseph Lanza, *Elevator Music: A Surreal History of Muzak, Easy-Listening, and Other Moodsong*. New York: St. Martin's Press, 1994.

Bruce McLeod, "Facing the Muzak," *Popular Music and Society* VII (spring 1979), 18–31.

Ronald E. Milliman, "The Influence of Background Music on the Behavior of Restaurant Patrons," *Journal of Consumer Research* XIII (September 1986), 286–9.

The Prerecorded Music Market: A Consumer Survey—1980. Burbank, CA: Warner Communications, 1981.

New Age Music

Patti Jean Birosik, *The New Age Music Guide: Profiles and Recordings of 500 Top New Age Musicians*. New York: Macmillan/Collier Books, 1989.

Dennis Hall, "New Age Music: A Voice of Liminality in Postmodern Popular Culture," *Popular Music and Society* XVIII (summer 1994), 13–21.

Susan Grove Hall, "New Age Music: An Analysis of an Ecstasy," *Popular Music and Society* XVIII (summer 1994), 23–33.

Henk N. Werkhoven, *The International Guide to New Age Music: A Comprehensive Guide to the Vast and Varied Artists and Recordings of New Age Music*. New York: Billboard Books, 1998.

New Wave Music

Peter Belstio and Bob Davis, *Hardcore California: A History of Punk and New Wave*. Berkeley, CA: Last Gasp Press of San Francisco, 1984.

David Bianco (comp.), *Who's New Wave in Music: An Illustrated Encyclopedia, 1976–1982 (the First Wave)*. Ann Arbor, MI: Pierian Press, 1985.

Colin Larkin (comp.), *The Virgin Encyclopedia of Indie and New Wave*. London: Virgin Books, 1998.

James Lull, "Popular Music: Resistance to New Wave," *Journal of Communication* XXXII (winter 1982), 121–31.

Myles Palmer, *New Wave Explosion: How Punk Rock Became New Wave Became the 80s*. London: Proteus Books, 1981.

Ira A. Robbins (ed.), *The Trouser Press Guide to New Wave Records*. New York: Scribner's, 1983.

Greg Shaw (comp.), *New Wave on Record: England and Europe, 1975–1978—A Discographical History*. Burbank, CA: Bomp Books, 1978.

Greg Shaw, "What's So New about the New Wave: A Hopefully Not Too Redundant Essay," *Waxpaper* II no. 9 (August 26, 1977), p. 8.

Pete Silverton and Paul Rambali, "The British New Wave, or Will There Always Be an England?" *Trouser Press* III (February/March 1977), 12–16.

Novelty Songs

Ken Barnes, "The Weird World of Beatle Novelties," *Who Put the Bomp!*, no. 13 (spring 1975), 13–15.

Ken Barnes, "The Weird World of Beatle Novelties," *Who Put the Bomp!*, no. 14 (fall 1975), 45.

Bill Cappelo, "Nervous Norvus," *Record Digest* I (July 1, 1978), 20–24.

Ace Collins, *Disco Duck and Other Adventures in Novelty Music: The True Stories behind the Greatest Novelty Hits of All Time*. New York: Berkley Boulevard Books, 1998.

B. Lee Cooper, "Review of *Dementia 2000! Dr. Demento's 30th Anniversary Collection*," *Rock and Blues News*, no. 10 (June-July 2000), 45.

B. Lee Cooper, "Review of *They Came From Outer Space: The Alien Songbook*," *Rock and Blues News*, no. 2 (February-March 1999), 42–43.

Don Cusic, "Comedy and Humor in Country Music," *Journal of American Culture* XVI (summer 1993), 45–50.

Warren Debenham (comp.), *Laughter on Record: A Comedy Discography*. Metuchen, NJ: Scarecrow Press, 1988.

Rush Evans, "Dr. Demento: A Doctorate in Record Collecting," *DISCoveries*, no. 136 (September 1999), 52–55.

George Gimarc and Pat Reeder, *Hollywood Hi-Fi: Over 100 of the Most Outrageous Celebrity Recordings Ever!* New York: St. Martin's Griffin, 1995.

Stacy Harris, *Comedians of Country Music.* Minneapolis, MN: Lerner, 1978.

Stephen Holden, "Randy Newman's Crass Menagerie: Stalking the Beast of Ignorance," *Musician*, no. 54 (April 1983), 72–77.

Peter Jones, "Calypso, Comedy, and The Creep," *The History of Rock*, no. 14 (1982), 267–70.

Howard Leib, "Tickle Your Funny Bone with One Foot of Comedy: 73 Records That Should Be Part of Your Collection," *Goldmine*, no. 514 (April 7, 2000), 36–38.

Lester S. Levy, *Flashes of Merriment: A Century of Humorous Songs in America, 1805–1905.* Norman: University of Oklahoma Press, 1971.

Ron Lofman, *Goldmine's Celebrity Vocals: Surprising, Unexpected, and Obscure Recordings by Actors, Sports Heroes, and Celebrities.* Iola, WI: Krause, 1994.

Michael T. Marsden, "Da Yoopers: Business Poets of Michigan's Upper Peninsula," *Popular Music and Society* XVIII (winter 1994), 1–6.

Dave Marsh, *Louie Louie: The History and Mythology of the World's Most Famous Rock 'n' Roll Song.* New York: Hyperion Books, 1993.

Jim McMullan, *Cheatin' Hearts, Broken Dreams, and Stomped on Love: The All-Time Funniest Country Music Titles.* New York: Dell, 1996.

Chuck Miller, "Alien Nation: The Story of Dickie Goodman," *Goldmine*, no. 447 (September 12, 1997), 144–4.

Chuck Miller, "Collectormania! The Jukebox of Dr. Demento," *Goldmine*, no. 541 (April 20, 2001), 22.

Chuck Miller, "Ray Stevens and His Streaks of Success: With 40 Years in Music, Stevens' Songs Are More than Just Novelties," *Goldmine*, no. 488 (April 9, 1999), 40–48, 58.

Chuck Miller, " 'Weird Al' Yankovic: The Crown Prince of Parody," *Goldmine*, no. 514 (April 7, 2000), 14–19, 50–54.

Jack Mirtle, with the assistance of Ted Hering (comps.), *Thank You Music Lovers: A Bio-Discography of Spike Jones and His City Slickers, 1941–1965.* Westport, CT: Greenwood, 1986.

Scott Montgomery, with Gary Norris and Kevin Walsh, "The Invisible Randy Newman: The Metric Music to Reprise Years, 1960–1995," *Goldmine*, no. 394 (September 1, 1995), 16–42, 56–75, 135–46, 152ff.

Bruce Nash and Allan Zullo, *The Wacky Top 40*. Holbrook, MA: Bob Adams, 1993.

Steve Otfinoski, *The Golden Age of Novelty Songs*. New York: Billboard Books/Watson-Guptill, 2000.

Alain Recaborde and Jeff Weiner, " 'Spell' Bound: The Wild Life of Screamin' Jay Hawkins," *Blues Access*, no. 42 (summer 2000), 18–22.

Ben Sandmel, "Whose Toot-Toot?" *Wavelength*, no. 56 (June 1985), 24–28.

Ronald L. Smith (comp.), *Comedy on Record: The Complete Critical Discography*. New York: Garland, 1988.

Ronald L. Smith, *Goldmine Comedy Record Price Guide*. Iola, WI: Krause, 1996.

Larry Stidom, "Sheb Wooley A.K.A. Ben Colder: The Purple People Eater Revisited," *Goldmine*, no. 65 (October 1981), 178–9.

Jeff Tamarkin, "Flying Saucer Rock 'n' Roll: A Space Odyssey," *Goldmine*, no. 197 (February 12, 1988), 22, 30, 129.

Jeff Tamarkin, "White House Funnies: Presidential Satire Records," *Goldmine*, no. 217 (November 18, 1988), 26–27, 83–85.

Michael A. Yahn, "The Music of the Marx Brothers," *Goldmine*, no. 363 (June 24, 1994), 14–28, 57–60, 106.

Jordan R. Young, *Spike Jones Off the Record: The Man Who Murdered Music*. Beverly Hills, CA: Past Times, 1994.

Orchestral Pop Music

John Covach and Walter Everett (eds.), *American Rock and the Classical Music Tradition*. Reading, England: Contemporary Music Review/Harwood Academic, 2000.

Reuben Musiker and Naomi Musiker, *Conductors and Composers of Popular Orchestral Music: A Biographical and Discographical Sourcebook*. Westport, CT: Greenwood, 1998.

Pop Music

Charles Boeckman, *And the Beat Goes On: A Survey of Pop Music in America*. Washington, D.C.: Robert B. Luce, 1972.

Don Breithaupt and Jeff Breithaupt, *Precious and Few: Pop Music in the Early '70s*. New York: St. Martin's Griffin, 1996.

Don Breithaupt and Jeff Breithaupt, *Night Moves: Pop Music in the Late '70s.* New York: St. Martin's Griffin, 2000.

Donald Clarke, *The Rise and Fall of Popular Music.* New York: St. Martin's Griffin, 1995.

B. Lee Cooper, "Review of *Discovering Great Singers of Classic Pop* by Roy Hemming and David Hajou," *Popular Culture in Libraries* II, no. 3 (1994), 109–10.

David Dachs, *Anything Goes: The World of Popular Music.* New York: Bobbs-Merrill, 1964.

John Gregory Dunne, *Crooning: A Collection.* New York: Simon & Schuster, 1990.

David Ewen, *All the Years of American Popular Music: A Comprehensive History.* Englewood Cliffs, NJ: Prentice Hall, 1977.

David Ewen, *The Life and Death of Tin Pan Alley: The Golden Age of American Popular Music.* New York: Funk and Wagnalls, 1964.

James J. Field, *American Popular Music, 1950–1975.* Philadelphia: Musical Americana, 1976.

Allen Forte, *The American Popular Ballad of the Golden Era, 1924–1950.* Princeton: Princeton University Press, 1995.

Charles Hamm, *Yesterdays: Popular Song in America.* New York: W. W. Norton, 1979.

Peter Gammond, *The Oxford Companion to Popular Music.* New York: Oxford University Press, 1991.

Tim Gracyk, with Frank Hoffmann, *Popular American Recording Pioneers, 1895–1925.* New York: Haworth Press, 2000.

Roy Hemming and David Hadju, *Discovering Great Singers of Classic Pop: A New Listener's Guide to the Sounds and Lives of Top Performers and Their Recordings, Movies, and Videos.* New York: Newmarket Press, 1991.

David Lee Joyner, *American Popular Music.* Dubuque, IA: Brown and Benchmark, 1993.

Hanif Kureishi and Jon Savage (eds.), *Faber Book of Pop.* London: Faber Books, 1995.

Margaret M. Mayer, *The American Dream: American Popular Music.* Santa Barbara, CA: Front Desk, 1994.

Jim Miller, "All-American Music," *Newsweek* CVIII (September 8, 1986), 62–63.

Gary E. Myers, *Do You Hear That Beat: Wisconsin Pop-Rock in the 50s and 60s.* Downey, CA: Hummingbird, 1995.

Tony Palmer, *All You Need Is Love: The Story of Popular Music.* New York: Grossman, 1976.

Michael Pitts and Frank Hoffmann, with the assistance of Dick Carty and Jim Bedoian, *The Rise of the Crooners: Gene Austin, Russ Columbo, Bing Crosby, Nick Lucas, Johnny Marvin, and Rudy Vallee.* Lanham, MD: Scarecrow Press, 2002.

Timothy E. Scheurer (ed.), *American Popular Music—Volume One: The 19th Century and Tin Pan Alley.* Bowling Green, OH: Bowling Green State University Popular Press, 1989.

Timothy E. Scheurer (ed.), *American Popular Music—Volume Two: The Age of Rock.* Bowling Green, OH: Bowling Green State University Popular Press, 1989.

Jo Stafford and B. Greeley, "A Great Thing's Been Lost to Rock and Roll—The American Pop Song," *Variety* CCXXXIII (January 29, 1964), 57.

Dean Tudor, *Popular Music: An Annotated Guide to Recordings.* Littleton, CO: Libraries Unlimited, 1984.

Don Tyler, *Hit Parade, 1920–1955: An Encyclopedia of the Top Songs of the Jazz, Depression, Swing, and Sing Eras.* New York: Quill/William Morrow, 1985.

Joel Whitburn (comp.), *Pop Memories, 1890–1954: The History of American Popular Music.* Menomonee Falls, WI: Record Research, 1986.

Adam White, "Philadelphia Pop," *The History of Rock*, no. 18 (1982), 341–3.

Power Pop

John Borack, "25 Essential Power Pop Albums," *Goldmine*, no. 484 (February 12, 1999), 26.

Progressive Rock

John Covach, "Echolyn and American Progressive Rock," *Contemporary Music Review* XVIII, no. 4 (2000), 13–61.

Kevin Holm-Hudson (ed.), *Progressive Rock Reconsidered.* New York: Routledge, 2002.

Jerry Lucky, *The Progressive Rock Files* (updated ed.). Burlington, Ontario: Collector's Guide, 2000.

Edward Macan, *Rocking the Classics: English Progressive Rock and the Counterculture.* New York: Oxford University Press, 1997.

Bill Martin, *Listening to the Future: The Time of Progressive Rock, 1968–1978.* Chicago: Open Court, 1997.

Joseph J. Shingler, "Renaissance of Progressive Rock: The Pioneers and the Revivalists," *DISCoveries* III (June 1990), 30–33.

Bradley Smith, *The Billboard Guide to Progressive Music.* New York: Billboard Books, 1997.

Paul Stump, *The Music's All That Matters: A History of Progressive Rock.* London: Quartet Books, 1997.

Barry Winton, "Progressive Rock," *Record Collector*, no. 115 (March 1989), 86–89.

Protest Music

Mary Ellison, *Lyrical Protest: Black Music's Struggle against Discrimination.* New York: Praeger Books, 1989.

Joe Ferrandino, "Rock Culture and the Development of Social Consciousness," *Radical America* III (November 1969), 11–34.

Peter Garrett, *Political Blues.* Sydney: Hodder and Stoughton, 1987.

Elizabeth J. Kizer, "Protest Song Lyrics as Rhetoric," *Popular Music and Society* IX, no. 1 (1983), 3–11.

Ralph E. Knupp, "A Time for Every Purpose under Heaven: Rhetorical Dimensions of Protest Music," *Southern Speech Communication Journal* XLVI (summer 1981), 377–89.

George H. Lewis, "Social Protest and Self Awareness in Black Popular Music," *Popular Music and Society* II (summer 1973), 327–33.

George H. Lewis, "Storm Blowing from Paradise: Social Protest and Oppositional Ideology in Popular Hawaiian Music," *Popular Music* X (January 1991), 53–67.

Robert G. Pielke, *You Say You Want a Revolution: Rock Music in American Culture.* Chicago: Nelson-Hall, 1986.

Ray Pratt, *Rhythm and Resistance: Explorations in the Political Uses of Popular Music.* New York: Praeger Books, 1990.

Robert Reid, "Music and Social Problems: A Poster Series," Portland, ME: J. Weston Walch, 1971.

Jerome L. Rodnitzky, "The Sixties between the Microgrooves: Using Folk and Protest Music to Understand American History, 1963–1973," *Popular Music and Society* XXIII (winter 1999), 105–22.

Robert A. Rosenstone, "The Times They are a-Changin': The Music of Protest," in *Old Government/New People: Readings for the New Politics* edited by Alfred de Grazia, R. Eric Weise, and John Appel. Glenview, IL: Scott Foresman, 1971, 96–110.

Psychedelic Rock

C. Baksa and J. D. Martignon (comps.), *The Midnight Records Book of 60's Punk and Psychedelic Compilations*. New York: Midnight Records, 1984.

Gary Burns, "Attack of the Psychedelic Garage Punks," *OneTwoThreeFour*, no. 4 (winter 1987), 58–65.

Jim DeRogatis, *Kaleidoscope Eyes: Psychedelic Rock From the '60s to the '90s*. Seacacus, NJ: Citadel Press Book, 1996.

James Henke, with Parke Puterbaugh, *I Want to Take You Higher: The Psychedelic Era, 1965–1969*. San Francisco: Chronicle Books/Rock and Roll Hall of Fame and Museum, 1997.

Michael Hicks, *Sixties Rock: Garage, Psychedelic, and Other Satisfactions*. Urbana: University of Illinois Press, 1999.

Barney Hoskyns, *Beneath the Diamond Sky: Haight Ashbury, 1965–1970*. Rochester, England: Bloomsbury Books, 1997.

Vernon Joynson (comp.), *The Acid Trip: A Complete Guide to Psychedelic Music*. Todmorden, England: Babylon Books, 1984.

Gene Sculatti and Davin Seay, *San Francisco Nights: The Psychedelic Music Trip, 1965–1968*. New York: St. Martin's Press, 1985.

Joel Selvin, *Summer of Love: The Inside Story of LSD, Rock and Roll, Free Love, and High Times in the Wild West*. New York: Cooper Square Press/Rowman and Littlefield, 1999.

Greg Shaw, "Psychedelic Rock: The World's Most Misunderstood Music," *Bomp!* no. 19 (October/November 1978), 32–33, 52.

Punk Rock

Isabelle Anscombe and Dike Blair, *Punk!* New York: Urizen Books, 1978.

Peter Belsito and Bob Davis, *Hardcore California: A History of Punk and New Wave*. Berkeley, CA: Last Gasp Press of San Francisco, 1983.

Dike Blair and Isabelle Anscombe (eds.), *Punk: Punk Rock/Punk Stance/Punk People/Punk Stars That Head the New Wave in England and America*. New York: Urizen Books, 1978.

Steven Blush, *American Hardcore: A Tribal History*. Los Angeles: Feral House, 2001.

Victor Bockris, *Beat Punks: New York's Underground Culture from the Beat Generation to the Punk Explosion*. New York: Da Capo Press, 1998.

Adrian Boot and Chris Salewicz, *Punk: The Illustrated History of a Music Revolution*. New York: Penguin Studio Books, 1996.

Julie Burchill and Tony Parsons, *"The Boy Looked at Johnny": The Obituary of Rock and Roll*. London: Pluto Press, 1978.

Stephen Colegrave and Chris Sullivan, *Punk: The Definitive Record of a Revolution*. New York: Thunder's Mouth Press, 2001.

Caroline Coon, *1988: The New Wave Punk Rock Explosion*. New York: Hawthorn Books, 1977.

Jude Davies, "The Future of 'No Future': Punk Rock and Postmodern Theory," *Journal of Popular Culture* XXIX, no. 4 (Spring 1996), 3–25.

Richard D. Dixon, Fred R. Ingram, Richard M. Levinson, and Catherine L. Putnam, "The Cultural Diffusion of Punk Rock in the United States," *Popular Music and Society* VI (spring 1979), 210–30.

Peter Doggett, "Punk—The First Wave," *Record Collector*, no. 125 (January 1990), 12–14.

Paul Fryer, "Punk and the New Wave of British Rock: Working Class Heroes and Art School Attitudes," *Popular Music and Society* X (winter 1986), 1–15.

Tricia Henry, "Punk and Avant-Garde Art," *Journal of Popular Culture* XVII (spring 1984), 30–36.

Clinton Heylin, *From the Velvets to the Voidoids: A Pre-Punk History for a Post-Punk World*. New York: Penguin Books, 1993.

Clinton Heylin, "Punk—The Indie Explosion," *Record Collector*, no. 125 (January 1990), 16–20.

Dave Laing, *One Chord Wonders: Power and Meaning in Punk Rock*. Milton Keynes, England: Open University Press, 1985.

Harold G. Levine and Steven H. Stumpf, "Statements of Fear through Cultural Symbols: Punk Rock as a Reflective Subculture," *Youth and Society* XIV (June 1983), 417–35.

Greil Marcus, *In the Fascist Bathroom: Punk in Pop Music, 1977–1992*. Cambridge: Harvard University Press, 1999.

James R. McDonald, "Suicidal Rage: An Analysis of Hardcore Punk Lyrics," *Popular Music and Society* XI (fall 1987), 91–102.

Gina Morris, *Happy Doin' What We're Doin': The Pub Rock Years, 1972–1975*. San Francisco: Nightbird Books, 1984.

Gina Morris, *Off-Beat: Pub Rock for the '80s*. San Francisco: Nightbird Books, 1985.

Myles Palmer, *New Wave Explosion: How Punk Rock Became New Wave Became the 80's*. London: Proteus Books, 1981.

John Reed, "Punk—The Compilations," *Record Collector*, no. 125 (January 1990), 22–24.

Deirdre Rockmake, "Punk Movement Now Ten Years Old and Collectible," *Goldmine*, no. 148 (March 28, 1986), 94–95.

Peter G. Ross, "An Organizational Analysis of the Emergence, Development, and Mainstreaming of British Punk Rock Music," *Popular Music and Society* XX (spring 1996), 155–73.

Roger Sabin (ed.), *Punk Rock: So What?* New York: Routledge, 1999.

Jon Savage, *England's Dreaming: Anarchy, Sex Pistols, Punk Rock, and Beyond*. New York: St. Martin's Griffin, 2001.

Julian Tanner, "Pop, Punk, and Subcultural Solutions," *Popular Music and Society* VI (spring 1978), 68–71.

Ragtime

Edward Berlin, *Ragtime: A Musical and Cultural History*. Berkeley: University of California Press, 1984.

Edward A. Berlin, *Reflections and Research on Ragtime*. Brooklyn, NY: Institute for Studies in American Music, 1987.

Rudi Blesh and Harriet Janis, *They All Played Ragtime* (4th ed.). New York: Oak, 1971.

John Edward Hasse (ed.), *Ragtime: Its History, Composers, and Music*. New York: Schirmer Books, 1985.

David A. Jasen and Gene Jones, *That American Rag: The Story of Ragtime from Coast to Coast*. New York: Schirmer Books, 2000.

Ross Laird, *Tantalizing Tingles: A Discography of Early Ragtime, Jazz, and Novelty Syncopated Piano Recordings, 1889–1934*. Westport, CT: Greenwood, 1995.

William J. Schafer and Johannes Riedel, *The Art of Ragtime: Form and Meaning of an Original Black American Art*. Baton Rouge: Louisiana State University Press, 1973.

Rap Music

Nathan D. Abrams, "Antonio's B-Boys: Rap, Rappers, and Gramsci's Intellectuals," *Popular Music and Society* XIX (winter 1995), 1–19.

Venise T. Berry, "Rap Music, Self Concept, and Low Income Black Adolescents," *Popular Music and Society* XIV (fall 1990), 89–107.

Michele N.-K. Collison, " 'Fight the Power': Rap Music Pounds Out a New Anthem for Many Black Students," *The Chronicle of Higher Education* XXXVI (February 14, 1990), A1, A29, 30.

J. D. Considine, "Fear of a Rap Planet: The Biggest Style of the Last Decade Has a Problem with Attitudes," *Musician*, no. 160 (February 1992), 34–43, 97.

Mark Costello and David Foster Wallace, *Signifying Rappers: Rap and Race in the Urban Present*. New York: Ecco Press, 1990.

William F. Danaher and Stephen P. Blackwelder, "The Emergence of Blues and Rap: A Comparison and Assessment of the Context, Meaning, and Message," *Popular Music and Society* XVII (winter 1993), 1–12.

Murran Forman, " 'Represent': Race, Space, and Place in Rap Music," *Popular Music* XIX (January 2000), 65–90.

Keith Elliot Greenberg, *Rap*. Minneapolis, MN: Lerner, 1988.

John Leland, with Marc Peyser and Farai Chideya, "Rap and Race," *Newsweek* XCIX (June 29, 1992), 46–52.

Judy McCoy, *Rap Music in the 1980s: A Reference Guide*. Metuchen, NJ: Scarecrow Press, 1992.

Judith McDonnell, "Rap Music: Its Role as an Agent of Change," *Popular Music and Society* XVI (fall 1992), 89–105.

David Mills, "Rap Music That Guns for Violence," *Insight* (September 25, 1989), 54–56.

Havelock Nelson and Michael A. Gonzales, *Bring the Noise: A Guide to Rap Music and Hip-Hop Culture*. New York: Harmony Books, 1991.

William Eric Perkins (ed.), *Droppin' Science: Critical Essays on Rap Music and Hip Hop Culture*. Philadelphia: Temple University Press, 1996.

Tricia Rose, *Black Noise: Rap Music and Black Culture in Contemporary America*. Hanover, NH: University Press of New England, 1994.

Tricia Rose, "Orality and Technology: Rap Music and Afro-American Cultural Resistance," *Popular Music and Society* XIII (winter 1989), 35–47.

Mike Royko, "Admit It, Execs, 'Cop Killer' Is Crap," *Lansing* [Michigan] *State Journal* (June 25, 1992), 8A.

David Samuels, "The Rap on Rap: The Black Music That Isn't Either," *New Republic* XI (November 1991), 24–29.

Adam Sexton (ed.), *Rap on Rap: Straight-up Talk on Hip-Hop Culture*. New York: Dell, 1995.

Jon Michael Spencer (eds.), *The Emergency of Black and the Emergence of Rap*. Durham, NC: Duke University Press, 1991.

Lawrence A. Stanley (ed.), *Rap: The Lyrics*. New York: Penguin Books, 1992.

Barbara Taylor (ed.), *The National Rap Directory*. Atlanta, GA: Rising Star Music, 1996.

David Toop, *The Rap Attack: African Jive to New York Hip Hop*. Boston: South End Press, 1984.

David Toop, *Rap Attack 2: African Pop to Global Hip-Hop*. Excelsior, MN: Serpent's Tail, 1992.

S. Craig Watkins, *Representing: Hip Hop Culture and the Production of Black Cinema*. Chicago: University of Chicago Press, 1998.

Reggae

Leonard Barrett, *The Rastafarians: Sounds of Cultural Dissonance*. Boston: Beacon Press, 1977.

Steve Barrow and Peter Dalton, *Reggae—100 Essential CDs: The Rough Guide*. London: Rough Guides, 1999.

Steve Barrow and Peter Dalton (edited by Orla Duane), *Reggae: The Rough Guide* (2d ed.). London: Rough Guides, 2001.

Kenneth Bilby, "The Impact of Reggae in the United States," *Popular Music and Society* V (spring 1977), 17–22.

Adrian Boot and Michael Thomas, *Jamaica: Babylon on a Thin Wire*. New York: Schocken Press, 1977.

Lloyd Bradley, *This Is Reggae Music: The Story of Jamaica's Music*. New York: Grove Press, 2000.

Stephen Davis (text) and Peter Simon (photos), *Reggae Bloodlines: In Search of the Music and Culture of Jamaica*. New York: Anchor Press/Doubleday, 1977.

Stephen Davis and Peter Simon, *Reggae International*. New York: Rogner and Bernhard/Random House, 1982.

Dick Hebdige, "Reggae, Rastas, and Rudies," in *Mass Communication and Society*, edited by James Curran, Michael Gurevitch, and Janet Woollacott. Beverly Hills, CA: Sage, 1979, 426–39.

Howard Johnson and Jim Pines, *Reggae: Deep Roots Music*. London: Proteus Books, 1982.

Colin Larkin (ed.), *The Guinness Who's Who of Reggae*. Enfield, England: Guinness, 1994.

Rebekah Michele Mulvaney, *Rastafari and Reggae: A Dictionary and Sourcebook* Westport, CT: Greenwood, 1990.

Robert Santelli, "Just What Is Reggae?" *Goldmine*, no. 85 (June 1983), 130, 148.

Robert Santelli, "Reggae History: Lesson 1," *Goldmine*, no. 71 (April 1982), 177.

Dave Thompson, *Reggae and Caribbean Music: The Essential Listening Companion*. San Francisco: Backbeat Books, 2002.

Timothy White, "The Waxpaper Chronicles—Volume Six: Reggae," *Waxpaper* III (March 3, 1978), 1–6.

James A. Winders, "Reggae, Rastafarians, and Revolution: Rock Music in the Third World," *Journal of Popular Culture* XVII (summer 1983), 61–73.

Rhythm and Blues

John Broven, *Rhythm and Blues in New Orleans*. Gretna, LA: Pelican, 1978.

Ashley Brown, "The Roots of Soul," *The History of Rock*, no. 17 (1982), 321–2.

B. Lee Cooper, "Review of *The Death of Rhythm and Blues* by Nelson George," *Popular Music and Society* XIII (summer 1989), 117–19.

B. Lee Cooper, "Review of *First Pressings: The History of Rhythm and Blues* (4 vols.) by Galen Gart," *Popular Music and Society* XIV (winter 1990), 110–12.

B. Lee Cooper, "Review of *I Hear You Knockin': The Sound of New Orleans Rhythm and Blues* by Jeff Hannusch," *Popular Music and Society* XI (winter 1987), 93–94.

B. Lee Cooper, "Review of *The Late Great Johnny Ace and the Transition from R & B to Rock 'n' Roll* by James M. Salem," *Popular Music and Society* XXIV (spring 2000), 119–21.

B. Lee Cooper, "Review of *The Rockin' 40's* (Hoy Hoy CD 40–5–01) by Morgan Wright," *Popular Music and Society* XVII (summer 1993), 134.

B. Lee Cooper, "Revisiting Rhythm 'n' Blues Royalty: A Review Essay," *Popular Music and Society* XX (fall 1996), 119–22.

Chip Deffaa, *Blue Rhythms: Six Lives in Rhythm and Blues*. Urbana: University of Illinois Press, 1996.

Peter Doggett, "Rhythm Boxes," *Record Collector*, no. 179 (July 1994), 116–18.

Joe Edwards (comp.), *Top 10's and Trivia of Rock and Roll and Rhythm and Blues, 1950–1980*. St. Louis, MO: Blueberry Hill, 1981.

Phyl Garland, "Basic Library of Rhythm-and-Blues," *Stereo Review* XLII (May 1979), 72–77.

Galen Gart (comp.), *First Pressings—Volume One, 1948–1950: Rock History as Chronicled in Billboard Magazine*. Milford, NH: Big Nickel, 1986.

Galen Gart (comp.), *First Pressings—Volume Two, 1951–1952: Rock History as Chronicled in Billboard Magazine*. Milford, NH: Big Nickel, 1986.

Galen Gart (comp.), *First Pressings: The History of Rhythm and Blues—Special 1950 Volume*. Milford, NH: Big Nickel, 1993.

Galen Gart (comp.), *First Pressings—The History of Rhythm and Blues: Volume One—1951*. Milford, NH: Big Nickel, 1991.

Galen Gart (comp.), *First Pressings—The History of Rhythm and Blues: Volume Two—1952*. Milford, NH: Big Nickel, 1992.

Galen Gart (comp.), *First Pressings—The History of Rhythm and Blues: Volume Three, 1953*. Milford, NH: Big Nickel, 1989.

Galen Gart (comp.), *First Pressings—The History of Rhythm and Blues: Volume Four, 1954*. Milford, NH: Big Nickel, 1989.

Galen Gart (comp.), *First Pressings—The History of Rhythm and Blues: Volume Five—1955*. Milford, Milford, NH: Big Nickel, 1990.

Galen Gart (comp.), *First Pressings—The History of Rhythm and Blues: Volume Six—1956*. Milford, NH: Big Nickel, 1991.

Galen Gart, *First Pressings: The History of Rhythm and Blues—Volume Seven—1957*. Milford, NH: Big Nickel, 1993.

Galen Gart (comp.), *First Pressings—The History of Rhythm and Blues: Volume 8—1958*. Milford, NH: Big Nickel, 1995.

Galen Gart, "The Inspirational Ballad: A Lost Artform in Rhythm n' Blue," *Goldmine*, no. 188 (October 9, 1987), 22, 86.

Nelson George, *The Death of Rhythm and Blues*. New York: Pantheon Books, 1988.

Nelson George, "The Rhythm and the Blues," *Billboard* XCVII (November 30, 1985), 42.

Tony Glover, "The Groovy Boom in R & B," *Sing Out* XVI (July 1966), 37–43.

Tony Glover, "R & B," *Sing Out: The Folk Song Magazine* XV (May 1965), 7–13.

Tony Glover, "R & B," *Sing Out!* XV (May 1965), 7–13.

Gary Graff, Josh Freedom du Lac, and Jim McFarlin (eds.), *Musichound R & B: The Essential Album Guide*. Detroit, MI: Visible Ink Press, 1998.

Hugh Gregory, *The Real Rhythm and Blues*. London: Blandford Books, 1998.

Peter Guralnick, *Feel Like Going Home: Portraits in Blues and Rock 'n' Roll*. New York: Outerbridge and Dienstrey, 1971.

Jeff Hannusch (aka Almost Slim), *I Hear You Knockin': The Sound of New Orleans Rhythm and Blues*. Ville Platte, LA: Swallow Press, 1985.

Jeff Hannusch, *The Soul of New Orleans: A Legacy of Rhythm and Blues*. Ville Platte, LA: Swallow Press, 2001.

Michael Haralambos, *Right On: From Blues to Soul in Black America*. New York: Drake, 1975.

Woodie King, Jr., "Searching for Brothers Kindred: Rhythm & Blues of the 1950's," *The Black Scholar* VI (November 1974), 19–30.

Jean-Charles Marion, "The Aesthetics of Lead Vocals: Upfront Variations in Style of the R & B Vocal Groups of the 50's," *Record Exchanger* II, no. 8 (1971), 16–17.

Portia K. Maultsby, "Rhythm and Blues (1945–1955): A Survey of Styles," from *Black American Popular Music: Rhythm and Blues, 1945–1955*. Washington, D.C.: National Museum of American History and the Smithsonian Institution, 1986, 6–23.

Tom McCourt, "Bright Lights, Big City: A Brief History of Rhythm and Blues, 1945–1957," *Popular Music and Society* IX (spring 1983), 1–18.

Lynn Ellis McCutcheon, *Rhythm and Blues: An Experience and Adventure in Its Origin and Development*. Arlington, VA: Beatty, 1971.

Bill Millar, "Rhythm and Blues," *The History of Rock*, no. 2 (1982), 29–32.

Doug Miller, "The Moan within the Tone: African Retentions in Rhythm and Blues Saxophone Style in Afro-American Popular Music," *Popular Music* XIV (May 1995), 155–74.

Al Pavlow (comp.), *Big Al Pavlow's The R & B Book: A Disc-History of Rhythm and Blues*. Providence, RI: Music House, 1983.

Lawrence N. Redd, *Rock Is Rhythm and Blues: The Impact of Mass Media*. East Lansing: Michigan State University Press, 1974.

Lawrence N. Redd, "Rock! It's Still Rhythm and Blues," *Black Perspectives in Popular Music* XIII (spring 1985), 31–47.

Mike Rowe, *Chicago Breakdown*. New York: Drake, 1975.

Arnold Shaw, *Honkers and Shouters: The Golden Years of Rhythm and Blues*. New York: Collier Books, 1978.

Arnold Shaw, *The Rock Revolution*. New York: Paperback Library, 1971.

Brian Ward, *Just My Soul Responding: Rhythm and Blues, Black Consciousness, and Race Relations*. Berkeley: University of California Press, 1998.

Pete J. Welding, "Rhythm and Blues in 1950," *Saturday Review* XXXIII (June 24, 1950), 49.

Jerry Wexler and David Ritz, *Rhythm and the Blues: A Life in American Music*. New York: Knopf, 1993.

Joel Whitburn (comp.), *Top R & B Singles, 1942–1999*. Menomonee Falls, WI: Record Research, 2000.

Timothy White, "Jerry Wexler: The Godfather of Rhythm and Blues," *Rolling Stone*, no. 331 (November 27, 1980), 48–52, 74–81.

Mark J. Zucker, "The Saga of Lovin' Dan: A Study in the Iconography of Rhythm and Blues Music of the 1950s," *Journal of Popular Culture* XVI (fall 1982), 43–51.

Rock 'n' Roll

Richard Aquila, *That Old-Time Rock and Roll: A Chronicle of an Era, 1954–1963*. Urbana: University of Illinois Press, 2000 (first published 1989).

B. Lee Cooper, "Review of *Shake, Rattle, and Roll—The Golden Age of American Rock 'n' Roll: Volume One—1952–1955* by Lee Cotton," *Popular Music and Society* XIII (fall 1989), 98–100.

B. Lee Cooper, "Review of *Reelin' and Rockin'—The Golden Age of American Rock 'n' Roll: Volume Two, 1956–1959* by Lee Cotton," *Popular Music and Society* XX (spring 1996), 225–6.

B. Lee Cooper, "Review of *What Was the First Rock 'n' Roll Record?* by Jim Dawson and Steve Propes," *Popular Music and Society* XVII (spring 1993), 115–16.

Jim Dawson and Steve Propes, *What Was the First Rock 'n' Roll Record?* Boston: Faber and Faber, 1992.

Colin Escott, with Martin Hawkins, *Good Rockin' Tonight: Sun Records and the Birth of Rock 'n' Roll*. New York: St. Martin's Press, 1991.

Pete Fornatale, *The Story of Rock 'n' Roll*. New York: William Morrow, 1987.

Bill Griggs, *The Evolution and Decline of 1950's Rock and Roll Music*. Lubbock, TX: William F. Griggs/Rockin' 50s Magazine, 1996.

Brock Helander, *Rock 'n' Roll to Rock: A Discography*. New York: B. Helander, 1978.

Michael Jarrett, "Concerning the Progress of Rock and Roll," *South Atlantic Quarterly* XC (fall 1991), 803–17.

Bob Kinder, *The Best of the First: The Early Days of Rock and Roll*. Chicago: Adams Press, 1986.

Mirek Kocandrle, *The History of Rock and Roll: A Selective Discography*. Boston: G. K. Hall, 1988.

Greil Marcus, *Mystery Train: Images of America in Rock 'n' Roll Music*. New York: E. P. Dutton, 1975.

Linda Martin and Kerry Segrave, *Anti-Rock: The Opposition to Rock 'n' Roll*. Hamden, CT: Archon Books, 1988.

Robert Palmer, *Rock and Roll: An Unruly History*. New York: Harmony Books, 1995.

Michael B. Smith, "25 Essential Rock 'n' Roll Albums of the '70s," *Goldmine*, no. 486 (March 12, 1999), 104.

Harry Sumrall, *Pioneers of Rock and Roll: 100 Artists Who Changed the Face of Rock*. New York: Billboard Books, 1994.

Nick Tosches, *Country: The Twisted Roots of Rock 'n' Roll*. New York: Da Capo Press, 1996.

Nick Tosches, *Unsung Heroes of Rock 'n' Roll: The Birth of Rock 'n' Roll in the Dark and Wild Years before Elvis*. New York: Scribner's, 1984.

Ritchie Yorke, *The History of Rock 'n' Roll*. New York: Methuen Books, 1976.

Rockabilly

Richard Blackburn (comp.) *Rockabilly: A Comprehensive Discography of Reissues*. New York: Blackburn, 1975.

B. Lee Cooper, "Review of *Go Cat Go! Rockabilly Music and Its Makers* by Craig Morrison," *Popular Music and Society* XXI (winter 1997), 145–8.

B. Lee Cooper and Wayne S. Haney, *Rockabilly: A Bibliographic Resource Guide*. Metuchen, NJ: Scarecrow Press, 1990.

Colin Escott, with Martin Hawkins, *Good Rockin' Tonight: Sun Records and the Birth of Rock }n' Roll*. New York: St. Martin's Press, 1991.

Dan Forte, "Rockabilly Revival," *Guitar Player* XVII (September 1983), 69.

Dan Forte, "Roots of Rockabilly," *Guitar Player* XVII (December 1983), 67–70, 96–98.

Timothy Frew, *Rockabilly: The Life, Times, and Music Series*. New York: Friedman/Fairfax, 1996.

Bob Garbutt, *Rockabilly Queens: The Careers and Recordings of Wanda Jackson, Janis Martin, and Brenda Lee*. Toronto, Ontario: Ducktail Press, 1979.

Jonathan Kamin, "The White R & B Audience and the Music Industry, 1952–1956," *Popular Music and Society* VI (summer 1978), 150–67.

Tom Lincoln and Dick Blackburn, *Guide to Rare Rockabilly and Rock 'n' Roll 45 RPMs*. Birmingham, AL: T. Lincoln/D. Blackburn, 1998.

Randy McNutt, *We Wanna Boogie: An Illustrated History of the American Rockabilly Movement*. Fairfield, OH: Hamilton Hobby Press, 1988.

Bill Millar, "Rockabilly: Was This the Purist Style in Rock?" *History of Rock*, no. 6 (1982), 101–3.

Craig Morrison, *Go Cat Go! Rockabilly Music and Its Makers*. Champaign: University of Illinois Press, 1996.

Robert K. Oermann and Mary A. Bufwack, "Rockabilly Women," *Journal of Country Music* VIII (May 1979), 65–94.

Billy Poore, *Rockabilly: A Forty-Year Journey*. Milwaukee, WI: Hal Leonard, 1998.

Rockabilly! Milwaukee, WI: Hal Leonard, 1993.

Greg Shaw, "The Rockabily Revival," *Who Put the Bomp!* no. 13 (spring 1975), 22–25.

Wayne Stierle, "Rockabilly Music? There's No Such Thing!" *DISCoveries* II (October 1989), 144.

Salsa

Vernon W. Boggs and Rolf Meyersohn, "The Profile of a Bronx Salsero: Salsa's Still Alive!" *Popular Music and Society* XII (winter 1988), 59–67.

Vernon W. Boggs, "Salsa Music: The Latent Function of Slavery and Racialism," *Popular Music and Society* XI (Spring 1987), 7–14.

Scott Heller, "Salsa: A Hybrid That Reflects the Globalization of Culture," *Chronicle of Higher Education* XLIV (May 1, 1998), A19–A22.

Felix M. Padilla, "Salsa: Puerto Rican and Latino Music," *Journal of Popular Culture* XXIV (summer 1990), 87–107.

Patria Román-Velazquez, "The Embodiment of Salsa: Musicians, Instruments, and the Performance of a Latin Style and Identity," *Popular Music* XVIII (January 1999), 115–31.

Show Music

Didier C. Deutsch (ed.), *MusicHound Soundtracks: The Essential Album Guide to Film, Television, and Stage Music*. Detroit, MI: Visible Ink Press, 2000.

Paul Filmer, Val Rimmer, and Dave Walsh, "Oklahoma! Ideology and Politics in the Vernacular Tradition of the American Musical," *Popular Music* XVIII (October 1999), 381–95.

Kurt Ganzl, *The Blackwell Guide to the Musical Theatre on Record*. Cambridge, MA: Basil Blackwell, 1990.

Kurt Ganzl, *The Encyclopedia of Musical Theatre—Three Volumes* (2d ed.). New York: Schirmer Books, 2001.

Thomas S. Hischak, *The American Musical Theatre Song Encyclopedia*. Westport, CT: Greenwood, 1995.

Thomas S. Hischak, *The American Musical Film Song Encyclopedia*. Westport, CT: Greenwood, 1999.

Colin Larkin (ed.), *The Guinness Who's Who of Stage Musicals*. Enfield, England: Guinness, 1994.

Richard Chigley Lynch (comp.), *Broadway, Movie, TV, and Studio Cast Musicals on Record: A Discography of Recordings, 1985–1995*. Westport, CT: Greenwood, 1996.

Jack Raymond, *Show Music on Record: The First 100 Years*. Washington, D.C.: Smithsonian Institution Press, 1992.

Ska

Chris Nickson, "The History of Jamaican Music: Part One—SKA and Rock Steady," *DISCoveries*, no. 112 (September 1997), 32–35.

Southern Rock

Marley Brant, *Southern Rockers: The Roots and Legacy of Southern Rock*. New York: Billboard Books, 1999.

Mike Butler, " 'Dixie Rock!': The Southern Rock Movement and White Male Culture in the Post-Civil Rights South. Master's thesis, University of Mississippi, 1996.

Mike Butler, " 'Luther King Was a Good Ole Boy': The Southern Rock Movement and White Male Identity in the Post-Civil Rights South," *Popular Music and Society* XXIII (summer 1999), 41–61.

Michael B. Smith, "25 Essential Southern Rock Albums," *Goldmine*, no. 482 (January 15, 1999), 48.

Surf Sounds

Peter Bart, "The California Sound," *Atlanta Monthly* CCXV (May 1965), 140, 142.

John Blair (comp.), *The Illustrated Discography of Surf Music, 1951–1965* (3d ed.). Ann Arbor, MI: Popular Culture, Ink., 1995.

John Blair and Bob Dalley, "Southern California Surf Revival Music up to Now," *Goldmine*, no. 86 (July 1983), 58–60.

George O. Carney, "Cowabunga! Surfer Rock and the Five Themes of Geography," *Popular Music and Society* XXIII (winter 1999), 3–29.

B. Lee Cooper, "Review of *The Illustrated Discography of Surf Music, 1961–1965* (2d ed., rev.) by John Blair," *Popular Music and Society* XI (spring 1987), 99–100.

Robert Dalley, "A Look at Surfin' 45 Rarities," *Goldmine*, no. 81 (February 1983), 176–7.

Robert Dalley, "1984: Banner Year for Surf Releases," *Goldmine*, no. 126 (May 24, 1985), 26, 30.

Robert J. Dalley, "Surfin' Guitars," *DISCoveries* II (June 1989), 128–9.

Gary Myers, "Surf Records," *Goldmine*, no. 315 (August 21, 1992), 26, 100.

Tim Neely, "25 Collectible Surf Records," *Goldmine*, no. 495 (July 16, 1999), 32.

Greg Shaw, "The Birth of Surf," *Who Put the Bomp!* no. 14 (fall 1975), 8–10, 46.

Greg Shaw, "Surf Music," *Stereo Review* XXXI (October 1973), 79–83.

Doug Sheppard, "Surf Guitar Summit: Five Big Kahunas of Surf Guitar Recount the Evolution of an Artform," *Goldmine*, no. 446 (August 29, 1997), 16–22, 42–50, 203.

Doug Sheppard, "Surf Guitar Tsunamis: The Top 40 LPs in Print," *Goldmine*, no. 446 (August 29, 1997), 32–38.

Larry Stidom, "Surfing, Hot Rods, and Other Music Trivia," *Goldmine*, no. 120 (March 1, 1985), 78.

Surfin' Records Checklist, 1956–1977. Jacksonville, IL: Ladd, 1978.

Swing

Kenneth J. Bindas, *Swing, That Modern Sound*. Jackson: University Press of Mississippi, 2001.

Gene Ferrett, *Swing Out: Great Negro Dance Bands*. New York: Da Capo Press, 1993.

Alex Green, "Swing Renaissance," *DISCoveries*, no. 128 (January 1999), 32–37.

Steve Knopper (eds.) *MusicHound Swing! The Essential Album Guide*. Detroit, MI: Visible Ink Press, 1999.

Degen Pener, *The Swing Book*. Boston: Back Bay Books/Little, Brown, 1999.

V. Vale and Marian Wallace (eds.), *Swing! The New Retro Renaissance*. San Francisco: V/Search, 1998.

Scott Yanow, *Swing*. San Francisco: Miller Freeman Books, 2000.

Techno-Rock

Simon Reynolds, *Generation Ecstasy: Into the World of Techno and Rave Culture*. Boston: Little, Brown, 1998.

Dan Sicko, *Techno Rebels: The Renegades of Electronic Funk*. New York: Billboard Books, 1999.

Jeff Walker, "The Waxpaper Chronicles—Volume Ten: Techno-Rock," *Waxpaper* III (September 15, 1978), 1–6.

Trad-Rock

Michael Hooker, "The Waxpaper Chronicles—Volume Eight: Trad-Rock," *Waxpaper* III (May 5, 1978) 1–8.

Tex-Mex Music

George H. Lewis, "Ghosts, Ragged but Beautiful: Influences of Mexican Music on American Country-Western and Rock 'n' Roll," *Popular Music and Society* XV (winter 1991), 85–103.

George H. Lewis, "La Pistola y El Corazan: Protest and Passion in Mexican-American Popular Music," *Journal of Popular Culture* XXVI (summer 1992), 51–67.

John Storm Roberts, "Tex-Mex and Zydeco: The Role of the Accordion," *High Fidelity* XXVIII (July 1978), 128.

Guadalupe San Miguel, Jr., *Tejano Proud: Tex-Mex Music in the Twentieth Century*. College Station: Texas A & M University, 2002.

Twist Music

"And Now Everybody Is Doing It: The Twist," *Life* LI (November 24, 1961), 75–78.

Mitchell S. Cohen, "When the Twisters Ruled—20 January 1962," *Let It Rock*, no. 29 (May 1975), 18–20.

Jim Dawson, "And the Twist Goes Round and Round," *Goldmine*, no. 389 (June 23, 1995), 42–58, 154.

Jim Dawson, *The Twist: The Story of the Song and Dance That Changed the World*. London: Faber and Faber, 1990.

Zydeco Music

Pat Nyhan, Brian Rollins, and David Bobb, *Let the Good Times Roll: A Guide to Cajun and Zydeco Music*. Portland, ME: Upbeat Books, 1997.

General International/World Musics

Muff Anderson, *Music in the Mix: The Story of South African Popular Music.* Athens: Ohio University Press, 1986.

Gerard H. Behague (ed.), *Music and Black Ethnicity: The Caribbean and South America.* New Brunswick, NJ: Transaction, 1994.

Andy Bennett, *Cultures of Popular Music.* Buckingham, England: Open University Press, 2001.

Jessica Berens, "Scots on the Rocks," *Spin* II (April 1986), 29–32.

Marcus Breen (eds.), *Missing in Action: Australian Popular Music in Perspective.* Kensington, Australia: Verbal Graphics, 1987.

Alejo Carpenter (translated by Alan West–Duran), *Music in Cuba.* Minneapolis: University of Minnesota Press, 2001.

Don Charles, "Conga with Your Coffee! A History of Cuban Music in the United States," *DISCoveries*, no. 130 (March 1999), 44–54.

Tony Clayton-Lea and Richie Taylor, *Irish Rock: Where It's Come from, Where It's at, Where It's Going.* Dublin, Ireland: Gill and Macmillan, 1992.

Paul Desruisseaux, "History of Jazz in the Soviet Union Gives a Sense of the Rhythm of Russian Life," *Chronicle of Higher Education* XXVI (July 20, 1983), 17–18.

John Einarson, "Winnipeg's British Connection: Liverpool, North American Style," *Goldmine*, no. 233 (June 30, 1989), 18–24, 36.

Ray Evans, "Shakin' at the Stadium: The Advent of Rock 'n' Roll in Australia," *Now Dig This*, no. 16 (July 1984), 12–15.

Juan Flores, *From Bomba to Hip-Hop: Puerto Rican Culture to Latino Identity.* New York: Columbia University Press, 2000.

Miroslav Foet, "Music Preferences of Youth in the Czechoslovak Socialist Republic in the 1980s," *Popular Music and Society* XIII (fall 1989), 1–4.

Charley Gerard, *Music from Cuba: Mongo Santamaria, Chocolate Armenteros, and Cuban Musicians in the United States.* Westport, CT: Praeger, 2001.

Ruth Glasser, *My Music Is My Flag: Puerto Rican Musicians and Their New York Communities, 1917–1940.* Berkeley: University of California Press, 1995.

Peter Goddard and Philip Kamin (comps.), *Shakin' All Over: The Rock 'n' Roll Years in Canada.* Toronto, Ontario: McGraw Hill Ryerson, 1989.

Ronnie Graham, *The Da Capo Guide to Contemporary African Music*. New York: Da Capo Press, 1988.

Philip Hayward (ed.), *From Pop to Punk to Postmodernism: Popular Music and Australian Culture From the 1960s to the 1990s*. Sydney: Allen and Unwin, 1992.

Dick Hebdige, *Cut 'n' Mix: Culture, Identity, and Caribbean Music*. New York: Methuen Books, 1987.

Kaj Holm, "Continental Cowboys: Country Music in Sweden," *Goldmine*, no. 101 (June 8, 1984), 47–49.

Dan Juma, "Africa: Land of Many Musics," *Goldmine*, no. 90 (November 1983), 188, 190, 192, 195.

Helmut Kallmann and Gilles Potvin (eds.), *Encyclopedia of Music in Canada* (2d ed.). Toronto, Ontario: University of Toronto Press, 1992.

Ytzhak Katz, "Shooting and Crying: The Politics of Israeli Protest Music," *Popular Music and Society* XII (winter 1988), 1–6.

Claire Levy, "The Influence of British Rock in Bulgaria," *Popular Music* XI (May 1992), 209–12.

George H. Lewis, "The Somersaults of Monkeys: Diffusion of Culture and Meaning across the Pacific Rim," *Journal of Popular Culture* XXX (summer 1996), 263–76.

Lars Lilliestam, "Musical Acculturation: 'Hound Dog' from Blues to Swedish Rock and Roll," *OneTwoThreeFour*, no. 8 (winter 1990), 37–63.

Peter Manuel, *Popular Musics of the Non-Western World: An Introductory Survey*. New York: Oxford University Press, 1988.

Jeremy Marre and Hannah Charlton, *Beats of the Heart: Popular Music of the World*. New York: Pantheon Books, 1985.

Carlos Alberto Martins, "Popular Music as Alternative Communication: Uruguay, 1973–1982," *Popular Music* VII (January 1988), 77–94.

Gunter Mayer, "Popular Music in the GDR," *Journal of Popular Culture* XVIII (winter 1984), 145–158.

Adam McGovern (eds.) *MusicHound World: The Essential Album Guide*. Detroit, MI: Visible Ink Press, 2000.

Noel McGrath (comp.), *Noel McGrath's Australian Encyclopedia of Rock*. Collingwood, Australia: Outback Press, 1978.

Noel McLaughlin and Martin McLoone, 'Hybridity and National Musics: The Case of Irish Rock Music," *Popular Music* XIX (April 2000), 181–99.

Martin Melhuish, *Heart of Gold: 30 Years of Canadian Pop Music*. Toronto, Ontario: Canadian Broadcasting Corporation, 1983.

William J. O'Callaghan, *Great Balls of Fire, or How I Grew to Love Rock and Roll under the Shadow of the A-Bomb*. Edmonton, Alberta: Plains, 1987.

Nuala O'Connor, *Bringing It All Back Home: The Influence of Irish Music*. London: BBC, 1991.

Dionizy Piatkowski, "The Blues in Poland," *Goldmine*, no. 250 (February 23, 1990), 96.

Uta G. Poiger, *Jazz, Rock, and Rebels: Cold War Politics and American Culture in a Divided Germany*. Berkeley: University of California Press, 2000.

Irina Pond, "Soviet Rock Lyrics: Their Content and Poetics," *Popular Music and Society* XI (winter 1987), 75–91.

Mark J. Prendergast, *Irish Rock: Roots, Personalities, Directions*. Dublin, Ireland: O'Brien Press, 1987.

Pedro Ramet and Sergei Zamascikov, "The Soviet Rock Scene," *Journal of Popular Culture* XXIV (summer 1990), 149–74.

Robert Rauth, "Back in the U.S.S.R.—Rock and Roll in the Soviet Union," *Popular Music and Society*, VIII nos. 3 and 4 (1982), 3–12.

John Storm Roberts, *Black Music of Two Worlds*. New York: William Morrow, 1974.

John Storm Roberts, *The Latin Tinge: The Impact of Latin American Music on the United States*. New York: Oxford University Press, 1979.

Deanna Campbell Robinson, Elizabeth B. Buck, and Marlene Cuthbert, *Music at the Margins: Popular Music and Global Cultural Diversity*. Newbury Park, CA: Sage, 1991.

Bob Roth, "Canadian and U.S. Pop Music," *The Magazine for Christian Youth!* IV (November 1988), 16–21.

Mark Rowland, "Russian Jazz," *Musician*, no. 68 (June 1984), 36–42.

Timothy W. Ryback, "Raisa Gorbachev is an Elvis Fan, and Other Reasons Why Scholars Should Study the Role of Rock in Eastern Europe," *Chronicle of Higher Education* XXXVI (June 6, 1990), 23A, 24A.

Timothy W. Ryback, *Rock around the Bloc: A History of Rock Music in Eastern Europe and the Soviet Union, 1954–1988*. New York: Oxford University Press, 1990.

John M. Schechter (eds.), *Music in Latin American Culture: Regional Traditions*. New York: Schirmer Books, 1999.

Phil Silverman, "Irish Biographer Says U.S. Armed Forces Radio Sparked His Lifelong Obsession with Little Richard and Rock Music," *Record Collector's Monthly*, no. 34 (February/March 1986), 1, 10–12.

James K. Skipper, Jr., "Musical Tastes of Canadian and American College Students: An Examination of the Massification and Americanization Theses," *Canadian Journal of Sociology* I (June 1975), 49–59.

Chris Spencer, *Who's Who of Australian Rock and Roll* (2d ed., rev. and expanded). Fitzroy, Australia: Five Mile Press, 1989.

Chris Stapleton and Chris May, *African All-Stars: The Pop Music of a Continent*. London: Quartet Books, 1987.

S. Frederick Starr, *Red and Hot: The Fate of Jazz in the Soviet Union, 1917–1980*. New York: Oxford University Press, 1983.

Sue Steward, *Musica! The Rhythm of Latin America—Salsa, Rumba, Merengue, and More*. San Francisco: Chronicle Books, 1999.

Philip Sweeney, *The Virgin Directory of World Music*. New York: Owl Books/Henry Holt, 1991.

Jeff Tamarkin, "Atlantic Canadian 'Roots'," *Goldmine*, no. 225 (March 10, 1989), 7, 79.

Jeff Tamarkin, "Australian Rock in the '80s: At the Scene Vinyl Survey—Part One," *Goldmine*, no. 172 (February 27, 1987), 14, 20–22, 28–30.

Timothy D. Taylor, *Global Pop: World Music, World Markets*. New York: Routledge, 1997.

Jeff Titon (ed.), *Worlds of Music: An Introduction to the Music of the World's Peoples* (2d ed.). New York: Schirmer Books, 1992.

Artemy Troitsky, *Back in the U.S.S.R.: The True Story of Rock in Russia*. London: Faber and Faber, 1988.

Artemy Troitsky, *Tusovka: Who's Who in the New Soviet Rock Culture*. London: Omnibus Press, 1990.

Clinton Walker, *The Next Thing: Contemporary Australian Rock*. Kenthurst, Australia: Kangaroo Press, 1984.

Christopher Alan Waterman, *JuJu: A Social History and Ethnography of an African Popular Music*. Chicago: University of Chicago Press, 1990.

Jim Wilkie, *Blue Suede Brogans: Scenes from the Secret Life of Scottish Rock Music*. Edinburgh, Scotland: Mainstream, 1991.

Ritchie Yorke, *Axes, Chops, and Hot Licks: The Canadian Rock Music Scene*. Edmonton, Canada: M. G. Hurtig, 1971.

Lawrence Zion, "The Impact of the Beatles on Pop Music in Australia, 1963–1966," *Popular Music* VI (October 1987), 291–311.

Nabeel Zuberi, *Sounds English: Transnational Popular Music*. Urbana: University of Illinois Press, 2001.

General Dance Music

Almost Slim, "Popeye," *Wavelength*, no. 92 (June 1988), 26.

Almost Slim, "The Popeye: Strong to the Finish," *Goldmine*, no. 216 (November 4, 1988), 73, 80.

Clive Anderson, "Dance, Dance, Dance," *The History of Rock*, no. 25 (1982), 481–3.

D. Duane Braun, *Toward a Theory of Popular Culture: The Sociology and History of American Music and Dance, 1920–1968*. Ann Arbor, MI: Ann Arbor, 1969.

R. M. Clark, "The Dance Party as a Socialization Mechanism for Black Urban Pre-Adolescents and Adolescents," *Sociology and Social Research* LVIII (1974), 145–54.

B. Lee Cooper, "Dancing: The Perfect Educational Metaphor," *Institute for Educational Management/Management Development Program Newsletter* VI (spring-summer 1990), 5.

B. Lee Cooper, "Review of *Land of 1000 Dances: The Ultimate Compilation of Hit Dances, 1958–1965*," *Rock and Blues News*, no. 5 (August-September 1999), 41–42.

Jim Dawson, *The Twist: The Story of the Song and Dance That Changed the World*. London: Faber and Faber, 1995.

Lynne Fauley Emery, *Black Dance in the United States from 1619 to 1970*. Palo Alto, CA: National Press Books, 1972.

Katrina Hazzard-Gordon, *Jookin': The Rise of Social Dance Formation in African-American Culture*. Philadelphia: Temple University Press, 1990.

Irene V. Jackson (ed.), *More Than Dancing: Essays on Afro-American Music and Musicians*. Westport, CT: Greenwood, 1985.

John Javna, *How to Jitterbug*. New York: St. Martin's Press, 1984.

Tony Leisner, *The Official Guide to Country Dance Steps*. Chicago: Domus Books, 1980.

Steven Levy, "Shag Dancing and Top Popping," *Rolling Stone*, no. 379 (September 30, 1982), 50–57.

George Lipsitz, "Land of a Thousand Dances: Youth, Minorities, and the Rise of Rock and Roll," *Recasting America: Culture and Politics in the Age of Cold War*, edited by Lary May. Chicago: University of Chicago Press, 1989, 267–84.

Carol Martin, *Dance Marathons: Performing American Culture in the 1920s and 1930s*. Jackson: University Press of Mississippi, 1994.

Cathleen McGuigan, with Mark D. Vehling, Jennifer Smith, Sherry Keene-Osborn, Barbara Burgower, and Nadine Joseph, "Breaking Out: America Goes Dancing," *Newsweek* CIV (July 2, 1984), 46–52.

Brian Rust (comp.), *American Dance Band Discography, 1917–1942* (2 vols.). New Rochelle, NY: Arlington House, 1975.

Brian Rust and Sandy Forbes, *British Dance Bands on Record, 1911–1945*. Harrow, England: General Gramophone, 1987.

Brian Rust, *The Dance Bands*. London: Ian Allan, 1972.

Doug Shannon, *Off the Record: Everything Related to Playing Recorded Dance Music in the Nightclub Industry*. Cleveland, OH: Pacesetting, 1985.

Marshall and Jean Stearns, *Jazz Dance: The Story of American Vernacular Dance*. New York: Da Capo Press, 1994 (first published 1968).

Michael Sturma, "The Politics of Dancing: When Rock 'n' Roll Came to Australia," *Journal of Popular Culture* XXV (spring 1992), 123–142.

Oscar Wednesday, "Dance Fever—Lambada vs. Vogueing: And the Winner Is. . ." *Request* (August 1990), 34–35.

Linda F. Wharton and Jack L. Daniel, "Black Dance: Its African Origins and Continuity," *Minority Voices* I (fall 1977), 73–80.

"The World of Dance Music," *Billboard* XCVI (August 11, 1984), D.1–17.

Chapter 4

Popular Music Reference Resources for Teachers, Librarians, Media Specialists, and Students

Music Bibliographies

Anthony J. Agostinelli, *The Newport Jazz Festival, Rhode Island, 1954–1971: A Bibliography, Discography, and Filmography*. Providence, RI: A. J. Agostinelli, 1977.

Richard N. Albert (comp.), *An Annotated Bibliography of Jazz Fiction and Jazz Fiction Criticism*. Westport, CT: Greenwood, 1996.

Mark W. Booth (comp.), *American Popular Music: A Reference Guide*. Westport, CT: Greenwood, 1983.

Mark W. Booth, "Music," in *Handbook of American Popular Culture—Volume Two* (2d ed.), edited by M. Thomas Inge. Westport, CT: Greenwood, 1989, 771–90.

Monica Burdex, Simon Frith, Stephen A. Fry, David Horn, Barbara James, Toru Mitsui, and Robert Springer (comps.), "Booklist," in *Popular Music 4*, edited by Richard Middleton and David Horn. New York: Cambridge University Press, 1984, 377–406.

Gary Carner (ed.), *Jazz Performers: An Annotated Bibliography of Biographical Materials*. Westport, CT: Greenwood, 1990.

Gilbert Chase, "Selected Bibliography," in *America's Music: From The Pilgrims to the Present* (3d ed.). Urbana: University of Illinois Press, 1987, 647–88.

B. Lee Cooper, "Bibliography of Popular Music Teaching Resources," *Popular Music and Society* XXIII (winter 1999), 123–9.

B. Lee Cooper, Simon Frith, Bernhard Hefele, Frank Hoffmann, David Horn, Toru Mitsui, Robert Springer, and Erzsebet Szeverenyi (comps.), "Booklist," *Popular Music* VI (October 1986), 361–85.

B. Lee Cooper, Simon Frith, Bernhard Hefele, Frank Hoffmann, David Horn, Toru Mitsui, Robert Springer, and Erzsebet Szeverenyi (comps.), "Booklist," *Popular Music* VI (October 1987), 361–85.

B. Lee Cooper, Simon Frith, Bernhard Hefele, Frank Hoffmann, David Horn, Toru Mitsui, Paul Oliver, Stan Rijuen, and Robert Springer (comps.), "Booklist," *Popular Music* VII (October 1988), 357–71.

B. Lee Cooper, Frank Hoffmann, Bernhard Hefele, Robert Springer, David Horn, and Toru Mitsui (comps.), "Booklist," *Popular Music* VIII (October 1989), 335–47.

B. Lee Cooper, Simon Frith, Bernhard Hefele, Frank Hoffmann, David Horn, Toru Mitsui, and Robert Springer (comps.), "Booklist," *Popular Music* IX (October 1990), 389–405.

B. Lee Cooper, Simon Frith, Bernhard Hefele, Frank Hoffmann, Toru Mitsui, Lynne Sharma, and Robert Springer (comps.), "Booklist," *Popular Music* X (October 1991), 361–78.

B. Lee Cooper, Frank Hoffmann, Simon Frith, Bernhard Hefele, David Horn, Jaap Gerritse, Antoine Hennion, and Toru Mitsui (comps.), "Booklist," *Popular Music* XI (October 1992), 385–404.

B. Lee Cooper, David Buckley, Simon Frith, Jaap Gerritse, Bernhard Hefele, Frank W. Hoffmann, and Toru Mitsui (comps.), "Booklist," *Popular Music* XII (October 1993), 331–52.

B. Lee Cooper, Jaap Gerriste, Bernhard Hefele, Frank Hoffmann, Toru Mitsui, and Motti Regev, "Booklist," *Popular Music* XIII (October 1994), 375–99.

B. Lee Cooper, Simon Frith, Paul Hansen, Bernhard Hefele, David Horn, and Toru Mitsui, "Booklist," *Popular Music* XIV (October 1995), 391–413.

B. Lee Cooper, Simon Frith, Bernhard Hefele, Dave Lang, and Toru Mitsui (comps.), "Booklist," *Popular Music* XV (October 1996), 371–96.

B. Lee Cooper, Bernhard Hefele, Dave Laing, and Toru Mitsui (comps.), "Booklist," *Popular Music* XVI (October 1997), 327–51.

B. Lee Cooper, Bernhard Hefele, Dave Laing, Toru Mitsui, and Christophe Pirenne (comps.), "Booklist," *Popular Music* XVIII (October 1998), 359–83.

B. Lee Cooper, Bernhard Hefele, Dave Laing, Toru Mitsui, and Christophe Pirenne (comps.), "Booklist," *Popular Music* XIX (October 1999), 425–46.

B. Lee Cooper, Bernhard Hefele, Dave Laing, Toru Mitsui, and Christophe Pirenne (comps.), "Booklist," *Popular Music* XIX (October 2000), 403–34.

B. Lee Cooper, Bernhard Hefele, Dave Laing, Toru Mitsui, and Christophe Pirenne (comps.), "Booklist," *Popular Music* XX (October 2001), 453–477.

B. Lee Cooper, "Discographies of Contemporary Music, 1965–1980: A Selected Bibliography," *Popular Music and Society* VII (fall 1980), 253–69.

B. Lee Cooper, "Examining a Decade of Rock Bibliographies, 1970–1979," *JEMF Quarterly* XVII (summer 1981), 95–101.

B. Lee Cooper, "Images of Women in Popular Song Lyrics: A Bibliography," *Popular Music and Society* XXII (winter 1998), 79–89.

B. Lee Cooper, Frank W. Hoffmann, and William L. Schurk, "The Music Magazine Reader's 'Hot 100': Popular Music Periodicals, 1950–1982," *JEMF Quarterly* XIX (spring 1983), 32–48.

B. Lee Cooper (comp.), "Popular Culture Research and Library Services: A Selected Bibliography," *Popular Culture Association Newsletter* XIX (May 1992), 5–7.

B. Lee Cooper, "Popular Music Bibliographies: Literary Resource Guides to Contemporary Songs, Singers, Styles, and Sounds from 1950–1980," *International Journal of Instructional Media* IX (1981–1982), 173–84.

B. Lee Cooper, *The Popular Music Handbook: A Resource Guide for Teachers, Librarians, and Media Specialists.* Littleton, CO: Libraries Unlimited, 1984.

B. Lee Cooper, "Popular Music in Print," *Popular Music and Society* XIX (winter 1995), 105–12.

B. Lee Cooper, "Popular Music in the Classroom: A Bibliography of Teaching Techniques and Instructional Resources," *International Journal of Instructional Media* X, no. 1 (1982–1983), 71–87.

B. Lee Cooper, "A Resource Guide to Studies in the Theory and Practice of Popular Culture Librarianship," *The Acquisitions Librarian*, no. 8 (1992), 131–46.

B. Lee Cooper, *A Resource Guide to Themes in Contemporary American Song Lyrics, 1950–1985*. Westport, CT: Greenwood, 1986.

B. Lee Cooper, "Resources for Teaching Popular Music: A Checklist," *Popular Culture Methods* III (spring 1976), 37–38.

B. Lee Cooper, "A Review Essay and Bibliography of Studies on Rock 'n' Roll Movies, 1955–1963," *Popular Music and Society* XVI (spring 1992), 85–92.

B. Lee Cooper, "Review of *Literature of American Music III, 1983–1992* by Guy A. Marco and *Checklist of Writings on American Music, 1640–1992* by Guy A. Marco," *Popular Music and Society* XXIII (spring 1999), 120–121.

B. Lee Cooper, "Review of *The Rock and Roll Reader's Guide: A Comprehensive Guide to Books by and about Musicians and Their Music* by Gary M. Krebs," *Popular Music and Society* XXIV (summer 2000), 158–9.

B. Lee Cooper, "Rock and Roll Teaching Approaches: A Bibliography of Studies Illustrating the Use of Popular Music in Interdisciplinary Teaching Situations." Cleveland, OH: Rock and Roll Hall of Fame and Museum/Cuyahoga Community College, 1997.

B. Lee Cooper, "Rock Discographies: Exploring the Iceberg's Tip," *JEMF Quarterly* XV (summer 1979), 115–20.

B. Lee Cooper, "Rock Discographies Revisited," *JEMF Quarterly* XVI (summer 1980), 89–94.

B. Lee Cooper and Wayne S. Haney, *Rock Music in American Popular Culture: Rock 'n' Roll Resources*. New York: Haworth Press, 1995.

B. Lee Cooper and Wayne S. Haney, *Rock Music in American Popular Culture II: More Rock 'n' Roll Resources*. New York: Haworth Press, 1997.

B. Lee Cooper and Wayne S. Haney, *Rock Music in American Popular Culture III: More Rock 'n' Roll Resources*. New York: Haworth Press, 1999.

B. Lee Cooper and Wayne S. Haney, *Rockabilly: A Bibliographic Resource Guide*. Metuchen, NJ: Scarecrow Press, 1990.

B. Lee Cooper, "Teaching with Popular Music Resources: A Bibliography of Interdisciplinary Instructional Approaches," *Popular Music and Society* XXII (summer 1998), 85–115.

David E. Cooper (comp.), *International Bibliography of Discographies: Classical Music and Jazz and Blues, 1962–1972—A Reference Book for Record Collectors, Dealers, and Libraries*. Littleton, CO: Libraries Unlimited, 1975.

Robert H. Cowden, *Popular Singers of the Twentieth Century: A Bibliography of Biographical Materials*. Westport, CT: Greenwood, 1999.

Deborah Crisp (comp.), *Bibliography of Australian Music: An Index of Monographs, Journal Articles, and Theses*. Armidale, Australia: Australian Music Studies Project, 1982.

Dominique-René De Lerma (comp.), *Bibliography of Black Music—Volume One: Reference Materials*. Westport, CT: Greenwood, 1981.

Dominique-René De Lerma (comp.), *Bibliography of Black Music—Volume Two: Afro-American Idioms*. Westport, CT: Greenwood, 1981.

Dominique-René De Lerma (comp.), *Bibliography of Black Music—Volume Three: Geographical Studies*. Westport, CT: Greenwood, 1982.

Dominique-René De Lerma (comp.), *Bibliography of Black Music—Volume Four: Theory, Education, and Related Studies*. Westport, CT: Greenwood, 1984.

R. Serge Denisoff, *American Protest Songs of War and Peace: A Selected Bibliography and Discography*. Los Angeles: Center for the Study of Armament and Disarmament, California State College, 1970.

R. Serge Denisoff and John Bridges, "The Battered and Neglected Orphan: Popular Music Research and Books," *Popular Music and Society* VIII (1981), 43–59.

R. Serge Denisoff, *Sing a Song of Social Significance* (2d ed.). Bowling Green, OH: Bowling Green State University Popular Press, 1983.

Mary Laverne Dimmick (comp.), *The Rolling Stones: An Annotated Bibliography* (rev. and enlarged ed.). Pittsburgh, PA: University of Pittsburgh Press, 1979.

Peter Doggett, "Beatle Books: The Good, the Bad, and the Unreadable," *Beatles Monthly Book*, no. 131 (March 1987), 17–21.

Peter Doggett, "Beatle Books: The Good, the Bad, and the Unreadable," *The Beatles Monthly Book*, no. 132 (April 1987), 32–35.

Peter Doggett and Mark Paytress, "The Rolling Stones: Books and Memorabilia," *Record Collector*, no. 111 (November 1988), 3–7.

Dr. Demento, "Everything You Ever Wanted to Read about Rock: The Complete Big Beat Reference Shelf," *Waxpaper* III (April 7, 1978), 20–22, 40–41.

Vincent Duckles (comp.), *Music Reference and Research Materials: An Annotated Bibliography* (3d ed.). New York, Schirmer Books, 1974.

William Reynolds Ferris (comp.), *Mississippi Black Folklore: A Research Bibliography and Discography*. Hattiesburg: University and College Press of Mississippi, 1971.

Samuel A. Floyd, Jr., and Marsha J. Reisser (comps.), *Black Music in the United States: An Annotated Bibliography of Selected Reference and Research Materials*. Millwood, NY: Kraus International, 1983.

Simon Frith, Stephen M. Fry, and David Horn (comps.), "Booklist," in *Popular Music 2*, edited by Richard Middleton and David Horn. New York: Cambridge University Press, 1982, 324–41.

Simon Frith and David Horn, with the assistance of Stephen M. Fry, Barbara James, Toru Mitsui, and Robert Springer (comps.), "Booklist," in *Popular Music 3*, edited by Richard Middleton and David Horn (New York: Cambridge University Press, 1983), 337–63.

Jeffrey N. Gatten, *Rock Music Scholarship: An Interdisciplinary Bibliography*. Westport, CT: Greenwood, 1995.

Jeffrey N. Gatten (comp.), *The Rolling Stone Index: Twenty-Five Years of Popular Culture, 1967–1991*. Ann Arbor, MI: Popular Culture, Ink., 1993.

Chris Geist, "Selected References and Indexes of Rock Music," *Popular Culture Methods* III (spring 1976), 38–39.

David D. Ginsburg, "State of the Art Survey of Reference Sources in Pop, Rock, and Jazz," *Reference Services Review* VI (July/September 1978), 5–16.

Robert Gottlieb (ed.), *Reading Jazz: A Gathering of Autobiography, Reportage, and Criticism, from 1919 to Now*. New York: Pantheon Books, 1996.

Michael H. Gray (comp.), *Bibliography of Discographies—Volume 3: Popular Music*. New York: R. R. Bowker, 1983.

Peter Grendysa (comp.), *Catalog-Index of Articles: Rhythm and Blues, Rock 'n' Roll, Blues, Pop, and Country, 1970–1984*. Caledonia, WI: Words on Music, 1984.

Stephen R. Groce, "The Sociology of Popular Music: A Selected and Annotated Bibliography of Recent Work," *Popular Music and Society* XVI (spring 1992), 49–80.

Stephen B. Groce and Jonathan S. Epstein, "Recent Theory and Research in the Sociology of Popular Music: A Selected and Annotated Bibliography," in *Adolescents and Their Music: If It's Too Loud, You're Too Old*, edited by Jonathan S. Epstein. New York: Garland, 1994, 329–88.

Gary Haggerty, *A Guide to Popular Music Reference Books: An Annotated Bibliography*. Westport, CT: Greenwood, 1995.

Bill Haines, "Rock and the Counter Culture: A Checklist," *Popular Culture Methods* II, no. 3 (1975), 12–14.

Ed Hanel (comp.), *The Essential Guide to Rock Books*. London: Omnibus Books, 1983.

Bill Harry, *Paperback Writers: The History of the Beatles in Print*. New York: Avon Books, 1985 (first published 1984).

Mary L. Hart, Brenda M. Eagles, and Lisa N. Howarth (comps.), *The Blues: A Bibliographic Guide*. New York: Garland, 1989.

James R. Heintze, *American Music Studies: A Classified Bibliography of Master's Theses*. Detroit, MI: Information Coordinators, 1985.

Don L. Hixon and Don A. Hennessee, *Women in Music: An Encyclopedic Bibliography* (2d ed.). Metuchen, NJ: Scarecrow Press, 1993.

Frank W. Hoffmann, *American Popular Culture: A Guide to the Reference Literature*. Englewood, CO: Libraries Unlimited, 1995.

Frank Hoffmann (comp.), *The Literature of Rock, 1954–1978*. Metuchen, NJ: Scarecrow Press, 1981.

Frank Hoffmann and B. Lee Cooper (comps.), *The Literature of Rock II, 1979–1983* (2 vols.). Metuchen, NJ: Scarecrow Press, 1986.

Frank Hoffmann and B. Lee Cooper (comps.), *The Literature of Rock III, 1984–1990*. Metuchen, NJ: Scarecrow Press, 1995.

David Horn (comp.), *The Literature of American Music in Books and Folk Music Collections: A Fully Annotated Bibliography*. Metuchen, NJ: Scarecrow Press, 1977.

David Horn, with Richard Jackson (comps.), *The Literature of American Music in Books and Folk Music Collections: A Fully Annotated Bibliography—Supplement One*. Metuchen, NJ: Scarecrow Press, 1988.

David Horn, Monica Burdex, Simon Frith, Stephen A. Fry, Bernhard Hefele, Toru Mitsui, Stan Rijuen, and Robert Springer (comps.), "Booklist," in *Popular Music 5: Continuity and Change*, edited by Richard Middleton and David Horn. New York: Cambridge University Press, 1985, 357–91.

M. Thomas Inge (ed.), *Concise Histories of American Popular Culture*. Westport, CT: Greenwood, 1982.

M. Thomas Inge (ed.), *Handbook of American Popular Culture—Three Volumes* (2d ed., rev. and enlarged). Westport, CT: Greenwood, 1989.

Roman Iwaschkin, *Popular Music: A Reference Guide*. New York: Garland, 1986.

Irene V. Jackson (comp.), *Afro-American Religious Music: A Bibliography and a Catalogue of Gospel Music*. Westport, CT: Greenwood, 1979.

Robert M. Jones (ed.), "Popular Music: A Survey of Books and Folios with an Index to Recently Reviewed Recordings," *Notes* XXXIV (September 1977), 216–21.

Hugo A. Keesing, "Annotated Bibliography of Pop/Rock Music," *Popular Culture Methods* III (spring 1976), 4–22.

Hugo A. Keesing (comp.), *Incomplete Bibliography of Pop/Rock Music*. Columbia, MD: H. A. Keesing, 1985.

Hugo A. Keesing, "Pop/Rock Writings: Trends and Uses," *Popular Culture Association Newsletter* X (July 1981), 20–22.

Donald Keenington and Danny L. Read, *The Literature of Jazz: A Critical Guide* (2d ed.). Chicago: American Library Association, 1980.

Gary M. Krebs, *The Rock and Roll Reader's Guide: A Comprehensive Guide to Books by and about Musicians and Their Music*. New York: Billboard Books, 1997.

Donald W. Krummel, *Bibliographical Handbook of American Music*. Urbana: University of Illinois Press, 1987.

D. W. Krummel, Jean Geil, Doris J. Dyen, and Deane L. Root, *Resources of American Music History: A Directory of Source Materials from Colonial Times to World War II*. Urbana: University of Illinois Press, 1981.

Josephine Langham and Janine Chrichley (comps.), *Radio Research: An Annotated Bibliography, 1975–1988* (2d ed.). Aldershot, England: Gower, 1989.

Ray M. Lawless, *Folk Singers and Folk Songs in America: A Handbook of Biography, Bibliography, and Discography*. New York: Duell, Sloan and Pearce, 1960.

George Lewis, Norm Cohen, Arnold Shaw et al. (comps.), "Black Music Bibliography," *Billboard* XCI (June 9, 1979), BM 32, 40–41.

George H. Lewis, "The Sociology of Popular Music: A Selected and Annotated Bibliography," *Popular Music and Society* VII (1979), 57–68.

Brady J. Leyser, with additional research by Pol Gosset (comps.), *Rock Stars/Pop Stars: A Comprehensive Bibliography, 1955–1994*. Westport, CT: Greenwood, 1994.

Beth MacLeod and David Ginsburg, "State of the Art Survey of Reference Sources in Music," *Reference Services Review* V (January/March 1977), 21–29.

Jessica MacPhail, *Yesterday's Papers: The Rolling Stones in Print, 1963–1984.* Ann Arbor, MI: Popular Culture, Ink., 1986.

Portia K. Maultsby, "Selective Bibliography: U.S. Black Music," *Ethnomusicology* XXIX (September 1975), 421–449.

Guy A. Marco, *Checklist of Writings on American Music, 1640–1992.* Lanham, MD: Scarecrow Press, 1996.

Guy A. Marco, *Literature of American Music III, 1983–1992.* Lanham, MD: Scarecrow Press, 1996.

Judy McCoy, *Rap Music in the 1980s: A Reference Guide.* Metuchen, NJ: Scarecrow Press, 1992.

Eddie S. Meadows (comp.), *Jazz Reference and Research Materials: A Bibliography.* New York: Garland, 1981.

Eddie S. Meadows, *Theses and Dissertations on Black American Music.* Beverly Hills, CA: Theodore Front, 1982.

Alan P. Merriam, with the assistance of Robert J. Benford, *A Bibliography of Jazz.* Philadelphia: American Folklore Society, 1954.

Jas Obrecht, "Guitar Books and Their Authors: From Research to Publication," *Guitar Player* XIII (October 1979), 79–98.

Steven Opdyke, *The Printed Elvis: The Complete Guide to Books about the King.* Westport, CT: Greenwood, 1999.

Robert G. Reisner (comp.), *The Literature of Jazz: A Preliminary Bibliography.* New York: New York Public Library, 1954.

Gilbert B. Rodman (comp.), "Everyday I Write the Book: A Bibliography of (Mostly) Academic Work on Rock and Pop Music," *Tracking: Popular Music Studies* II (spring 1990), 17–50.

Gilbert B. Rodman (comp.), "Everyday I Write the Book: A Bibliography of (Mostly) Academic Work on Rock and Pop Music," *Tracking: Popular Music Studies* III (winter 1990), 18–39.

Gilbert B. Rodman (comp.), *Everyday I Write the Book: A Bibliography of (Mostly) Academic Work on Rock and Pop Music.* Champaign, IL: G. B. Rodman/Institute of Communications Research, 1992.

Neil V. Rosenberg, "Rock Books: An Incomplete Survey (Part 1)," *JEMF Quarterly* VIII (spring 1972), 48–56.

Neil V. Rosenberg, "Rock Books: An Incomplete Survey (Part II), *JEMF Quarterly* VIII (summer 1972), 109–16.

Timothy E. Scheurer (comp.), "The Best Books on Popular Music Since 1971: A Bibliography," *Popular Music and Society* XXI (spring 1997), 117–21.

John Shepherd, David Horn, Dave Laing, et al. (eds.), *Popular Music Studies: A Select International Bibliography*. London: Mansell Books, 1997.

JoAnn Skowronski (comp.), *Black Music in America: A Bibliography*. Metuchen, NJ: Scarecrow Press, 1981.

Paul Taylor (comp.), *Popular Music Since 1955: A Critical Guide to the Literature*. New York: Mansell, 1985.

Carol D. Terry, *Here, There, and Everywhere: The First International Beatles Bibliography, 1962–1982*. Ann Arbor, MI: Popular Culture, Ink., 1985.

Carol D. Terry, *Sequins and Shades: The Michael Jackson Reference Guide*. Ann Arbor, MI: Pierian Press, 1987.

Kimberly R. Vann, *Black Music in Ebony: An Annotated Guide to the Articles on Music in Ebony Magazine, 1945–1985* (CBRM Monographs no. 2). Chicago: Center for Black Music Research, 1990.

Laura Vazquez and William L. Schurk (comps.), "Bibliography of Books, Book Chapters, and Articles by R. Serge Denisoff," *Popular Music and Society* XXI (spring 1997), 141–46.

James Von Schilling, "Records and The Recording Industry," in *Handbook of American Popular Culture—Volume Three* (2d ed.), edited by M. Thomas Inge (Westport, CT: Greenwood, 1989), 1155–83.

Donald E. Walker and B. Lee Cooper, *Baseball and American Culture: A Thematic Bibliography of over 4,500 Works*. Jefferson, NC: McFarland, 1995.

Mark Wallgren, "The Beatles: The Year in Print," *Goldmine*, no. 347 (November 12, 1993), 82–84.

Chas 'Dr. Rock' White and B. Lee Cooper (comps.), "Bibliography," in *Killer!* by Jerry Lee Lewis and Charles White (London: Century Books, 1993), 267–71.

Peter Winkler, "Pop Music's Middle Years," *Music Educators Journal* LXVI (December 1979), 26–33, 90–93.

Stephen Wolter and Karen Kimber, *The Who in Print: An Annotated Bibliography, 1965 through 1990*. Jefferson, NC: McFarland, 1992.

Carolyn E. Wood (comp.), *The Literature of Rock 'n' Roll: A Special Collection*. Cambridge, MA: Charles B. Wood III Antiquarian Booksellers, 1991.

Ronald Zalkind (comp.), *Contemporary Music Almanac 1980/1981*. New York: Schirmer Books, 1980.

Music Books

Michael Bane, *White Boy Singin' The Blues: The Black Roots of White Rock.* New York: Da Capo Press, 1992 (first published 1982).

Martha Bayles, *Hole in Our Soul: The Loss of Beauty and Meaning in American Popular Music.* New York: Free Press 1994.

Carl Belz, *The Story of Rock* (2d ed.). New York: Harper and Row, 1972.

Andy Bennett, *Popular Music and Youth Culture: Music, Identity, and Place.* New York: St. Martin's Press, 2000.

William Benzon, *Beethoven's Anvil: Music in Mind and Culture.* New York: Basic Books, 2001.

Michael T. Bertrand, *Race, Rock and Elvis.* Urbana: University of Illinois Press, 2000.

Alan Betrock, *Girl Groups: The Story of a Sound.* New York: Delilah Books, 1982.

Lars Bjorn, with Jim Gallert, *Before Motown: A History of Jazz in Detroit, 1920–1960.* Ann Arbor: University of Michigan Press, 2001.

Mark W. Booth, *The Experience of Songs.* New Haven, CT: Yale University Press, 1981.

Stanley Booth, *Rythm Oil: A Journey through the Music of the American South.* New York: Da Capo Press, 2000 (first published 1991).

B. A. Botkin, *The American People: Stories, Legends, Tales, Traditions, and Songs.* New Brunswick, NJ: Transaction, 1998.

David Brackett, *Interpreting Popular Music.* Berkeley: University of California Press, 2000.

Bill Brewster and Frank Broughton, *Last Night a DJ Saved My Life: The History of the Disc Jockey.* New York: Grove Press, 2000 (first published 1999).

Cecil Brown, *Stagolee Shot Billy.* Cambridge: Harvard University Press, 2003.

John Butt, *Playing with History: The Historical Approach to Musical Performance.* New York: Cambridge University Press, 2002.

Steve Chapple and Reebee Garofalo, *Rock 'n' Roll Is Here to Pay: The History and Politics of the Music Industry.* Chicago: Nelson-Hall, 1977.

Gilbert Chase, *America's Music: From the Pilgrims to the Present* (rev. 3d ed.). Urbana: University of Illinois Press, 1992.

Peter G. Christenson and Donald F. Roberts, *It's Not Only Rock and Roll: Popular Music in the Lives of Adolescents*. Hampton, England: Hampton Press, 1997.

Ian Christe, *Sound of The Beast: The Complete Headbanging History of Heavy Metal*. New York: Harper Entertainment, 2003.

Robert Christgau, *Grown Up All Wrong: 75 Great Rock and Pop Artists from Vaudeville to Techno*. Cambridge: Harvard University Press, 1998.

Donald Clarke, *The Rise and Fall of Popular Music: A Narrative History from the Renaissance to Rock 'n' Roll*. New York: St. Martin's Press, 1995.

John Clemente, *Girl Groups: Fabulous Females That Rocked the World*. Iola, WI: Krause, 2000.

Nik Cohn, *A Wop Bop Loo Bop A Lop Bam Boom: The Golden Age of Rock*. New York: Da Capo Press, 1996.

Ace Collins, *Stories behind the Best-Loved Songs of Christmas*. Grand Rapids, MI: Zondervan Press, 2001.

Stuart Colman, *They Kept on Rockin': The Giants of Rock 'n' Roll*. Poole, England: Blandford Press, 1982.

B. Lee Cooper (ed.), *American Culture Interpreted through Popular Music: Interdisciplinary Teaching Approaches*. Bowling Green, OH: Popular Music and Society/Bowling Green State University Popular Press, 2000.

B. Lee Cooper, *Images of American Society in Popular Music: A Guide to Reflective Teaching*. Chicago: Nelson-Hall, 1982.

B. Lee Cooper, "The Objectives of Teaching Survey History Courses in American High Schools and Colleges: A Content Analysis of Articles from Selected Periodicals, 1939–1969." Unpublished doctoral dissertation, Ohio State University, Columbus, 1971.

B. Lee Cooper, *The Popular Music Handbook: A Resource Guide for Teachers, Librarians, and Media Specialists*. Littleton, CO: Libraries Unlimited, 1984.

B. Lee Cooper, *Popular Music Perspectives: Ideas, Themes, and Patterns in Contemporary Lyrics*. Bowling Green, OH: Bowling Green State University Popular Press, 1991.

B. Lee Cooper, *A Resource Guide to Themes in Contemporary American Song Lyrics, 1950–1985*. Westport, CT: Greenwood, 1986.

B. Lee Cooper and Wayne S. Haney, *Response Recordings: An Answer Song Discography, 1950–1990*. Metuchen, NJ: Scarecrow Press, 1990.

B. Lee Cooper and Wayne S. Haney, *Rock Music in American Popular Culture: Rock 'n' Roll Resources*. New York: Harrington Park Press, 1995.

B. Lee Cooper and Wayne S. Haney, *Rock Music in American Popular Culture II: More Rock 'n' Roll Resources*. New York: Haworth Press, 1997.

B. Lee Cooper and Wayne S. Haney, *Rock Music in American Popular Culture III: More Rock 'n' Roll Resources*. New York: Haworth Press, 1999.

B. Lee Cooper and Wayne S. Haney, *Rockabilly: A Bibliographic Resource Guide*. Metuchen, NJ: Scarecrow Press, 1990.

Lee Cotten, *Shake, Rattle, and Roll—The Golden Age of American Rock 'n' Roll: Volume One, 1952–1955*. Ann Arbor, MI: Pierian Press, 1989.

Lee Cotten, *Reelin' and Rockin': The Golden Age of American Rock 'n' Roll—Volume Two: 1956–1959*. Ann Arbor, MI: Popular Culture, Ink., 1995.

Lee Cotten, *Twist and Shout: The Golden Age of American Rock 'n' Roll—Volume Three, 1960–1963*. Sacramento, CA: High Sierra Books, 2002.

David Crosby and David Bender, *Stand and Be Counted: Making Music, Making History—The Dramatic Story of the Artists and Events That Changed America*. New York: HarperCollins, 2000.

Jim Curtis, *Rock Eras: Interpretations of Music and Society, 1954–1984*. Bowling Green, OH: Bowling Green State University Popular Press, 1987.

Adam Cussow, *Seems Like Murder Here: Southern Violence and the Blues Tradition*. Chicago: University of Chicago Press, 2002.

Bill Dahl, *Motown: The Golden Years*. Iola, WI: Krause, 2001.

James Dawes, *The Language of War: Literature and Culture in the U.S. from The Civil War through World War II*. Cambridge: Harvard University Press, 2002.

Anthony DeCurtis and James Henke, with Holly George-Warren (eds.), *The Rolling Stone Illustrated History of Rock and Roll* (2d ed.). New York: Random House/Rolling Stone Press, 1992.

Bill DeMain, *Behind the Muse: Pop and Rock's Greatest Songwriters Talk about Their Work and Inspiration*. Cranberry Township, PA: Tiny Ripple Books, 2001.

R. Serge Denisoff, *Inside MTV*. New Brunswick, NJ: Transaction, 1991.

R. Serge Denisoff, *Sing a Song of Social Significance* (2d ed.). Bowling Green, OH: Bowling Green State University Popular Press, 1983.

R. Serge Denisoff, *Solid Gold: The Popular Record Industry*. New Brunswick, NJ: Transaction, 1975.

R. Serge Denisoff and William D. Romanowski, *Risky Business: Rock in Film*. New Brunswick, NJ: Transaction, 1991.

R. Serge Denisoff, with the assistance of William L. Schurk, *Tarnished Gold: The Record Industry Revisited*. New Brunswick, NJ: Transaction, 1986.

Robin Denselow, *When the Music's Over: The Story of Political Pop*. London: Faber and Faber, 1990.

Dave DiMartino, *Singer-Songwriters: Pop Music's Performer-Composers, from A to Zevon*. New York: Billboard Books, 1994.

Spencer Drate (ed.), *45 RPM: A Visual History of the Seven-Inch Record*. New York: Princeton Architectural Press, 2002.

Janell R. Duxbury, *Rockin' the Classics and Classicizin' the Rock: A Selectively Annotated Discography*. Westport, CT: Greenwood, 1985.

Janell R. Duxbury (comp.), *Rockin' the Classics and Classicizin' the Rock: A Selectively Annotated Discography—First Supplement*. Westport, CT: Greenwood, 1991.

Editors of *Goldmine* Magazine (comps.), *Goldmine Classic Rock Digest: 25 Years of Rock 'n' Roll*. Iola, WI: Krause, 1998.

Editors of *Goldmine* Magazine, *Goldmine Roots of Rock Digest*. Iola, WI: Krause, 1999.

John Einarson, *Desperados: The Roots of Country Rock*. New York: Cooper Square Press, 2001.

Mary Ellison, *Lyrical Protest: Black Music's Struggle against Discrimination*. New York: Praeger Books, 1989.

Howard Elson, *Early Rockers*. New York: Proteus Books, 1982.

Philip H. Ennis, *The Seventh Stream: The Emergency of Rock }n' Roll in American Popular Music*. Hanover, NH: Wesleyan University Press, 1992.

Colin Escott (ed.), *All Roots Lead to Rock: Legends of Early Rock 'n' Roll*. New York: Schirmer Books, 1999.

Colin Escott, *Roadkill on the Three-Chord Highway: Art and Trash in American Popular Music*. New York: Routledge, 2002.

Colin Escott, *Tattooed on Their Tongues: A Journey through the Backrooms of American Music*. New York: Schirmer Books, 1996.

Ron Eyerman and Andrew Jamison, *Music and Social Movements: Mobilizing Traditions in the Twentieth Century*. New York: Cambridge University Press, 1998.

Benjamin Filene, *Romancing the Folk: Public Memory and American Roots Music*. Chapel Hill: University of North Carolina Press, 2000.

Jon W. Finson, *Voices That Are Gone: Themes in 19th-Century American Popular Song*. New York: Oxford University Press, 1994.

Bill Flanagan, *Written in My Soul: Conversations with Rock's Great Songwriters*. Chicago: Contemporary Books, 1987.

Murray Forman, *The 'Hood Comes First: Race, Space, and Place in Rap and Hip-Hop*. Middletown, CT: Wesleyan University Press, 2002.

Johan Fornas, Ulf Lindberg, and Ove Servhede (translated by Jan Teelano), *In Garageland: Rock, Youth, and Modernity*. New York: Routledge, 1995.

Pete Fornatale and Bill Ayres, *All You Need Is Love . . . and 99 Other Life Lessons from Classic Rock Songs*. New York: Fireside Books, 1998.

Peter T. Fornatale and Frank R. Scatoni, *Who Can It Be Now? The Lyrics Game That Takes You Back to the '80s . . . One Line at a Time*. New York: Fireside Books/Simon & Schuster, 1998.

Allen Forte, *The American Popular Ballad of the Golden Era, 1924–1950*. Princeton: Princeton University Press, 1995.

Ted Fox, *In the Groove: The Men behind the Music*. New York: St. Martin's Press, 1986.

Jim Fricke and Charlie Ahearn, *Yes Yes Y'All: The Experience Music Project Oral History of Hip-Hop's First Decade*. Oxford, England: Perseus Press, 2002.

Paul Friedlander, *Rock and Roll: A Social History*. Boulder, CO: Westview Press, 1996.

Simon Frith, *Music for Pleasure: Essays in the Sociology of Pop*. New York: Routledge, Chapman, and Hall, 1988.

Simon Frith, *Performing Rites: On the Value of Popular Music*. Cambridge: Harvard University Press, 1996.

Simon Frith, *The Sociology of Rock*. London: Constable, 1978.

Simon Frith, *Sound Effects: Youth, Leisure, and the Politics of Rock 'n' Roll*. New York: Pantheon Books, 1981.

Simon Frith and Howard Horne, *Art into Pop*. New York: Methuen Books, 1987.

Philip Furia, *Poets of Tin Pan Alley: A History of America's Great Lyricists*. New York: Oxford University Press, 1990.

Gillian G. Gaar, *She's a Rebel: The History of Women in Rock and Roll*. Seattle, WA: Seal Press, 1992.

Paul Gambaccini, *Masters of Rock*. London: Omnibus Press, 1982.

Paul Gambaccini, *Track Records: Profiles of 22 Rock Stars*. North Pomfret, VT: David and Charles, 1986 (first published 1985).

Peter Gammond, *The Oxford Companion to Popular Music*. New York: Oxford University Press, 1993.

Bryan K. Garman, *A Race of Singers: Whitman's Working-Class Hero from Guthrie to Springsteen*. Chapel Hill: University of North Carolina Press, 2000.

Reebee Garofalo, *Rockin' Out: Popular Music in the USA*. Boston: Allyn and Bacon, 1997.

Holly George-Warren and Patricia Romanowski (eds.), *The Rolling Stone Encyclopedia of Rock and Roll: Revised and Updated for the 21st Century* (3d ed.). New York: Fireside/Rolling Stone Press Book, 2001.

Holly George-Warren and Editors of *Rolling Stone* (comps.), *Rolling Stone: The Decades of Rock and Roll*. San Francisco: Chronicle Books, 2001.

Charlie Gillett, *The Sound of the City: The Rise of Rock and Roll* (2d ed.). New York: Da Capo Press, 1996.

H. L. Goodall, Jr., *Living in the Rock 'n' Roll Mystery: Reading Context, Self, and Others as Clues*. Carbondale: Southern Illinois University Press, 1991.

Theodore Gracyk, *I Wanna Be Me: Rock Music and the Politics of Identity*. Philadelphia: Temple University Press, 2001.

Theodore Gracyk, *Rhythm and Noise: An Aesthetics of Rock*. Durham, NC: Duke University Press, 1996.

Michael Gray and Roger Osborne, *The Elvis Atlas: A Journey through Elvis Presley's America*. New York: Henry Holt, 1996.

Jeff Green, *The Green Book of Songs by Subject: The Thematic Guide to Popular Music* (4th ed.). Nashville, TN: Professional Desk References, 1995.

Lucy Green, *How Popular Musicians Learn: A Way ahead for Music Education*. Burlington, VT: Ashgate, 2002.

Hugh Gregory, *A Century of Pop: From Vaudeville to Rock, Big Bands to Techno—A Hundred Years of Music That Changed the World*. Chicago: A Cappella Books/Chicago Review Press, 1998.

Charlotte Greig, *Will You Still Love Me Tomorrow? Girl Groups from the '50s On.* London: Virago Press, 1989.

Lawrence Grossberg, *Dancing in Spite of Myself: Essays on Popular Culture.* Durham, NC: Duke University Press, 1997.

Peter Gurlanick, *Feel Like Going Home: Portraits in Blues and Rock 'n' Roll.* Boston: Back Bay Books/Little, Brown, 1999.

Peter Guralnick, *Lost Highway: Journeys and Arrivals of American Musicians.* Boston: Back Bay Books/Little, Brown, 1999.

Peter Guralnick, *Sweet Soul Music: Rhythm and Blues and the Southern Dream of Freedom.* Boston: Back Bay Books/Little, Brown, 1999.

Neil Haislop, Tad Lathrop, and Harry Sumrall, *Giants of Country Music: Classic Sounds and Stars, from the Heart of Nashville to the Top of the Charts.* New York: Billboard Books, 1995.

Charles E. Hamm, Bruno Nettl, and Ronald Byrnside, *Contemporary Music and Music Cultures.* Englewood Cliffs, NJ: Prentice Hall, 1975.

Charles Hamm, *Music in the New World.* New York: W. W. Norton and Company, 1983.

Charles Hamm, *Putting Popular Music in Its Place.* Cambridge: Cambridge University Press, 1995.

Jeff Hannusch, *I Hear You Knockin': The Sound of New Orleans Rhythm and Blues.* Ville Platte, LA: Swallow Press, 1985.

Jeff Hannusch, *The Soul of New Orleans: A Legacy of Rhythm and Blues.* Ville Platte, LA: Swallow Press, 2001.

Phil Hardy and Dave Laing, *The Faber Companion to 20th-Century Popular Music.* London: Faber and Faber, 1990.

Dave Harker, *One for the Money: Politics and the Popular Song.* London: Hutchinson, 1980.

James F. Harris, *Philosophy at 33 1/3 R.P.M.: Themes of Classic Rock Music.* La Salle, IL: Open Court Press, 1993.

David Hatch and Stephen Millward, *From Blues to Rock: An Analytical History of Pop Music.* Manchester, England: Manchester University Press, 1989.

Amy Henderson, *Red, Hot and Blue: A Smithsonian Salute to the American Musical.* Washington, D.C.: Smithsonian Institution Press, 1996.

Herb Hendler, *Year by Year in the Rock Era: Events and Conditions Shaping the Rock Generations That Reshaped America.* Westport, CT: Greenwood, 1983.

Don J. Hibbard and Carol Kaleialoha, *The Role of Rock: A Guide to the Social and Political Consequences of Rock Music*. Englewood, NJ: Prentice Hall, 1983.

Gerri Hirshey, *Nowhere to Run: The Story of Soul Music*. New York: Penguin Books, 1984.

Frank W. Hoffmann, *American Popular Culture: A Guide to the Reference Literature*. Englewood, CO: Libraries Unlimited, 1995.

Frank W. Hoffmann, *The Literature of Rock, 1954–1978*. Metuchen, NJ: Scarecrow Press, 1981.

Frank W. Hoffmann (comp.), *Popular Culture and Libraries*. Hamden, CT: Library Professional/Shoe String Press, 1984.

Frank W. Hoffmann and William G. Bailey, *Arts and Entertainment Fads*. Binghamton, NY: Haworth Press, 1990.

Frank Hoffmann and B. Lee Cooper, *The Literature of Rock II, 1979–1983—With Additional Material for the Period 1954–1978* (2 vols.). Metuchen, NJ: Scarecrow Press, 1986.

Frank Hoffmann and B. Lee Cooper, *The Literature of Rock III, 1984–1990—With Additional Material for the Period 1954–1983*. Metuchen, NJ: Scarecrow Press, 1995.

John A. Jackson, *American Bandstand: Dick Clark and the Making of a Rock 'n' Roll Empire*. New York: Oxford University Press, 1997.

John A. Jackson, *Big Beat Heat: Alan Freed and the Early Years of Rock and Roll*. New York: Schirmer Books, 1991.

David A. Jasen, *Tin Pan Alley—The Composers, the Songs, the Performers, and Their Times: The Golden Age of American Popular Music from 1886 to 1956*. New York: Donald I. Fine, 1988.

Robert Jourdain, *Music, the Brain, and Ecstasy: How Music Captures Our Imagination*. New York: Quill/HarperCollins, 2002 (first published 1997).

Bruce F. Kawin, *Telling It Again and Again: Repetition in Literature and Film*. Ithaca, NY: Cornell University Press, 1972.

Charles Keil and Steven Feld, *Music Grooves*. Chicago: University of Chicago Press, 1994.

Rick Kennedy and Randy McNutt, *Little Labels—Big Sound*. Bloomington: Indiana University Press, 1999.

Kit Kiefer (ed.), *They Called It Rock: The Goldmine Oral History of Rock 'n' Roll, 1950–1970*. Iola, WI: Krause, 1991.

Michael Kilgarriff, *"Sing Us One of the Old Songs": A Guide to Popular Song, 1860–1920*. New York: Oxford University Press, 1999.

Stephen A. King, *Reggae, Rastafari, and the Rhetoric of Social Control*. Jackson: University Press of Mississippi, 2002.

Daniel Kingman, *American Music: A Panorama* (2d ed.). New York: Schirmer Books, 1990.

Paul Kingsbury and the Staff of the Country Music Hall of Fame and Museum, *Vinyl Hayride: Country Music Album Covers, 1947–1989*. San Francisco: Chronicle Books, 2003.

David Konow, *Bang Your Head: The Rise and Fall of Heavy Metal*. New York: Three Rivers Press, 2002.

M. William Krasilovsky and Sidney Shemel, *This Business of Music: The Definitive Guide to the Music Industry* (8th ed.). New York: Billboard Books, 2000.

Barry Lazell, with Dafydd Rees and Luke Crampton (eds.), *Rock Movers and Shakers: An A to Z of the People Who Made Rock Happen*. New York: Billboard Books, 1989.

Lawrence W. Levine, *Black Culture and Black Consciousness: Afro-American Folk Thought from Slavery to Freedom*. New York: Oxford University Press, 1977.

Lawrence W. Levine, *Highbrow/Lowbrow: The Emergence of Cultural Hierarchy in America*. Cambridge: Harvard University Press, 1988.

Grace Lichtenstein and Laura Dankner, *Musical Gumbo: The Music of New Orleans*. New York: W. W. Norton, 1993.

George Lipsitz, *American Studies in a Moment of Danger*. Minneapolis: University of Minnesota Press, 2001.

George Lipsitz, *Dangerous Crossroads: Popular Music, Postmodernism, and the Poetics of Place*. New York: Verso Books, 1994.

George Lipsitz, *Rainbow at Midnight: Labor and Culture in the 1940s*. Urbana: University of Illinois Press, 1994.

George Lipsitz, *Time Passages: Collective Memory and American Popular Culture*. Minneapolis: University of Minnesota Press, 1990.

Herbert I. London, *Closing the Circle: A Cultural History of the Rock Revolution*. Chicago: Nelson-Hall, 1984.

Brian Longhurst, *Popular Music and Society*. Cambridge, England: Polity Press, 1995.

Michael Lydon, *Rock Folk: Portraits from the Rock 'n' Roll Pantheon*. New York: Dial Press, 1971.

Michael Lydon and Ellen Mandel, *Boogie Lightning: How Music Became Electric*. New York: Da Capo Press, 1980.

Bob Macken, Peter Fornatale, and Bill Ayres, *The Rock Music Source Book*. Garden City, NY: Doubleday, 1980.

Bill C. Malone, *Southern Music—American Music*. Lexington: University Press of Kentucky, 1979.

Greil Marcus, *Mystery Train: Images of America in Rock 'n' Roll Music* (3rd rev. ed.). New York: Plume (Penguin) Books, 1990.

Greil Marcus, *The Old, Weird America: The World of Bob Dylan's Basement Tapes*. New York: Picador/Henry Holt , 1997.

Dave Marsh, with Lee Ballinger, Sandra Choron, Wendy Smith, and Daniel Wolff, *the First Rock and Roll Confidential Report: Inside the Real World of Rock and Roll*. New York: Pantheon Books, 1985.

Dave Marsh, *Fortunate Son*. New York: Random House, 1985.

Dave Marsh, *The Heart of Rock and Soul: The 1001 Greatest Singles Ever Made*. New York: New American Library, 1989.

Linda Martin and Kerry Segrave, *Anti-Rock: The Opposition to Rock 'n' Roll*. New York: Da Capo Press, 1993.

Perry Meisel, *The Cowboy and the Dandy: Crossing over from Romanticism to Rock and Roll*. New York: Oxford University Press, 1999.

Bob Merlis and Davin Seby, *Heart and Soul: A Celebration of Black Music Style in America, 1930–1975*. New York: Billboard Books, 2002.

Richard Middleton, *Studying Popular Music*. Milton Keynes, England: Open University Press, 1989.

James Miller, *Flowers in the Dustbin: The Rise of Rock and Roll, 1947–1977*. New York: Simon & Schuster, 1999.

Jim Miller (ed.), *The Rolling Stone Illustrated History of Rock and Roll*. New York: Random House/Rolling Stone Press, 1976.

Jim Miller (ed.), *The Rolling Stone Illustrated History of Rock and Roll* (2d ed.). New York: Random House/Rolling Stone Press Book, 1980.

Allan F. Moore, *Rock: The Primary Text* (2d ed.). Burlington, VT: Ashgate, 2001.

Craig Morrison, *Go Cat Go! Rockabilly Music and Its Makers*. Champaign: University of Illinois Press, 1996.

Bert Muirhead, *The Record Producers File: A Directory of Rock Album Producers, 1962–1984*. Poole, England: Blandford Press, 1984.

Brian Murdoch, *Fighting Songs and Warring Words: Popular Lyrics of Two World Wars*. London: Routledge, 1990.

Philip Norman, *The Road Goes on Forever: Portraits from a Journey through Contemporary Music*. New York: Fireside Book, 1982.

Jas Obrecht (ed.), *Blues Guitar: The Men Who Made the Music*. San Francisco: Guitar Player International Books, 1990.

Jas Obrecht (ed.), *Rollin' and Tumblin': The Postwar Blues Guitarists*. San Francisco: Miller Freeman Books, 2000.

Tim O'Brien and Mike Savage, *Naked Vinyl: Bachelor Album Cover Art*. New York: Universe, 2002.

Jim O'Neal and Amy Van Singel (eds.), *The Voice of the Blues: Classic Interviews from Living Blues Magazine*. New York: Routledge, 2002.

Katherine Orloff, *Rock 'n' Roll Woman*. Los Angeles: Nash, 1974.

John Orman, *The Politics of Rock Music*. Chicago: Nelson-Hall, 1984.

Guy Oseary, *Jews Who Rock*. New York: St. Martin's Griffin, 2001.

Robert Palmer, *Dancing in the Street: A Rock and Roll History*. London: BBC Books, 1996.

David R. Pichaske, *A Generation in Motion: Popular Music and Culture in the Sixties*. Granite Falls, Minnesota: Ellis Press, 1989.

Robert G. Pielke, *You Say You Want a Revolution: Rock Music in American Culture*. Chicago: Nelson-Hall, 1986.

George Plasketes, *Images of Elvis Presley in American Culture, 1977–1997*. New York: Haworth Press, 1997.

Gerald Posner, *Motown: Music, Money, Sex, and Power*. New York: Random House, 2002.

John Potter, *Vocal Authority, Singing Style, and Ideology*. New York: Cambridge University Press, 1998.

Sabrina P. Ramet and Gordana P. Crnkovic (eds.), *Kazaaam! Splat! Ploof! The American Impact on European Popular Culture Since 1945*. Lanham, MD: Rowman and Littlefield, 2003.

Robert R. Raulkner, *Music on Demand: Composers and Careers in the Hollywood Film Industry*. New Brunswick, NJ: Transaction, 2003 (first published 1983).

Alan Reder and John Baxter, *Listen to This! Leading Musicians Recommend Their Favorite Artists and Recordings*. New York: Hyperion Books, 1999.

Teresa L. Reed, *The Holy Profane: Religion in Black Popular Music*. Lexington: University Press of Kentucky, 2003.

Dafydd Rees and Luke Crampton, *VH1 Music First Rock Stars Encyclopedia* (rev. ed.). New York: DK, 1999.

Simon Reynolds, *Generation Ecstasy: Into the World of Techno and Rave Culture*. New York: Routledge, 1999 (first published 1998).

Walter Rimler, *Not Fade Away: A Comparison of Jazz Age with Rock Era Pop Song Composers*. Ann Arbor, MI: Pierian Press, 1984.

Jody Rosen, *White Christmas: The Story of an American Song*. New York: Scribner, 2002.

John Ryan, *The Production of Culture in the Music Industry: The ASCAP-BMI Controversy*. Lanham, MD: University Press of America, 1985.

Russell Sanjek (updated by David Sanjek), *Pennies from Heaven: The American Popular Music Business in the Twentieth Century*. New York: Da Capo Press, 1996.

Nicholas Schaffner, *The British Invasion: From the First Wave to the New Wave*. New York: McGraw-Hill, 1982.

Timothy E. Scheurer, *Born in the U.S.A.: The Myth of America in Popular Music From Colonial Times to the Present*. Jackson: University Press of Mississippi, 1991.

Quentin J. Schultze, Roy M. Anker, James D. Bratt, William D. Romanowski, John W. Worst, and Lambert Zuidervaart, *Dancing in the Dark: Youth, Popular Culture, and the Electronic Media*. Grand Rapid, MI: William B. Eerdmans, 1991.

Arnold Shaw, *The Rockin' '50s: The Decade That Transformed the Pop Music Scene*. New York: Hawthorn Books, 1974.

Dan Sicko, *Techno Rebels: The Renegades of Electronic Funk*. New York: Billboard Books, 1999.

Steve Simels, *Gender Chameleons: Androgeny in Rock 'n' Roll*. New York: Arbor House, 1985.

Joe Smith (Edited by Mitchell Fink), *Off the Record: A Oral History of Popular Music*. New York: Warner Books, 1988.

Kathleen E. R. Smith, *God Bless America: Tin Pan Alley Goes to War*. Lexington: University Press of Kentucky, 2003.

Wes Smith, *The Pied Pipers of Rock 'n' Roll: Radio Deejays of the '50s and '60s*. Marietta, GA: Longstreet Press, 1989.

Anthony Stecheson and Anne Stecheson (comps.), *Stecheson Classified Song Directory*. Hollywood, CA: Music Industry Press, 1961.

Anthony Stecheson and Anne Stecheson (comps.), *The Supplement to the Stecheson Classified Song Directory*. Hollywood, CA: Music Industry Press, 1978.

Ken Stephenson, *What to Listen for in Rock: A Stylistic Analysis*. New Haven, CT: Yale University Press, 2002.

Larry Stidom (comp.), *IZATSO?! Larry Stidom's Rock 'n' Roll Trivia and Fact Book*. Indianapolis, Indiana: L. Stidom, 1986.

Larry Stidom, *They're Coming to Take Us Away (Ha, Ha): An Illustrated Discography of the 45-RPM Novelty Record*. Indianapolis, Indiana: L. Stidom, 2000.

Joe Stuessy and Scott D. Lipscomb, *Rock and Roll: Its History and Stylistic Development* (3d ed.). Paramus, NJ: Prentice Hall, 1998.

David P. Szatmary, *Rockin' in Time: A Social History of Rock-and-Roll* (2d ed.). Englewood Cliffs, NJ: Prentice Hall, 1991.

Nick Talevski, *Tombstone Blues: The Encyclopedia of Rock Obituaries*. New York: Omnibus Press, 1999.

Nick Talevski, *The Unofficial Encyclopedia of the Rock and Roll Hall of Fame*. Westport, CT: Greenwood, 1998.

Nicholas Tawa, *A Music for the Millions: Antebellum Democratic Attitudes and the Birth of American Popular Music*. New York: Pendragon Press, 1984.

Nicholas E. Tawa, *Serenading the Reluctant Eagle: American Musical Life, 1925–1945*. New York: Schirmer Books, 1984.

Nicholas E. Tawa, *Sweet Songs for Gentle Americans: The Parlor Song in America, 1790–1860*. Bowling Green, OH: Bowling Green State University Popular Press, 1980.

Nicholas E. Tawa, *The Way to Tin Pan Alley: American Popular Song, 1866–1910*. New York: Schirmer Books, 1990.

Dave Thompson, *The Dark Reign of Gothic Rock: In the Reptile House with the Sisters of Mercy, Bauhaus, and the Cure*. London: Helter Skelter, 2002.

Dave Thompson, *Funk*. San Francisco: Backbeat Books, 2001.

Storm Thorgerson and Aubrey Powell (comps.), *100 Best Album Covers*. New York: DK, 1999.

John Tobler and Stuart Grundy, *The Record Producers*. New York: St. Martin's Press, 1982.

Nick Tosches, *Country: Living Legends and Dying Metaphors in America's Biggest Music* (rev. ed.). New York: Scribner's, 1985.

Nick Tosches, *Unsung Heroes of Rock 'n' Roll: The Birth of Rock in the Wild Years Before Elvis*. New York: Da Capo Press, 1999.

Paul Trynka (ed.), *The Electric Guitar*. London: Virgin Books, 2002 (first published 1993).

Steve Turner, *Amazing Grace: The Story of America's Most Beloved Song*. New York: HarperCollins, 2002.

Richie Unterberger, *Turn! Turn! Turn! The '60s Folk-Rock Revolution*. San Francisco: Backbeat Books, 2002.

Peter Van Der Merwe, *Origins of the Popular Style: The Antecedents of Twentieth-Century Popular Music*. Oxford, England: Clarendon Press, 1989.

Graham Vulliamy and Ed Lee (eds.), *Pop Music in School* (rev. ed.). Cambridge: Cambridge University Press, 1980.

Graham Vulliamy and Ed Lee (eds.), *Pop, Rock and Ethnic Music in School*. Cambridge: Cambridge University Press, 1982.

Dorothy Wade and Justine Picardie, *Music Man: Ahmet Ertegun, Atlantic Records, and the Triumph of Rock 'n' Roll*. New York: W. W. Norton, 1990.

Steve Waksman, *Instruments of Desire: The Electric Guitar and the Shaping of Musical Experience*. Cambridge: Harvard University Press, 1999.

Donald E. Walker and B. Lee Cooper, *Baseball and American: Culture: A Bibliographic Guide for Teachers and Librarians*. Jefferson, NC: McFarland, 1995.

Ed Ward, Geoffrey Stokes, and Ken Tucker, *Rock of Ages: The Rolling Stone History of Rock and Roll*. New York: Rolling Stone Press/Summit Books, 1996.

Dick Weissman, *Music Making in America*. New York: Frederick Ungar, 1982.

Pete Welding and Toby Byron (eds.), *Bluesland: Portraits of Twelve Major American Blues Masters*. New York: Dutton/Penguin Books, 1991.

Joel Whitburn (comp.), *A Century of Pop Music: Year-by-Year Top 40 Rankings of the Songs and Artists That Shaped a Century*. Menomonee Falls, WI: Record Research, 1999.

Joel Whitburn (comp.), *Pop Hits 1940–1954*. Menomonee Falls, WI: Record Research, 1994.

Joel Whitburn (comp.), *Pop Memories, 1890–1954: The History of American Popular Music*. Menomonee Falls, WI: Record Research, 1986.

Joel Whitburn (comp.), *Top Adult Contemporary 1961–2001*. Menomonee Falls, WI: Record Research, 2002.

Joel Whitburn (comp.), *Top Country Singles, 1944–2001*, Menomonee Falls, WI: Record Research, 2002.

Joel Whitburn (comp.), *Top Pop Albums, 1955–2001*. Menomonee Falls, WI: Record Research, 2002.

Joel Whitburn (comp.), *Top Pop Singles, 1955–2002*. Menomonee Falls, WI: Record Research, 2003.

Joel Whitburn (comp.), *Top R & B Singles, 1942–1999*. Menomonee Falls, WI: Record Research, 2000.

Timothy White, *Music to My Ears: The Billboard Essays—Profiles of Popular Music in the '90s*. New York: Henry Holt, 1996.

Timothy White, *Rock Lives: Profiles and Interviews*. New York: Henry Holt, 1990.

Timothy White, *Rock Stars*. New York: Stewart, Tabori, and Chang, 1984.

Albin J. Zak III, *The Poetics of Rock: Cutting Tracks, Making Records*. Berkeley: University of California Press, 2001.

Music Anthologies

Tony Bennett, Simon Frith, Lawrence Grossberg, John Shepherd, and Graeme Turner (eds.), *Rock and Popular Music: Politics/Policies/Institutions*. London: Routledge, 1993.

Kenneth J. Bindas (ed.), *America's Musical Pulse: Popular Music in the Twentieth-Century Society*. Westport, CT: Greenwood, 1992.

Ray B. Browne and Ronald J. Ambrosetti (eds.), *Continuities of Popular Culture: The Present in the Past and the Past in the Present and Future*. Bowling Green, OH: Bowling Green State University Popular Press, 1993.

Ray B. Browne and Pat Browne (eds.), *The Guide to United States Popular Culture*. Bowling Green, OH: Bowling Green State University Popular Press, 2001.

George O. Carney (ed.), *Fast Food, Stock Cars, and Rock-n-Roll: Place and Space in American Pop Culture*. Lanham, MD: Rowman and Littlefield, 1995.

George O. Carney (ed.), *The Sounds of People and Places: A Geography of American Folk and Popular Music* (3d ed.). Lanham, MD: Rowman and Littlefield, 1994.

John Covach and Graeme M. Boone (eds.), *Understanding Rock: Essays in Musical Analysis*. New York: Oxford University Press, 1997.

Anthony DeCurtis (ed.), *Present Tense: Rock and Roll and Culture*. Durham, NC: Duke University Press, 1992.

R. Serge Denisoff and Richard A. Peterson (eds.), *The Sounds of Social Change: Studies in Popular Culture*. Chicago: Rand McNally, 1972.

Kevin J. H. Dettmar and William Richey (eds.), *Reading Rock and Roll: Authenticity, Appropriation, Aesthetics*. New York: Columbia University Press, 1999.

Jacqueline Cogdell Djedje and Eddie S. Meadows (eds.), *California Soul: Music of African Americans in the West*. Berkeley: University of California Press, 1998.

Jim Driver (ed.), *The Mammoth Book of Sex, Drugs, and Rock 'n' Roll*. New York: Carroll and Graf, 2001.

Paul Du Noyer (ed.), *The Story of Rock 'n' Roll: The Year-by-Year Illustrated Chronicle*. Miami, FL: Music Book Services/Carlton Books, 1995.

Jonathan Eisen (ed.), *The Age of Rock: Sounds of the American Cultural Revolution*. New York: Vintage Books, 1969.

Jonathan Eisen (ed.), *The Age of Rock/2: Sights and Sounds of the American Cultural Revolution*. New York: Vintage Books, 1970.

Jonathan Eisen (ed.), *Twenty-Minute Fandangos and Forever Changes: A Rock Bazaar*. New York: Vintage Books, 1971.

Jonathan S. Epstein (ed.), *Adolescents and Their Music: If It's Too Loud, You're Too Old*. New York: Garland, 1994.

Alison J. Ewbank and Fouli T. Papageorgiou (eds.), *Whose Master's Voice? The Development of Popular Music in Thirteen Cultures*. Westport, CT: Greenwood, 1997.

Ben Fong-Torres (ed.), *The Rolling Stone Rock 'n' Roll Reader*. New York: Bantam Books, 1974.

Ben Fong-Torres (comp.), *What's That Sound? The Contemporary Music Scene from the Pages of Rolling Stone*. Garden City, NY: Doubleday Anchor Books, 1976.

Simon Frith (ed.), *Facing the Music*. New York: Pantheon Books, 1988.

Simon Frith (ed.), *World Music, Politics, and Social Change: Papers from the International Association for the Study of Popular Music*. Manchester, England: Manchester University Press, 1989.

Simon Frith and Andrew Goodwin (eds.), *On Record: Rock, Pop, and the Written Word*. New York: Pantheon Books, 1990.

Simon Frith, Andrew Goodwin, and Lawrence Grossberg (eds.), *Sound and Vision: The Music Video Reader*. New York: Routledge, 1993.

Reebee Garofalo (ed.), *Rockin' the Boat: Mass Music and Mass Movements*. Boston: South End Press, 1992.

Charlie Gillett and Simon Frith (eds.), *Beat Goes On: Rock File Reader*. London: Pluto Press, 1996.

Douglas Gomery (ed.), *Media in America: The Wilson Quarterly Reader* (rev. ed.). Washington, D.C.: Woodrow Wilson Center Press, 1998.

Robert Gottlieb and Robert Kimball (eds.), *Reading Lyrics*. New York: Pantheon Books, 2000.

Archie Green (ed.), *Songs about Work: Essays in Occupational Culture for Richard A. Reuss*. Bloomington: Indiana University Press, 1993.

Peter Guralnick (ed.), *Da Capo Best Music Writing 2000: The Year's Best Writing on Rock, Pop, Jazz, Country, and More*. New York: Da Capo Press, 2000.

C. Lee Harrington and Denise D. Bielby (eds.), *Popular Culture: Production and Consumption*. Malden, MA: Blackwell, 2001.

Clinton Heylin (ed.), *The Penguin Book of Rock and Roll Writing*. New York: Penguin Books, 1992.

Nick Hornby (ed.), *Da Capo Best Music Writing 2001: The Year's Finest Writing on Rock, Pop, Jazz, Country, and More*. New York: Da Capo Press, 2001.

M. Thomas Inge (ed.), *Handbook of American Culture—Three Volumes* (2d ed., rev. and enlarged) Westport, CT: Greenwood, 1989.

M. Thomas Inge (ed.), *Handbook of American Popular Literature.* Westport, CT: Greenwood, 1988.

Karen Kelly and Evelyn McDonnell (eds.), *Stars Don't Stand Still in the Sky.* New York: New York University Press, 1999.

Paul Kingsbury and Alan Axelrod (eds.), *Country: The Music and the Musicians.* New York: Abbeville Press, 1988.

Paul Kingsbury (ed.), *The Country Reader: Twenty-Five Years of the Journal of Country Music.* Nashville, TN: Country Music Foundation Press/Vanderbilt University Press, 1996.

Spencer Leigh (comp.), *Speaking Words of Wisdom.* Liverpool, England: Cavern City Tours, 1991.

Richard Leppert and Susan McClary (eds.), *Music and Society: The Politics of Composition, Performance, and Reception.* Cambridge: Cambridge University Press, 1987.

Jonathan Lethem (ed.), *Da Capo Best Music Writing 2002: The Year's Finest Writing on Rock, Pop, Jazz, Country, and More.* New York: Da Capo Press, 2002.

George H. Lewis (ed.), *Side-Saddle on the Golden Calf: Social Structure and Popular Culture in America.* Pacific Palisades, CA: Goodyear, 1972.

Kip Lornell and Anne K. Rasmussen (eds.), *Musics of Multicultural America: A Study of Twelve Musical Communities.* New York: Schirmer Books, 1997.

Robert Love (ed.), *The Best of Rolling Stone: Twenty-Five Years of Journalism on the Edge.* New York: Doubleday, 1993.

James Lull (ed.), *Popular Music and Communication.* Newbury Park, CA: Sage, 1987.

James Lull (ed.), *Popular Music and Communication* (2d ed.). Newbury Park, CA: Sage, 1992.

Greil Marcus (ed.), *Stranded: Rock and Roll for a Desert Island.* New York: Da Capo Press, 1996.

George Martin (ed.), *Making Music: The Guide to Writing, Performing, and Recording.* London: Pan Books, 1983.

Elizabeth West Marvin and Richard Hermann (eds.), *Concert Music, Rock, and Jazz since 1945: Essays and Analytical Studies.* Rochester, New York: University of Rochester Press, 1995.

Evelyn McDonnell and Ann Powers (eds.), *Rock She Wrote: Women Write about Rock, Pop, and Rap*. New York: Delta Books, 1995.

William McKeen (ed.), *Rock and Roll Is Here to Stay: An Anthology*. New York: W. W. Norton , 2000.

Melton A. McLaurin and Richard A. Peterson (eds.), *You Wrote My Life: Lyrical Themes in Country Music*. Philadelphia: Gordon and Breach, 1992.

Angela McRobbie (ed.), *Zoot Suits and Second-Hand Dresses: An Anthology of Fashion and Music*. Winchester, MA: Unwin Hyman Books, 1989.

Richard Middleton and David Horn (eds.), *Popular Music 1: Folk or Popular? Distinctions, Influences, Continuities*. Cambridge: Cambridge University Press, 1981.

Richard Middleton and David Horn (eds.), *Popular Music 2: Theory and Method*. Cambridge: Cambridge University Press, 1982.

Richard Middleton and David Horn (eds.), *Popular Music 3: Producers and Markets*. Cambridge: Cambridge University Press, 1983.

Richard Middleton and David Horn (eds.), *Popular Music 4: Performers and Audiences*. Cambridge: Cambridge University Press, 1984.

Richard Middleton (ed.), *Reading Pop: Approaches to Textual Analysis in Popular Music*. Oxford: Oxford University Press, 2000.

Charles Nanry (ed.), *American Music: From Storyville to Woodstock*. New Brunswick, NJ: Transaction, 1972.

Jas Obrecht (ed.), *Blues Guitar: The Men Who Made the Music*. San Francisco: Guitar Player International Books, 1990.

Jas Obrecht (ed.), *Rollin; and Tumblin': The Postwar Blues Guitarists*. San Francisco: Miller Freeman Books, 2000.

Barbara O'Dair (ed.), *Trouble Girls: The Rolling Stone Book of Women in Rock*. New York: Random House, 1997.

Michael A. Oliker and Walter P. Krolikowski (eds.), *Images of Youth: Popular Culture as Educational Ideology*. New York: Peter Lang, 2001.

Jim O'Neal and Amy Van Singel (eds.), *The Voice of the Blues: Classic Interviews from Living Blues Magazine*. New York: Routledge, 2002.

Tom Pendergast and Sara Pendergast (eds.), *St. James Encyclopedia of Popular, Culture—Five Volumes*. Detroit, MI: St. James Press, 2000.

Richard A. Peterson (ed.), *The Production of Culture*. Beverly Hills, CA: Sage, 1976.

Marianne Philbin (ed.), *Give Peace a Chance: Music and the Struggle for Peace*. Chicago: Chicago Review Press, 1983.

Playboy's Music Scene. Chicago: Playboy Press, 1972.

Janet Podell (ed.), *Rock Music in America* (vol. LVIII, no. 6 from *The Reference Bookshelf*). New York: H. W. Wilson, 1987.

Editors of *Ramparts*, *Conversations with the New Reality: Readings in the Cultural Revolution*. San Francisco: Canfield Press, 1971.

Editors of *Ramparts*, with the assistance of Richard H. Dodge (comps.), *Divided We Stand*. San Francisco: Canfield Press, 1970.

Steve Redhead, with Derek Wynne and Justin O'Connor (eds.), *The Clubcultures Reader: Readings in Popular Cultural Studies*. Malden, MA: Blackwell, 1997.

Pauline Rivelli and Robert Levin (eds.), *The Rock Giants*. New York: World, 1970.

Andrew Ross and Tricia Rose (eds.), *Microphone Fiends: Youth Music and Youth Culture*. New York: Routledge 1994.

Ron Sakolsky and Fred Wei-Han Ho (eds.), *Sounding Off! Music as Subversion/Resistance/Revolution*. Brooklyn, NY: Autonomedia, 1995.

Tony Scherman (ed.), *The Rock Musician—15 Years of Interviews: The Best of Musician Magazine*. New York: St. Martin's Press, 1994.

Timothy E. Scheurer (ed.), *American Popular Music—Volume One: The Nineteenth Century to Tin Pin Alley*. Bowling Green, OH: Bowling Green State University Popular Press, 1989.

Timothy E. Scheurer (ed.), *American Popular Music—Volume Two: The Age of Rock*. Bowling Green, OH: Bowling Green State University Popular Press, 1989.

David Schwarz, Anahid Kassabian, and Lawrence Siegel (eds.), *Keeping Score: Music, Disciplinarity, Culture*. Charlottesville: University Press of Virginia, 1997.

Jane and Michael Stern, *Encyclopedia of Pop Culture: An A to Z of Who's Who and What's What, from Aerobics to Bubble Gum to Valley of the Dolls and Moon Unit Zappa*. New York: HarperCollins, 1992.

Will Straw, Stacey Johnson, Rebecca Sullivan, and Paul Friedlander (eds.), *Popular Music: Style and Identity*. Montreal, Quebec: Centre for Research on Canadian Cultural Industries and Institutions, 1995.

Thomas Swiss, John Sloop, and Andrew Herman (eds.), *Mapping the Beat: Popular Music and Contemporary Theory*. Oxford: Blackwell Books, 1997.

James L. Thomas (ed.), *Nonprint in the Secondary Curriculum: Readings for Reference*. Littleton, CO: Libraries Unlimited, 1982.

Elizabeth Thomson and David Gutman (eds.), *The Lennon Companion: Twenty-Five Years of Comment*. New York: Macmillan Books, 1988.

Wiley Lee Umphlett (ed.), *Mythmakers of the American Dream: The Nostalgic Vision in Popular Culture*. Lewisburg, PA: Bucknell University Press, 1983.

Reinhold Wagnleitner and Elaine Tyler May (eds.), *"Here, There and Everywhere": The Foreign Politics of American Popular Culture*. Hanover, NH: University Press of New England, 2000.

Pete Welding and Toby Byron (eds.), *Bluesland: Portraits of Twelve Major American Blues Masters*. New York: Dutton/Penguin Books, 1991.

Sheila Whiteley (ed.), *Sexing the Groove: Popular Music and Gender*. New York: Routledge, 1997.

Charles R. Wilson and William Ferris (eds.), *Encyclopedia of Southern Culture*. Chapel Hill: University of North Carolina Press, 1989.

Charles K. Wolfe and James E. Akenson (eds.), *Country Music Annual 2001*. Lexington: University Press of Kentucky, 2001.

Charles K. Wolfe and James E. Akenson (eds.), *Country Music Annual 2002*. Lexington: University Press of Kentucky: 2002.

Music Articles and Chapters

Paul Ackerman, "The Poetry and Imagery of Country Songs," *Billboard* XC (March 18, 1978), CMA 22, 42.

Martha Bayles, "Rock 'n' Roll Has Lost Its Soul: And What's Needed to Save It," *UTNE Reader*, no. 60 (November/December 1993), 100–9.

M. Elizabeth Blair and Eva M. Hyatt, "Home Is Where the Heart Is: An Analysis of Meanings of the Home in Country Music," *Popular Music and Society* XVI (winter 1992), 69–82.

Mark Booth, "The Art of Words in Songs," *Quarterly Journal of Speech* LXII (1976), 242–9.

Gary Burns, "Trends in Lyrics in the Annual Top Twenty Songs in the United States, 1963–1972," *Popular Music and Society* IX (1983), 25–39.

Gary Burns, "Visualizing 1950s Hits on *Your Hit Parade*," *Popular Music* XVII (May 1998), 139–52.

Ronald E. Butchart and B. Lee Cooper, "Perception of Education in the Lyrics of American Popular Music, 1950–1980," *American Music* V (fall 1987), 271–81.

James T. Carey, "The Ideology of Autonomy in Popular Lyrics: A Content Analysis," *Psychiatry* XXXII (May 1969), 150–64.

George O. Carney, "Cowabunga! Surfer Rock and the Five Themes of Geography," *Popular Music and Society* XXIII (winter 1999), 3–29.

James W. Chesebro, Davis A. Foulager, Jay E. Nachman, and Andrew Yannelli, "Popular Music as a Mode of Communication, 1955–1982," *Critical Studies in Mass Communication* II (1985), 115–35.

William J. Clark, " 'The Kids Really Fit': Rock Text and Rock Practice in Bill Haley's *Rock around the Clock*," *Popular Music and Society* XVIII (winter 1994), 57–75.

Norm Cohen, "Tin Pan Alley's Contribution to Folk Music," *Western Folklore* XXIX (September 1970), 9–20.

Sara Cohen, "Ethnography and Popular Music Studies," *Popular Music* XII (May 1993), 123–38.

Richard Cole, "Top Songs of the Sixties: A Content Analysis of Popular Lyrics," *American Behavioral Scientist* XIV (January 1971), 389–400.

B. Lee Cooper, "Audio Musicology: A Discography of Tributes to Musical Styles and Recording Artists," *International Journal of Instructional Media* XXVI, no. 4 (1999), 459–67.

B. Lee Cooper, "Building, Burning, Crossing . . . and Feelin' Groovy: Examining the Human Condition through Bridge Songs," *International Journal of Instructional Media* XXVII, no. 3 (2000), 315–26.

B. Lee Cooper, "Christmas Songs as American Cultural History: Audio Resources for Classroom Investigation, 1940–1990," *Social Education* LIV (October 1990), 374–9.

B. Lee Cooper, "Cover Recordings by DOT Artists," *Popular Music and Society* XX (summer 1996), 199–204.

B. Lee Cooper, "Formal Education as a Lyrical Target: Images of Schooling in Popular Music, 1955–1980," in *Images of Youth: Popular Culture as Educational Ideology*, edited by Michael A. Oliker and Walter P. Krolikowski. New York: Peter Lang, 2001, 73–95.

B. Lee Cooper, "From Johnny Ace to Frank Zappa: Debating the Meaning of Death in Rock Music—A Review Essay," *Popular Culture in Libraries* III, no. 1 (1995), 51–75.

B. Lee Cooper, "From 'Love Letters' to 'Miss You': Popular Recordings, Epistolary Imagery, and Romance during War Time, 1941–1945," *Journal of American Culture* XIX (winter 1996), 15–27.

B. Lee Cooper, "I'll Fight for God, Country, and My Baby: Persistent Themes in American Wartime Songs," *Popular Music and Society* XVI (summer 1992), 95–111.

B. Lee Cooper, "The Image of the Outsider in Contemporary Lyrics," *Journal of Popular Culture* XII (summer 1978), 168–78.

B. Lee Cooper, "It's Still Rock and Roll to Me: Reflections on the Evolution of Popular Music and Rock Scholarship," *Popular Music and Society* XXI (spring 1997), 101–8.

B. Lee Cooper, "Mick Jagger as Herodotus and Billy Joel as Thucydides? A Rock Music Perspective, 1950–1985," *Social Education* XLIX (October 1985), 596–600.

B. Lee Cooper, "Oral History, Popular Music, and American Railroads, 1920–1980," *Social Studies* LXXIV (November/December 1983), 223–31.

B. Lee Cooper, "Please Mr. Postman: Images of Written Communication in Contemporary Lyrics," *International Journal of Instructional Media* XXIII, no. 1 (1996), 79–89.

B. Lee Cooper, "Popular Music: An Untapped Resource for Teaching Contemporary Black History," *Journal of Negro Education* XLVIII (winter 1979), 20–36.

B. Lee Cooper, "Popular Music in Print," *Popular Music and Society* XIX (winter 1995), 105–12.

B. Lee Cooper, "Popular Records as Oral Evidence: Creating an Audio Time Line to Examine American History, 1955–1987," *Social Education* LIII (January 1989), 34–40.

B. Lee Cooper, "Popular Songs, Military Conflicts, and Public Perceptions of the United States at War," *Social Education* LVI (March 1992), 160–8.

B. Lee Cooper, "Processing Health Care Images from Popular Culture Resources: Physicians, Cigarettes, and Medical Metaphors in Contemporary Recordings," *Popular Music and Society* XVII (winter 1993), 105–24.

B. Lee Cooper, "Promoting Social Change through Audio Repetition: Black Musicians as Creators and Revivalists, 1953–1978," *Tracking: Popular Music Studies* II (winter 1989), 26–46.

B. Lee Cooper, "Repeating Hit Tunes, A Cappella Style: The Persuasions as Song Revivalists, 1967–1982," *Popular Music and Society* XIII (fall 1989), 17–27.

B. Lee Cooper, "Revising 'Oldies But Goodies' Playlists: Radio Programming, Market Expansion, and America's Musical Heritage," *Rock and Blues News*, no. 2 (February–March 1999), 19–20.

B. Lee Cooper, "Rhythm 'n' Rhymes: Character and Theme Images from Children's Literature in Contemporary Recordings, 1950–1985," *Popular Music and Society* XIII (spring 1989), 53–71.

B. Lee Cooper, "Rumors of War: Lyrical Continuities, 1914–1991," in *Continuities of Popular Culture*, edited by Ray B. Browne and Ronald J. Ambrosetti. Bowling Green, OH: Bowling Green State University Popular Press, 1993, 121–42.

B. Lee Cooper, "Sex, Songs, and Censorship: A Thematic Taxonomy of Popular Recordings for Music Librarians and Sound Recording Archivists," *Popular Culture in Libraries* II, no. 4 (1994), 11–47.

B. Lee Cooper, "The Sky Is Crying: Tales Told in Tearful Tunes," *Popular Music and Society,* XXVII (February 2004), 107–15.

B. Lee Cooper, "Squeezing Sugar from the Phone: Rock, Blues, and Pop Telephone Songs," *Rock and Blues News*, no. 4 (May-June 1999), 26–28.

B. Lee Cooper, "Sultry Songs as High Humor," *Popular Music and Society* XVII (spring 1993), 71–85.

B. Lee Cooper, "A Taxonomy of Tributes on Compact Discs," *Popular Music and Society* XX (summer 1996), 204–217.

B. Lee Cooper, "Teardrops in the Night: A Discography of Crying Theme Recordings, 1950–2000," *International Journal of Instructional Media* XXIX, no. 3 (2002), 345–54.

B. Lee Cooper, "Terror Translated into Comedy: The Popular Music Metamorphosis of Film and Television Horror, 1956–1991," *Journal of American Culture* XX (fall 1997), 31–42.

B. Lee Cooper, "Wise Men Never Try: A Discography of Fool Songs, 1945–1995," *Popular Music and Society* XXI (summer 1997), 115–31.

B. Lee Cooper, "Women's Studies and Popular Music Stereotypes," *Popular Music and Society* XXIII (winter 1999), 31–43.

B. Lee Cooper, Patty Falk, and William L. Schurk, "From Piccolo Pete to the Piano Man: Music Instruments Referenced in Sound Recordings," *International Journal of Instructional Media* XXVIII, no. 3 (2001), 319–26.

B. Lee Cooper and Larry S. Haverkos, "An Error in Punctuation," in *Stellar 3: Science Fiction Stories*, edited by Judy-Lynn del Rey. New York: Ballantine Books, 1977, 108–15.

B. Lee Cooper and Larry S. Haverkos, "Roll Over Beethoven," *Garfield Lake Review* (spring 1987), 77–81.

B. Lee Cooper and Larry S. Haverkos, "Total Recall," *Garfield Lake Review* (spring, 1990), 15–18.

B. Lee Cooper and William L. Schurk, "Singing, Smoking, and Sentimentality: Cigarette Imagery in Contemporary Recordings," *Popular Music and Society* XXIII (fall 1999), 79–88.

B. Lee Cooper and William L. Schurk, "There's a Surfeit of Java in Rio: Coffee Songs as Teaching Resources," *International Journal of Instructional Media* XXVI (1999), 231–6.

B. Lee Cooper and William L. Schurk, "You're the Cream in My Coffee: A Discography of Java Jive," *Popular Music and Society* XXIII (summer 1999), 91–100.

B. Lee Cooper and Donald E. Walker, "Baseball, Popular Music and Twentieth-Century American History," *Social Studies* LXXXI (May-June 1990), 120–4.

B. Lee Cooper and Donald E. Walker, with the assistance of William L. Schurk, "The Decline of Contemporary Baseball Heroes in American Popular Recordings," *Popular Music and Society* XV (summer 1991), 49–62.

Laura E. Cooper and B. Lee Cooper, "The Pendulum of Cultural Imperialism: Popular Music Interchanges Between the United States and Britain, 1943–1967," in *Kazaaam! Splat! Ploof! The American Impact on European Popular Culture Since 1945*, edited by Sabrina P. Ramet and Gordana P. Crnkovic. Lanham, MD: Rowman and Littlefield, 2003, 69–82.

Helen Davies, "All Rock and Roll Is Homosocial: The Representation of Women in the British Rock Music Press," *Popular Music* XX (October 2001), 301–19.

Sheila Davis, "The Facts of Life: Updated," *Billboard* XCVII (October 5, 1985), 10.

Sheila Davis, "Pop Lyrics: A Mirror and a Molder of Society," *ETC.* XLII (summer 1985), 167–9.

R. Serge Denisoff, "Rock Music—The Sound and the Fury," in *Sociology: Theories in Conflict*. Belmont, CA: Wadsworth, 1972, 231–6.

Dr. Demento, "Summertime Blues from Percy Faith to Alice Cooper: A History of the Summer Song," *Waxpaper* III (June 2, 1978), 18–19, 28.

Howard A. Doughty, "Rock: A Nascent Protean Form," *Popular Music and Society* II (winter 1973), 155–65.

Peter Dunbar-Hall, "Rock Songs as Messages: Issues of Health and Lifestyle in Central Australian Aboriginal Communities," *Popular Music and Society* XX (summer 1996), 43–67.

Ralph Eastman, "Country Blues Performance and the Oral Tradition," *Black Music Research Journal* VIII (fall 1998), 161–76.

Roger Elbourne, "A Mirror of Man? Traditional Music as a Reflection of Society," *Journal of American Folklore* LXXXIX (October-December 1976), 463–8.

Bruce C. Elrod, "Music from the Confederate Scrapbook," *DISCoveries* II (February 1989), 112–13.

Larry Etling, "O Canada, We Stand on Guard for Thee: Protecting the Canadian Music Industry," *Journal of American Comparative Cultures* XXV (spring-summer 2002), 134–8.

Joe Ferrandino, "Rock Culture and the Development of Social Consciousness," in *Side Saddle on the Golden CA: Social Structure and Popular Culture in America*, edited by George H. Lewis. Pacific Palisades, CA: Goodyear Company, 1972, 263–90.

Jon Fitzgerald, "Songwriters in the U.S. Top Forty, 1963–1966," *Popular Music and Society* XXI (winter 1997), 85–110.

Jon Fitzgerald, "When the Brill Building Met Lennon-McCartney: Continuity and Change in the Early Evolution of the Mainstream Pop Song," *Popular Music and Society* XIX (spring 1995), 59–77.

Cathleen C. Flanagan, "The Use of Commercial Sound Recordings in Scholarly Research," *ARSC Journal* XI, no. 1 (1979), 3–17.

Warren G. French, "Pop Songs vs. the Blues: Comments on Hayakawa's Article," *ETC: A Review of General Semantics* XII (winter 1955), 127–33.

Paul Friedlander, "The Rock Window: A Systematic Approach to an Understanding of Rock Music," *Tracking: Popular Music Studies* I (spring 1988), 42–51.

Doris B. Garey, "Are 'Mature' Songs Possible?" *ETC: A Review of General Semantics* XIII (winter 1955), 133–5.

Bryan Garman, "The Ghost of History: Bruce Springsteen, Woody Guthrie, and The Hurt Song," *Popular Music and Society* XX (summer 1996), 69–120.

Lionel Grady and Richard Baxter, "Attitudes about the Business Community as Expressed in the Popular Music of 1983," *Popular Music and Society* X (spring 1985), 51–58.

Barry Keith Grant, "Purple Passages or Fiestas in Blue? Notes toward an Aesthetic of Vocalese," *Popular Music and Society* XVIII (spring 1994), 125–43.

Charles F. Gritzner, "Country Music: A Reflection of Popular Culture," *Journal of Popular Culture* XI (fall 1978), 857–64.

Stephen B. Groce and John Lynx Wiler, "The Silent Performance: Audience Perceptions of Musicians' Nonverbal Behavior," *Popular Music and Society* XVIII (spring 1994), 105–21.

Patricia A. Hall, "From 'The Wreck of the Number Nine' to 'The Wreck on the Highway': A Preliminary Comparison of Traditional Folksong and Commercial Country Song Composition and Composers," *Journal of Country Music* VII (January 1978), 60–73.

F. Hannett, "The Haunting Lyric: The Personal and Social Significance of American Popular Songs," *Psychoanalytic Quarterly* XXXIII (1964), 226–69.

Jeff Hannusch, "The Legend of Jody," *Living Blues*, no. 163 (June 2002), 21–22.

James E. Harmon, "Meaning in Rock Music: Notes toward a Theory of Communication," *Popular Music and Society* II (fall 1972), 18–32.

Bill Harry, "The Birth of Mersey Beat: A Personal Recollection," *Goldmine*, no. 585 (December 27, 2002), 48–49.

Bill Harry, "Liverpool: The Capital City of Music," *Goldmine*, no. 583 (November 29, 2002), 19–20.

Bill Harry, "The Road to 'Love Me Do': The Record That Started It All Marks Its 40th Anniversary," *Goldmine*, no. 581 (November 1, 2002), 18–19.

S. I. Hayakawa, "Popular Songs vs. The Facts of Life," *ETC: A General Review of Semantics* XII (winter 1955), 83–95.

Kenneth R. Hey, "I Feel a Change Comin' On: The Counter-Cultural Image of the South in Southern Rock 'n' Roll," *Popular Music and Society* V (spring 1977), 93–99.

Paul M. Hirsch, "Sociological Approaches to the Pop Music Phenomenon," *American Behavioral Scientist* XIV (January-February, 1971), 371–87.

Paul Hirsch, John Robinson, Elizabeth Keogh Taylor, and Stephen B. Withey, "The Changing Popular Song: An Historical Overview," *Popular Music and Society* I (winter 1972), 83–93.

Lawrence Hoffman, "The Blues Harp: The Classic Era," *Living Blues*, no. 167 (March/April/May 2003), 113–23.

Paul Dennis Hoffmann, "Rock and Roll and JFK: A Study of Thematic Changes in Rock and Roll Lyrics since the Assassination of John F. Kennedy," *Popular Music and Society* X (summer 1985), 59–79.

Carl B. Holmberg, "On the Rhetoric of Popular Song: 'Y' Ain't Juzz Whizzlin' 'Dixie'," *Popular Music and Society* IX (winter 1984), 27–33.

Thomas W. Hutchinson and C. Edward Wotring, "Musical Preferences Among Clientele of a Non-Thematic Night Club: A Study of Diversification," *Popular Music and Society* XVII (fall 1993), 43–62.

Peter Ingham and Toru Mitsui, "The Search for Sweet Georgia Brown: A Case for Discographical Detection," *Popular Music* VI (October 1987), 273–83.

Ian Inglis, " 'The Beatles are Coming!': Conjecture and Conviction in the Myth of Kennedy, America, and The Beatles," *Popular Music and Society* XXIV (summer 2000), 93–108.

Ian Inglis, "Conformity, Status, and Innovation: The Accumulation and Utilization of Idiosyncrasy Credits in the Career of The Beatles," *Popular Music and Society* XIX (fall 1995), 41–74.

Ian Inglis, "Synergies and Reciprocities: The Dynamics of Musical and Professional Interaction between the Beatles and Bob Dylan," *Popular Music and Society* XX (winter 1996), 53–63.

James R. Irvine and Walter G. Kirkpatrick, "The Musical Form in Rhetorical Exchange: Theoretical Considerations," *Quarterly Journal of Speech*, LVIII (October 1972), 272–84.

Larry Jaffee, "The Politics of Rock," *Popular Music and Society* XI (winter 1987), 19–30.

Doyle Paul Johnson, "Tuning into Fantasy: Some Notes on Music, Brain Structure, and Social Reality," *Popular Music and Society* XIII (spring 1989), 83–98.

Brenda Johnson-Grau, "Prodigal Songs on a Lost Highway: Records in Rock and Roll," *OneTwoThreeFour*, no. 7 (winter 1989), 21–36.

Brenda Johnson-Grau, "Impersonating the Popular," *OneTwoThreeFour*, no. 6 (summer 1988), 46–55.

Jonathan Kamin, "Parallels in the Social Reactions to Jazz and Rock," *Journal of Jazz Studies* II (December 1974), 95–125.

Jonathan Kamin, "Taking the Roll Out of Rock 'n' Roll: Reverse Acculturation," *Popular Music and Society* II (fall 1972), 1–17.

Jonathan Kamin, "The White R & B Audience and the Music Industry, 1952–1956," *Popular Music and Society* IV (fall1975), 170–87.

I. M. Knickerbockers (aka B. Lee Cooper), "Does Howard A. Dewitt Really Exist?" *DISCoveries*, no. 72 (May 1994), 10–12.

Paul R. Kohl, "Looking through a Glass Onion: Rock and Roll as a Modern Manifestation of Carnival," *Journal of Popular Culture* XXVII (summer 1993), 143–61.

Paul R. Kohl, "Reading between the Lines: Music and Noise in Hegemony and Resistance," *Popular Music and Society* XXI (fall 1997), 3–17.

Paul R. Kohl, "A Splendid Time Is Guaranteed for All: The Beatles as Agents of Carnival," *Popular Music and Society* XX (winter 1996), 81–88.

Spencer Leigh, "Before Beatlemania: British Success on the U.S. Charts before The Beatles," *Goldmine*, no. 576 (August 23, 2002), 57–59, 79.

Stuart Lenig, "The Theatre of Rock," *Popular Music and Society* XVII (spring 1993), 1–21.

George H. Lewis, "Across the Borderline: The Outlaws of Country Music," *Popular Music and Society* XXI (summer 1997), 139–42.

George H. Lewis, "Country Music Lyrics," *Journal of Communications* XXVI (autumn 1976), 37–40.

George H. Lewis, "Cultural Socialization and the Development of Taste Cultures and Culture Classes in American Popular Music: Existing Evidence and Proposed Research Directions," *Popular Music and Society* IV (spring 1975), 226–41.

George H. Lewis, "Duelin' Values: Tension, Conflict, and Contradiction in Country Music," *Journal of Popular Culture* XXIV (spring 1991), 103–17.

George H. Lewis, "Lap Dancer or Hillbilly Deluxe: The Cultural Constructions of Modern Country Music," *Journal of Popular Culture* XXXI (winter 1997), 163–73.

George H. Lewis, "Mapping the Fault Lines: The Core Values Trap in Country Music," *Popular Music and Society* IX (winter 1984), 7–16.

302 \ 4—Popular Music Reference Resources

George L. Lewis, "The Meaning's in the Music and the Music's in Me: Popular Music as Symbolic Communication," *Theory, Culture, and Society* I (fall 1983), 133–41.

George H. Lewis, "The Pop Artist and His Product: Mixed-up Confusion," *Journal of Popular Culture* IV (fall 1970), 327–38.

George H. Lewis, "Tied to the Land: The Interaction of Popular and Folk Elements in Regionally Based Music," *Popular Music and Society* XIV (fall 1990), 59–69.

George H. Lewis, "Uncertain Truths: The Promotion of Popular Culture," *Journal of Popular Culture* XX (winter 1986), 31–44.

John Limeberry, "Idealism down on the Farm: Is the Rhetoric of Country Music Changing?" *Popular Music and Society* XVIII (fall 1994), 33–51.

Herbert London, "The Charles Reich Typology and Early Rock Music," *Popular Music and Society* I (winter 1972), 65–72.

Bill C. Malone, "Country Music, the South, and Americanism," *Mississippi Folklore Register* X (spring 1976), 54–66.

Bunny Matthews, "Mysteries of New Orleans Revealed: It's Our Party," *Wavelength*, no. 71 (September 1986), 21–23.

James R. McDonald, "Rock and Memory: A Search for Meaning," *Popular Music and Society* XVII (fall 1993), 1–17.

Richard Middleton, "Popular Music Analysis and Musicology: Bridging the Gap," *Popular Music* XII (May 1993), 177–190.

David A. Milberg, "Rock-a-Bye Babies: Songs That Made Hitting the Charts Child's Play," *DISCoveries*, no. 87 (August 1995), 36–40.

David A. Milberg, "Saluting Summer: Pop Music's Second Most Favorite Time of the Year," *DISCoveries*, no. 62 (July 1993), 31–35.

Richard E. Miller, "The Music of Our Sphere: Apocalyptic Visions in Popular Music of the Eighties," *Popular Music and Society* XI (fall 1987), 75–90.

George A. Moonoogian, "Ain't Nothin' but a Hound Dog," *Whiskey, Women, and. . .*, no. 14 (June 1984), 4–10.

Harold F. Mosher, Jr., "The Lyrics of American Pop Music: A New Poetry," *Popular Music and Society* I (spring 1972), 167–76.

Tim Murphy, "The When, Where, and Who of Pop Lyrics: The Listener's Prerogative," *Popular Music* VIII (May 1989), 185–93.

George Nettleton, "Researching Rock 'n' Roll: The Researcher Can Be You," *Rockin' 50s*, no. 65 (August-September 2002), 20–21.

Irene J. Nexica, "Music Marketing: Tropes of Hybrids, Crossovers, and Cultural Dialogue through Music," *Popular Music and Society* XXI (fall 1997), 61–82.

Jolanta Pekacz, "Did Rock Smash the Wall? The Role of Rock in Political Transition," *Popular Music* XIII (January 1994), 41–49.

Richard A. Peterson, "Five Constraints on the Production of Culture: Law, Technology, Market, Organizational Structure, and Occupational Careers," *Journal of Popular Culture* XVI (fall 1982), 143–53.

Richard A. Peterson and David G. Berger, "Cycles in Symbol Production: The Case of Popular Music," *American Sociological Review* XL (April 1975), 158–73.

Richard Phelps, "Songs of the American Hobo," *Journal of Popular Culture* XVII (fall 1983), 1–21.

Barbara J. Phillips, "Defining Trade Characters and Their Role in American Popular Culture," *Journal of Popular Culture* XXIX (spring 1996), 143–58.

George M. Plasketes and Julie Grace Plasketes, "From Woodstock Nation to Pepsi Generation: Reflections on Rock Culture and the State of Music, 1969–Present," *Popular Music and Society* XI (summer 1987), 25–52.

Robin Platts, "It's for You: The Songs the Beatles Gave Away," *Goldmine*, no. 399 (November 10, 1995), 60–68.

Ray Pratt, "Popular Music, Free Space, and the Quest for Community," *Popular Music and Society* XIII (winter 1989), 59–76.

Raymond S. Rodgers, "Images of Rednecks in Country Music: The Lyrical Persona of a Southern Superman," *Journal of Regional Cultures* I (spring 1982), 71–81.

Robert L. Root, Jr., "A Listener's Guide to the Rhetoric of Popular Music," *Journal of Popular Culture* XX (summer 1986), 15–26.

E. Anthony Rotundo, "Jews and Rock and Roll: A Study in Cultural Contrast," *American Jewish History* LXXII (spring 1982), 82–107.

Donna Rouner, "Rock Music Use as a Socializing Function," *Popular Music and Society* XIV (spring 1990), 97–107.

William Ruhlmann, "A Century on Record: The 1960s . . . and Then the Beatles Happened," *Goldmine*, no. 566 (April 5, 2002), 19–20, 53, 56.

John Ryan, Legare H. Calhoun, III, and William M. Wentworth, "Gender or Genre? Emotion Models in Commercial Rap and Country Music," *Popular Music and Society* XX (summer 1996), 121–54.

David Sanjek, "Pleasure and Principles: Issues of Authenticity in the Analysis of Rock 'n' Roll," *Tracking: Popular Music Studies* IV (spring 1992), 12–21.

Timothy E. Scheurer, "The Beatles, the Brill Building, and the Persistence of Tin Pan Alley in the Age of Rock," *Popular Music and Society* XX (winter 1996), 89–102.

J. G. Schuberk, "Beginning of the End: Paul McCartney's 1970 Lawsuit Calling for the Dissolution of the Beatles," *Goldmine*, no. 322 (November 27, 1992), 22–24, 28, 30, 34ff.

Alvin Scodel, "Changes in Song Lyrics and Some Speculations on National Character," *Merrill-Palmer Quarterly of Behavior and Development* VII (January 1961), 39–47.

S. Lee Seaton and Karen Ann Watson, "Counter-Culture and Rock: A Cantometric Analysis of Retribalization," *Youth and Society* IV (September 1972), 3–19.

Shirley Seltzer, "Quo Vadis, Baby? Changing Adolescent Values as Reflected in the Lyrics of Popular Music," *Adolescence* XI (fall 1976), 419–29.

David R. Shumway, "Rock and Roll as a Cultural Practice," *South Atlantic Quarterly* XC (fall 1991), 753–69.

M. L. Corbin Sicoli, "Mid Life Music: Mid Life Message?" *Popular Music and Society* XV (spring 1991), 69–80.

Michael W. Singletary, "Some Perceptions of the Lyrics of Three Types of Recorded Music: Rock, Country, and Soul," *Popular Music and Society* IX (spring 1983), 51–63.

Stephen A. Smith, "Sounds of the South: The Rhetorical Saga of Country Music Lyrics," *Southern Speech Communication Journal* XLV (winter 1980), 164–72.

Richard S. Sorrell, " 'My Life Was Saved by Rock and Roll': Personal Reflections on the Age of Rock Music," *Popular Music and Society* XV (spring 1991), 81–89.

Larry Stidom, "The First Cheating Song," *Goldmine*, no. 78 (November 1982), 190.

Robynn J. Stilwell, "In the Air Tonight: Text, Intertextuality, and the Construction of Meaning," *Popular Music and Society* XIX (winter 1995), 67–103.

Rodney W. Stith and Ik-Whan Kwon, "Discriminant Analysis Approach to the Measurement of Commercial Performance of Contemporary Popular Music," *Popular Music and Society* XV (winter 1991), 33–46.

William E. Studwell, "American College Fight Songs: History and Historiography," *Popular Music and Society* XIX (fall 1995), 125–30.

William E. Studwell, "Circus Music and Drinking Songs: United States Manifestations of Two Age Old Recreations: An Essay and Bibliography," *Music Reference Services Quarterly* IV (fall 1996), 57–62.

William E. Studwell, "Circus Songs in America: A Historical and Bibliographic Glance Back to a Popular Recreation of Days Gone By," *Popular Culture in Libraries* V (summer 1999), 29–34.

William E. Studwell, "Tracking Down the Elusive College Fight Song: A Problem for Libraries," *Popular Culture in Libraries* II, no. 4 (1994), 49–52.

Thomas Swiss, "Representing Rock: Poetry and Popular Music," *Popular Music and Society* XVIII (summer 1994), 1–12.

David Temperly, "Syncopation in Rock: A Perceptual Perspective," *Popular Music* XVIII (January 1999), 19–40.

Dave Thompson, "The Demented Genius of Joe Meek: One of the Greatest Producers of All Time, He Was Also, Perhaps, the Strangest," *Goldmine*, no. 453 (December 5, 1997), 56–74, 144.

Dave Thompson, "Let It Bleed . . . The Beatles Slam the Rolling Stones, Stones Bash Beatles: The Heated '60s Rivalry between Two of the World's Greatest Rock Bands," *Goldmine*, no. 581 (November 1, 2002), 14–17.

Peter Thorpe, "I'm Movin' On: The Escape Theme in Country and Western Music," *Western Humanities Review* XXIV (autumn 1970), 307–18.

Donald E. Walker and B. Lee Cooper, "Baseball Cards, Hispanic Players, and Public School Instruction," *Popular Culture in Libraries* I (1993), 85–104.

Donald E. Walker and B. Lee Cooper, "Black Players and Baseball Cards: Exploring Racial Integration with Popular Culture Resources," *Social Education* LV (March 1991), 169–73, 204.

John Wanzenried and Robert Henley Woody, "Country and Western Song Lyrics: Intensional and Extensional Orientations," *Popular Music and Society* V (1977), 89–92.

John W. Wanzenried and Robert Henley Woody, "Personality Factors and Preference for Rock and Country Lyrics," *Popular Music and Society* VI (1979), 302–12.

Alan Wells, "Popular Music: Emotional Use and Management," *Journal of Popular Culture* XXIV (summer 1990), 105–17.

Alan West and Colin Martindale, "Creative Trends in the Content of Beatles Lyrics," *Popular Music and Society* XX (winter 1996), 103–25.

Joseph Witek, "Blindness as a Rhetorical Trope in Blues Discourse," *Black Music Research Journal* VIII (fall 1988), 177–93.

Arnold S. Wolfe, Chuck Miller, and Heather O'Donnell, "On the Enduring Popularity of Cream's 'Sunshine of Your Love': Sonic Synecdoche of the Psychedelic 60s," *Popular Music* XVIII (May 1999), 259–76.

Charles Wolfe, "Nuclear Country: The Atomic Bomb in Country Music," *Journal of Country Music* VI (January 1978), 4–22.

Mark J. Zucker, "The Saga of Lovin' Dan: A Study in the Iconography of Rhythm & Blues Music of the 1950s," *Journal of Popular Culture* XVI (fall 1982), 43–51.

Songbooks, Lyric Anthologies, and Discographies

Alan Aldridge (ed.), *The Beatles Illustrated Lyrics*. New York: Black Dog and Leventhal, 1999 (first published 1969, 1971).

American Song: The Complete Musical Theatre Companion, 1990–1994 (2d ed.). New York: Schirmer Books, 1995.

Amy Appleby (comp.), *America's All—Time Favorite Songs*. New York: AMSCO, 1991.

Hazel Arnett (ed.), *I Hear America Singing! Great Folk Songs from the Revolution to Rock*. New York: Praeger, 1975.

Bob Atkinson (ed.), *Songs of the Open Road: The Poetry of Folk Rock and the Journey of the Hero*. New York: New American Library, 1974.

Janette Beckman and B. Adler, *Rap: Portraits and Lyrics of a Generation of Black Rockers*. New York: St. Martin's Press, 1991.

Chuck Berry, *Chuck Berry—The Golden Decade, 1955–1965*. New York: ARC Music, n.d.

Stephen Bishop, *Songs in the Rough—From Heartbreak Hotel to Higher Love: Rock's Greatest Songs in Rough-Draft Form*. New York: St. Martin's Press, 1996.

John Blair and Stephen J. McParland, *The Illustrated Discography of Hot Rod Music, 1961–1965*. Ann Arbor, MI: Popular Culture, Ink., 1990.

Bob Blanksy (comp.), *The Motown Era*. Detroit, MI: Jobete Music, 1971.

Ken Bloom, *Tin Pan Alley: The Complete Popular Song Companion—Three Volumes*. New York: Facts on File, 1997.

M. J. Bristow (ed.), *State Songs of America*. Westport, CT: Greenwood, 2000.

Scott Buchanan (ed.), *Rock 'n' Roll: The Famous Lyrics*. New York: Harper Perennial Books, 1994.

Colin Campbell and Allan Murphy, *Things We Said Today: The Complete Lyrics and a Concordance to the Beatles' Songs, 1962–1970*. Ann Arbor, MI: Pierian Press, 1980.

Guy Carawan and Candie Carawan, *We Shall Overcome! Songs of the Southern Freedom Movement*. New York: Oak, 1963.

Joyce Cheney, Marcia Deihl, and Deborah Silverstein, *All Our Lives: A Women's Songbook*. Baltimore: Diana Press, 1976.

Bruce L. Chipman (comp.), *Hardening Rock: An Organic Anthology of the Adolescence of Rock 'n' Roll*. Boston: Little, Brown, 1972.

Barbara Cohen-Stratyner (ed.), *Popular Music, 1900–1919: An Annotated Guide to American Popular Songs*. Detroit, MI: Gale Research, 1988.

Ace Collins, *The Stories behind Country Music's All-Time Greatest 100 Songs*. New York: Boulevard Books, 1996.

Contemporary: 100 Solid Gold Hits. Milwaukee, WI: Hal Leonard, n.d.

B. Lee Cooper and Wayne S. Haney, *Response Recordings: An Answer Song Discography, 1950–1990*. Metuchen, NJ: Scarecrow Press, 1990.

Ed Cray, *The Erotic Muse: American Bawdy Songs* (2d ed.). Urbana, IL: University of Illinois Press, 1999.

David Dalton (ed.), *Rolling Stones: An Unauthorized Biography in Words, Photographs, and Music*. New York: AMSCO Music, 1972.

Matt Damsker (ed.), *Rock Voices: The Best Lyrics of an Era*. New York: St. Martin's Press, 1980.

Barbara Dane and Irwin Silber (comps.), *The Vietnam Songbook*. New York: Guardian, 1969.

Charles W. Darling (comp.), *The New American Songster: Traditional Ballads and Songs of North America*. Lanham, MD: University Press of America, 1983.

Ted Dicks (ed.), *A Decade of the Who: An Authorized History in Music, Paintings, Words, and Photographs*. London: Fabulous Music, 1977.

Landon Gerald Dowdey (comp.), *Journey to Freedom: A Casebook with Music*. Chicago: Swallow Press, 1969.

Bob Dylan, *Bob Dylan: Lyrics, 1962–1985*. New York: Knopf, 1985.

Bob Dylan, *Bob Dylan Song Book*. New York: M. Witmark, n.d.

Bob Dylan (compiled by Ronnie Ball and Milton Okun), *The Songs of Bob Dylan: From 1966 through 1975*. New York: Knopf, 1976.

Duncan Emrich (comp.), *American Folk Poetry: An Anthology*. Boston: Little, Brown, 1974.

Lyle Engel, *America's Greatest Hit Songs*. New York: Grosset and Dunlap, 1962.

Philip S. Foner, *American Labor Songs of the Nineteenth Century*. Urbana: University of Illinois Press, 1975.

Will Friedwald, *Stardust Melodies: A Biography of Twelve of America's Most Popular Songs*. New York: Pantheon Books, 2002.

Ira Gershwin, *Lyrics on Several Occasions*. New York: Viking Press, 1973.

Tom A. Glazer (ed.), *A New Treasury of Folk Songs* (2d ed.). New York: Bantam Books, 1964.

Tom Glazer (ed.), *Songs of Peace, Freedom, and Protest*. Greenwich, CT: Fawcett, 1970.

Richard Goldstein (ed.), *The Poetry of Rock*. New York: Bantam Books, 1969.

William D. Goodfellow, *Where's That Tune? An Index to Songs in Fakebooks*. Metuchen, NJ: Scarecrow Press, 1990.

Robert Gottlieb and Robert Kimball (eds.), *Reading Lyrics*. New York: Pantheon Books, 2000.

Gary Graff (ed.), *Popular Music 2000: Volume 25*. Detroit, MI: Gale Research, 2001.

Gary Graff (ed.), *Popular Music 2001: Volume 26*. Detroit, MI: Gale Research, 2002.

Gary Graff (ed.), *Popular Music 2002: Volume 27*. Detroit, MI: Gale Research, 2003.

Barbara Farris Graves and Donald J. McBain (eds.), *Lyric Voices: Approaches to the Poetry of Contemporary Song*. New York: John Wiley, 1972.

Archie Green, *Only a Miner: Studies in Recorded Coal—Mining Songs*. Urbana: University of Illinois Press, 1972.

W[illiam] C[hristopher] Handy (edited by Jerry Silverman), *Blues: An Anthology* (2d ed.). New York: Macmillan, 1972.

Thomas Hischak, *Film It with Music: An Encyclopedic Guide to the American Movie Musical*. Westport, CT: Greenwood, 2001.

Thomas S. Hischak, *Word Crazy: Broadway Lyricists from Cohan to Sondheim*. Westport, CT: Greenwood, 1991.

Barney Hoskyns, *Say It One Time for the Broken Hearted: The Country Side of Southern Soul*. London: Fontana Books, 1987.

Stan Hugill, *Shanties from the Seven Seas: Shipboard Work—Songs and Songs Used as Work—Songs from the Great Days of Sail* (rev. ed.). London: Routledge and Kegan Paul, 1984.

Gale Huntington, *Songs that the Whalemen Sang*. Barre, MA: Barre Gazette, 1964.

Bruce Jackson, *Wake Up Dead Man: Afro-American Worksongs from Texas Prisons*. Cambridge: Harvard University Press, 1972.

Darryl James (ed.), *So Whatcha Sayin'? The Lyrics to Fifty of Rap's Best Songs*. New York: St. Martin's Press, 1996.

Michael Kilgarriff, *"Sing Us One of the Old Songs": A Guide to Popular Song, 1860–1920*. New York: Oxford University Press, 1999.

Roger Lax and Frederick Smith (comps.), *The Great Song Thesaurus* (2d ed.). New York: Oxford University Press, 1988.

The Legal Fake Book (rev. ed.). New York: Warner Brothers, 1979.

Richard Lewine and Alfred Simon (comps.), *Songs of the American Theater: A Comprehensive Listing of More than 12,000 Songs, Including Selected Titles from Film and Television Productions*. New York: Dodd, Mead , 1973.

John A. Lomax and Alan Lomax (comps.), *American Ballads and Folk Songs*. New York: Macmillan, 1967.

John A. Lomax and Alan Lomax (comps.), *Folk Song U.S.A.* New York: American Library, 1975.

Alan Lomax (comp.), *Hard Hitting Songs for Hard-Hit People*. New York: Oak, 1967.

Leslie Lowe (comp.), *Directory of Popular Music, 1900–1965*. Droitwich, England: Peterson, 1975.

Julius Mattfeld (comp.), *Variety Musical Cavalcade—1620–1969* (3d ed.). Englewood Cliffs, NJ: Prentice Hall, 1971.

Paul C. Mawhinney (ed.), *Musicmaster: The CD-5 Singles Directory from the Beginning to 1992—Alphabetically Listed by Artist/Title*. Pittsburgh, PA: Record-Rama Sound Archives, 1992.

Paul C. Mawhinney (ed.), *Musicmaster: The 45 R.P.M. Singles Directory/Supplement—44 Years of Recorded Music from 1948 to 1992 Listed Alphabetically by Artist*. Pittsburgh, PA: Record-Rama Sound Archives, 1992.

David Morse (comp.), *Grand Father Rock: The New Poetry and the Old*. New York: Dell, 1972.

Jim Morse and Nancy Mathews (comps.), *Survival Songbook*. San Francisco: Sierra Club, 1971.

Tim Neely (comp.), *Goldmine Standard Catalog of Rhythm and Blues Records*. Iola, WI: Krause, 2002.

A. X. Nicholas (ed.), *The Poetry of Soul*. New York: Bantam Books, 1971.

A. X. Nicholas (ed.), *Woke Up This Mornin': Poetry of the Blues*. New York: Bantam Books, 1973.

Robert F. O'Brien (ed.), *School Songs of America's Colleges and Universities: A Directory*. Westport, CT: Greenwood, 1991.

Carol Offen (ed.), *Country Music: The Poetry*. New York: Ballantine Books, 1977.

Harry Oster (comp.), *Living Country Blues*. New York: Minerva Books, 1975.

Richard Peck (ed.), *Sounds and Silences: Poetry for Now*. New York: Dell, 1970.

Bruce Pollock (ed.), *Popular Music—1970–1974. An Annotated Index of American Popular Songs,* vol. 7. Detroit, MI: Gale Research, 1984.

Bruce Pollock (ed.), *Popular Music—1975–1979. An Annotated Index of American Popular Songs,* vol. 8. Detroit, MI: Gale Research, 1984.

Bruce Pollock (ed.), *Popular Music: 1980–1984—An Annotated Index of American Popular Songs,* vol. 9. Detroit, Michigan: Gale Research, 1986.

Bruce Pollock (ed.), *Popular Music: 1985, An Annotated Index of American Popular Songs,* vol. 10. Detroit, MI: Gale Research, 1986.

Bruce Pollock (ed.), *Popular Music: 1986, An Annotated Index of American Popular Songs,* vol. 11. Detroit, MI: Gale Research, 1987.

Bruce Pollock (ed.), *Popular Music: 1987, An Annotated Index of American Popular Songs,* vol. 12. Detroit, MI: Gale Research, 1988.

Bruce Pollock (ed.), *Popular Music: 1988, An Annotated Index of American Popular Songs,* vol. 13. Detroit, MI: Gale Research, 1989.

Bruce Pollock (ed.), *Popular Music: 1989, An Annotated Index of American Popular Songs,* vol. 14. Detroit, MI: Gale Research, 1990.

Bruce Pollock, *Popular Music: 1990, An Annotated Index of American Popular Songs,* vol. 15. Detroit, MI: Gale Research, 1991.

Bruce Pollock (ed.), *Popular Music: 1991, An Annotated Index of American Popular Songs,* vol. 16. Detroit, MI: Gale Research, 1992.

Bruce Pollock (ed.), *Popular Music: 1992, An Annotated Index of American Popular Songs,* vol. 17. Detroit, MI: Gale Research, 1993.

Bruce Pollock (ed.), *Popular Music: 1993, An Annotated Index of American Popular Songs,* vol. 18. Detroit, MI: Gale Research, 1994.

Bruce Pollock (ed.), *Popular Music: 1994,An Annotated Index of American Popular Songs,* vol. 19. Detroit, MI: Gale Research, 1995.

Bruce Pollock (ed.), *Popular Music: 1995, An Annotated Index of American Popular Songs,* vol. 20. Detroit, MI: Gale Research, 1996.

Bruce Pollock (ed.), *Popular Music: 1996, An Annotated Index of American Popular Songs,* vol. 21. Detroit, MI: Gale Research, 1997.

Bruce Pollock (ed.), *Popular Music: 1997, An Annotated Index of American Popular Songs,* vol. 22. Detroit, MI: Gale Research, 1998.

Bruce Pollock (ed.), *Popular Music: 1998, An Annotated Index of American Popular Songs,* vol. 23. Detroit, MI: Gale Research, 1999.

Bruce Pollock (ed.), *Popular Music: 1999,An Annotated Index of American Popular Songs,* vol. 24. Detroit, MI: Gale Research, 2000.

Bruce Pollock, *The Rock Songs Index.* New York: Scribner's, 1997.

David Proctor, *Music of the Sea.* London: Her Majesty's Stationery Office, 1992.

Ethel Raim and Irwin Silber (eds.), *American Favorite Ballads: Tunes and Songs as Sung by Pete Seeger.* New York: Oak, 1961.

Theodore Raph (comp.), *The Songs We Sang: A Treasury of American Popular Music.* New York: A. S. Barnes, 1964.

The Real Little Best Fake Book Ever for Keyboard, Vocal, Guitar, and All 'C' Instruments (2d ed.). Milwaukee, WI: Hal Leonard, n.d.

Richard A. Reuss (ed.), Songs of American Labor, Industrialization, and the Urban Work Experience: A Discography. Ann Arbor, MI: Labor Studies Center in the Institute of Labor and Industrial Relations at the University of Michigan, 1983.

Rock 'n' Roll: 100 of the Best. Milwaukee, WI: Hal Leonard, n.d.

Betsy Ryan (ed.), *Sounds of Silence.* New York: Scholastic Book Services, 1972.

Eric Sackheim (comp.), *The Blues Line: A Collection of Blues Lyrics.* New York: Schirmer Books, 1975.

Louis M. Savary (ed.), *Popular Song and Youth Today: Fifty Songs—Their Meaning and You.* New York: Association Press, 1971.

John Anthony Scott (comp.), *The Ballad of America: The History of the United States in Song and Story.* New York: Bantam Books, 1966.

Pete Seeger, *American Favorite Ballads.* New York: Oak, 1961.

Pete Seeger and Bob Reiser, *Carry It On! The Story of America's Working People in Song and Picture.* Bethlehem, PA: Sing Out, 1991.

Bob Shannon and John Javna, *Behind the Hits: Inside Stories of Classic Pop and Rock and Roll.* New York: Warner Books, 1986.

Nat Shapiro and Bruce Pollock (eds.), *Popular Music: 1920–1979—A Revised Cumulation,* vol. 3. Detroit, MI: Gale Research, 1985.

Nat Shapiro, (Editor), *Popular Music—An Annotated Index of American Popular Songs: Volume Three, 1960–1964.* New York: Adrian Press, 1967.

Nat Shapiro (ed.), *Popular Music—An Annotated Index of American Popular Songs: Volume Six, 1965–1969.* New York: Adrian Press, 1973.

Fred Silber and Irwin Silber (eds.), *Folksinger's Wordbook.* New York: Oak, 1973.

Irwin Silber (ed.), *Songs America Voted By.* Harrisburg, PA: Stackpole Books, 1971.

Jerry Silverman (comp.), *Folk Blues* (rev. ed.). New York: Oak, 1968.

Paul Simon, *Paul Simon—Greatest Hits, etc.* New York: Charing Cross Music, 1977.

Paul Simon, *The Songs of Paul Simon.* New York: Knopf/Big Bells, 1972.

William L. Simon (ed.), *Reader's Digest Festival of Popular Songs.* Pleasantville, NY: Reader's Digest Association, 1977.

Stephanie Spinner (ed.), *Rock Is Beautiful: An Anthology of American Lyrics, 1953–1968.* New York: Dell, 1970.

Lawrence A. Stanley (ed.), *Rap—The Lyrics: The Words to Rap's Greatest Hits*. New York: Penguin Books, 1992.

Jeff Sultanof (editorial director), *The Most Fantastic Fakebook in the World*. Secaucus, NJ: Warner Brothers, 1992.

Steve Turner, *A Hard Day's Write: The Stories behind Every Beatles' Song*. New York: HarperCollins, 1994.

Jerry L. Walker (ed.), *Favorite Pop/Rock Lyrics*. New York: Scholastic Book Services, 1969.

Jerry L. Walker (ed.), *Pop/Rock Lyrics 2*. New York: Scholastic Book Services, 1970.

Jerry L. Walker (ed.), *Pop/Rock Lyrics 3*. New York: Scholastic Book Services, 1971.

Jerry L. Walker (ed.), *Pop/Rock Songs of the Earth*. New York: Scholastic Book Services, 1972.

Alan Warner, *Who Sang What in Rock 'n' Roll: 500 Revered, Revived, and Much Recorded Songs from the Rock Era*. London: Blandford Press, 1990.

Ian Whitcomb, *Tin Pan Alley: A Pictorial History (1919–1939), with Complete Words and Music of Forty Songs*. New York: Two Continents/Paddington Press, 1975.

Wanda Willson Whitman (ed.), *Songs That Changed the World*. New York: Crown, 1970.

Allen J. Wiener (comp.), *The Beatles: A Recording History*. Jefferson, NC: McFarland, 1986.

Richard Wolfe (comp.), *Legit Professional Fake Book: More than 1010 Songs*. New York: Big 3 Music, n.d.

Woodstock. New York: Warner Brothers, 1970.

John W. Work (ed.), *American Negro Songs and Spirituals*. New York: Bonanza Books, 1940.

Paul Zollo, *Songwriters on Songwriting* (expanded ed.). New York: Da Capo Press, 1997.

Song and Performer Popularity Charts

George Albert and Frank Hoffmann (comps.), *The Cashbox Black Contemporary Singles Charts, 1960–1984*. Metuchen, NJ: Scarecrow Press, 1986.

George Albert and Frank Hoffmann (comps.), *The Cashbox Country Singles Charts, 1958–1982*. Metuchen, NJ: Scarecrow Press, 1984.

Barry Alfonso, *The Billboard Guide to Contemporary Christian Music*. New York: Billboard Books, 2002.

Bruce Anderson, Peter Hesbacher, K. Peter Etzkorn, and R. Serge Denisoff, "Hit Record Trends, 1940–1977," *Journal of Communication* XXX (spring 1980), 31–43.

Peter E. Berry, ". . . *And the Hits Just Keep on Comin'*." Syracuse, NY: Syracuse University Press, 1977.

The Billboard Illustrated Encyclopedia of Rock. New York: Billboard Books, 2003 (first published 2002).

Ken Bloom (comp.), *American Song: The Complete Companion to Tin Pan Alley Song,* vol. 3. New York: Schirmer Books, 2001.

Ken Bloom (comp.), *American Song: The Complete Companion to Tin Pan Alley Song,* vol. 4. New York: Schirmer Books, 2001.

Dick Bradley, "Charting Success," *The History of Rock*, no. 3 (1982), 59–60.

Fred Bronson, *The Billboard Book of Number One Hits* (rev. and updated 4th ed.). New York: Billboard Books/Watson-Guptill, 1997.

Fred Bronson, *Billboard's Hottest Hot 100 Hits* (rev. and enlarged ed.). New York: Billboard Books, 1995.

Elston Brooks, *I've Heard Those Songs Before: The Weekly Top Ten Tunes for the Past Fifty Years*. New York: Morrow/Quill Paperbacks, 1981.

Elston Brooks, *I've Heard Those Songs Before—Volume Two: The Weekly Top Ten Hits of the Last Six Decades*. Fort Worth, TX: Summit Group, 1991.

Tim Brooks, "Review of *Pop Memories* by Joel Whitburn," *ARSC Journal* XXI (spring 1990), 134–41.

John H. Chipman (comp.), *Index to Top—Hit Tunes, 1900–1950*. Boston: Bruce Humphries, 1962.

Robert Christgau, *Christgau's Consumer Guide: Albums of the '90s*. New York: St. Martin's Griffin, 2000.

Barry Cohen and Jim Quirin (comps.), *Rock One Hundred: An Authoritative Ranking of the Most Popular Songs for Each Year, 1954 through 1991* (5th ed.). Los Angeles: Chartmasters, 1992.

Barbara Cohen-Stratyner (ed.), *Popular Music, 1900–1919: An Annotated Guide to American Popular Songs*. Detroit, MI: Gale Research, 1988.

B. Lee Cooper, "Review of *Billboard's American Rock 'n' Roll in Review* by Jay Warner," *Popular Music and Society* XXIV (summer 2000), 151–2.

B. Lee Cooper, "Review of *The Golden Age of Top 40 Music (1955–1973) on Compact Disc* by Pat Downey," *Popular Music and Society* XVI (winter 1992), 92–93.

B. Lee Cooper, "Searching for the Most Popular Songs of the Year . . . with Menomonee Joel, Big Al, Louisiana Jim, and Bayou Barry," *Popular Culture in Libraries* I, no. 2 (1993), 125–30.

Demitri Coryton and Joseph Murrels, *Hits of the '60s: The Million Sellers.* London: Batsford Press, 1990.

Andrew J. Csida, "The Hot 100—How It Is Compiled," *Billboard* LXXXI (September 20, 1969), 60ff.

Andrew J. Csida, "How the 'Top LP's' Chart Is Compiled," *Billboard* LXXXI (September 20, 1969), 34.

Joe and June Bunny Csida, "Charting the Hit Songs, Artists and Records: From Spotlighting Song Successes in 1903 to the Complex, Total Coverage Charts of 1976," *Billboard* LXXXVIII (July 4, 1976), 10ff.

Pat Downey, George Albert, and Frank Hoffmann, *Cash Box Pop Singles Charts, 1950–1993.* Englewood, CO: Libraries Unlimited, 1994.

Pat Downey, *Top 40 Music on Compact Disc, 1955–1994.* Boulder, CO: Pat Downey Enterprises, 1996.

Carl Drake, *The Country Music Consultant Guide to Vintage Hits, 1950–1980.* Springfield, IL: Stranger Productions, 1981.

Joseph Edwards (comp.), *Top 10's and Trivia of Rock and Roll and Rhythm and Blues, 1950–1980.* St. Louis, MO: Blueberry Hill, 1981.

Gunter Ehnert, *Hit-Records: British Chart Singles, 1950–1965.* Hamburg, Germany: Taurus Press, 1995.

Bruce C. Elrod (ed.), *Your Hit Parade and American Top 10 Hits: A Week-by-Week Guide to the Nation's Favorite Music, 1935–1994* (4th ed.). Ann Arbor, MI: Popular Culture, Ink., 1994.

Lyle Kenyon Engel (comp.), *500 Songs That Made the All Time Hit Parade.* New York: Bantam Books, 1964.

Charles F. Faber (comp.), *Greatest Country Music Hits of All Time.* Lexington, KY: C. F. Faber, 1974.

Christopher G. Feldman, *The Billboard Book of No. 2 Singles.* New York: Billboard Books/Watson-Guptill, 2000.

Gary Lynn Ferguson (comp.), *Song Finder: A Title Index to 32,000 Popular Songs in Collections, 1854–1992*. Westport, CT: Greenwood, 1995.

Paul Gambaccini, Tim Rice, and Jonathan Rice (comps.), *British Hit Albums* (5th ed.). Enfield, England: Guinness 1992.

Paul Gambaccini, Tim Rice, and Jonathan Rice (comps.), *British Hit Singles* (8th ed.). Enfield, England: Guinness, 1991.

Paul Gambaccini (comp.), *Rock Critics' Choice: The Top 200 Albums*. New York: Quick Fox, 1978.

Paul Gambaccini, *The Top 100 Rock 'n' Roll Albums of All Time*. New York: Harmony Books, 1987.

Paul Gambaccini, Tim Rice, and Jonathan Rice (comps.), *U.K. Top 1,000 Singles*. Enfield, England: Guinness, 1990.

Nelson George, *Top of the Charts—The Most Complete Listing Ever: The Top 10 Records and Albums for Every Week of Every Year from 1970*. Piscataway, NJ: New Century, 1983.

Bob Gilbert and Gary Theroux (comps.), *Top Ten: 1956–Present*. New York: Fireside Books, 1982.

Charlie Gillett (ed.), *Rock File*. London: New English Library, 1972

Steven Goldberg, "Statistical Fraud and the Million Seller, ´Record Exchanger II (January-February 1971), 12–13.

Stewart Goldstein and Alan Jacobson (comps.), *Oldies But Goodies: The Rock 'n' Roll Years*. New York: Mason/Charter, 1977.

Ernest A. Hakanen, "Counting Down to Number One: The Evolution of the Meaning of Popular Music Charts," *Popular Music* XVII (January 1998), 95–111

Roy Hall, *The Chum Chart Book, 1957–1983: A Complete Listing of Every Charted Record*. Rexdale, Ontario: Stardust Productions, 1984.

Charles Hamm, *Yesterdays: Popular Song in America*. New York: W. W. Norton , 1979.

Patricia Pate Havlice (comp.), *Popular Song Index*. Metuchen, NJ: Scarecrow Press, 1975.

Patricia Pate Havlice (comp.), *Popular Song Index—First Supplement*. Metuchen, NJ: Scarecrow Press, 1978.

Patricia Pate Havlice (comp.), *Popular Song Index—Second Supplement*. Metuchen, NJ: Scarecrow Press, 1984.

Patricia Pate Havlice (comp.), *Popular Song Index—Third Supplement.* Metuchen, NJ: Scarecrow Press, 1989.

Peter Hesbacher, "*Record World* and *Billboard* Compared: Singles Hits, 1969–1979," *Popular Music and Society* VIII (summer 1982), 101–12.

Peter Hesbacher, Robert Downing, and David G. Berger, "Sound Recording Popularity Charts: A Useful Tool for Music Research," *Popular Music and Society* VI (summer 1978), 118–31.

Tom Hibbert, *The Perfect Collection.* New York: Proteus Books, 1982.

Frank Hoffmann and George Albert, with assistance from Lee Ann Hoffmann (comps.), *The Cash Box Album Charts, 1955–1974.* Metuchen, NJ: Scarecrow Press, 1988

Frank Hoffmann and George Albert, with assistance from Lee Ann Hoffmann (comps.), *The Cash Box Album Charts, 1975–1985.* Metuchen, NJ: Scarecrow Press, 1987.

Frank Hoffmann and George Albert (comps.), *The Cash Box Black Contemporary Album Charts, 1975–1987.* Metuchen, NJ: Scarecrow Press, 1989.

Frank Hoffmann and George Albert (comps.), *The Cash Box Country Album Charts, 1964–1988.* Metuchen, NJ: Scarecrow Press, 1989.

Frank Hoffman (comp.), *The Cash Box Singles Charts, 1950–1981.* Metuchen, NJ: Scarecrow Press, 1983.

Frank Hoffmann, "Joel Whitburn and the Record Research Archives," *Popular Culture in Libraries* II, no. 2 (1994), 27–39.

John Humphries, *British Pop Singles, 1975–1984: Title Index.* Hastings, England: J. Humphries, 1985.

Wesley Hyatt, *The Billboard Book of Number One Adult Contemporary Hits.* New York: Billboard Books, 1999.

William G. Hyland, *The Song Is Ended: Songwriters and American Music, 1906–1950.* New York: Oxford University Press, 1995.

Arthur L. Iger, *Music of the Golden Age, 1900–1950 and Beyond: A Guide to Popular Composers and Lyricists.* Westport, CT: Greenwood, 1998.

Chris Ingham and Daniel Lane, *The Book of Metal: The Most Comprehensive Encyclopedia of Metal Music Ever Created.* New York: Thunder's Mouth Press, 2002.

Jim Irvin (ed.), *The Mojo Collection: The Greatest Albums of All Time.* Edinburgh, Scotland: Mojo Books, 2000.

Dick Jacobs and Harriet Jacobs, *Who Wrote That Song?* (2d ed., updated and expanded). Cincinnati, OH: Writer's Digest Books, 1994.

Wayne Jancik, *The Billboard Book of One-Hit Wonders* (rev. and expanded ed.). New York: Billboard Books/Watson-Guptill, 1997.

David A. Jasen, *Tin Pan Alley: The Composers, The Performers, and Their Times—The Golden Age of American Popular Music From 1886 to 1956*. New York: Donald I. Fine, 1988.

David A. Jasen and Gene Jones, *Spreadin' Rhythm Around: Black Popular Songwriters, 1880–1930*. New York: Schirmer Books, 1998.

Tony Jasper (comp.), *British Record Charts, 1955–1978*. London: MacDonald and Janes, 1979.

Tony Jasper, *The 70's: A Book of Records*. London: MacDonald Futura, 1980.

Tony Jasper (ed.), *The Top Twenty Book, 1955–1990* (5th ed.). London: Blandford Press, 1991.

Derek Jewell, *The Popular Voice: A Musical Record of the 60s and 70s*. London: Andre Deutsch, 1980.

Thomas N. Jewell, "Rock: The Best Recordings of 1979," *Library Journal* CV (February 15, 1980), 473–80.

Thomas N. Jewell, "Rock: The Best Recordings of 1980," *Library Journal* CVI (February 15, 1981), 419–28.

Thomas N. Jewell, "Rock: The Best Recordings of 1981," *Library Journal* CVII (February 15, 1982), 402–9.

Thomas N. Jewell, "Rock: The Best Recordings of 1982," *Library Journal* CVIII (May 1, 1983), 871–8.

Kenneth Aaron Kantor, *The Jews on Tin Pan Alley: The Jewish Contribution to American Popular Music, 1830–1940*. New York: KTAU House, 1982.

Lenny Kaye, "The 'Nuggets' Compilations," *Record Collector*, no. 84 (August 1986), 40–41.

Colin Larkin (comp.), *All-Time Top 1,000 Albums: The World's Most Authoritative Guide to the Perfect Record Collection*. London: Virgin Books, 1999.

Colin Larkin, *The Virgin Encyclopedia of Popular Music* (3d ed.). London: Virgin Books, 1999.

Roger Lax and Frederick Smith, *The Great Song Thesaurus* (2d ed., updated and expanded). New York: Oxford University Press, 1989.

Spencer Leigh, "100 Steps to Rock 'n' Roll," *Record Collector*, no. 176 (April 1994), 22–31.

George H. Lewis, "Dimensions of Popularity: A Comparison of *Billboard* and *The Gavin Report* Singles Charts, 1970–1979," *Popular Music and Society* IX (summer 1983), 54–60.

Len Lyons (comp.), *The 101 Best Jazz Albums: A History of Jazz on Records*. New York: William Morrow, 1980.

Dave Marsh, *The Heart of Rock and Soul: The 1001 Greatest Singles Ever Made*. New York: Da Capo Press, 1999.

Dave McAleer (comp.), *The All Music Book of Hit Albums: The Top 10 U.S. and U.K. Album Charts from 1960 to the Present Day*. San Francisco: Miller Freeman Books, 1995.

Dave McAleer (comp.), *The Book of Hit Singles: Top 20 Charts From 1954 to the Present Day*. San Francisco: Backbeat Books, 2001.

Dave McAleer, *Encyclopedia of Hits: The 1950s*. London: Blandford Press, 1997.

Dave McAleer, *Encyclopedia of Hits: The 1960s*. London: Blandford Books, 1996.

Dave McAleer, *The Omnibus Book of British and American Hit Singles, 1960–1990*. London: Omnibus Press, 1990.

Dave McAleer, (comp.), *Warner Book of Hit Singles*. Boston: Little, Brown, 1995.

J. J. Med, *25 Years of Popular Hits*. Tampa, FL: J. J. Med, 1981.

Betty T. Miles, Daniel J. Miles, and Martin J. Miles (comps.), *The Miles Chart Display of Popular Music—Volume I: Top 100, 1955–1970*. Boulder CO: Convex Industries, 1981.

Daniel J. Miles, Betty T. Miles, and Martin J. Miles (comps.), *The Miles Chart Display of Popular Music—Volume II: 1971–1975*. New York: Arno Press, 1977.

Charles Miron (comp.), *Rock Gold: All the Hit Charts from 1955 to 1976*. New York: Drake, 1977.

Jeffery J. Mondak, "Cultural Heterogeneity in Capitalist Society: In Defense of Repetition on the *Billboard* Hot 100," *Popular Music and Society* XIII (fall 1989), 45–58.

Max Morath, *The NPR [National Public Radio] Curious Listener's Guide to Popular Standards*. New York: Grand Central Press/Perigee Books, 2002.

Tim Morse, *Classic Rock Stories: The Stories Behind the Greatest Songs of All Time*. New York: St. Martin's Griffin, 1998.

John Morthland, *The Best of Country Music*. Garden City, NY: Dolphin/Doubleday, 1984.

Bert Muirhead and Mark Hagen, *The Hit Songwriter's File: A Directory of Writers, Artists, and Their Chart Hits, 1955–1985*. Poole, England: Blandford Press, 1986.

Joseph Murrells (comp.), *The Book of Golden Discs: The Records That Sold a Million* (rev. ed.). London: Barrie and Jenkins, 1978.

Joseph Murrells (comp.), *Million Selling Records from the 1900s to the 1980s: An Illustrated Directory*. New York: Arco, 1984.

Music/Records/200: Billboard's July 4, 1976 Spotlight on America. New York: Billboard, 1976.

Tim Neely, "*Billboard's* Hot 100: Changing Soon," *Goldmine*, no. 476 (October 23, 1998), 46.

Thomas E. Noonan, "Pop Charts: Industry's Measure of Performance," *Billboard* LXXXI (December 27, 1969), 112–14.

Stephen Nugent and Charlie Gillett (comps.), *Rock Almanac: Top Twenty American and British Singles and Albums of the '50s, '60s and '70s*. Garden City, NY: Anchor Press/Doubleday, 1976.

Roger Osborne (comp.), *The Complete NME Album Charts*. London: Boxtree Books, 1995.

Roger Osborne (comp.), *Forty Years of NME Charts*. London: Boxtree Books, 1992.

Martin Parker, "Reading the Charts—Making Sense with the Hit Parade," *Popular Music* X (May 1991), 205–217.

Al Pavlow, *Big Al Pavlow's Rhythm 'n' Blues Book: A Disc—History of Rhythm 'n' Blues*. Providence, RI: Music House, 1983.

Al Pavlow, *Big Al Pavlow's R&B Files, 1940–1949*. Providence, RI: Music House, 2001.

Al Pavlow, *Big Al Pavlow's R&B Files, 1950–1959*. Providence, RI: Music House, 1995.

Al Pavlow, *Hot Charts Artist Index, 1940–1959*. Providence, RI: Music House, 1995.

Al Pavlow, *Hot Charts Title Index, 1940–1959*. Providence, RI: Music House, 1995.

Al Pavlow (comp.), *Hot Charts 1940*. Providence, RI: Music House, 1994.

Al Pavlow (comp.), *Hot Charts 1941*. Providence, RI: Music House, 1994.

Al Pavlow (comp.), *How Charts 1942*. Providence, RI: Music House, 1994.

Al Pavlow (comp.), *Hot Charts 1943*. Providence, RI: Music House, 1994.

Al Pavlow (comp.), *Hot Charts 1944*. Providence, RI: Music House, 1994.

Al Pavlow (comp.), *Hot Charts 1945*. Providence, RI: Music House, 1994.

Al Pavlow (comp.), *Hot Charts 1946*. Providence, RI: Music House, 1994.

Al Pavlow (comp.), *Hot Charts 1947*. Providence, RI: Music House, 1994.

Al Pavlow (comp.), *Hot Charts 1948*. Providence, RI: Music House, 1994.

Al Pavlow (comp.), *Hot Charts 1949*. Providence, RI: Music House, 1994.

Al Pavlow (comp.), *Hot Charts 1950*. Providence, RI: Music House, 1990.

Al Pavlow (comp.), *Hot Charts 1951*. Providence, RI: Music House, 1990.

Al Pavlow (comp.), *Hot Charts 1952*. Providence, RI: Music House, 1990.

Al Pavlow (comp.), *Hot Charts 1953*. Providence, RI: Music House, 1990.

Al Pavlow (comp.), *Hot Charts 1954*. Providence, RI: Music House, 1990.

Al Pavlow (comp.), *Hot Charts 1955*. Providence, RI: Music House, 1991.

Al Pavlow (comp.), *Hot Charts 1956*. Providence, RI: Music House, 1991.

Al Pavlow (comp.), *Hot Charts 1957*. Providence, RI: Music House, 1991.

Al Pavlow (comp.), *Hot Charts 1958*. Providence, RI: Music House, 1992.

Al Pavlow (comp.), *Hot Charts 1959*. Providence, RI: Music House, 1992.

John Politis, "Discography—Three Decades of Top Country Records," *Rockingchair* IV (October 1980), 4–5.

Bruce Pollock, *When Rock Was Young: A Nostalgic Review of the Top 40 Era*. New York: Holt, Rinehart and Winston, 1981.

Daffyd Rees and Barry Lazell (comps.), *The Complete NME Singles Charts*. London: Boxtree Books, 1995.

H. Kandy Rohde, with research assistance from Laing Ned Kandel, *The Gold of Rock and Roll, 1955–1967*. New York: Arbor House, 1970.

Tom Roland, *The Billboard Book of Number One Country Hits*. New York: Billboard Books/Watson-Guptill, 1991.

Rikky Rooksby, *Inside Classic Rock Tracks: Songwriting and Recording Secrets of 100 Great Songs, from 1960 to the Present Day*. San Francisco: Backbeat Books, 2001.

Craig Rosen, *The Billboard Book of Number One Albums: The Inside Story Behind Pop Music's Blockbuster Records*. New York: Billboard Books, 1996.

William Ruhlmann, "The *Billboard* Charts Lose Their 'Biblical' Status," *Goldmine*, no. 291 (September 20, 1991), 7.

Robert Santelli, *The Best of the Blues: The 101 Essential Albums*. New York: Penguin Books, 1997.

Jimmy Savile and Tony Jasper, *Nostalgia Book of Hit Singles*. London: Frederick Muller, 1982.

Henry Schipper, *Broken Record: The Inside Story of the Grammy Awards*. Secaucus, NJ: Birch Lane Press Books, 1992.

Jim Sernoe, " 'Here You Come Again': Country Music's Performance on the Pop Singles Charts from 1955 to 1996," *Popular Music and Society* XXII (spring 1998), 17–39.

Bob Shannon and John Javna, *Behind the Hits: Inside Stories of Classic Pop and Rock and Roll*. New York: Warner Books, 1986.

Nat Shapiro and Bruce Pollock (eds.), *Popular Music, 1920–1979—A Revised Cumulation* (3 vols.). Detroit, MI: Gale Research, 1985.

Nat Shapiro (ed.), *Popular Music—An Annotated Index of American Popular Songs: Volume One, 1950–1959*. New York: Adrian Press, 1964.

Doug Sheppard, "Burning Down the Hotel California: An Indictment of VH1's Top 100 and Rock's Most Undeserving Icons," *DISCoveries*, no. 161 (October 2001), 14A–15A.

Clive Solomon (comp.), *Record Hits: The British Top 50 Charts, 1954–1976*. London: Omnibus Press, 1977.

William Studwell, *The American Song Reader*. New York: Harrington Park Press, 1997.

William Studwell, *The Popular Song Reader: A Sampler of Well-Known Twentieth-Century Songs*. New York: Haworth Press, 1994.

William E. Studwell and D. F. Lonergan, *The Classic Rock and Roll Reader*. New York: Haworth Press, 1999.

William E. Studwell and Bruce R. Schueneman, *State Songs of the United States: An Annotated Anthology*. New York: Haworth Press, 1997.

Bruce Sylvester, "25 Great Folk Revival Albums Not Limited to the 1960s," *Goldmine*, no. 554 (October 19, 2001), 54.

John F. Tanner (comp.), *Hits through the Years: 1952*. Whitley Bay, Tyne and Wear: JFT-Valid Records, 1989.

John F. Tanner (comp.), *Hits through the Years: 1963*. Whitley Bay, Tyne and Wear: JFT-Valid Records, 1989.

John F. Tanner (comp.), *Hits throughout the Years: 1976*. Whitley Bay, Tyne and Wear: JFT-Valid Records, 1989.

Frank C. Tharin, Jr. (comp.), *Chart Champions: 40 Years of Rankings and Ratings*. San Francisco: Chart Champions, 1980.

Gary Theroux and Bob Gilbert, *The Top Ten: 1956 to the Present*. New York: Simon & Schuster, 1982.

Don Tyler, *Hit Parade: An Encyclopedia of the Top Songs of the Jazz, Depression, Swing, and Sing Eras*. New York: Quill Books, 1985.

Jay Warner, *Billboard's American Rock 'n' Roll in Review*. New York: Schirmer Books, 1997.

Joel Whitburn (comp.), *Album Cuts, 1955–2001*. Menomonee Falls, WI: Record Research, 2002.

Joel Whitburn (comp.), *The Billboard Book of Top 40 Albums: The Complete Chart Guide to Every Album in the Top 40 Since 1955* (rev. and enlarged edition). New York: Billboard Books, 1991.

Joel Whitburn (comp.), *The Billboard Book of Top 40 Country Hits: Country Music's Hottest Records, 1944 to the Present*. New York: Billboard Books, 1996.

Joel Whitburn (comp.), *The Billboard Book of Top 40 Hits: Complete Chart Information about Artists and Their Songs, 1955–2000*. New York: Billboard Books, 2000.

Joel Whitburn (comp.), *Billboard Hot 100 Charts: The Sixties*. Menomonee Falls, WI: Record Research, 1990.

Joel Whitburn (comp.), *Billboard Hot 100 Charts: The Seventies*. Menomonee Falls, WI: Record Research, 1990.

Joel Whitburn (comp.), *Billboard Hot 100 Charts: The Eighties*. Menomonee Falls, WI: Record Research, 1991

Joel Whitburn (comp.), *Billboard Hot 100 Charts: The Nineties*. Menomonee Falls, WI: Record Research, 2000.

Joel Whitburn (comp.), *Billboard Pop Album Charts, 1965–1969*. Menomonee Falls, WI: Record Research, 1994.

Joel Whitburn (comp.), *The Billboard Pop Charts, 1955–1959*. Menomonee Falls, WI: Record Research, 1992.

Joel Whitburn (comp.), *Billboard Top 10 Album Charts, 1963–1998*. Menomonee Falls, WI: Record Research, 1999.

Joel Whitburn (comp.), *Billboard Top 10 Singles Charts, 1955–2000*. Menomonee Falls, WI: Record Research, 2001.

Joel Whitburn (comp.), *Billboard Top 1,000 Singles, 1955–2000:The 1,000 Biggest Hits of the Rock Era*. Milwaukee, WI: Hal Leonard, 2001.

Joel Whitburn (comp.), *Billboard's Top 2000, 1955–1985: The 2000 Biggest Hits of the Rock Era*. Menomonee Falls, WI: Record Research, 1986.

Joel Whitburn (comp.), *Billboard Top 3000+, 1955–1990*. Menomonee Falls, WI: Record Research, 1990.

Joel Whitburn (comp.), *Bubbling Under: Singles and Albums*. Menomonee Falls, WI: Record Research, 1998.

Joel Whitburn (comp.), *1997 Billboard Music Yearbook*. Menomonee Falls, WI: Record Research, 1998.

Joel Whitburn (comp.), *1998 Billboard Music Yearbook*. Menomonee Falls, WI: Record Research, 1999.

Joel Whitburn (comp.), *2000 Billboard Music Yearbook*. Menomonee Falls, WI: Record Research, 2001.

Joel Whitburn (comp.), *2001 Billboard Music Yearbook*. Menomonee Falls, WI: Record Research, 2002.

Joel Whitburn (comp.), *2002 Billboard Music Yearbook*. Menomonee Falls, WI: Record Research, 2003.

Joel Whitburn (comp.), *Billboard Pop Hits: Singles and Albums, 1940–1954*. Menomonee Falls, WI: Record Research, 2002.

Joel Whitburn (comp.), *A Century of Pop Music: Year-by-Year Top 40 Rankings of the Songs and Artists That Shaped a Century*. Menomonee Falls, WI: Record Research, 1999.

Joel Whitburn (comp.), *Country Annual, 1944–1997*. Menomonee Falls, WI: Record Research, 1998.

Joel Whitburn (comp.), *Daily #1 Hits, 1940–1992*. Menomonee Falls, WI: Record Research, 1993.

Joel Whitburn (comp.), *Pop Hits 1940–1954*. Menomonee Falls, WI: Record Research, 1994.

Joel Whitburn (comp.), *Pop Hits Singles and Albums, 1940–1954*. Menomonee Falls, WI: Record Research, 2003.

Joel Whitburn (comp.), *Pop Memories, 1890–1954: The History of American Popular Music*. Menomonee Falls, WI: Record Research, 1986.

Joel Whitburn (comp.), *Pop Singles Annual, 1955–1990*. Menomonee Falls, WI: Record Research, 1991.

Joel Whitburn (comp.), *Rock Tracks: Album Rock (1981–1995) and Modern Rock (1988–1995)*. Menomonee Falls, WI: Record Research, 1995.

Joel Whitburn (comp.), *Rock Tracks: Mainstream Rock (1981–2002) and Modern Rock (1988–2002)*. Menomonee Falls, WI: Record Research, 2003.

Joel Whitburn (comp.), *Top Adult Contemporary, 1961–2001*. Menomonee Falls, WI: Record Research, 2002.

Joel Whitburn (comp.), *Top Country Albums, 1964–1997*. Menomonee Falls, WI: Record Research, 1998.

Joel Whitburn (comp.), *Top Country Singles, 1944–2001*. Menomonee falls, WI: Record Research, 2002.

Joel Whitburn (comp.), *Top Pop Albums, 1955–2002*. Menomonee Falls, WI: Record Research, 2003.

Joel Whitburn (comp.), *Top Pop Singles, 1955–2002*. Menomonee Falls, WI: Record Research, 2003.

Joel Whitburn (comp.), *Top Pop Singles CD Guide, 1955–1979*. Menomonee Falls, WI: Record Research, 1995.

Joel Whitburn (comp.), *Top R&B Albums, 1965–1998*. Menomonee Falls, WI: Record Research, 1999.

Joel Whitburn (comp.), *Top R&B Singles, 1942–1999*. Menomonee Falls, WI: Record Research, 2000.

Joel Whitburn (comp.), *Top 1000 X 5: Five Top 1000 Rankings of America's Favorite Hits*. Menomonee Falls, WI: Record Research, 1996.

Adam White, *The Billboard Book of Gold and Platinum Records*. New York: Billboard Books, 1990.

Adam White and Fred Bronson, *The Billboard Book of Number One Rhythm and Blues Hits*. New York: Billboard Books/Watson-Guptill, 1993.

John R. Williams, *This Was Your Hit Parade, 1935–1950*. Rockland, ME: Courier-Gazette, 1973.

Paul Williams, *Rock and Roll: The 100 Best Singles*. New York: Carroll and Graf, 1993.

Chris Woodford, "The Rock 'n' Roll Years," *Now Dig This*, no. 100 (July 1991), 18–19.

Ritchie Yorke, *Axes, Chops, and Hot Licks: The Canadian Rock Music Scene*. Edmonton, Alberta: M. G. Hurtig, 1971.

Library Resources, Archival Collections, and Other Specialized Popular Music Sources

Richard B. Allen, "New Orleans Jazz Archive at Tulane," *Wilson Library Bulletin* XL (March 1966), 619–23.

"The Archive of New Orleans Music," *Wavelength*, no. 107 (September 1989), 31.

Anne Lowrey Bailey, "Scholars at Mississippi Center Preserve and Promote the Culture of the South," *Chronicle of Higher Education* XXXIV (August 3, 1988), A4–A6.

Bill Barol, "One of Each, Please," *Newsweek* CIX (April 6, 1987), 54–55.

Bonna J. Boettcher and William L. Schurk, "From Games to Grunge: Popular Culture Research Collections at Bowling Green State University," *Notes* (June 1998), 849–59.

John S. Brecher, "Is Clyde McCoy a Piece of History? Maybe So. But Again, Maybe Not," *Wall Street Journal* CLXXX (September 12, 1972), 1, 36.

Tim Brooks, "ARSC: Association for Recorded Sound Collections—An Unusual Organization," *Goldmine*, no. 81 (February 1983), 22–23.

Ray B. Browne, "Libraries at the Crossroads: A Perspective on Libraries and Culture," *Drexel Library Quarterly* XVI (July 1980), 12–23.

Wanda Bryant, "Music Resources on the Internet," *Popular Music and Society* XX (spring 1996), 93–122.

B. Lee Cooper, "An Opening Day Collection of Popular Recordings: Searching for Discographic Standards," in *Twentieth-Century Popular Culture in Museums and Libraries*, edited by Fred E. H. Schroeder. Bowling Green, OH: Bowling Green University Popular Press, 1981, 228–55.

B. Lee Cooper, "From the Outside Looking In: A Popular Culture Researcher Speaks to Librarians," *Popular Culture in Libraries* I (1993), 37–46.

B. Lee Cooper, "Huntin' for Discs with Wild Bill: William L. Schurk—Sound Recordings Artist," *ARSC Journal* XIV, no. 3 (1982), 9–19.

B. Lee Cooper, "Information Services, Popular Culture, and the Librarian: Promoting a Contemporary Learning Perspective," *Drexel Library Quarterly* XVI (July 1980), 24–42.

B. Lee Cooper (comp.), "Popular Culture Research and Library Services: A Selected Bibliography," *Popular Culture Association Newsletter* XIX (May 1992), 5–7.

B. Lee Cooper, "A Resource Guide to Studies in the Theory and Practice of Popular Culture Librarianship," *The Acquisitions Librarian*, no. 8 (1992), 131–146.

B. Lee Cooper, "Sex, Songs, and Censorship: A Thematic Taxonomy of Popular Recordings for Music Librarians and Sound Recording Archivists," *Popular Culture in Libraries* II, no. 4 (1994), 11–47.

B. Lee Cooper, "Tapping a Sound Recording Archive for War Song Resources to Investigate America's Major Military Involvements, 1914–1991," *Popular Culture in Libraries* I, no. 4 (1993), 71–93.

B. Lee Cooper, Frank W. Hoffmann, and William L. Schurk, "A Guide to Popular Music Periodicals of the Rock Era, 1953–1983," *International Journal of Media* XI, no. 4 (1983–1984), 369–81.

B. Lee Cooper, Michael Marsden, Barbara Moran, and Allen Ellis, "Popular Culture Materials in Libraries and Archives," *Popular Culture in Libraries* I, no. 1 (1993), 5–35.

B. Lee Cooper and William L. Schurk, "A Haunting Question: Should Sound Recordings Archives Promote the Circulation of Horror Material?" *Popular Culture in Libraries* I, no. 3 (1993), 45–58.

Bruce Dudley, "Comic Books and Rock 'n' Roll: The Artifacts of Our Society," *At Bowling Green: News for Alumni* VIII (February 1978), 3–7.

Allen Ellis (ed.), *Popular Culture and Acquisitions*. Binghamton, NY: Haworth Press, 1992.

Allen Ellis and Doug Highsmith, "Popular Culture and Libraries," *College and Research Library News* LI (May 1990), 410–13.

Jannette Fiore, "Popular Culture and the Academic Library: The Nye Collection," *Drexel Library Quarterly* XVI (July 1980), 53–64.

Samuel A. Floyd, "Center for Black Music Research–Columbia College Chicago," *Sonneck Society Bulletin* XVI (spring 1990), 3–6.

Christopher D. Geist, Ray B. Browne, Michael T. Marsden, and Carole Palmer (comps.), *Directory of Popular Culture Collections*. Phoenix, AZ: ORYX Press, 1989.

Frank J. Gillis, "The Association for Recorded Sound Collections," *Folklore and Folk Music Archivist* IX (winter 1966/1967), 55–58.

Douglas Green, "Country Music's Solid Foundation," *Billboard* XC (March 18, 1978), CMA–12, 42.

Peter Grendysa, "The Rhythm and Blues Foundation: Who's Jiving Who?" *Goldmine*, no. 223 (February 10, 1989), 7.

Bob Groom, "The Blues Archive at Ole Miss," *Living Blues*, no. 68 (1986), 14–16.

David Hamilton, "For Sound Collectors, ARSC Is the Answer," *High Fidelity* XXVIII (June 1978), 30–32.

Chris Hartlaub, "University of Mississippi Blues Archive: A Five Year Celebration," *DISCoveries* II (December 1989), 103.

Leta Hendricks, "A Review of Rap Sound Recordings in Academic and Public Libraries," *Popular Music and Society* XXI, no. 2 (summer 1997), 91–114.

Brad Hill, *The Virtual Musician: A Complete Guide to Online Resources and Services*. New York: Schimer Books/Simon & Schuster Macmillan, 1996.

Frank Hoffmann, "Popular Music Collections and Public Libraries," *Southeastern Librarian* XXIII (winter 1974), 26–31.

Frank W. Hoffmann, *Popular Culture and Libraries*. Hamden, CT: Library Professional (Shoe String Press), 1984.

Steve Jones, "Music and the Internet," *Popular Music* XIX (April 2000), 217–30.

Tim LaBorie (issue ed.), "Collecting Popular Music," *Drexel Library Quarterly* XIX (winter 1983), 1–164.

David Lance (ed.), *Sound Archives: A Guide to Their Establishment and Development*. London: International Association of Sound Archives, 1983.

Larry N. Landrum, *American Popular Culture: A Guide to Information Sources*. Detroit, MI: Gale Research, 1982.

Chuck Miller, "ARSC—A Society for Record Collectors, Historians, Audiophiles, and Musicologists," *Goldmine*, no. 545 (June 15, 2001), 20.

Barbara B. Moran, "Popular Culture and Library Education," *Journal of Education for Library and Information Science* XXVI (summer 1985), 42–64.

James Briggs Murray, "Understanding and Developing Black Popular Music Collections," *Drexel Library Quarterly* XIX (winter 1983), 4–54.

Angus Paul, "New Research Center in Chicago Strives to Preserve and Promote the Legacy of Black Music," *Chronicle of Higher Education* XXXIII (January 28, 1987), 6–7, 10.

John Politis, "Rock Music's Place in the Library," *Drexel Library Quarterly* XIX (winter 1983), 78–92.

Jean Rosenblatt, "From Rock 'n' Roll to Zydeco: Eclectic Archives of Popular Music at Bowling Green State University," *Chronicle of Higher Education* XXXVII (February 6, 1991), 6B–7B.

Janet K. Schroeder, "Studying Popular Culture in the Public Library: Suggestions for Cooperative Programs," *Drexel Library Quarterly* XVI (July 1980), 65–72.

Fred E. H. Schroeder (ed.), *Twentieth-Century Popular Culture in Museums and Libraries*. Bowling Green, OH: Bowling Green State University Popular Press, 1981.

William L. Schurk, "A Description of the Sound Recordings Archive at Bowling Green State University," *ARSC Journal* XIV, no. 3 (1982), 5–8.

William L. Schurk, "Popular Culture and Libraries: A Practical Perspective," *Drexel Library Quarterly* XVI (July 1980), 43–52.

William L. Schurk, "Uncovering the Mysteries of Popular Recordings Collection Development," *The Acquisitions Librarian*, no. 8 (1992), 91–98.

Richard Skelly, "Send Two Copies of Each, Please: Archive of Contemporary Music Preserves Popular Music for All Eternity," *Goldmine*, no. 305 (April 3, 1992), 120, 126.

Lee Anne Snook, "Stuff 'n' Such: Popular Culture Experts Tell Who Saves What, and Why," *At B. G.* XVIII (summer 1988), 10–12.

Gordon Stevenson, "Popular Culture and the Public Library," in *Advances in Librarianship* VII, edited by Melvin J. Voight and Michael H. Harris. New York: Academic Press, 1977, 177–229.

Gordon Stevenson, "Popular Culture Studies and Library Education," *Journal of Education for Librarianship* XV (April 1977), 235–250.

Gordon Stevenson, "Race Records: Victims of Benign Neglect in Libraries," *Wilson Library Bulletin*, L (November 1975), 224–32.

Gordon Stevenson, "Sound Recordings," in *Advances in Librarianship* (vol. V), edited by Melvin J. Voight and Michael H. Harris. New York: Academic Press, 1975, 279–320.

Gordon Stevenson (ed.), "Trends in Archival and Reference Collections of Recorded Sound," *Library Trends* XXI (July 1972), 1–155.

Gordon Stevenson, "The Wayward Scholar: Resources and Research in Popular Culture," *Library Trends* XXV (April 1977), 779–818.

William E. Studwell, "American Popular Culture, Music, and Collection Development in Libraries: Some Comments and Five Examples," *Popular Culture in Libraries* I, no. 2 (1993), 19–27.

Alan Ward, *A Manual of Sound Archive Administration*. Aldershot, England: Gower, 1990.

George Ware, "A Rallying Cry for a Strong Black Music Association," *Billboard* XCVIII (March 22, 1986), 10.

Beverly T. Watkins, "A Folklorist's Material on More than 400 Cultures to Be Available on a Multimedia 'Global Jukebox'," *Chronicle of Higher Education* XXXVIII (May 13, 1992), 21A–22A.

Wayne A. Wiegand, "Popular Culture: A New Frontier for Academic Libraries," *Journal of Academic Librarianship* V (September 1979), 200–4.

Wayne A. Wiegand (ed.), "Popular Culture and Libraries" (entire issue), *Drexel Library Quarterly* XVI (July 1980), 1–99.

Wayne A. Wiegand (ed.), *Popular Culture and the Library: Proceedings of Symposium II*. Lexington: University of Kentucky College of Library Science, 1978.

Wayne A. Wiegand, "Taste Cultures and Librarians: A Position Paper," *Drexel Library Quarterly* XVI (July 1980), 1–11.

Artist Index

Author Index

333

Hopkins, Jerry, 120, 132, 142, 215
Horn, David, 6, 263–4, 268–9, 272, 291
Horn, Richard, 198
Hornby, Nick, 289
Horne, Howard, 277
Horner, Bruce, 46
Horricks, Raymond, 17
Horsley, A. Doyne, 29
Horstman, Dorothy, 205
Hoskyns, Barney, 81, 101, 170, 205,
    242, 309
Hosum, John, 135
Hotchner, A. E., 175
Houston, Craig, 38
Howard, Jay R., 223
Howarth, Lisa N., 269
Howells, David, 9
Howlett, Kevin, 154
Hudak, Glenn M., 6
Hudson, Kathleen, 205
Huff, W. A. Kelly, 165
Hugh, Gregory, 99
Hugill, Stan, 309
Hugunin, Marc, 6, 18
Hume, Martha, 101
Humphrey, Clark, 81
Humphries, John, 317
Humphries, Patrick, 177
Huntington, Gale, 309
Hurwitz, Robert, 234
Hussey, Dermott, 157
Huston, Bruce, 172, 219
Hutchinson, Thomas W., 300
Hutchon, Kathryn, 46
Hutson, Cecil Kirk, 29
Hyatt, Eva M., 293
Hyatt, Wesley, 317
Hyden, Colleen, 85
Hyland, William G., 89, 317
Hyman, Laurence J., 201

Iger, Arthur, 89, 317
Iglauer, Bruce, 150
Ignatz, Kaptin, 137
Inciardi, James A., 22
Inge, M. Thomas, 269, 290
Ingham, Chris, 317
Ingham, Peter, 300

Inglis, Ian, 118, 300
Ingram, Fred R., 243
Ingrassia, Thomas A., 183
Irvine, James R., 79, 300
Irwin, Jim, 317
Isaacs, Alan, 101
Isler, Scott, 35, 130, 142, 171
Ivory, Steven, 184
Iwaschkin, Roman, 269

Jablonski, Edward, 101
Jackson, Blair, 139
Jackson, Bruce, 309
Jackson, Irene V., 230, 261, 270
Jackson, John A., 18, 54, 137, 280
Jackson, Michael, 144
Jackson, Richard, 128, 144, 269
Jacobs, Arthur, 101
Jacobs, Dick, 89, 192, 318
Jacobs, Harriet, 89, 318
Jacobs, Philip, 76
Jacobson, Alan, 316
Jacobson, Jake, 69
Jaffee, Larry, 18, 132, 215, 300
James, Barbara, 263, 268
James, Darryl, 309
James, David E., 40
James, Richard S., 43
James, Sally, 44
James, Steve, 81
Jamison, Andrew, 277
Jancik, Wayne, 89, 101, 140, 173, 150,
    225, 318
Janis, Harriet, 244
Jaret, Charles, 32
Jarrett, Michael, 251
Jasen David A., 89–90, 244, 280, 318
Jasper, Tony, 101, 181, 231, 318, 322,
Javna, John, 261, 312, 322
Jeffries, Neil, 101, 232
Jenkinson, Philip, 25
Jensen, Joli, 125, 205
Jensen, Richard J., 156
Jepsen, Jorgen Grunnet, 115, 211
Jewell, Derek, 318
Jewell, Thomas N., 318
Jochem, Phil, 6
Johansson, Thomas, 54

Topic Index

367

About the Authors

B. LEE COOPER is Provost and Vice President for Academic Affairs at Newman University in Wichita, Kansas.

REBECCA A. CONDON is School Library Media Specialist at Canton Elementary School in Canton, Georgia.